Presented to:

From:

A WORLD OF WONDERS

"He does great things past finding out,
Yes, wonders without number."
Job 9:10

DOUG BATCHELOR

God's Message Is Our Mission
www.amazingfacts.org

P.O. Box 1058
Roseville, CA 95678-8058

Phone: (916) 434-3880
Fax: (916) 434-3889
Order Dept.: (800) 538-7275

Graphic Design: Erin Engle, Haley Trimmer
Additional Design: Greg Solie • Altamont Graphics

And His name will be called Wonderful ..." (Isaiah 9:6).

Life is full of wonders because we have a wonderful God. I am fascinated with the wonders of creation. From the Pleiades constellation to the tiny proton, the hand of God touches the universe everywhere. But it's not just in nature that we see the works of God. Through the stories of people—even the strange ones—we can learn about how the Lord works in us and through us.

A World of Wonders is a daily devotional that comes out of my personal interest in collecting amazing facts that illustrate Bible truths. As a pastor, I'm always looking for ways to point people to Christ. In this devotional you will find stories about driven people like Anna Jarvis, the woman who helped establish Mother's Day as a holiday. You'll read about historic discoveries, like the Rosetta Stone, and learn about fascinating creatures, like the walking catfish. Each page will give you a deeper glimpse into the wonderful Word of God.

This devotional is categorized by 12 different topics, so each month you will find a new category of interesting facts and stories. Some are stories more about people or stunning feats and accomplishments. Other topics tell of wonders in the natural world like birds, insects, the heavens, or mammals. Each devotional concludes with a spiritual lesson to guide you in your walk with the Lord.

Job was a godly and righteous man who faced trials greater than you or I will ever see. As he wrestled to understand God's leading, Job looked to the wonders around him. He reflected on the stars and the great creatures of the deep. He studied the mountains and the animals, and it reminded him of the immensity of God and the humbleness of people.

As you read through *A World of Wonders*, it is my prayer that you too will look to the Lord and exclaim, "He does great things past finding out, yes, wonders without number" (Job 9:10).

Doug Batchelor

World History

"These things I have spoken to you, that in Me you may have peace. In the world you will have tribulation; but be of good cheer, I have overcome the world."
John 16:33

January 1 EMPTY TANKS

"For this reason we ... do not cease to pray for you, and to ask that you may be filled with the knowledge of His will in all wisdom and spiritual understanding; that you may walk worthy of the Lord, fully pleasing Him, being fruitful in every good work" (Colossians 1:9, 10).

On July 23, 1983, Air Canada Flight 143 ran out of fuel at 41,000 feet. The new Boeing 767 jet was only halfway through its trip from Montreal to Edmonton when the aircraft's warning system sounded in the cockpit, indicating a fuel problem on the left side. The pilots naturally assumed that a fuel pump had failed, and turned off the alarm. But then a few moments later a second fuel alarm sounded, followed by a loud bong, and then both engines starving for fuel went silent. Obviously this stunned the pilots and terrified the 63 passengers.

Without any engine power most of the cockpit instruments went blank, leaving only a few battery-powered basics. Still disbelieving the jet could be out of fuel, the pilots scrambled to restart the engines. When they saw this was futile they began frantically searching charts for any landing strip within gliding distance that would be long enough to accommodate their rapidly descending jet. They turned towards the nearest landing site, a closed airbase at Gimli, Manitoba, 20 miles away. What the pilots didn't know was that the decommissioned runway was being used that day as a drag racing strip and was full of cars, campers ... and people.

Without regular engine power, the hydraulic steering became very stiff. Captain Bob Pearson performed a difficult side-slip maneuver to line up the silently descending aircraft with the runway. As the 767 main gear touched down the captain stood on the brakes. Then the nose wheel collapsed, sending sparks flying 300 feet into the air as the aircraft plowed down the runway. Shocked spectators, racers, and kids on bicycles scattered, clearing the runway. Miraculously, the crew was able to safely land the jumbo jet and no one was hurt. The subsequent investigation revealed that someone had miscalculated the fuel load. Canadian airlines had recently adopted the metric system in place of the imperial system.

It takes power to fly an airplane up into the blue sky. It also takes power for the Christian to "walk worthy of the Lord." If the fuel tank is empty and the engines are not running, you will glide downward like the Gimli Glider. Fortunately, the pilots of Flight 143 made a safe landing. But how many people will crash and burn because they are not filled with the power of the Holy Spirit?

"Again, the kingdom of heaven is like treasure hidden in a field, which a man found and hid; and for joy over it he goes and sells all that he has and buys that field" (Matthew 13:44).

Peter Whatling, a farmer from the town of Hoxne in England, lost a hammer in his field in November of 1992. Of course he wanted to find the hammer, but more importantly, a hammer lying in a farm field can do a lot of damage to mowers and harvesting equipment. So Whatling asked his friend Eric Lawes to try and find it with his metal detector. Instead, Lawes found something he wasn't looking for: 24 bronze coins, 565 gold coins, almost 15 thousand silver coins, and nearly 200 silver and gold pieces of jewelry and tableware—all dating back to around A.D. 408. It was the largest hoard of Roman silver and gold from this era ever discovered in the United Kingdom.

It is believed the treasure was hidden as the Roman Empire was crumbling and losing control of Britain. The treasure was buried in a couple of wooden chests that rotted away, leaving behind their two silver locks. The careful burial suggests that the owner intended to come back and recover it later, but obviously something went wrong. Since British law requires such finds to be reported to the authorities, Whatling and Lawes immediately called the police. The next day a team of archaeologists came and excavated the treasure, which became the property of the British government. British law also required the government to pay the finders of the treasure its fair market value, so Whatling and Lawes evenly split the equivalent of $2.8 million dollars. And the hammer? It too was found and is now displayed alongside the treasure at the British Museum.

Can you imagine the joy of finding treasure worth millions of dollars? Would you be tempted to sell everything you have in order to obtain that treasure? God's kingdom is something like that! When we search His words in the Bible, we find the treasure of salvation—"the exceeding riches of His grace" (Ephesians 2:7). When we get a glimpse of His grace, the world will mean very little to us—all that matters is having more of Jesus and His truth! Would you like to trade in your worn-out hammer for His treasure chest?

THE $500,000 BATH

"Then Peter said to them, 'Repent, and let every one of you be baptized in the name of Jesus Christ for the remission of sins; and you shall receive the gift of the Holy Spirit'" (Acts 2:38).

In 1851, Maha Mongkut, also known as Rama IV, ascended the throne as the king of Siam (now better known as Thailand). Mongkut was a true monarch, with total power over his five and a half million subjects. But he was also different from previous Siamese kings. Before becoming king he spent 27 years traveling as a Buddhist priest, studying English, French, and Latin as well as Siamese and Sanskrit. This made him friendlier toward the West, inviting European diplomats to his coronation and introducing Western innovations into his kingdom. Despite his open-mindedness about other cultures, in his personal life Mongkut adhered to royal Siamese tradition, having 82 children by 39 wives. Nine thousand women lived in his harem, kept apart from the world in a separate city.

Mongkut was also very devoted to Buddhist tradition. This is why he spent half a million dollars for a single ritual bath for his son. The Temple of the Bath is a beautiful pool surrounded by four smaller pagodas, all encrusted with heavy plates of gold and gems. In the center is the fabulous marble and gold swimming pool. The king built the Golden Temple on the Menam River in 1887 at a cost of $500,000. After the solemn bath was administered to the prince, the structure was never occupied again.

The Bible invites us to experience a cleansing bath that removes more than dirt from our bodies. Baptism is a ritual that demonstrates our belief that when we confess our sins to God, we can be assured that Jesus washes away all sin from our hearts. We are plunged beneath the waters to publicly signify our allegiance to our King in heaven.

Christ led the way by His own example. But he wasn't baptized in a gold- and marble-plated pool decorated with gemstones. Jesus was immersed in the muddy Jordan River. This pleased His Heavenly Father. Baptism symbolizes Jesus' death, burial, and resurrection. When we are baptized, we accept the work of Christ for our salvation. Jesus paid to wash away our sins by shedding His own blood. That's why the most expensive bath in the world is baptism!

"Then I was given a reed like a measuring rod. And the angel stood, saying, 'Rise and measure the temple of God, the altar, and those who worship there'" (Revelation 11:1).

We hear a lot these days about banking corruption, but the problem isn't new. In eleventh-century England, people were plagued by the dishonesty of creditors. To overcome this abuse, in the year A.D. 1100, Henry I, son of William the Conqueror, started a system known as the "tally," from the Latin word for "stick." A tally stick was about nine feet long and a half inch wide. Every time money changed hands, lines were drawn across the face of a stick, indicating the amount of the loan. On two sides, the value of the "tally" was carved into the wood. It was then split lengthwise and each person received a half of the stick as proof of the transaction, with the creditor retaining one half and the debtor getting the other, an exact "carbon copy."

It was practically impossible to counterfeit a tally, and those who tried lost their heads! The wood grain was as unique as a fingerprint. Notches and ink inscriptions had to match. This could only happen if both pieces came from the same split tally stick. When compared they had to "tally," which is where we get the word for reckoning. The British Empire used tally sticks for over 700 years. Then in 1843, because a new banking system and currency were introduced, all the tally sticks in England were collected and burned. Yet the term lives on, since it is from the German word for "stick" that we get the word "stock," a security for creditors of a business we hear about on Wall Street.

The book of Revelation speaks of God's people being measured with a stick. What is the Lord's "tally stick"? James writes, "For whoever shall keep the whole law, and yet stumble in one point, he is guilty of all" (James 2:10). If we are preparing for Jesus' soon coming, then "when He is revealed, we shall be like Him" (1 John 3:2). In other words, God's law and our hearts will tally!

Before Jesus comes let us take stock of our lives. He covered the debt of our sin that we might receive the free gift of salvation. As we come closer to Jesus our characters will be a copy of His. It's a transaction that can never be counterfeited.

January 5 DISCOURAGING WORDS

"Then she said to him, 'How can you say, "I love you," when your heart is not with me? You have mocked me these three times, and have not told me where your great strength lies.' And it came to pass, when she pestered him daily with her words and pressed him, so that his soul was vexed to death" (Judges 16:15, 16).

The Battle of Stalingrad during World War II was arguably the bloodiest battle in human history, with combined casualties estimated above 1.5 million. In 1942 the German army, with the Axis forces, had nearly captured the sprawling Russian city. But by 1943, after months of brutal house-to-house fighting, the Russian military defending Stalingrad managed to turn the tables and surround Hitler's Sixth Army—the besiegers became the besieged.

In addition to a heavy bombing campaign, the Russians placed powerful loudspeakers within the listening range of German soldiers. A series of sound tactics were used to discourage the German troops. For example, they played the loud, monotonous ticking of a clock, followed by a voice saying, "A German dies every seven seconds on the Eastern Front." The propaganda voice then intoned, "Stalingrad, mass grave of Hitler's army!" and then creepy tango music would start blaring across the empty frozen wasteland. Demoralized and starved, 91,000 German soldiers eventually surrendered.

Samson, the mighty judge of Israel, surrendered the secret of his strength when Delilah pestered him over and over. Her words eventually broke him down until "his soul was vexed to death that he told her all his heart" (v. 16, 17). Discouraging words have a powerful force on our lives. We don't even need to audibly hear them. They can bring us down just by thinking negative thoughts.

Wise Solomon penned, "The light of the eyes rejoices the heart, and a good report makes the bones healthy" (Proverbs 15:30), and Paul encouraged, "Finally, brethren, whatever things are true, whatever things are noble, whatever things are just, whatever things are pure, whatever things are lovely, whatever things are of good report, if there is any virtue and if there is anything praiseworthy—meditate on these things" (Philippians 4:8).

Do not surrender to the enemy by listening to negative words or an evil report. Think and talk faith! Repeat the promises of God. Believe in the Bible and stand firm against discouraging words.

"And the Lord God said, 'It is not good that man should be alone; I will make him a helper comparable to him.'" (Genesis 2:18).

Probably the only healthy man in modern history who never saw the form or heard the voice of a woman was Mihailo Tolotos. Mihailo was a monk who died in 1938 at the age of 82 in one of the monasteries atop Mount Athos, in Greece. When his mother passed away during his birth, Mihailo was taken the next day to Athos, a piece of land jutting out into the Aegean Sea. The monk never once, throughout his entire life, left this monastic colony, which for more than 900 years has strictly excluded all females, animals as well as humans. This tradition dates back to the founding of the monastery nine centuries earlier.

Is it good for man to be alone? Not according to Genesis 2:18. But with the rising divorce epidemic it might make you wonder if marriage is still a good idea. Jesus quotes Genesis 2:24 and says, "For this reason a man shall leave his father and mother and be joined to his wife, and the two shall become one flesh" (Matthew 19:5), supporting the institution of marriage.

The apostle Paul certainly does not insist on everyone getting married, and supports celibacy as a positive lifestyle for serving the Lord (see 1 Corinthians 7:7). But would Paul recommend a lifetime of seclusion? In an interesting application of Genesis 2:24, the apostle says, "For we are members of His body, of His flesh and His bones. 'For this reason a man shall leave his father and mother and be joined to his wife, and the two shall become one flesh.' This is a great mystery, but I speak concerning Christ and the church" (Ephesians 5:30-32).

In the Bible, a woman is used as a symbol for God's people. "I have likened the daughter of Zion to a lovely and delicate woman" (Jeremiah 6:2). God's church is described as a woman in Revelation 12:1. Perhaps Paul's counsel to Mihailo Tolotos would be to stay connected to God's people and not live in isolation from the body of Christ. It is not good for anyone to be separated from the church, especially as we near the time of Jesus' return.

"And let us consider one another in order to stir up love and good works, not forsaking the assembling of ourselves together ... so much more as you see the Day approaching" (Hebrews 10:24, 25).

LIVING WITH THE DEAD

"He who has the Son has life; he who does not have the Son of God does not have life" (1 John 5:12).

Around the 14th century A.D., thousands of poor and homeless people who were seeking shelter began squatting in tombs in an area of Cairo, Egypt. Can you imagine living in a tomb with the dead? It would be repulsive to most of us, yet the City of the Dead is a real place that I saw years ago while visiting the northern part of Cairo. It's actually the strangest cemetery I've ever seen. The word "cemetery" is, in fact, a misnomer because this graveyard is teeming with life and activity.

Over a period of hundreds of years, the great rulers of ages past built acres and acres of huge and elaborate mausoleums and tombs. At that time, tradition dictated that each tomb be built with its own "party room"—which eventually became habitations for the homeless. The 1992 Cairo earthquake forced even more people to live in the City of the Dead, often in family tombs.

Strangely, this cemetery, which measures about four miles in length, is now classified as a suburb of Cairo. It has its own zip code, post office, police station, shops, electricity, running water, and sewer system. It's also rather creative how the residents made use of the smaller gravestones by turning them into washing lines or tables. People actually live and conduct their lives in and around these tombs—working, sleeping, cooking, and eating—surrounded by their silent, macabre neighbors.

The Bible teaches there are only two classes of people, the living and the dead. You might think this is an obvious statement but, according to the Word of God, not all of the living are alive and not all of the dead are dead. Jesus said, "Let the dead bury their own dead, but you go and preach the kingdom of God" (Luke 9:60). On another occasion, He said, "... have you not read what was spoken to you by God, saying, 'I am the God of Abraham, the God of Isaac, and the God of Jacob'? God is not the God of the dead, but of the living."

Jesus offers us this promise: "I am the resurrection and the life. He who believes in Me, though he may die, he shall live" (John 11:25). Aren't you glad God gives us that kind of reassurance of eternal life with Him?

"And they said to me, 'The survivors who are left from the captivity in the province are there in great distress and reproach. The wall of Jerusalem is also broken down, and its gates are burned with fire'" (Nehemiah 1:3).

Around A.D. 122 Roman Emperor Hadrian ordered the construction of a wall in northern Britain, then part of the Roman Empire, to keep out the unconquered Caledonians of Scotland. Built out of stone and turf and measuring about 117 kilometers (73 miles) in length, the wall linked a series of forts and watchtowers. The Romans rebuilt Hadrian's Wall several times throughout the 200s and 300s and used it as a fortification until about 400. The wall extended from Solway Firth to the mouth of the Tyne River and was about 6 meters (20 feet) high and about 2.4 meters (8 feet) wide. A military road ran along the south side of the wall, and a series of heavily garrisoned forts and sentry posts were built along its length. The wall also marked the frontier of Roman civil jurisdiction.

A few parts of Hadrian's Wall remain standing in present-day Great Britain, especially in the mid-section. You can actually follow a path or ride your bicycle along the wall. It is the most popular attraction for tourists in Northern England. One government organization that manages historic sites in England calls Hadrian's Wall "the most important monument built by the Romans in Britain." On March 13, 2010, the route of the wall was lit by 500 gas beacons, flares, and torches at 250-meter intervals. Over 1,000 volunteers helped with the celebration of the 1,600th anniversary of the end of Roman rule in Britain.

The Bible tells us about another famous wall that was built to keep enemies out. When Babylon sacked Jerusalem, the army broke down the walls and burned the gates of the city. Years later Nehemiah hears a report of the condition of Jerusalem that not only makes him sad, but motivates him to do something about it. He was a cupbearer for King Artaxerxes and, after much prayer, an opportunity opens for Nehemiah to ask for help in restoring the walls of this beloved city. By God's grace the reconstruction was completed in only 52 days!

The Lord wants to protect you from the devil. Like a broken-down wall, our hearts need repair. God wants to build up your life so that you are resistant to enemy attacks by Satan. Just as Hadrian's Wall stretched from coast to coast, the Lord wants to completely protect you with His care.

THE SAVIOR OF JOHN SMITH

"Therefore My Father loves Me, because I lay down My life that I may take it again" (John 10:17).

Legends grow with the passing of time, and the story of Pocahontas seems to have become more embellished since Captain John Smith first wrote about this famous Native American woman who saved his life.

According to Smith, a Jamestown leader, a group of Powhatan's warriors captured him in December 1607. He was then taken to Powhatan, who forced him to kneel before him to be executed. Just as Powhatan's men were about to crack his skull with wooden clubs, Powhatan's young daughter, Pocahontas, ran and threw her body over Smith's. She convinced her father to spare his life. Smith was then treated to a huge feast and let go.

But historians debate the details of what happened. Some compare different accounts of John Smith and believe he tended to exaggerate stories and wanted to enhance Pocahontas's standing. Others think Powhatan may have been staging a special ceremony his people used to adopt someone into their tribe. In other words, Pocahontas may have simply been "playing the savior" in the ritual of symbolically making the Englishman an adopted son of Powhatan.

The story of Pocahontas is fun to read and has become a part of American folklore. Movies and books have taken the storyline and romanticized it until we are not sure where truth ends and fable begins. But there is a story of a savior who laid down his life to redeem a people who were captured and sentenced to die. Jesus Christ, God's only Son, came to our Earth and was willingly crucified that we might live.

The father of Pocahontas, so the story goes, was going to execute John Smith. Pocahontas willingly laid down her life to save Smith. Her life was spared, but Christ's life was not. Jesus threw Himself over our world to protect us, not from a Father seeking to execute us, but from the results of sin. He received the death blows that we might be set free. We have a Savior and His name is Jesus. Have you accepted Christ's sacrifice?

"For [the LORD] is coming to judge the earth. With righteousness He shall judge the world, and the peoples with equity" (Psalm 98:9).

Fabian von Schlabrendorff was born in Germany in 1907. Though he trained as a lawyer, he eventually joined the German army before World War II. Realizing that Adolph Hitler was insane and destroying Europe, he joined the resistance. On March 13, 1943, during a visit by Hitler to an army center headquarters in Russia, Schlabrendorff smuggled a time bomb onto an aircraft meant to carry Hitler back to Germany. The bomb did not detonate, and even though Schlabrendorff was able to retrieve the bomb without being detected, he was eventually arrested after a second assassination attempt.

Schlabrendorff was sent to a Gestapo prison where he was tortured, but he refused to give any details of his own or others' involvement with the resistance. Early in 1945, Schlabrendorff was brought before a Nazi court. The evidence against him was weak, but the judge, Roland Freisler, was infamous for handing down death sentences in almost every case. In fact, in his three years on the court, Freisler was responsible for as many death sentences as all the other judges combined over the eleven years the court existed. However, while Schlabrendorff waited for his trial to begin, an American air raid bomb hit the courthouse. The judge was killed, still holding Schlabrendorff's file.

A month later, when Schlabrendorff's trial was rescheduled, a different judge actually acquitted him, but he was still shuffled from one concentration camp to another until U.S. forces liberated his camp in May of 1945. In a unique twist of fate, he became a judge in the very country where he stood trial for treason.

The Bible teaches that a similar reversal of roles will happen again. Jesus was once condemned to death in an unfair trial, but we know that when He comes again, it will be as a righteous judge. As Peter told Cornelius, "It is [Jesus] who was ordained by God to be Judge of the living and the dead" (Acts 10:42). But Peter didn't stop there, because the best news of all is that our judge is also our redeemer: "Whoever believes in Him will receive remission of sins" (Acts 10:42, 43). Why not trust your case to Him?

January 11 THE GREAT SURRENDER

"I have been crucified with Christ; it is no longer I who live, but Christ lives in me ..." (Galatians 2:20).

Masada, which means "fortress" in Hebrew, is a mountaintop stronghold in the Judean desert, built on a rocky mesa rising abruptly 2,000 feet above the nearby Dead Sea. It was renovated by Herod the Great between 37 and 31 B.C. When Jerusalem was taken by the Romans in A.D. 70, the last remaining rebels, a Jewish sect known as the Zealots, revolted and seized the fortress in their last stand against Roman rule. They refused to surrender.

With plenty of food and water, this group of about 1,000 men, women, and children led by Eleazar ben Jair, held off the whole Roman army for more than two years. After this long siege, 15,000 Roman soldiers from the Tenth Legion raised an enormous Earth ramp and broke through the walls. They found the bodies of over 960 men, women, and children, victims of a suicide pact to keep the Romans from taking them as slaves. All but seven killed themselves rather than yield to their enemies.

The Masada site was rediscovered in 1842 and extensively excavated by archaeologist Higael Yadin between 1963 and 1965. Today tourists may hike up the Snake Path on the eastern side or take a cable car to the top. Because of the dry climate, Masada has remained largely untouched by humans for over 2,000 years. A museum now displays findings, and tours are given daily, telling the story of the zealots who refused to give in.

There are certainly times in which we should fearlessly stand against the enemy. But there is also a time to surrender—not to the devil, but to Christ. When Paul shared the gospel with the Corinthians, he wrote, "The message of the cross is foolishness to those who are perishing, but to us who are being saved it is the power of God" (1 Corinthians 1:18). To the world it seems preposterous to worship a God who laid down His life. Yet, in the same way we may find life when we die to self and humble ourselves before God.

Our Bible text for today calls us to be just like Jesus and be crucified with Him. It is not our physical bodies that must climb upon a cross and die. We must surrender self. By laying down our rights, our desire to be first, and the lusts of our flesh, we receive salvation. When we admit defeat in the battle with self, we win the war by surrendering to Jesus.

"And do not be conformed to this world, but be transformed by the renewing of your mind, that you may prove what is that good and acceptable and perfect will of God" (Romans 12:2).

We've all heard the true account of the Mutiny on the Bounty, but one aspect of the story that deserves retelling is the transformation wrought by one incredible book.

Shortly after the famous mutiny in 1789, nine mutineers with six Tahitian men and 12 women went ashore on Pitcairn Island—a tiny island in the southern Pacific Ocean. They burned the Bounty and established a colony. Things went along all right for a short time. In some respects, it seemed like they were living in a paradise. But some of the mutineers treated the Tahitians disrespectfully and war broke out between them, eventually resulting in the deaths of most of the men on both sides.

After that, peace reigned again briefly, until one of the sailors began distilling alcohol from a native plant. Most of the surviving settlers drank excessively. Soon the little colony was plunged into debauchery, vice, and murder.

Ten years later, only one man—John Adams—survived, surrounded by 10 native women and a bushel of half-breed children. One day this sailor discovered a Bible in an old chest from the Bounty. He began to read it and then teach it to the others. The result was that his own life and, ultimately, the lives of all those on the island were dramatically transformed. In fact, when Pitcairn Island was visited in 1808 by an American whaling ship, the previously crime-consumed colony had become a thriving community with no jail, no whiskey, no laziness, and no crime.

Today the descendants of this colony still live in a moralistic society on one of the most isolated islands in the world. Can Bible principles really transform a culture from vice and crime to tranquility today? I believe they can. The Word of God draws us away from conformity to the world with all of its trouble and vices. By reading and studying the Bible our minds are renewed; they are transformed to become more and more like the mind of Christ. We find that we have peace in our hearts, conformity to God's will, and a saving relationship with Him. Now that is real paradise!

January 13 A SMASHING ENTRANCE

"For Satan himself transforms himself into an angel of light" (2 Corinthians 11:14).

The first recorded roller skates, called skaites, were built in 1760 by a Belgian musical instrument maker named John-Joseph Merlin. Each skate had only two wheels, which were aligned one in front of the other along the center of the shoe. The crude design was based on the ice skates of Merlin's day, which were strapped to the shoes.

Soon after inventing the skates, Merlin decided to wear them to make a spectacular entrance at a costume party. A master violinist, Merlin intended to roll into the party while playing his violin. Unfortunately, he had neglected to master the fine art of stopping on skates, and when the big moment came he went careening through the room and crashed into a very valuable full-length mirror, breaking it and his violin and injuring himself. His entrance was indeed spectacular, though it did not have the desired effect of increasing the popularity of his new invention!

Did you know that in the near future the devil is planning to make his own spectacular appearance masquerading as Jesus Christ? But unlike John-Joseph Merlin, Satan has been practicing his dramatic entrance for 6,000 years! The Bible says that the coming deception will include "great signs and wonders," convincingly designed in order to "deceive, if possible, even the elect" (Matthew 24:24).

How can we avoid being deceived? The answer is threefold. First, we must stay close to Jesus. The Bible tells us that the only way to resist the devil is to "draw near to God" (James 4:7, 8). Second, we must test every religious teaching by searching the Scriptures diligently: "To the law and to the testimony! If they do not speak according to this word, it is because there is no light in them" (Isaiah 8:20). Third, we must pray for the discernment that the Holy Spirit can give, because spiritual things are "spiritually discerned" (1 Corinthians 2:14). As we do these three things, we can rest in Jesus' promise to His disciples: "My Father, who has given them to Me, is greater than all; and no one is able to snatch them out of My Father's hand" (John 10:29).

"Our friend Lazarus sleeps, but I go that I may wake him up" (John 11:11).

The Catacombs of Rome are a network of underground chambers and galleries that were used as burial places by the early Christians of the ancient Mediterranean world. During times of persecution, the catacombs became places of refuge because burial places were sacrosanct by Roman law. When churches above ground were destroyed by imperial order, worshipers met in the catacomb chapels. By the 3rd century A.D. Christians had carved 600 miles of tombs in volcanic rock in the area around Rome.

As Christianity gained converts and burials multiplied, the catacombs were expanded into honeycombs of galleries. The soft rock around Rome is perfect for making tunnels. When one level was no longer sufficient, staircases were dug and a second, third, or even fourth level of galleries was excavated below. Archeologists estimate that approximately three million Christians were interred in the catacombs around Rome.

Romans preferred cremation, but the Christians followed the practice of interring the dead in catacombs. They called them koimeteria, or "sleeping places." This shows death, for a Christian, was merely sleep before resurrection, a state of temporary unconsciousness. The Bible repeatedly speaks of the dead "sleeping," such as the kings of Israel and Judah "sleeping with their forefathers" (see 1 Kings 2:10 and 2 Chronicles 21:1 for examples).

When God created Adam from the dust of the Earth, the Lord breathed life into the first man and he "became a living being" (Genesis 2:7). At death the opposite of this creation takes place. When the breath of man returns to God, the body returns to the Earth and becomes dust again. The person or soul has no conscious existence apart from the body. Nothing in the Bible teaches a "soul" survives as a conscious entity after a person dies. In fact, the Bible says, "The soul who sins shall die" (Ezekiel 18:20).

When Jesus spoke to His disciples about their friend Lazarus sleeping, the disciples responded, "Lord, if he sleeps he will get well" (John 11:12). Notice the next verse. "However, Jesus spoke of his death, but they thought that He was speaking about taking rest in sleep. Then Jesus said to them plainly, 'Lazarus is dead'" (verses. 13, 14). And so, when our loved ones die, they rest in their graves or tombs until the second coming of Christ. Wouldn't it be interesting to be near the catacombs on that day?

January 15 THE PIGGY BANK

"But now, O Lord, You are our Father; we are the clay, and You our potter; and all we are the work of Your hand" (Isaiah 64:8).

Squirrels gather nuts. Dogs bury bones. Camels store food and water so they can travel across vast deserts. And pigs ... well, pigs save nothing. They bury nothing. They store nothing. So why do we save our spare coins in a piggy bank? A little history.

During the Middle Ages, in about the 15th century, metal was very expensive and seldom used for household wares. Instead, dishes and pots were made of cheap orange clay called pygg. Whenever housewives could save an extra coin, they dropped it into one of their clay jars or pots. They called this their pygg bank. Over the next two hundred years, people forgot that "pygg" referred to the earthenware material, but the "piggy bank" retained its name.

Around the 17th century an unknown potter thought to shape a "pygg" jar to look just like a real "pig." Of course, the piggy banks appealed to customers and delighted children. But the first piggy banks only had a slot in the top with no access hole in the bottom. Banks and savings institutions would often give piggy banks to children in an attempt to encourage them to save. People would drop their spare coins in the top and then literally break it open when it was full or some emergency arose. That's where we get the saying "Break the bank."

Isaiah says in our Bible text for today that God is the potter and we are the clay. The apostle Paul expands on this idea when he describes the message of the gospel being spread by simple people. "But we have this treasure in earthen vessels that the excellence of the power may be of God and not of us" (2 Corinthians 4:7). In other words, the precious treasure inside is of more value than the container. The piggy bank is not as important as the coins it holds.

I'm sure looking forward to the day when our earthly bodies will be laid aside, these vessels of clay, and a new heavenly body will be given to us. But something that will not change is the treasure of the gospel in our hearts.

"These words the LORD spoke to all your assembly, in the mountain from the midst of the fire, the cloud, and the thick darkness, with a loud voice; and He added no more. And He wrote them on two tablets of stone and gave them to me" (Deuteronomy 5:22).

Everyone knows the ancient Egyptians possessed great scientific and engineering knowledge. But for more than 1,500 years, the history of this great civilization had remained a baffling secret. Even though Egypt's history was written everywhere, it remained locked up in a mysterious writing called hieroglyphics. The Egyptians had used hieroglyphics for nearly 3,500 years, but no one in the modern world could decipher the meaning of the strange pictures and symbols. The Arabs who live in Egypt today are not the same race who built the pyramids so even they had no idea how to read the odd writings.

Then in 1799, while helping to extend an old Ottoman fort near Rosetta, a small city near Alexandria, a young French officer named Pierre-Francois Bouchard found an interesting block of black basalt stone. It measured three feet nine inches long, two feet four inches wide, and eleven inches thick. What is now considered a priceless archeological treasure which dates to 196 B.C.—and is said to be the most-visited item in the British Museum—had been used as common building material!

On this stone was etched a decree written in three distinct bands of language—Egyptian hieroglyphs, Egyptian demotic, and ancient Greek. Scholars quickly realized that the same message was written in these three languages.

After years of careful examination a brilliant young scholar and linguist named Jean-Francois Champollion, in 1824, was able to decipher the hieroglyphics by comparing the ancient texts on the Rosetta Stone. Understanding hieroglyphics unlocked the mysteries and history of ancient Egypt.

The Bible is often compared to a rock that unlocks the plan of salvation. For those willing to listen, it explains the deepest spiritual mysteries and deciphers the real meaning of life. It reveals the Savior of the world and brings hope to millions of people of all nations.

Sadly, the Word of God, which is the most priceless treasure we have, is often ignored and unappreciated, as was the Rosetta Stone for so many years. Why not read the Bible today and see what treasures are hidden in its precious pages?

January 17 THE LAST LIVING DRAGON

"He laid hold of the dragon, that serpent of old, who is the Devil and Satan, and bound him for a thousand years" (Revelation 20:2).

Flying dragons are prominent in many legends and stories from around the world. Often there is a kernel of truth in legends, and this appears to be the case with flying dragons. Paleontologists have found amazing fossil evidence all over the globe of giant flying reptiles called pterosaurs, or "winged lizards." Pterosaurs were flying reptiles, some with a wingspan of around 40 feet. That's about the size of a small Cessna airplane! They appear to be the largest flying animals that ever lived on Earth. The biggest of the pterosaurs weighed around 550 pounds. By comparison, the heaviest flying bird alive today, a kori bustard, is only 44 pounds. The bones of a pterosaur were lightly built and hollow to aid with flight.

Pterosaurs often had necks as long as 10 feet and legs as tall as seven feet. To someone watching from the ground, the long legs trailing behind a flying pterosaur might have looked like a dragon's pointed tail. Pterosaurs also had large brains and eyes, with a long, thin beak and toothless jaws. On their heads were bony crests, which some believe acted as a rudder in flight. Other scientists have surmised that the hollow chambers in the skull could have contained chemicals like the bombardier beetle that sprayed a fiery liquid from their mouths. We can't tell from the bones, but it is even possible that some of these extinct dragons were red.

Some of these creatures may have survived the flood. In the 5th century B.C. the Greek historian Herodotus wrote about "winged serpents" living in Arabia. But the Bible tells us that at least one dragon still exists today—the dragon also known as "the Devil and Satan" (Revelation 20:2). While some people believe that the devil is just a religious legend, the Bible makes it quite clear that he not only exists, but seeks to "deceive the whole world" and destroy those "who keep the commandments of God and have the testimony of Jesus Christ" (Revelation 12:9, 17). But the devil is not left unchecked, nor will he prevail. After being bound for a thousand years, he too will become extinct: "The devil, who deceived them, was cast into the lake of fire and brimstone" (Revelation 20:10).

"In the beginning was the Word, and the Word was with God, and the Word was God" (John 1:1).

During the days of the Persian Empire the grand vizier was typically the most influential officer in the realm. He was second in authority only to the sultan himself, who often left politics to others so he could indulge in palace pleasures. The grand vizier served much like a prime minister, with complete powers of attorney and was the leader of the imperial council.

In the 10th century, the grand vizier of Persia, Abdul Kassem Ismael, carried his library with him whenever he went on official business. The 117,000-volume collection was carried by 400 camels that had been trained to walk in alphabetical order! This was to simplify locating official documents for the librarians quickly pulling a book for their master.

The Bible exalts Jesus Christ as the Grand Ruler of the universe. Because of Christ's willingness to come to this Earth, Paul writes, "Therefore God also has highly exalted Him and given Him the name which is above every name, that at the name of Jesus every knee should bow ..." (Philippians 2:9,10). Much like a giant library, Jesus is not only called "the Alpha and the Omega" (Revelation 1:8), but John tells us regarding the works of Christ, "And there are also many other things that Jesus did, which if they were written one by one, I suppose that even the world itself could not contain the books that would be written" (John 21:25).

Jesus is called "the Word." He knew the written Word of God because the library of Scripture pointed to Himself. After His death and resurrection, Jesus appeared to two men walking on the road to Emmaus. They were confused about the recent events in Jerusalem. Christ pointed them to the Bible to encourage their faith. Luke writes, "And beginning at Moses and all the Prophets, He expounded to them in all the Scriptures the things concerning Himself" (Luke 24:27).

The Bible is like a walking library. Everything in this sacred library points to Jesus' life and work to save people. No matter which book you pull out and open, it tells of Christ. No matter where you are in the world, you can open the Word of God and find that all of Scripture testifies of Him (John 5:39). And you don't need 400 camels to carry around this amazing book!

January 19 THE WICKED BIBLE

"For assuredly, I say to you, till heaven and earth pass away, one jot or one tittle will by no means pass from the law till all is fulfilled. Whoever therefore breaks one of the least of these commandments, and teaches men so, shall be called least in the kingdom of heaven; but whoever does and teaches them, he shall be called great in the kingdom of heaven" (Matthew 5:18, 19).

Most of us know that the first book ever printed on a printing press was the Bible. But the quality and methods of printing in those early years were very primitive in comparison to today. This led to many printing errors in these early Bibles; although they did not cause any serious theological confusion, some of them were still worth a smile.

That is, until 1631, when King Charles I ordered 1,000 Bibles from an English printer named Robert Barker. Only after the Bibles were delivered did anyone notice a serious mistake. In Exodus 20:14, a very small word was forgotten by the printers—the word "not." That might seem like a small mistake in a book with over 700,000 words. But Exodus 20:14 happens to be one of the Ten Commandments. This little error changed the seventh commandment to say "Thou shalt commit adultery"!

This legendary edition became known as the "Wicked Bible." King Charles was not amused by the infamous printing blunder. He ordered the Bibles recalled and destroyed, took away Barker's license to print Bibles, and fined him 300 pounds (that was a lifetime of wages in those days). It is believed that only 11 of the original 1,000 Bibles exist today.

Robert Barker's mistake was an innocent one; he didn't intend to tamper with the Ten Commandments. But the Bible tells us that the Beast power would deliberately try to change God's law. The prophet Daniel wrote, "He shall speak pompous words against the Most High, shall persecute the saints of the Most High, and shall intend to change times and law" (Daniel 7:25).

But Jesus told us that God's law cannot be changed, not even "one jot or one tittle." As a reflection of God's character, it is unalterable. Whatever happens, God's law stands solid and immovable.

"And in vain they worship Me, teaching as doctrines the commandments of men.' For laying aside the commandment of God, you hold the tradition of men ..." (Mark 7:7, 8).

Years ago in the old Russian Empire the ruling czar, Nicholas II, was strolling through his vast palace gardens when he came upon a lonely guard standing at attention in a secluded corner of the great meandering gardens. "What are you guarding?" asked the inquisitive ruler. "To tell you the truth, O Great Sovereign, I have no idea, but the captain of the guard ordered me to this post," the sentry replied.

Czar Nicholas then summoned the captain and made further inquiries as to what was being guarded. The captain of the guard replied, "O Great Sovereign, there are clear written regulations specifying that a guard was to be assigned to that precise corner at all times and this has been done as long as I can remember." The curious czar then ordered a search to find out why.

The palace archives finally yielded the answer. Years before, Catherine the Great had planted a special rose bush in that corner, and she had firmly ordered a sentry to be posted there to guard it so nothing might disturb or damage it. Now, one hundred years later, even though the rose bush had died long before, sentries were still guarding the now barren corner of dirt, even though no one knew why!

Traditions of faith can be valuable. They may be useful in preserving special experiences or ideals handed down by family or culture. However, we should be careful in what we spend our time guarding! Many religions zealously defend rituals which have lost their meaning. People may faithfully stand by traditions but not know why.

There is a more serious concern regarding traditions that Jesus warned us about. If a custom should ever stand in conflict with the commandments of God, it should be thrown out. Christ told us that holding such traditions makes "the word of God of no effect" (Mark 7:13). It's a good idea to reflect on the traditions we keep. Do they conflict with God's law? If so, we are stepping away from the Bible. It's like standing guard over a dead bush.

THE GIVER OF WISDOM

"And men of all nations, from all the kings of the earth who had heard of his wisdom, came to hear the wisdom of Solomon" (1 Kings 4:34).

Born of slave parents in Diamond Grove, Missouri, George Washington Carver was rescued from Confederate kidnappers as an infant. He began his education in Newton County in southwest Missouri, where he worked as a farmhand and studied in a one-room schoolhouse. Throughout his formal education, Carver was the only African-American student at each school he attended. An excellent student, he thrived in the educational environment, impressed his teachers, and went on to earn a master's degree from Iowa State College.

Carver is perhaps to this day the nation's best known African-American scientist. In the period between 1890 and 1910, the cotton crop had been devastated by the boll weevil. At Tuskegee Institute, Carver had developed his crop rotation method, which alternated nitrate-producing legumes—such as peanuts and peas—with cotton, which depletes the soil of its nutrients.

Carver advised the cotton farmers to cultivate peanuts. Following Carver's lead, southern farmers soon began planting peanuts one year and cotton the next. While many of the peanuts were used to feed livestock, large surpluses quickly developed. Carver then invented over 300 different uses for the extra peanuts—from cooking oil to shampoo, from milk to printer's ink.

When he discovered that the sweet potato and the pecan also enriched depleted soils, Carver found almost 20 uses for these crops, including making synthetic rubber and material for paving highways. His accomplishments earned him world renown as a plant expert, scientist, and inventor, and he received many honors.

While some people, such as George Washington Carver, seem to have an extra measure of wisdom, we can all increase our wisdom. The Bible clearly identifies the true source: "For the LORD gives wisdom; from His mouth come knowledge and understanding" (Proverbs 2:6). God wants us to have wisdom. His Word tells us, "If any of you lacks wisdom, let him ask of God, who gives to all liberally and without reproach, and it will be given to him" (James 1:5).

George Washington Carver had great faith in God and knew Jesus as his Savior. He was also a humble man. Because he understood that all wisdom comes from God, he rightly gave God the credit for all of his skills, talents, and accomplishments.

"And Jesus answered and said to them: 'Take heed that no one deceives you. For many will come in My name, saying, "I am the Christ," and will deceive many"' (Matthew 24:4, 5).

Legend has it that when the Greeks were unable to capture the city of Troy, even after imposing a 10-year siege, they finally resorted to a clever stratagem. The Greek army pretended to sail away and left on the shore a huge, hollow wooden horse as an apparent victory gift. However, the gift was actually filled with several armed warriors!

Sinon, a Greek warrior, is the only volunteer to be "left behind" and become a spy inside Troy. The Greeks pretend to sail away, but plan to come back under the cover of night. Sinon then tells the people of Troy that the horse is a gift to the god Athena to atone for their evil acts against their city. He then persuades the Trojans to bring the horse within the city walls, saying it will mysteriously make Troy invincible. That night Sinon releases the troops hiding in the gigantic horse. After killing the Trojan guards, they open the gates to the waiting Greek soldiers, and Troy is captured and burned.

There are various accounts of different characters who try to warn the Trojans not to accept the gift horse. A Trojan priest expresses, in Virgil's famous poetic words, "Beware of Greeks bearing gifts," but is strangled by the god Poseidon before the townspeople hear and believe his warning. Modern historians suggest the horse may have originally been a battering ram. Others think an earthquake provided the necessary break down of walls for soldiers to enter the city. Today we think of a "Trojan horse" as any deceptive strategy used to trick people into bringing an enemy into one's protected space—such as innocently opening a computer file and infecting your hard drive.

The Trojan horse is a clear illustration for the work of Satan in seeking to deceive people just before Jesus returns. Christ warns us that in the last days "many will come in My name, saying, 'I am the Christ,' and will deceive many" (Matthew 24:5). The devil will not try to send false Christs only once or twice. Many deceivers will come. Jesus tells us to be careful. Like Virgil's famous words, we too should "beware of the devil bearing gifts!"

January 23 A KING'S RANSOM

"Stand fast therefore in the liberty by which Christ has made us free, and do not be entangled again with a yoke of bondage" (Galatians 5:1).

In A.D. 1532, Francisco Pizarro, with around 160 men, entered the heart of the Inca Empire in search of gold. The Conquistadors eventually found their way into the presence of the young Inca king, Atahuallpa. That's when a Spanish friar, traveling with Pizarro, told the Inca monarch his people must renounce their gods. When Atahuallpa asked them upon what authority they were making this demand, the Catholic friar handed him a Bible. Atahuallpa held the book next to his ear, trying to listen to its pages. At last he asked: "Why doesn't the book say anything to me?" And he threw it violently to the ground.

The Spanish used this insult as an excuse to attack and massacre the crowds of unarmed people, and the handsome king was arrested. It is, indeed, astonishing to think how a small army like Pizarro's, with only 62 horsemen and 102 infantry, were able to attack an empire of at least five million people. But they had the latest technology in deadly weapons—guns and mechanical crossbows and horses—that terrified the natives.

King Atahuallpa, now understanding that the Spanish wanted gold, came up with his plan to free himself. He told Pizarro he would give, for his release, enough gold and silver vessels to fill three large rooms. The Spaniards thought this was impossible, but the gold-hungry Pizarro agreed. So Atahuallpa decreed that his realm be ransacked to fill one room 18-by-22-feet with gold stacked to a height of a little more than eight feet. In addition, two equal-sized rooms would be filled with silver! By July of 1533, more than 24 tons of exquisite treasure had been collected, worth at least 267 million dollars at today's values. The Spaniards did not honor their promise. They kept Atahuallpa imprisoned for another year, using him to control the Inca Empire, and then killed him.

How sad that the largest ransom ever paid for a man's freedom was in vain! Sadder still, there are millions of people who have had a king's ransom paid for their freedom and they choose to remain in prison! It doesn't have to be this way. Jesus is waiting to release us from the prison of sin. "Therefore if the Son makes you free, you shall be free indeed" (John 8:36). Will you accept this freedom today?

"O Jerusalem, Jerusalem, the one who kills the prophets and stones those who are sent to her! How often I wanted to gather your children together, as a hen gathers her chicks under her wings, but you were not willing. See! Your house is left to you desolate; for I say to you, you shall see Me no more till you say, 'Blessed is He who comes in the name of the LORD!'" (Matthew 23:37-39).

The state of Israel has only 0.8 percent of the world's population and is the world's 100th smallest country. Yet they can claim the following amazing accomplishments:

- Twenty-four percent of Israel's workforce holds university degrees and 12 percent hold advanced degrees. That's the highest ratio for its population in the world.
- Aside from the United States, Israel has the largest number of start-up companies in the world.
- Israel's economy of $100 billion is larger than all of its immediate neighbors combined.
- Israel has the highest average standard of living in the Middle East, even exceeding that of the United Kingdom.
- Israel has the world's second highest number of new books per capita.
- Israel has the highest percentage in the world of home computers per capita.
- The cell phone was developed in Israel by Motorola.
- Israel is the only country in the world that entered the 21st century with a net gain in its number of trees.
- With an aerial arsenal of over 250 F-16s, Israel has the largest fleet of fighter aircraft outside of the United States.
- Relative to its population, Israel is the largest immigrant-absorbing nation on Earth.
- Israel has more museums per capita than any other country in the world.

It would certainly seem that God is blessing this little country! But why then is this unique nation so embattled? What will their end result be as a nation? Christ wept over Jerusalem and foretold their future. God has not rejected individuals of Jewish descent. But the Lord has turned away from Israel as His representative nation. Yet, the tears of Christ, when He wept over Jerusalem, are tears He weeps for you and me if we will not turn to Him.

THE MOTHER OF ALL CITIES

"And Babylon, the glory of kingdoms, the beauty of the Chaldeans' pride, will be as when God overthrew Sodom and Gomorrah. It will never be inhabited, nor will it be settled from generation to generation" (Isaiah 13:19, 20).

Aside from Israel, Iraq is the land most often mentioned in the Bible. Some familiar Bible names for this historic region are Eden, Shinar, Babylon, Assyria, Mesopotamia, Nineveh, and parts of ancient Persia. It is sometimes known as the Fertile Crescent and cradle of civilization. The adventures of Bible characters like Esther, Jonah, Daniel, and Ezekiel all took place in this historic land. On two occasions the people of God have been carried off to the land of Iraq. The ten tribes were carried off into Assyria in 721 B.C. Then Nebuchadnezzar destroyed Jerusalem in 587 B.C. and drove its inhabitants of Judah into 70 years of captivity. This is one reason Saddam Hussein revered King Nebuchadnezzar as his hero. Hussein longed to duplicate the feat of conquering Israel and ruling the Arab nations!

In fact, Saddam once had himself photographed in a replica of the war chariot of Nebuchadnezzar, and tried to convince people he was the reincarnation of the ancient king of Babylon. (The Bible also tells us that Nebuchadnezzar went insane for seven years.) History records Babylon was conquered by the Persians and then the Greeks. After the death of Alexander the Great the city of Babylon began to fade. Ultimately, the once great city ceased to be inhabited and the ruins were swallowed by the Euphrates River and shifting sand of the Iraqi desert.

Many Christians firmly believe that Babylon must be rebuilt before the last events of prophecy can be fulfilled. But the prophet Isaiah clearly promised, "It will never be inhabited ... But wild beasts of the desert will lie there, and their houses will be full of owls ..." (Isaiah 13:20, 21). Saddam Hussein desperately wanted to prove the Jewish prophet wrong and vainly spent millions trying to rebuild the ruins of ancient Babylon in an effort to restore it to a thriving metropolis. Saddam's grand plans to restore Babylon have been repeatedly thwarted by war, and now he is gone.

If the Bible says Babylon will never be rebuilt, then what is the last-day Babylon spoken of in the book of Revelation? Revelation 17:5 speaks of Babylon as "the mother of harlots and of the abominations of the earth." If Christ's church is represented as a pure woman (see Revelation 12:1), then what else could Babylon represent but fallen apostate churches?

"I know your works, that you are neither cold nor hot. I could wish you were cold or hot. So then, because you are lukewarm, and neither cold nor hot, I will vomit you out of My mouth" (Revelation 3:15, 16).

On September 22, 1840, Captain Brighton of the whaling ship *Hope* claimed to have happened upon a strange sight—a ship frozen in the ice of the Drake Passage near Antarctica. Boarding the ship, Captain Brighton found that the crew had died some years before, but their bodies had been perfectly preserved by the frigid temperatures of the Antarctic sea. They were frozen solid—some in their hammocks as if asleep. The captain of the Jenny was sitting at his desk in front of his log book, his pen still in his hand. The last entry read: "No food for 71 days. I am the only one left alive." According to the date, the schooner Jenny had been floating among the icebergs for thirteen years.

While this account is unsubstantiated and likely only a sea-faring legend, it is thought provoking. Do we have churches with a temperature problem? Jesus warned that His church at the end of time would think that they are rich and in need of nothing, but in reality they are "wretched, miserable, poor, blind, and naked" (Revelation 3:17). Thankfully, Jesus also provided a solution: "I counsel you to buy from Me gold refined in the fire, that you may be rich; and white garments, that you may be clothed, that the shame of your nakedness may not be revealed; and anoint your eyes with eye salve, that you may see" (Revelation 3:18).

The gold Jesus refers to is a loving faith, the kind that can endure tough trials. He offers us His white garments of righteousness—His life lived out within us (Isaiah 61:10), but first we need to look to Jesus so our blind eyes can see our true condition. When we realize how our spiritual pride has blinded us and how poor we really are, we might well ask how a poor man can afford gold and new clothes. That's the best part! Jesus intends for us to buy from Him "without money" because He's paid the price (Isaiah 55:1).

Good news like this can thaw even the hardest heart!

January 27 BERSERKERS

"So then, my beloved brethren, let every man be swift to hear, slow to speak, slow to wrath; for the wrath of man does not produce the righteousness of God" (James 1:19, 20).

Ancient Norse history speaks in the old sagas of a fearsome class of warriors called Berserkers. According to reports, Berserkers would dress themselves in the skins of bears or wolves to exploit the fear common people had for wild animals.

Before entering battle, Berserkers would whip themselves up into a sort of crazed frenzy, biting their shields and howling like animals, possibly aided by psychoactive drugs. While in this trance-like condition, they were ferocious fighters and seemingly impervious to pain. Swords and knives seemed to have little impact on them. In their rage, Berserkers made formidable enemies; they even attacked the boulders and trees of the forest and it was not uncommon for them to kill their own people during their rampage. Their irrational and violent behavior showed that they were totally out of control.

It was often said the Berserker seemed to change into bestial form, or at least to assume the ferocious nature of the wolf or bear. One writer reports, "... they went without coats of mail, and acted like mad dogs and wolves." It is believed the myth of werewolves originates with these wild Norse warriors. And you probably figured out that these enraged Scandinavian fighters gave rise to the English word "berserk" to describe someone who is overcome with an uncontrolled rage. Now here's a question: If Christians lose their temper and fly off the handle, are they really Christians when they act berserk?

The Scriptures tell us, "A wise man fears and departs from evil, but a fool rages ..." and "He who is slow to anger is better than the mighty, and he who rules his spirit than he who takes a city" (Proverbs 14:16; 16:32). And Peter advises: "... add to your faith virtue, to virtue knowledge, to knowledge self-control ..." (2 Peter 1:5-7).

Self-control is an important part of Christian character. Only by controlling our temper can we reflect Christ to others. If we're really living for Christ, rather than acting impulsively in response to anger, we will be developing the fruit of His Spirit. "But the fruit of the Spirit is love, joy, peace, longsuffering, kindness, goodness, faithfulness, gentleness, self-control. Against such there is no law" (Galatians 5:22, 23).

"You shall make of these an incense, a compound according to the art of the perfumer, salted, pure, and holy. And you shall beat some of it very fine, and put some of it before the Testimony in the tabernacle of meeting where I will meet with you. It shall be most holy to you" (Exodus 30:35, 36).

Josephine de Beauharnais was the first wife of Napoleon Bonaparte and the first empress of the French. She received many love letters from Napoleon, and many of them still exist. Her chateau was known for a magnificent rose garden. She watched over it very carefully and collected roses from around the world. Because she did not produce an heir for the king, Napoleon divorced her, but never forgot her.

The chateau near Paris, long inhabited by Josephine, still exudes the strong odor of musk with which the empress used to douse her person in life. Her favorite essence was the Houbigant musk perfume manufactured in Paris. The castle, now a museum, changed hands many times after Napoleon's ex-wife died in it in 1814. But no effort of the subsequent owners has ever succeeded in eradicating the strong and penetrating scent which clings to the walls, imprinting the empress's personality on her residence forever.

Napoleon was so enamored of the sweet smell of success that he used 54 bottles of cologne a month and carried them with him to his battlefields. Houbigant fragrances could be found in his campaign chest during the years he went out to conquer Europe. One would think that on a windy day the odor would have alerted the enemy of his presence!

The Bible talks about perfume in reference to the Old Testament sanctuary altar of incense. God gave careful instructions on how to make this fragrant substance using gum resins and spices. The specific recipe was sacred and not to be used for general purposes (see Exodus 30:34-38). This incense was burned morning and evening on the altar that stood in the Holy Place in front of the curtain that separated it from the Most Holy Place.

This golden altar of incense was seen by John in vision in heaven standing before God. On it an angel burned incense, which was mingled with the prayers of the saints (Revelation 8:3) and represents the ministry of Christ. Like Josephine and Napoleon, it would be well for us to "douse" ourselves every day, not with cologne or perfume, but with the sweet savor of prayer.

January 29 THE LEFT OR RIGHT

"And He will set the sheep on his right hand, but the goats on the left" (Matthew 25:33).

Have you ever wondered why in some countries the drivers use the right side of the road and in others—like Great Britain—they use the left? Well, the theory is that in olden days the nobility would ride their horses on the left of the road so their sword hand, usually the right hand, would be on the same side as an oncoming horseman. Naturally, with armed nobility riding around, it made sense for peasants to walk on the right, facing the oncoming traffic. For many years this was the case in the U.K. and Europe.

But remember that during the French revolution many of the aristocrats were executed. Even after the revolution it was a bad idea to be mistaken for nobility. So everyone in France started to travel on the right side of the road. Then along came Napoleon, who carried this practice with him as he conquered large parts of Europe and built the first international road system since the Romans. But because of his defeat at Waterloo, Napoleon never made it to England. Therefore, the U.K. and all its territories continued riding on the left. Today the words "right" and "left" have also come to represent opposite extremes in politics and religion, generally in reference to liberal or conservative views and practices.

Did you know that the Bible teaches that right and left extremes will come together in the last days to worship the beast and its image? Revelation 13 talks about "small and great, rich and poor, free and slave" receiving a mark of allegiance to the beast. This power will attempt to unite all mankind in a defiant stance against God. When good and evil play out their final struggle, no one will be immune from making a choice one way or the other. Everyone will worship either God or the beast.

According to Scripture, the confrontation won't last long. Every person from every nation will be gathered before Christ, "and He will separate them one from another, as a shepherd divides his sheep from the goats" (Matthew 25:32). Great things are in store for the sheep on the right, for they will inherit the kingdom of God (verse 34). I want to be sure I'm at the right hand of Jesus on that day, don't you?

"And the LORD God said, 'It is not good that man should be alone'" (Genesis 2:18).

Alexander Selkirk was a quick-tempered, hardened sailor and pirate. In 1703, he joined William Dampier on a privateering expedition, plundering Spanish merchant ships in the Pacific. After a quarrel with the captain over the seaworthiness of their ship, the hotheaded Selkirk demanded to be left ashore on the uninhabited island of Juan Fernandez, 400 miles west of Chile. However, when Selkirk realized that none of the crew would join him, he had a moment of regret and begged the captain to be let on the ship—but the captain refused. So Selkirk was left alone with a few basic supplies: clothes, bedding, flint, a pound of gunpowder, bullets, a hatchet, a knife, a kettle, his navigation tools, and a Bible. What Selkirk thought might be a few days until the next ship came by stretched into nearly four and a half years.

The first months were a difficult adjustment. The nights were terrifying: the bellowing calls of sea lions, tree limbs breaking in the frequent storms, and the hordes of rats gnawing on his feet as he tried to sleep. Selkirk was depressed and even contemplated suicide. He was almost glad to be hungry because it diverted his thoughts. However, in time, Selkirk's mood improved. He kept busy building a hut, catching wild goats to eat, and taming the feral cats (which eventually helped with the rats). In addition to watching for passing ships, Selkirk spent time singing hymns, praying, and reading his Bible. He later remarked that he was a better Christian on the island than ever before, or, as it seems, after. In 1709, Selkirk was rescued by another English ship. It was then that he learned the fate of his old crewmates: the ship sank soon after leaving Juan Fernandez, most of the crew was killed, and the rest were captured by the Spanish.

As the poet John Milton wrote, "Loneliness is the first thing which God's eye named, not good." God knew that we would need human companionship and gave us marriage, family, and friendship for that purpose. But during those abandoned-at-sea moments when marriages fail, families misunderstand us, and friends desert us, we can find the Companion that Selkirk found—the One who promises "I will not leave you nor forsake you" (Joshua 1:5).

MIRROR IN THE OCEAN

"For Satan himself transforms himself into an angel of light" (2 Corinthians 11:14).

On August 4, 1914, the magnificent British luxury liner RMS *Carmania* was three days out of New York City with 800 passengers on her way to Liverpool when she learned from another ship that England had declared war on Germany. As soon as the *Carmania* arrived in Liverpool the British Admiralty assumed command. Within one week of entering port as a first-class cruise liner, the *Carmania* was converted into a warship in service of the Royal Navy.

On September 2, the *Carmania* was assigned to the West Indies with orders to scout the vicinity for enemy ships. Three days later the lookout sighted a ship off the coast of Trinidad. At that point the *Carmania* crew might have thought they entered the Twilight Zone. The ship they spied in the distance from the decks of the *Carmania* was ... the *Carmania*! Or at least a ship that bore her name and looked exactly like her. The other vessel was in fact a German luxury liner called the *Cap Trafalgar* that had also been converted into a warship and then disguised in every outward detail as the *Carmania*.

Because of the short-range guns which had been installed on the German ship, she could only be effective in battle if she could get close enough to the enemy. So the *Cap Trafalgar* was disguised as the British liner *Carmania*, and that was the German ship's downfall. On September 14, the disguised *Cap Trafalgar* was attacked and sunk by the real *Carmania*.

The incredible mirror encountered in the ocean by the *Carmania* was a two-way mirror. Just as the *Cap Trafalgar* was redesigned—even to the dismantling of one smoke stack—to look like the *Carmania*, the *Carmania* was also redesigned and repainted so that she could get closer to the enemy. In the process a dummy smoke stack was added to the British ship. That's right! When the two vessels coincidentally met in mid-Atlantic on September 14, 1914, each was masquerading as the other!

The Bible teaches in the last days Satan will perform his masterpiece of impersonation. Jesus warned of false christs coming (Matthew 24:24-26), but God's people will not be caught off guard for they know the Scriptures. The devil cannot counterfeit the universal coming of Christ (see v. 27). If we study the Bible we will detect the deceiver and not be fooled, even if the outward details look like the real thing.

Health & Human Biology

*"So God created man in His own image;
in the image of God He created him;
male and female He created them."
Genesis 1:27*

February 1 THE LOVE APPLE

"Oh, taste and see that the LORD is good; blessed is the man who trusts in Him!" (Psalm 34:8).

In 1820, a crowd of curious people gathered around the county courthouse in Salem, New Jersey. The county fair was in progress, and they jostled one another in eager anticipation, for they were about to witness a daring feat. Soon a man appeared on the steps, holding in one hand a piece of poisonous fruit that had been part of the fair's decorations. As he held it up for them to see, members of the crowd whispered excitedly to one another. "Is he really going to eat it?" some asked in disbelief.

The man was Colonel Robert Gibbon Johnson, and the fruit was a tomato. Returning Spanish conquistadors brought the first tomato seeds from Peru to Italy. Upon arrival, the Italians believed the heart-shaped tomato was an aphrodisiac—thus tomato in Italian, poma amoris, means "love apple." Love apples were often tokens of courtship. Young men gave them to their girlfriends, who would wear the seeds in sachets around their necks. The fruit was admired for its beauty, but because of its relation to deadly nightshade the tomato was regarded as poison by Americans and no one would dream of eating it.

The crowd gasped in horror as Colonel Johnson deliberately placed the tomato in his mouth and ate it with apparent relish. They waited breathlessly, expecting soon to see him collapse, writhing in dying agony, on the courthouse steps. But nothing happened. Instead, praising the color and texture, he ate a second tomato, explaining that tomatoes were delicious either cooked or raw. He then invited the onlookers to join him in his meal, and a few of the braver ones went forward. Soon they too were relishing the tomatoes' flavor.

The news rapidly spread, and eventually tomatoes became a widely accepted article of diet, providing a primary source of minerals and vitamins A and C. Today the United States grows about 9 million metric tons of tomatoes yearly and there are more varieties of tomatoes sold than of any other fruit.

The Bible teaches that the devil is a master of deception in convincing people to fear what is good and eat what is bad. But once we taste the goodness of the Lord and learn to trust in Him, He will help us discern between what is bad and what is good. He will be our Guide.

"In the middle of its street, and on either side of the river, was the tree of life, which bore twel fruits, each tree yielding its fruit every month. The leave tree were for the healing of the nations" (Revel 2).

Deadly malaria een killing people since the beginning
of written histo until the middle of the 17th century
ffecti scovered. Jesuit missionaries in Peru
Indians in treating malaria with a tea
Vhile no one knows for sure how the
lausible legend which supplies

gle and burning
ater and threw
h p of the bitter water
of the quina-quina tree,
Much to the man's surprise, he
rning. He eventually found his way
le a full recovery. He told everybody
quina-quina bark, and the quinine
treat 742, the tree was renamed cinchona
by a Swedish botan he Countess of Chinchon, who may
have been the first Eu an extract of the bark to treat her
malaria. Quinine was stil rred treatment for malaria until the
1940s, and it is still used in ce egions of the world because of its low
cost. Quinine has also been used to treat arthritis and lupus.

The Bible speaks of another tree that has healing properties: the tree of life. This tree, which has two trunks, one on either side of the river of life, bears 12 different kinds of fruit. Poetically, Revelation tells us that its leaves are for healing the nations. In other words, all that divides us here on Earth will be healed as people from all nations of the world gather under its branches.

February 3 SLEEPWALKING CHRISTIANS

"And do this, knowing the time, that now it is high time to awake out of sleep; for now our salvation is nearer than when we first believed" (Romans 13:11).

Sleepwalking, also known as somnambulism, is a troubling condition where individuals, mostly children, arise in a state of low consciousness and perform various activities normally performed while awake. These activities can be as harmless as sitting up in bed, walking to the bathroom, and cleaning, or as hazardous as driving, starting fires, walking in traffic, or cooking. The person's eyes might be open but have a glassy "look right through you" expression. These sleepwalking episodes can last as little as 30 seconds or as long as 30 minutes.

In 2005, a 34-year-old computer expert was reportedly caught sleepwalking by his wife. He was mowing the lawn at 2 a.m. ... naked. Rebekah Armstrong was awakened by a noise coming from the garden. When she realized her husband, Ian, was not in bed she went downstairs and looked outside to see what was happening. Rebekah found Ian was mowing the lawn in his birthday tuxedo. She was afraid to wake him up because she had heard it could be dangerous to disturb someone in a sleepwalking trance. So she just unplugged the electric mower, went back to bed and let him go through the motions. Later Ian came wandering back to bed. In the morning he didn't believe Rebekah when she told him what he'd been up to. "It wasn't until I told him to look at the soles of his feet that he finally believed me—they were filthy."

Is it possible to be a sleepwalking Christian? I don't mean physically getting out of bed and walking around in a state of unconsciousness. Can Christians be spiritually asleep, walking through life in a low state of awareness about the things of God? Absolutely! Jesus' parable of the ten virgins describes a group (representing the church) who were awaiting the coming of the bridegroom (Jesus). Notice, "But while the bridegroom was delayed, they all slumbered and slept" (Matthew 25:5).

Do you know what divides these sleeping saints into two different groups? Half of them, though slumbering, still had made preparations for the coming of the bridegroom. When the midnight cry was heard, part of the group had extra oil (representing the Holy Spirit) and were immediately ready to follow the wedding party. Are you making necessary preparations for Jesus' soon coming?

"He gives power to the weak, and to those who have no might He increases strength" (Isaiah 40:29).

Eugen Sandow, a Prussian man born in 1867, is known as "the father of modern bodybuilding." Besides performing feats of strength with barbells, Sandow was one of the first individuals to develop his muscles to exact proportions. He greatly admired the classical Greek and Roman statues. When he visited museums containing these statues, he would carefully measure them. He then used these figures to build his physique to the same proportions, which he considered the "Grecian ideal." Eventually, more people became interested in bodybuilding, and Sandow later created a gym and shared his knowledge on how to develop muscles. He is credited with initiating and popularizing the fitness craze that continues to this day.

Sandow's strength and muscles were only moderate compared to those of modern body builders. Take, for example, Isaac Nesser, who holds the record for the largest naturally obtained muscular chest and arms. His chest measures 74 inches around and his arms bulge at 29 inches in circumference. He has bench pressed as much as 820 pounds and curls barbells up to 315 pounds.

This is impressive, but a small feat compared with the exploits of Samson. According to the Bible, he was the strongest man who ever lived, and he killed thousands of the enemies of his people. When he was tied up with new rope, he simply broke free. Another time he picked up the gates of a city and carried them to the top of a hill. He even killed a lion with his bare hands! How many people do you know who could do that? Can you imagine the size of Samson's muscles? Yet, when it came to spiritual muscle, for most of his life Samson was a real wimp, chasing after heathen women and making other disastrous moral choices.

The Scriptures tell us that God is the one who gives us strength, both physical and spiritual. "The LORD will give strength to His people ..." (Psalm 29:11). "The LORD is my strength and my shield ..." (Psalm 28:7). "It is God who arms me with strength ..." (Psalm 18:32).

God strengthens our spiritual muscle through regular prayer and Bible study, through trusting His promises and sharing His goodness with others. And like Sandow with his statues, we have an "ideal"—Jesus—and He will empower us to be like Him.

February 5 MR. UNFORGETTABLE

"I will never forget Your precepts, for by them You have given me life" (Psalm 119:93).

When Kim Peek was born in 1951, his parents knew he was different. He had an enlarged head, and tests revealed that his left and right brain hemispheres were not separated like most people, forming a great single "data storage" area. Kim's motor skills and physical development proved slow, and he did not walk until age four. But early on his parents noticed other remarkable abilities. By 20 months Kim was able to memorize every book that was read to him. By age three Kim was reading the dictionary. Since that time until his death in 2009, Kim had read and could clearly recall over 12,000 books!

Peek was called a "mega-savant" because his photographic memory made him a virtual genius in about 15 different subjects. Known as "Kimputer" to many, his vast knowledge included: world and American history, British monarchs, Bible history, geography (he was acquainted with all main roads and highways in the U.S. and Canada), professional sports statistics (for baseball, basketball, football, Kentucky Derby winners, etc.), the history of the space program, movies and music themes, the complete works of Shakespeare, telephone area codes, major zip codes, and all TV stations and their markets. He could identify most classical music compositions and tell the date the music was written and the composer's birth date and place of birth and death. He especially enjoyed calendar calculations. If you told him your birth date, he would tell you the day of the week you were born and what the day of the week will be when you turn 65 so you can retire.

Kim struggled with simple tasks like dressing and shaving himself or finding the silverware drawer at home. Still, it was his encyclopedic memory that became the inspiration for the 1988 Oscar-winning movie *Rain Man*, portrayed by Dustin Hoffman. In his later life, when home in Utah, Kim spent afternoons at the Salt Lake City Public Library poring over books, even memorizing phone books. It only took him about eight seconds to read an average page and he read two pages at a time—one with his left eye the other with his right.

If you had a photographic memory, what would you want to remember? King David provides the perfect answer in today's Bible text. What could be more important than to keep in mind all of God's law. David also wrote: "Your word I have hidden in my heart, that I might not sin against You" (Psalm 119:11).

"...[N]ow it is high time to awake out of sleep; for now our salvation is nearer than when we first believed" (Romans 13:11).

Did you know that one hour of sleep deprivation increases the number of highway accidents by 8 percent and an hour of extra sleep decreases them by 8 percent? It's true, and studies have shown that it happens every year during the daylight saving time changes.

Getting a good night's rest is nothing to snore at. Your efficiency driving after you have been awake for 18 hours is the same as driving after you have had two alcoholic drinks. When you have been awake for 24 hours your driving efficiency is equivalent to driving under the influence of 4-6 drinks!

Are Americans sleeping less than their great-grandparents? Yes. An estimated 60 million Americans have trouble sleeping. Today, because of artificial lights, TV, the Internet, and the caffeine craze, people are sleeping about one hour less than their great-grandparents did. This figure might not be startling in itself—but considering that proper sleep is one of the most important elements in the process of healing, America is also in for a disease-ridden wake up call.

So, what's wrong with a little caffeine to keep you awake? The hormone adenosine induces relaxation to help us sleep, but caffeine blocks the communication between adenosine and the brain, keeping you "awake" and shutting off the body's defense against exhaustion-related injury. Alcohol also robs the body of deep sleep. Tobacco users miss out on deeper sleep due to nicotine withdrawal during the night. And anti-depressants (even sleeping pills) can also decrease levels of REM sleep, a type of sleep that keeps your mind healthy.

Optimum performance comes with nine hours of sleep each night. Sending your kids to bed early is no longer a "because I said so" event. According to one study, school-age children who had less than nine hours of sleep had dramatically higher rates of obesity and increased temperament issues. And those going to bed after 9 p.m. were the most at risk for developing these complications.

Getting enough sleep is important when it comes to performance, but Jesus said there is a time to stay awake at any cost. Paul explains, "Therefore let us cast off the works of darkness, and let us put on the armor of light. Let us walk properly, as in the day, not in revelry and drunkenness" (Romans 13:13, 14). When we properly get our rest, physically and spiritually in Christ, we will be able to function with clear minds.

February 7

"But when the king came in to see the guests, he saw a man there who did not have on a wedding garment" (Matthew 22:11).

Man is different from every other creature in regard to clothing. All of God's other creatures were "born with their clothes on," so to speak. Shrimp and snakes slough off their old clothes and grow new ones. Some animals even shed their old clothes periodically and develop new ones. Man is the only creature whose clothes must come from the outside.

Most of us have never felt much of a debt of gratitude for our clothing, but some people owe their lives to what they were wearing! For instance, in order to survive the extreme temperatures and vacuum of space, astronauts need special spacesuits. These suits supply them with oxygen, maintain pressure, monitor their blood pressure and heart rhythm, and keep their bodies at controlled temperatures. Without the Earth's atmosphere to filter the sunlight, the side of the suit facing the Sun may be heated to a temperature as high as 248 degrees F; the other side, exposed to darkness of deep space, may get as cold as minus 160 degrees F. Paradoxically, the suit's life-support system has to remove the heat and sweaty moisture generated by the working astronaut. This is usually accomplished by circulating cool water through an undergarment worn next to the astronaut's skin.

When Neil Armstrong went on the historic Apollo 11 mission as the first man to land on the moon, his suit was specially designed to provide a life-sustaining environment with relative comfort for up to 115 hours outside the spacecraft, or for 14 days in an unpressurized mode. Astronauts must put an enormous amount of trust in their spacesuits. One described the eerie feeling he got after realizing that while outside the space capsule, there was just one-quarter of an inch of material between him and eternity. Now that's important clothing!

Jesus once told a story about a king who provided wedding garments for all his guests. When he walked through the banquet hall he was surprised to find one person without the special clothing he provided. "So he said to him, 'Friend, how did you come in here without a wedding garment?' And he was speechless" (Matthew 22:12). When Jesus comes back to our Earth, will you be ready to make a trip to heaven because you have on the special garment of His righteousness?

"Then Jesus, moved with compassion, stretched out His hand and touched him, and said to him, 'I am willing; be cleansed'" (Mark 1:41).

In 1915, Dr. Henry D. Chapin reported that in infant-care homes throughout the U.S. nearly every child under two years died. The mortality rate was almost 100 percent. Knowing the babies were given adequate nourishment and cleanliness, he wondered what the problem was. He then discovered the policy at the time was "no coddling of the babies was allowed." The babies died from lack of touch.

During WWII, an orphanage in London was a warehouse for a wave of unwanted babies. Children there were only given essential care like clothing, food, and shelter. It was all they could do just to attend to the many physical needs that were obvious. At this particular orphanage, the mortality rate was high. Fifty percent of all babies that came in died within a year and a half of their arrival. They simply did not know then, what we know today, about the importance of human touch and the role it plays in the physical, as well as emotional, well-being of babies.

Someone came up with the idea of touching the babies more, not just when they were fed or clothed. All workers, from the janitor to the director, were ordered to reach down and stroke or gently touch every baby they passed in the course of their day. They were not required to pick them up or spend any significant amount of time being physical. They just had to touch. The results of this new mandate were astonishing. Within two years, the mortality rate of infants brought to the orphanage dropped from 50 percent to 15 percent.

The 13th-century historian Salimbene described an experiment made by the German emperor Frederick II, who wanted to know what language children would speak if raised without hearing any words at all. Babies were taken from their mothers and raised in isolation. The result was that they all died. Salimbene wrote in 1248, "They could not live without caressing." Nor can anyone else. Human babies definitely need tender loving care to survive. Untouched adults may not die physically, but they will experience emotional and social atrophy.

Could this be why everywhere Jesus went He touched people? Whether He was blessing children or healing a leper, Jesus made it a point to reach out and lovingly touch people. Who will you bless today with your touch of Christian love?

TYPHOID MARY

"The woman was arrayed in purple and scarlet ... having in her hand a golden cup full of abominations" (Revelation 17:4).

Mary Mallon, also known as Typhoid Mary, was an Irish immigrant who was the first known healthy carrier of typhoid fever in the United States. She was born in Ireland in 1869 and immigrated alone to the U.S. in 1883 when she was only 15. She apparently contracted typhoid fever at some point but only suffered a mild case, resisting the bacteria enough to appear healthy but still being very capable of spreading the disease to others. Mary loved to cook, so she obtained employment between 1900 and 1907 in private homes around New York City as a household cook.

While cooking in a house in Mamaroneck, New York, for less than two weeks, the residents came down with typhoid. She then worked in Manhattan in 1901, and members of that family developed typhoid, and the laundress died. In 1904, she took another position on Long Island. Within two weeks, four of 10 family members were hospitalized with typhoid. She changed employment, and three more households were infected. Apparently, the disease was frequently transmitted by Mary's favorite recipe, a dessert of iced peaches.

After careful investigation, George Soper identified Mary as a carrier. But Mary stubbornly refused to believe someone not sick could spread disease and rejected requests for testing. The New York City Health Department tried to reason with Mary but she was convinced that the law was wantonly persecuting her because she was a working-class Irish immigrant. It required several police officers to place her into custody. The New York City health inspector tested her and confirmed she was a rare case of a healthy carrier. So they isolated her for three years at a hospital.

Later she was reluctantly released on the condition that she would not work with food. However, in 1915 she returned to cooking, at a New York hospital no less, and infected 25 people, two of whom died. Public health authorities again seized and confined Mary in quarantine for the remaining 23 years of her life. When she died in 1938 of pneumonia, the autopsy revealed that she was still actively carrying typhoid. In the end she had infected at least 51 people with the disease, three of whom died.

The Bible teaches about another woman who deliberately spreads deadly false teachings. John writes that she had "in her hand a golden cup full of abominations" (Revelation 17:4). We can avoid the infection of sin when we only drink of the pure water of life.

"Is anyone among you sick? Let him call for the elders of the church, and let them pray over him, anointing him with oil in the name of the Lord" (James 4:14).

Did you know that nearly 80 percent of Americans believe spiritual faith and prayer can help people recover from illness or injury? In a survey of 269 doctors in the American Academy of Family Physicians, 99 percent said religious beliefs can contribute to healing. When asked about personal experiences, 63 percent said God had intervened to improve their own medical conditions.

"Many Americans rely on prayer and spirituality for the benefit of health," said Stephen E. Straus, MD, former director of the National Center for Complementary and Alternative Medicine (NCCAM) at the National Institutes of Health (NIH). Indeed, a 2004 survey of more than 31,000 adults conducted by researchers at the National Center for Health Statistics and NCCAM found that prayer was the most commonly used practice among all the approaches mentioned in the survey.

In one study in the *American Journal of Health Promotion* (May-Jun 2005) it was discovered that people who pray have more favorable health-related behaviors, have less preventive care visits, and are more satisfied with the services of their medical care. About 47 percent of the subjects in this study prayed for their health and 90 percent believed that prayer improved their health.

So compelling is the evidence for the "faith factor" that even prestigious medical journals like the *Archives of Internal Medicine* have developed spiritual questionnaires to assess a patient's level of trust in God. Science indeed has recognized what every person of faith has known intuitively for centuries—trusting God can be very beneficial to your health!

Paul encourages the Philippian believers to pray about everything. What is the result? "And the peace of God, which surpasses all understanding [expectations] will guard your hearts and minds through Christ Jesus" (Philippians 4:7). James actually gives us clear instructions on praying for the sick. "Is anyone among you sick? Let him call for the elders of the church, and let them pray over him, anointing him with oil in the name of the Lord. And the prayer of faith will save the sick, and the Lord will raise him up" (James 5:14, 15).

Sometimes God chooses to miraculously heal our bodies, but what is assured is that our sins will be forgiven and we will enjoy everlasting life. We are safe in God's hands when we pray.

February 11 WATER GIVES LIFE

"Whoever drinks of this water will thirst again, but whoever drinks of the water that I shall give him will never thirst" (John 4:13).

About 100 years ago, a pile of bones was found on a sand dune in Saudi Arabia. Evidently, a man had died while lost in the desert. In one of the pockets of his tattered clothes was a scribbled note that read, "Dying of thirst. I cannot go on any longer." The lost soul had apparently assembled a small makeshift shelter there and, without water, sat down to die. Tragically, his remains were found right across a sand dune from a lush oasis—he died from thirst only a few hundred yards from artesian springs. Millions today are slowly dying from dehydration simply because they do not drink enough water.

About 83 percent of your blood is water. If that ratio drops just 5 percent, you will no longer be able to see. Another 10 percent and you will be unable to hear. A 12 percent reduction leads to your blood thickening, making it impossible for your heart to pump, which leads to death. On the other hand, a camel can lose 40 percent of the water content in its blood and do just fine!

Drinking other beverages (fruit juice, coffee, tea, etc.) does not provide the same health benefits as plain water. In fact, research has shown that women who consumed large quantities of non-water beverages increased their risk of a fatal heart attack by two-and-a-half times. The same study showed that men increased their risk by 50 percent!

Unless you are proactive in your daily intake of water, dehydration could become a way of life. It is little wonder that 75 percent of Americans are chronically dehydrated. In 37 percent the thirst sensation is so impaired it is mistaken for feelings of hunger. But you can do too much of a good thing. Drinking too much water is rare, but it can happen. Forcing yourself to drink massive amounts of water can cause low blood sodium levels and lead to brain swelling and even death.

Water is so important that Jesus used it as an illustration of Himself. When talking to the Samaritan woman at the well, Christ compared the message of salvation He brings with life-giving water. He added, "But the water that I shall give him will become in him a fountain of water springing up into everlasting life" (John 4:14). Every time you drink a glass of water, remember that Jesus is the ultimate thirst quencher!

"But Daniel purposed in his heart that he would not defile himself with the portion of the king's delicacies, nor with the wine which he drank ..." (Daniel 1:8).

Many people love to eat pancakes for breakfast. Did you know one of the tallest (it keeps growing!) stacks of pancakes on record is 29.5 inches high set by chefs Sean McGinlay and Natalie King of Glagow's Hilton Grosvenor Hotel. It contained 672 pancakes made with 100 eggs, 17 pints of milk, 11 pounds of flour, and 6.6 pounds of butter. But if you think that's big, the largest pancake made weighed three tons! The Co-operative Union Ltd of Manchester, England, created a pancake measuring 49 feet, 2.55 inches in diameter on August 13, 1994. It contained an estimated two million calories!

The most pancakes ever made by an individual in one hour is 956 and goes to Steve Hamilton of Indiana. He claims to have flipped over 34 million pancakes in his lifetime. If they were laid end to end they would stretch from Los Angeles to Springfield, Illinois. And the most pancakes made in eight hours by a group of 300 volunteer cooks is 76,382. Thirty-eight griddles were used to cook almost 6,000 pounds of batter. People who ate them up used about 136 gallons of maple syrup and 365 pounds of butter. There is actually no official record for the number of pancakes people have eaten at one sitting since the Guinness Book of World Records tends to track things that people don't normally enjoy eating in large quantities (like garlic cloves or onions). Some say the unofficial record is 72. (I like pancakes, but that is going just a little too far!)

Obviously, overeating pancakes for breakfast is not good for your health. But, did you know that skipping breakfast could be deadly? In one study, skipping breakfast was linked to an increased risk of premature death. By far, the best meal to skip, or at least minimize, is dinner. Another study reported better weight loss, improvement in diabetic conditions, and increased thyroid efficiency among a group of 595 people who consumed their last meal of the day by 3:00 p.m.

Wise eating can make a difference in your body and spirit. Daniel knew this when he turned away from eating the rich foods offered to him in Babylon. He challenged the steward overseeing him and his friends to let them only eat simple food. The result? "And at the end of ten days their features appeared better and fatter in the flesh than all the young men who ate the portion of the king's delicacies" (Daniel 1:15). So, eat a healthy breakfast and enjoy better health!

February 13 CLEARING THE AIR

"He gives to all life, breath, and all things" (Acts 17:25).

The air we breathe is more than oxygen. It is a mixture of different gases that cover the Earth in a layer that is over 400 miles high, called the atmosphere. Air is made up of approximately 78 percent nitrogen, 21 percent oxygen, and small amounts of argon, hydrogen, carbon dioxide, and some others. Oxygen is our body's most important physical need. Each breath we take brings this life-sustaining gas into our lungs. Oxygen is then diffused into our bloodstream, where it is transported all over the body through our red blood cells.

We all know that unless we are breathing we will die. But not many realize that poor breathing habits can affect your health. You can breathe better by using your lungs more effectively. Ideally, breathing should expand the lungs through lowering the diaphragm (a muscle separating the lungs from the abdominal organs). This can be accomplished by relaxing the abdominal muscles when you breathe in. The idea is to expand your upper lung area as well as your lower lung area, resulting in an increased lung function—deeper breathing. This makes a more efficient oxygen/carbon dioxide exchange. In fact, the practice of deep breathing is one of the simplest ways of preventing certain types of pneumonia.

Typically the best air to breathe is found in the great out-of-doors, especially out in the country away from polluted city air. Some people might think indoor air isn't so bad, but studies have shown it can be five times more polluted than outdoor air, which is bad considering that most people spend 90 percent of their time indoors. A simple remedy for improving indoor air quality is by "clearing the air." Throw open the windows and let fresh air circulate through your home. Better yet, keep some windows open so that there is a constant supply of clean air coming through. If you live in the city, open your windows and air out your home at night since smog levels are lower after sunset.

God gives "breath to all," not just physically, but spiritually as well. The Bible says, "And when He had said this, He [Jesus] breathed on them, and said to them, 'Receive the Holy Spirit'" (John 20:22). The Greek word for "spirit" is the same word for "wind" or "air." Just as we need fresh air to live, we also need God's Spirit to truly live the Christian life.

"Awake, you who sleep, arise from the dead, and Christ will give you light" (Ephesians 5:14).

Michelle Funk was only left alone for a few minutes that day in June 1986. It was long enough. She fell into the icy, runoff-swollen waters of Bell Canyon Creek, which winds through southeast Salt Lake County near her parents' home. Sixty-six minutes later, when a diver pulled Michelle from the creek approximately 150 feet from where she had fallen in, she was lifeless. Her small body was frozen by the 40 degree water. It was the icy temperature of the water, along with its cleanliness, that allowed Michelle to be saved by doctors at Primary Children's Medical Center in Salt Lake City. She was rushed to the hospital, where a machine warmed up her blood. When her temperature reached 91 degrees F her heart started beating and she opened her eyes. Michelle entirely recovered and showed no signs of her traumatic experience.

The resuscitation of this two-and-a-half-year-old girl, submerged for more than an hour, was rare. Even the *Journal of the American Medical Association* described it as "miraculous." It was not only the longest documented submersion with a positive outcome (she grew in a healthy and normal way), but it's also the first successful use of a heart-lung bypass machine to re-warm a child whose temperature had dropped extremely low from hypothermia.

What is amazing about this story is that the doctor that saved her life, Dr. Bolte, pondered the idea of using a heart-lung machine to warm the blood of victims of hypothermia just a few months before Michelle's accident. When she arrived at the hospital, they worked for three hours to warm her up. After coming back to life it was another two months before she was able to return home.

Though many children die from drowning, usually from backyard swimming pools that do not have protective fences, there are some fortunate cases like Michelle's. Someday, when Jesus returns, all those who are asleep in death will be miraculously resurrected and live forever. Even the Old Testament prophets described this spectacular day. "Your dead shall live; together with my dead body they shall arise. Awake and sing, you who dwell in dust; for your dew is like the dew of herbs, and the earth shall cast out the dead" (Isaiah 26:19).

Not everyone will have another chance like Michelle to awaken from being close to death. But we all may have hope in the resurrection if we seek to follow the Lifegiver.

February 15 A RUTHLESS TERRORIST

"Who has woe? Who has sorrow? Who has contentions? Who has complaints? Who has wounds without cause? Who has redness of eyes? Those who linger long at the wine, those who go in search of mixed wine. Do not look on the wine when it is red, when it sparkles in the cup, when it swirls around smoothly; at the last it bites like a serpent, and stings like a viper" (Proverbs 23:29-32).

In the next 24 hours a ruthless terrorist will be responsible for nearly ...

... half of all the homicides in North America.

... half of all the people who will die on the highways.

... half of all the people who will be admitted to the hospital.

... half of all the people who will incarcerated in jail or prison.

... half of all the people who will be involved in domestic violence.

... half of all the nation's birth defects.

His chemical attacks will cause untold misery and sorrow to thousands of families. Sadly, the government is looking the other way because this terrorist is paying them hush money. Worse still, even many professed Christians are defending and harboring this cold-hearted terrorist. Who is this deadly villain who is devastating our homes and nation?

Alcohol is the one responsible for all this hardship and tragedy. God wants us to have healthy, happy lives, and He has repeatedly warned us against alcoholic beverages. The Bible says, "Wine is a mocker, strong drink is a brawler, and whoever is led astray by it is not wise" (Proverbs 20:1).

Samson's mother was warned not to drink wine or similar products, because her yet unborn son was to be set aside in service to God. Similarly, John the Baptist was set aside for a special purpose. When he was conceived, his father was told, "For he will be great in the sight of the Lord, and shall drink neither wine nor strong drink" (Luke 1:15).

The same guidelines apply to us because we've all been set aside for a special purpose. We've all been chosen by God as ambassadors for Christ. Only in soberness can we reflect Jesus' love to others.

"But although He had done so many signs before them, they did not believe in Him, that the word of Isaiah the prophet might be fulfilled, which he spoke ... 'He has blinded their eyes and hardened their hearts, lest they should see with their eyes, lest they should understand with their hearts and turn, so that I should heal them'" (John 12:37, 38, 40).

Did you know that you don't technically see with your eyes or hear with your ears? Your eyes and ears simply transmit light and vibrating molecules of air to your nerves, which then send impulses to the brain, where sight and sound are interpreted. All this might help to explain some of the strangest documented phenomena in medical history: the cases of those who, though blind or blindfolded, were nevertheless able to "see."

For example, in the 1890s doctors in New York described how blind Mollie Fancher could read regular printed books using only her fingertips. In Italy, a neurologist wrote about a blind girl who could see with her left earlobe and the tip of her nose. Doctors have documented cases of those who could see with their fingertips, cheeks, or even their abdomens. In 1960, 14-year-old Margaret Foos of Ellerson, Virginia, underwent elaborate tests conducted by experts. Securely blindfolded, Margaret read randomly selected passages of print, identified colors and objects, and even played a game of checkers. In Russia, medical researchers reported the case of Rosa Kuleshova who, in rigidly controlled experiments, was able to read newsprint and sheet music with her fingertips and elbow.

How is this possible? No one knows for certain. Some have posited that these individuals were abnormally sensitive to the amount of heat absorbed by different colors: sightless reading could be possible because black print absorbs more heat and is warmer than the surrounding white page.

The Bible speaks about those who, though able to see perfectly, are blind to spiritual truth because they prefer to live in darkness. For example, John tells of some who believed in Jesus but did not follow Him because they preferred the good opinion of men over the good opinion of God (John 12:42, 43). The good news is that no one needs to live in darkness. Jesus longs to heal our spiritual blindness if we will only allow Him.

February 17 NATURAL SUPERGLUE

"But take careful heed to ... love the Lord your God ... to hold fast to Him, and to serve Him with all your heart ..." (Joshua 22:5).

Sandcastle worms live along the shallow seas off the California coast that stretches from Baja, California in the south to Sonoma County in the north. These tiny sea creatures are also known as honeycomb worms because they build clusters of tube-shaped homes in colonies. The micro-cities are situated in places where wave action will swirl up tiny pieces of sand and broken bits of sea shells. The feathery worms catch these particles and then, like miniature masons, cement them one grain at a time to the tube opening. To enable them to do this, God has created these little creatures with the perfect formula for producing a sturdy underwater adhesive. After catching a grain of sand, the worm will secrete two little dabs of glue onto the particle, then stick it onto the end of the tube. It holds it there for about 25 seconds, wiggling it a little to see if the glue is set, and then it lets go. This amazing glue is designed to set up and harden within 30 seconds after the worm secretes it.

One grain of sand at a time these clever creatures build big, reef-like colonies that look like stacks of organ pipes. Now, after years of studying the sandcastle worm, scientists from the University of Utah have succeeded in duplicating their miraculous adhesive and invented underwater super glue. Doctors have long sought a medical adhesive to repair moist bones shattered in accidents or battlefield injuries. The traditional method of repairing shattered bones is to use mechanical connectors like wires, pins, nails, and screws for support until they grow together and can bear weight. Up until now there has never been glue that would work in the wet environment of the body during surgery. The new glue will help doctors repair bone. After the bone re-grows, the non-toxic glue gradually dissolves.

Did you know the Bible speaks of a super glue that will keep families together? "Therefore a man shall leave his father and mother and be joined to his wife, and they shall become one flesh" (Genesis 2:24). The Bible word "join" comes from the Hebrew word "daw-bak," which means "cling" or "adhere"—in other words, glue! God's super glue is what we need to build homes that will last for eternity.

"He who is faithful in what is least is faithful also in much" (Luke 16:10).

In September 1862, Confederate General Robert E. Lee made his greatest effort to carry the Civil War into the North. This climaxed with the Battle of Antietam, which became the bloodiest and perhaps the most decisive battle in the War Between the States.

On the morning of September 17, a Union commander named Colonel Hayes ordered his men to the firing line before sunrise and without breakfast. It was crucial that they prevent the advance of the Confederate army from crossing into the North. By afternoon the soldiers were exhausted and famished. A 19-year-old mess sergeant, known as Billy, took pity on the hungry men and loaded up a wagon with buckets of coffee and food rations. He then drove the wagon under fire to reach the men. The famished soldiers, surprised and grateful for the food, sent up a loud cheer for Billy. They wolfed down the food and then turned back to the fight with renewed strength. When Colonel Hayes learned what Billy had done for his men, he recommended Billy be promoted to the rank of second lieutenant. The colonel who promoted Billy was Rutherford B. Hayes, who became the nineteenth president of the United States ... and Billy, the mess sergeant, was William McKinley, who became our twenty-fifth president.

Later, Hayes remarked that "McKinley was a man of rare capacity, especially for a boy of his age ... the night was never too dark; the weather was never too cold; there was no sleet, or storm, or hail, or snow, or rain that was in the way of his prompt and efficient performance in every duty."

Though the duties in front of us today may not seem great, if we perform them faithfully it will soon become apparent to those around us that we can be trusted with greater things. And even if we're never given earthly recognition for our efforts, Paul reminds us that whatever we do, we should "do it heartily, as to the Lord and not to men" (Colossians 3:23). If we do that, we can be confident that we'll hear our Commander say, "'Well done, good and faithful servant; you were faithful over a few things, I will make you ruler over many things. Enter into the joy of your lord'" (Matthew 25:21).

BULLETPROOF WASHINGTON

"A thousand may fall at your side, and ten thousand at your right hand; but it shall not come near you" (Psalm 91:7).

On July 9, 1755, during the French and Indian War, a force of 1,500 British soldiers was ambushed in the open by a small force of French and American Indian fighters shooting fr[illegible] The British soldiers—trained for European war—made ea[illegible] to shoulder in their bright red uniforms. A[illegible] more exposed on horseback, high above the [illegible] perfect targets. The slaughter continued [illegible] percent of the British soldiers were cut dow[illegible]

One by one, the chief's marksmen shot t[illegible] horses until only one remained. Amazingly, [illegible] at this one man. Twice the young lieutena[illegible] under him. Twice he grabbed another hor[illegible] were fired by the sharpshooters. Still, the [illegible] native warriors stared in disbelief. Their r[illegible] realized that a mighty power must be shiel[illegible] "Stop firing! This one is under the special protection of the Great Spi[illegible]

Eventually the lieutenant colonel gathered the remaining British troops and led them to safety. That evening, as the last of the wounded were being cared for, the officer noticed an odd tear in his coat. It was a bullet hole! He rolled up his sleeve and looked at his arm directly under the hole. There was no mark on his skin. Amazed, he took off his coat and found three more holes where bullets had passed through his coat but stopped before they reached his body. Nine days after the battle, the young lieutenant colonel wrote his brother: "By the all-powerful dispensations of Providence I have been protected beyond all human probability or expectation; for I had four bullets through my coat, and two horses shot under me yet escaped unhurt, although death was leveling my companions on every side!"

The 23-year-old officer went on to become the commander in chief of the Continental Army and the first president of the United States. During the years that followed in his long career, this man, George Washington, was never once wounded in battle. Washington also escaped flying bullets on four other occasions and survived contracting diphtheria, malaria, smallpox, and tuberculosis.

"You are the light of the world. A city that is set on a hill cannot be hidden. Nor do they light a lamp and put it under a basket, but on a lampstand, and it gives light to all who are in the house. Let your light so shine before men, that they may see your good works and glorify your Father in heaven"(Matthew 5:14-16).

Did you know that as you are reading this right now you are glowing? That's right; it has recently been discovered that human bodies emit a visible light in extremely small quantities at levels that rise and fall through the day.

Research has shown that this light is about 1,000 times fainter than the levels we can see with our naked eyes. In fact, virtually all living creatures emit varying amounts of weak light, which is thought to be a byproduct of biochemical reactions involving free radicals. This light is different from the red glow of body heat captured by infrared cameras. In fact, infrared cameras show some of the hottest body parts give off very little light.

To learn more about this light, scientists in Japan used extremely sensitive cameras capable of detecting a single photon, the smallest unit of light. For three days, five healthy young men were placed bare-chested in front of the cameras. They sat in perfectly dark, light-proof rooms for 20 minutes every three hours from 10 a.m. to 10 p.m. The researchers found the body glow of the men rose and fell over the day, with its lowest point at 10 a.m. and its peak at 4 p.m.

The findings suggest these light emissions are linked to our fluctuating metabolic rhythms. Since this faint light is linked with metabolism, these findings suggest that in the future special cameras that can spot a person's light emissions may help identify medical conditions. It was also discovered that our faces glow more than the rest of the body, possibly because facial circulation is more dense and closer to the surface.

Did you know the Bible also speaks about a man with a glowing face? It says that when Moses came down from the mountain after speaking with God, "the skin of his face shone" (Exodus 34:30).

Spend time with God and you will emit a spiritual glow. With His help we can become lights in the darkness, reflecting the "true Light which gives light to every man coming into the world" (John 1:9).

THE CROWBAR CASE

"He causes all, both small and great, rich and poor, free and slave, to receive a mark on their right hand or on their foreheads ..." (Revelation 13:16).

On September 13, 1848, a 25-year-old railroad foreman in Vermont, named Phineas P. Gage, was packing explosive powder in a hole with an iron rod. Unfortunately, someone forgot to put the sand in the hole over the powder. A spark flew and there was a powerful blast. The 13-pound tamping iron, over one inch thick and three feet long, was propelled with the force of a bullet, through Gage's head. It entered under his left cheekbone, went through his brain, and then out the top of his head. Amazingly, this traumatic accident did not kill Phineas. In fact, he regained his physical strength and lived for another 13 years. He seemed mentally sound; he could speak and do physical tasks just as well, and his memory seemed unimpaired. But friends and family knew he was no longer the same man.

Before the accident he was a well-loved, responsible worker. He was known by all as a pious, reverent, and dependable man with high morals. But after the accident Phineas experienced a major moral decline. He became very short-tempered, rude, foul-mouthed, and lost all respect for spiritual things. It seemed as though all of his ethical filters had been turned off. As a result he had difficulty keeping jobs. Around 1850 he spent about a year as a sideshow attraction with P. T. Barnum's New York museum, putting his injury and the tamping iron on display. Gage kept the iron rod throughout his life as a souvenir and even had it buried with him in death. In medical circles, his story became known as the "crowbar case."

In 1867 his skull and the original rod that pierced it were exhumed. Both became part of the exhibition at the Harvard Medical School Museum in Boston, where it remains today. Phineas' traumatic accident cost him his personality, his moral standards, and his commitment to loved ones. Researchers have concluded that he had lost an important part of his brain called the "frontal lobe." The frontal lobe, behind the forehead, is the largest section of the brain and is responsible for moral reasoning, judgment, social behavior, and most of all, spirituality.

It is interesting that in the book of Revelation, the enemy of God, the beast, seeks to place a mark on the foreheads of all, while the 144,000 have God's name "written on their foreheads" (Revelation 14:1). Which mark represents the controlling force in your life?

What a powerful example of our Bible text for today!

"Hypocrites! Well did Isaiah prophesy about you, saying, 'These people draw near to Me with their mouth, and honor Me with their lips, but their heart is far from Me'" (Matthew 15:7, 8).

It has been discovered there are several factories based in North America that are producing and selling weapons of mass destruction. In case you're wondering, I'm talking about tobacco and the lethal habit of cigarette smoking. And the saddest part is, this deadly and expensive international health hazard is easily preventable.

Tobacco was once considered a cure for many ailments, including headache, toothache, arthritis, stomachaches, wounds, and bad breath. It was made into a tea and even rolled into pills in order to serve as a medicinal herb. A Spanish doctor, Nicolas Monardes, first described its medicinal potential in a 1577 book called *Joyful News out of the New Found World*. His views were accepted for more than two centuries.

Every year, four million people die worldwide from smoking-related diseases. That's approximately one person every 8 seconds. Every minute 10 million cigarettes are sold worldwide; that's 15 billion cigarettes sold every day. Smoking costs the United States over $150 billion each year in healthcare costs, including $81 billion in productivity losses and over $75 billion in excess medical expenditures. Smoking is directly responsible for 87 percent of lung cancer, and causes most cases of emphysema and chronic bronchitis. Smoking is also a major factor in coronary heart disease and stroke and has been linked to a variety of other health disorders, including infertility and peptic ulcers. Smoking in pregnancy accounts for an estimated 20 to 30 percent of low-birth-weight babies, and some 10 percent of all infant deaths.

It's estimated that one out of every five teens between 13 and 15 years old smokes. Evidence also indicates that half of the people who start smoking as adolescents will go on to smoke for 15 to 20 years. Yet tobacco companies continue to invest millions of dollars in effective advertising encouraging young people to begin a lifelong addiction to smoking.

Still, the tobacco companies in America continue to manufacture and use these weapons of mass destruction. The greatest irony is that tobacco companies like Philip Morris pretend to discourage people from smoking on one hand while they continue to profit from peddling their deadly poison on the other. They are very much talking from both sides of their mouth. In today's Key Bible Text, Jesus describes people who give double-talk as hypocrites.

February 23 A BABY BORN TWICE

"[U]nless one is born again, he cannot see the kingdom of God" (John 3:3).

When Chad and Keri McCartney say their infant daughter, Macie Hope, has been born again, they aren't referring to religion—their miracle baby really was born twice! During Keri's 23rd week of pregnancy, the couple went to their obstetrician's office for a simple ultrasound procedure to determine if they would be having a little boy or girl. The couple brought their four children along to hear the good news.

At that time it was discovered that the McCartney's baby girl had a noncancerous but deadly tumor growing off her tailbone. The fast-growing tumor, as large as the baby, was robbing vital blood from their baby. Without medical intervention their unborn child had no chance. The Texas Children's Hospital in Houston was one of only three hospitals in the world that could perform such a specialized and risky surgery. After being told that there was less than a 10 percent chance the baby was going to make it, the parents wanted to pick a fitting name before the perilous procedure. They chose Macie Hope. Faced with a dismal future, Keri said, "Hope was all we had."

The "first birth" was about six months into Keri's pregnancy, when fetal surgeons led by Dr. Darrell Cass gently took the tiny 5-ounce baby from Keri's womb to remove the tumor. The surgery went flawlessly. Then back into mommy she went to heal and grow for two more months. Then Macie was born the second time on May 3, 2008, when the McCartney's welcomed their perfectly healthy baby girl into the world.

Did you know the Bible teaches that if you are only born once you will die twice? But if you are born twice you will die only once? While explaining the plan of salvation to one of Israel's most gifted teachers, Jesus plainly outlined for Nicodemus what must happen: "Jesus answered and said to him, 'Most assuredly, I say to you, unless one is born again, he cannot see the kingdom of God'" (John 3:3). Nicodemus seems confused and says, "How can a man be born when he is old? Can he enter a second time into his mother's womb and be born?" (v. 4). Though baby Macie did just that, Jesus was speaking of the miracle of salvation in the heart. The spiritual birth, marked by baptism in water, symbolizes a new life in Christ. This second birth does not happen under a surgeon's knife, but through the work of the Holy Spirit.

"... for the Lamb who is in the midst of the throne will shepherd them and lead them to living fountains of waters" (Revelation 7:17).

Have you heard these water statistics?

1. By some estimates, about 75 percent of people in the U.S. are "chronically dehydrated."
2. Perhaps one-third of people in the U.S. have a sensation of thirst so weak that it's often mistaken for hunger. Maybe this is why one study revealed that a glass of water will shut down nighttime hunger pangs for most people.
3. Even a small amount of dehydration can slow a person's metabolism down. For this reason, lack of water is the primary cause of fatigue during the day.
4. A 2 percent drop in body water can cause fuzzy short-term memory, difficulty with basic math, and trouble focusing on a computer screen or on a printed page (by the time a person feels thirsty, the body has already lost about 1 percent of its water volume).
5. Drinking sufficient water every day decreases the risk of colon cancer, bladder cancer, and very possibly other cancers. The American Cancer Society recommends drinking at least 8 cups of liquid a day.

It's obvious that proper water intake can eliminate or ease a whole host of common health problems. This shouldn't be surprising, since our bodies are up to 75 percent water. Water plays a role in almost every body function, carrying nutrients and oxygen to every cell, helping us to breathe, cushioning and protecting our vital organs and joints, converting food into energy, and removing waste.

While water is the cure for physical dehydration, the Bible teaches that living water will save us from spiritual dehydration! When Jesus met the Samaritan woman at Jacob's well, He asked her for a drink. When she tried to change the subject, He offered her "living water" (John 4:10). It all sounded good to the woman who asked about the source of such water.

Jesus told her, "Whoever drinks of this water will thirst again, but whoever drinks of the water that I shall give him will never thirst. But the water that I shall give him will become in him a fountain of water springing up into everlasting life" (verses 13, 14).

If you're thirsty today, He invites you to come to Him and drink.

February 25 XERODERMA PIGMENTOSUM

"And the light shines in the darkness, and the darkness did not comprehend it" (John 1:5).

Long before the initials "XP" were chosen as the name for a Microsoft operating system, XP was short for a very rare incurable skin disease, found mostly among children, called Xeroderma Pigmentosum. The nature of the incurable malady prevents skin cells from repairing once they have become sun-damaged. In healthy people, our skin and eye surfaces are always healing and repairing themselves from the damage resulting from normal exposure to sunlight. But not so for those who suffer with XP. Only about one in one million children are affected by this life-threatening disease, but due to their extremely severe sensitivity to UV rays, those afflicted by XP are 1,000 times more likely to develop skin cancers or lose their sight than healthy children.

In order to prolong their lives, children affected by XP must take very radical measures to avoid all direct and indirect sunlight. That even includes light from fluorescent bulbs. In order to decrease their chances of cancer, they must virtually live their lives hiding from the light behind sunglasses, slathered in sunscreen, sequestered in dim shadows and darkness. These children of the moon can only come out to play after dark and live in virtual fear of daylight! It is so sad to hear how these children with XP must spend their lives in the dark.

While there is currently no cure for those afflicted with Xeroderma Pigmentosum, there is a cure for God's children who are imprisoned in spiritual darkness. Jesus said, "I am the light of the world. He who follows Me shall not walk in darkness, but have the light of life" (John 8:12). While the scribes and Pharisees prided themselves in having great light, they actually lived in darkness. The disease of sin made them uncomfortable with being in the presence of Jesus, the light of the world.

But there are those who want to be in the light. "The people who walked in darkness have seen a great light; those who dwelt in the land of the shadow of death, upon them a light has shined" (Isaiah 9:2). I sure look forward to the day when not only will Christ shine upon our world in the fullness of His glory, but heal all the children who suffer from diseases like XP.

"Knowing that you were not redeemed with corruptible things, like silver or gold, from your aimless conduct received by tradition from your fathers, but with the precious blood of Christ, as of a lamb without blemish and without spot" (1 Peter 1:18, 19).

James Harrison is an Australian man who holds the world record for blood donations, having donated blood over 1,000 times. When Harrison was 13 years old, he went through a major surgery and required 13 liters of blood. Afterward, realizing that donated blood had saved his life, he pledged to begin donating his own blood when he turned 18. Soon after he started donating, it was discovered that his blood contains a rare antibody that can save babies from dying of Rhesus disease—a disorder where the Rh-positive blood of the mother is incompatible with the Rh-negative blood of her unborn child.

Rhesus disease often results in a miscarriage or stillbirth and sometimes causes brain damage in newborns. Harrison was asked to undergo a series of tests to help create a vaccine for the disease. Since then, the Anti-D vaccine created with his blood plasma has been given to hundreds of thousands of women. It's estimated that Harrison's blood has saved around 2.2 million babies—a gift that has affected the lives of several women close to Harrison. Joy Barnes, a worker at a Red Cross blood bank where Harrison has donated, received the vaccine after having two miscarriages. She said, "Without him I would never have been able to have a healthy baby." Best of all, one of the babies saved was Harrison's own grandson!

Harrison says, "I've never thought about stopping. Never." Even after his wife of 56 years passed away, he was back in the hospital a week later to donate. Harrison has been nicknamed the "man with a golden arm" and has received the Order of Australia medal for his contributions.

Just as 2.2 million babies would have died without Harrison's gift, all humanity would have died without Jesus' saving blood. It is only Christ's death on the cross that redeems us—we can't redeem ourselves with any amount of gold or silver. Just as Harrison planned from boyhood to donate his blood, Jesus was "foreordained before the foundation of the world" as our sacrificial lamb (1 Peter 1:20). And just as Harrison never plans to stop donating blood, Jesus' gift of salvation isn't limited to a select few. There is no sinner that His blood can't save!

February 27 RIP VAN WINKLE

"Behold, I tell you a mystery: We shall not all sleep, but we shall all be changed" (1 Corinthians 15:51).

Most Americans are acquainted with Washington Irving's short story about Rip Van Winkle. It is a tale about an early American villager of Dutch descent who escapes his nagging wife by wandering up in the mountains of New York. After some bizarre adventures, he falls asleep and wakes up 20 years later only to find out that his wife and his best friends have died. Rip Van Winkle is a fanciful fairytale, but there is a real story much like it.

In 1984, 20-year-old Terry Wallis, married and with a six-week-old girl, was involved in a serious car wreck in Mountain View, Arkansas. The driver died instantly; Terry went into a coma. His family hoped it wouldn't last long and that he'd soon recover. Well, he didn't. And for 19 long years he existed in a semi-vegetative state in which he had to be constantly cared for. Then, much to everyone's incredible surprise, on June 13, 2003, Terry suddenly awoke in his hospital bed and uttered his first words, which were, "Mom," "Pepsi," and then "Milk."

Strangely, Terry began talking as if nothing had happened, as if he had been in the coma for just a few days, not 19 years. In his mind it was still 1984, Ronald Reagan was president, the Berlin Wall still stood, cell phones were the size of bricks, the Internet was largely unknown, and the Twin Towers were still standing. He thought that Bill Clinton was still the governor of his state, and that he was still only 20 years old. In addition, the last he remembered, his daughter was an infant, not the 19-year-old young woman who stood beside his bed. Doctors are still mystified regarding this "mental resurrection."

Sadly, Terry's body has severely atrophied after 19 years in bed, but the Bible teaches that there is a real resurrection coming, in which all those who have been "asleep" in Jesus will arise to eternal life with new glorified bodies! Paul writes, "... in a moment, in the twinkling of an eye, at the last trumpet. For the trumpet will sound, and the dead will be raised incorruptible, and we shall be changed" (1 Corinthians 15:52). Though time has passed, the dead in Christ will feel as if they have only been asleep in their graves for a short time.

"... and the swine, though it divides the hoof, having cloven hooves, yet does not chew the cud, is unclean to you" (Leviticus 11:7).

Most people think the deadliest plague in history was the bubonic plague that killed two million victims a year. Actually, the deadliest plague occurred in the 20th century! And it started right here in the USA. It was the influenza of 1918 that hit right after World War I.

The war killed nine million men in four years, but this killer flu took at least 25 million lives in one year. In the first year, nearly 20 million cases were reported in the United States alone, accounting for almost one million deaths. That's more than were killed during World War I, World War II, the Korean War, and the Vietnam War combined.

It all started on March 11, 1918, at Camp Funston, Kansas, when a company cook reported to the infirmary with typical flu symptoms. By noon, 107 soldiers were sick. Within two days, 522 people were sick, many gravely ill with severe pneumonia, the deadliest part of the sickness. Reports started coming in from other military bases. Within a week, every state in the Union had been infected by this airborne killer. In two months it spread to South America, Europe, Africa, and Asia.

The United States had the lowest death toll. But a large percentage of the Eskimo population was wiped out in Nome, Alaska. Eighty to 90 percent of the Samoan population was infected, many survivors dying from starvation, too weak to feed themselves. The disease seemed to peak within three weeks of entering a given city, then subsided. In the end, it's estimated 25 to 35 million people died worldwide.

Eighteen months after the disease appeared, the flu bug vanished, leaving a mystery as to its source, until March 1997, when Armed Forces Institute of Pathology researchers found specimens that 1918 Army doctors had preserved. It appears the virus started from birds, passed to pigs, and then to humans. These are the deadliest of all viruses because when the hearty pig immune system kicks into action the virus is forced to mutate. Both the deadly Asian flu (1957) and the Hong Kong flu (1968) came from mutated pig viruses.

The scary part is that hog farms continue to breed pigs for food near populated areas. It could happen again! Perhaps this is one of the reasons God said people should not eat pigs. His laws are always intended to bless us.

February 29 FACIAL RECOGNITION

"The LORD looks from heaven; He sees all the sons of men" (Psalm 33:13).

Forget ID badges, passwords, and access cards. Pretty soon, to get in and out of your office, you might start using something you can't forget or misplace: your face. Facial recognition technology, once the subject of science fiction, has now started to appear in real-life public places. A camera will capture images of people who pose or simply walk by, and then software matches those pictures with images stored in a database. All types of institutions that need greater security have recently begun to use facial recognition to verify identity. Currently more than 100 casinos across the country have facial recognition systems in operation. The city of Tampa uses it in outdoor cameras to spot missing children and lawbreakers.

University scientists have been working on facial recognition technology for over a decade. With financial support from the U.S. Defense Department, scientists are attempting to find a technology that can spot criminals or terrorists at airports and border crossings. Companies began commercializing the technology in the mid-'90s. It made headlines when word got out that authorities used it at the Super Bowl in Tampa to search for felons and terrorists among the crowd of 100,000 spectators. Electronic readers can be affixed to entryways, keyboards, laptops, and even mobile phones. Companies often do not need to install anything beyond the new software because most already have pictures of employees on file and cameras in place, making it cheaper than iris-reading setups.

Here's how it works. Computer software measures a face according to its peaks and valleys—such as the tip of the nose, the depth of the eye sockets—which are known as nodal points. Even though a human face has 80 nodal points, programs only require 14 to 22 to achieve recognition with 99 percent accuracy. The program concentrates on the inner region of the face, which runs from temple to temple and just over the lip, called the "golden triangle." The software matches face prints in the existing file with those of the people passing in front of the cameras.

Did you know the Bible teaches that recognition technology has actually been around for thousands of years? When Abraham sent Hagar and Ishmael away, Hagar cried out to God for help. When the Angel of the Lord came to her and encouraged her, "Then she called the name of the LORD who spoke to her, You-Are-the-God-Who-Sees; for she said, 'Have I also here seen Him who sees me?'" (Genesis 16:13). The Lord, from the heavens, can see our every move.

Earth, Weather, & Plants

"He calms the storm,
So that its waves are still."
Psalm 107:29

March 1 THE DOLDRUMS

"After these things I saw four angels standing at the four corners of the earth, holding the four winds of the earth, that the wind should not blow on the earth, on the sea, or on any tree" (Revelation 7:1).

Nothing was so feared by seamen in the days when ocean vessels were driven by wind and sail than the doldrums. The doldrums is a part of the ocean near the equator, abounding with prolonged calms and light, baffling winds. The old sailing vessels, when caught in doldrums, would sometimes lie helpless for days and weeks, waiting for the wind to begin to blow. There the weather is hot, humid, and extremely dispiriting, sometimes driving the irritable sailors to violence or insanity.

The doldrums in the Pacific Ocean were famously described in the "Rime of the Ancient Mariner" by Samuel Taylor Coleridge:

All in a hot and copper sky,
The blood Sun, at noon,
Right up above the mast did stand,
No bigger than the Moon.
Day after day, day after day,
We stuck, nor breath nor motion;
As idle as a painted ship
Upon a painted ocean.

The low-pressure area around the equator, where the winds are often calm, is called the Intertropical Convergence Zone. With the winds absent, the sea has no swells, so on a clear day the sky is reflected in the water. The same happens at night so that sailors feel as if they are floating in space. The word actually comes from the word *dold* (which means "stupid") and *rums* (a noun suffix found in words like "tantrum"), which seems to describe how people caught in them might go crazy.

The children of Israel, when they turned away from conquering Canaan the first time, wandered in the wilderness for 40 years. It was like being in the doldrums. David describes their experience: "They wandered in the wilderness in a desolate way; they found no city to dwell in. Hungry and thirsty, their soul fainted in them. Then they cried out to the Lord in their trouble, and He delivered them out of their distresses" (Psalm 107:4-6). Someday soon the winds that have been held back from blowing on this Earth will be loosened and the final events of Earth's history will be rapidly fulfilled. Will you be on board God's ship moving quickly toward the Promised Land?

"Therefore, if anyone is in Christ, he is a new creation; old things have passed away; behold, all things have become new" (2 Corinthians 5:17).

The word "volcano" comes from a small island called Vulcano in the Mediterranean off the northern coast of Sicily, which gets its name from the blacksmith of the Roman gods—the god of fire—Vulcan. Thousands of years ago, the people who lived in this area believed that Vulcano was actually the forge chimney of Vulcan.

But volcanoes are not just a colorful legend; they are one of the most powerful and potentially destructive forces on Earth. For example, the 1980 explosion of Mount St. Helens in Washington State was estimated at 500 times more powerful than the force of the atomic bomb that destroyed Hiroshima. There are over 500 known active volcanoes on Earth, with around 1,500 that are potentially active, and that's not counting those that lie beneath the sea. Unfortunately, about 500 million people live within the "danger range" of these active volcanoes. The biggest volcano on Earth is Hawaii's Mauna Loa. It rises more than 30,000 feet, nearly 5.7 miles above its base on the Pacific sea floor.

For years it was generally accepted and taught by geologists that volcanoes developed slowly over long eons. That was until 1963 when, off the coast of Iceland, the world witnessed a volcano virtually grow up out of the ocean in a matter of months. By 1967 the new volcanic island of Surtsey was transformed into a "mature" island with wide sandy beaches, pebbles, vegetation, birds, and many other features that would suggest great geological age. When the geologists wandered about the island they were mystified and found it hard to believe that this was a volcano whose age was still measured in months and not millennia!

In like manner, many people believe it would take years for them to turn from their sinful habits and live a Christian life. But they may be underestimating the miraculous power of God to quickly give them a new birth. The Lord promises, "I will give you a new heart and put a new spirit within you; I will take the heart of stone out of your flesh and give you a heart of flesh" (Ezekiel 36:26). God's Word says that the time for salvation is now. The same God who gives volcanoes their tremendous power can give you a new direction in an instant—the moment you accept Him into your heart.

March 3 THE GREAT STORM

"Then I saw another sign in heaven, great and marvelous: seven angels having the seven last plagues, for in them the wrath of God is complete" (Revelation 15:1).

The deadliest natural disaster in American history occurred just 300 miles west of New Orleans, where Hurricane Katrina came ashore in 2005. The unnamed category 4 hurricane struck over a century ago on September 8, 1900, ripping into Galveston, Texas, killing somewhere between 6,000 and 12,000 men, women, and children and wiping away three-quarters of the city.

However, the fatal storm did not come without warning. People in Galveston knew that there was a major storm brewing in the Gulf of Mexico. Days before the hurricane reached Texas, Galveston received telegraph reports telling of a fierce storm that caused havoc in the Caribbean. One day before the hurricane arrived barometric pressure dropped rapidly, and warning flags were raised as huge waves pounded the shore. But less than half the population evacuated the island, and some sightseers even came over from Houston to view the powerful surf. People's attitude of complacency greatly increased the number of fatalities. Wind speeds measured 100 mph before the instruments were blown away. The winds would eventually reach 150 mph.

One of the first buildings to succumb to the storm was St. Mary's Orphanage that stood near the beach. Of the 93 children and 10 nuns, the only survivors were three boys who managed to cling to an uprooted tree. About 50 people sought shelter in the home of Isaac Cline. Battered by the heavy winds and a 16-foot tidal wave, it collapsed, and all but 18 perished, including Isaac Cline's wife, May. Strangely, Isaac Cline worked for the U.S. Weather Bureau and had dismissed concerns that a hurricane could someday devastate Galveston. He discouraged the town from building a sea wall. One in six Galveston residents died in the disaster. A few months after the hurricane, Galveston began construction on a 17-foot-high, 3-mile-long sea wall and raised the ground level of the entire city.

Did you know that the Bible forecasts a terrible storm just before the coming of Jesus, concluding with a great rescue from above? Like the unheeded flags that were raised on the Galveston beach to warn of the coming storm, we must be responsible to be prepared. God has given us many signs of the times. Will you listen to His counsel to watch and be ready?

"He shall be like a tree planted by the rivers of water, that brings forth its fruit in its season, whose leaf also shall not wither; and whatever he does shall prosper" (Psalm 1:3).

Roots are the underground branches that spread out beneath plants and trees as anchors. They provide water and nutrients from the soil to feed the plant. Some roots are familiar, like carrots, potatoes, and radishes. But because roots are usually out of sight, many people don't realize how long and vast they can be. An alfalfa plant only two or three feet high may have roots reaching out as far as 30 feet. If you lay all the roots of a corn plant end to end, the resulting strand could be up to 500 feet long. Roots of the giant California redwoods have been known to occupy as much as 50,000 cubic feet of subsoil. Cavers in South Africa found a tree with the deepest-reaching root so far: a wild fig tree with a root that extended nearly 400 feet into the ground!

In addition, roots can be incredibly strong. It's common knowledge that, given enough time, roots can crack foundations, snap water lines, and lift sidewalks. Once they find even the tiniest crack, a rootlet can break through compacted soil, stone, or concrete and even push aside large boulders. For example, when tree roots become wedged in granite, it is the hard granite that splits while the comparatively fragile-looking root stubbornly continues to grow.

And why are roots so tenacious? They're looking for water. While some plants like cacti have swollen roots that store water for the dry months, most roots reach out long distances in search of water to transport back to the plant. Plants flourish where there is plenty of water, which is why the trees growing along a stream look more vibrant than the ones growing farther away.

The Bible teaches that a person who delights in the law of the Lord "shall be like a tree planted by the rivers of water" (Psalm 1:3). Would you like to prosper in whatever you do? Then let meditating on God's Word become your delight!

March 5 THE SARGASSO SEA

"So the great dragon was cast out, that serpent of old, called the Devil and Satan, who deceives the whole world ..." (Revelation 12:7).

One of the most interesting places in the world is actually out in the middle of the ocean. The Sargasso Sea does not even have a coastline but is a separate sea located in the middle of the North Atlantic, between the West Indies and the Azores. The warm waters of the Sargasso Sea cover some 2 million square miles and are encircled by the Gulf Stream, causing the oval-shaped sea to move in a slow, clockwise drift. This makes the 3-mile-deep waters exceptionally clear and blue, with a higher than normal salt content.

The Sargasso Sea is filled with seaweed. Early Portuguese navigators named the sea "sargaco," the word for grape, after the bulbous little floats on the Sargassum seaweed. Although one-third of the Atlantic's plankton is produced there, the Sargasso Sea is known as "the floating desert" because the Sargassum seaweed lacks the nutrients to attract commercially valuable fish. But many small marine animals, including tiny crabs, shrimp, and octopuses, live on and among the seaweed.

One of the most amazing facts about the Sargasso Sea is that it serves as the international meeting place for eels. Drawn by unknown forces, each fall millions of these snakelike fish migrate from Europe, the Mediterranean, and the United States to mate, spawn, and die. Some eels have even left their freshwater homes and crossed miles of land, breathing through their skin, to reach the ocean that they might swim to the Sargasso Sea and breed. Once the eggs hatch, their inch-long, transparent larvae, known as "glass eels," make the long journey back to continental streams and rivers.

For hundreds of years naturalists wondered where eels came from. When it was discovered that virtually all the eels in the Western Hemisphere migrated to the Sargasso Sea, it was an amazing revelation. In the same way, many have wondered where sin and evil spawned. The Bible tells us about one of the highest angels in heaven, named Lucifer, who turned from God and was eventually cast out.

"How you are fallen from heaven, O Lucifer, son of the morning! How you are cut down to the ground, you who weakened the nations! For you have said in your heart: 'I will ascend into heaven, I will exalt my throne above the stars of God ... I will be like the Most High'" (Isaiah 14:12-14). It is no secret where sin came from.

"So Jesus said to them, '...if you have faith as a mustard seed, you will say to this mountain, "Move from here to there," and it will move; and nothing will be impossible for you'" (Matthew 17:20).

Would you like to know some fascinating facts about seeds? Did you know a turnip seed, under the right conditions, can increase its weight 15 times a minute? And in rich soil, after sprouting, turnip seeds may increase their weight up to 15,000 times a day. Some seeds are viable for hundreds years. For example, seeds of the Oriental lotus have been known to germinate 3,000 years after dispersal.

The world's largest seeds resemble giant coconuts, and for centuries were thought to come from the sea because they often washed up on the shores around the Indian Ocean. Consequently, those who found them called them sea coconuts. But in the 18th century it was discovered that the seeds came from tall nut palms that grew only on the Seychelles Islands. For years, Eastern kings and Asian potentates eagerly sought the seeds, which weigh upwards of 40 pounds, thinking that they could be used as antidotes to poison.

Amazingly enough there are few forces more powerful than a growing squash seed. In one experiment, a squash 18 days old was harnessed on a lever in such a way that in its growing process it lifted 50 pounds! Nineteen days later it raised 5,000 pounds!

Seeds are incredible in their abilities. Perhaps this is why Jesus said if you have "faith as a mustard seed," you can move mountains (Matthew 17:20). What is this seed of faith that can move mountains? The human race—from the days of our first parents to the present time—is full of unbelief. Even to His own disciples Jesus said, "Why are you so fearful? How is it that you have no faith?" (Mark 4:40). It seems that it's much easier for us to doubt than to believe, but we need to believe in order to be saved.

So how do we get faith? The book of Acts speaks of the faith that comes through Jesus (Acts 3:16), and Paul tells us "it is the gift of God" (Ephesians 2:8). Only God can give us the faith we need to believe in Him and trust His promises. Won't you ask Him for that faith right now?

March 7 HAILSTONES

"Have you entered the treasury of snow, or have you seen the treasury of hail?" (Job 38:22).

We've all enjoyed stepping outside after a hailstorm and scooping up a handful of the cold pellets on a summer day, but hail can be deadly. Most of the time hail stays small and is harmless. Sometimes conditions can produce large stones that can destroy crops, strip trees of foliage, damage roofs, and break car windows. As a pilot, I'm also aware of how quickly hail can damage an airplane! In the spring of 1986, hail the size of grapefruit fell in Bangladesh, killing over 90 people.

Hail is formed in thunderhead clouds when warm summer air from the ground rises and cools. As the temperature of this air drops and loses its ability to hold moisture, it releases it and forms puffy-looking clouds. The interaction of rising air creates updrafts with vertical wind speeds of over 110 mph. Hail grows in the storm cloud's main updraft, where most of the cloud is, in the form of "super-cooled" water molecules which then attach themselves to particles and freeze. Often a hailstone will connect with other stones until the weight of the hail overcomes the updraft wind and it falls from the sky.

The size of hail is best measured with a ruler for accuracy. But most of us don't carry rulers around when we encounter hail. So, common household objects or coins are used to quickly determine size—such as a dime, penny, nickel, or pea, grape, golf ball, or cantaloupe. The most common area for hail in the United States is in an area where Colorado, Nebraska, and Wyoming meet. It's known as "Hail Alley." The city that gets the most hail in the U.S. is Cheyenne, Wyoming. It averages nine to 10 hailstorms every year! The largest hailstone on record in the U.S. fell on July 23, 2010, in Vivian, South Dakota. This whopper stone had an eight-inch diameter and weighed 1.93 pounds. I don't think an umbrella would protect you from this storm!

The Bible actually predicts the mother of all hailstorms as happening in the future when the seven last plagues fall on the Earth. The Bible explains the seventh plague: "And great hail from heaven fell upon men, each hailstone about the weight of a talent" (Revelation 16:21). A talent weighs about 75 pounds. Only those under the care of God's mighty hand will be protected from these disasters. Are you living under the Lord's shelter every day?

March 8

"The nations were angry, and Your wrath has come, and the time of the dead, that they should be judged, and that You should reward Your servants the prophets and the saints, and those who fear Your name, small and great, and should destroy those who destroy the earth" (Revelation 11:18).

The most densely concentrated area of life on the planet is the tropical rainforest. In fact, researchers found that just a 4-mile-square patch of rainforest contains as many as 1,500 species of flowering plants, 750 species of trees, 125 mammal species, 400 species of birds, 100 species of reptiles, 60 species of amphibians, and 150 different species of butterflies. A single pond in Brazil is home to more fish species than can be found in all of Europe's rivers, while the fish species in the Amazon River outnumber those in the Atlantic Ocean! But of the estimated 5 million species in the rainforest, only a small percentage has been named, much less studied.

The rainforest is also a cornucopia of produce, with over 3,000 varieties of fruit. Fruits like avocados, coconuts, figs, oranges, lemons, grapefruit, bananas, guavas, pineapples, mangoes, and tomatoes all originated in tropical rainforests. Even so, the rainforest's bounty is largely undiscovered by the Western world: of the 3,000 varieties, Westerners only use around 200.

In addition, the rainforest contains a pharmaceutical gold mine. Nearly half of our medicinal compounds come from the plant life in the tropical rainforest, including drugs for childhood leukemia and heart disease. Yet these riches are largely unmined, as less than 1 percent of tropical plants and trees have been tested by scientists.

Rainforests are a living dynamo of animals, plants, and medicines, but instead of discovering and enjoying its bounty, man is destroying it at the rate of 1 acre every minute. While rainforests used to cover fifteen percent of the Earth's land area, today they cover less than seven percent. In the book of Jeremiah, God expresses His displeasure over how Israel treated the Promised Land: "I brought you into a bountiful country, to eat its fruit and its goodness. But when you entered, you defiled My land And made My heritage an abomination" (Jeremiah 2:7). The book of Revelation makes it plain that God will eventually "destroy those who destroy the earth" (Revelation 11:18). As the Earth's caretakers, shouldn't we do our best to preserve His bountiful country?

March 9 RAINING FISH

"These all died in faith, not having received the promises ..." (Hebrews 11:13).

You have probably heard the expression "raining cats and dogs." While there is no record of the sky ever showering canines and felines, other creatures have rained from the sky. For example, on March 5, 2000, farmers tending their fields in southern Ethiopia reported seeing, and smelling, an unusual downpour on their drought-stricken land. Suddenly they were being pelted by millions of falling fish. For a country crippled by famine, this was a welcome and unexpected answer to their prayers.

Reports of falling fish, frogs, tomatoes, and even coal date back to antiquity. In the first century, Pliny the Elder mentioned storms of frogs and fish. Jellyfish reportedly fell from the sky in Bath, England, in 1894. Worms dropped from the sky in Jennings, Louisiana, on July 11, 2007, and spiders fell out of the sky on April 6, 2007, in Salta Province, Argentina!

The phrase "It's raining cats and dogs" probably comes from an era when animals walked on the thatched roofs of homes that became soft during rainstorms, and the household pet came through the roof. Actually, most countries have strange expressions for heavy rain. In Bosnia they say, "It's raining crowbars." In Czech it's "wheelbarrows," and the Dutch say, "It's raining like kittens." That's probably better than the Serbians, who refer to "axes," or the Welsh, who speak of it raining like "old ladies and sticks!"

Meteorologists say it is more common than you might think for cloud bursts to open and release a hail of small fish, snails, or tadpoles. Weather experts explain these freak showers occur because powerful updrafts generated during thunderstorms form mini-tornadoes. If the storm brews out at sea, or crosses a river or lake, the tornado can suck up small fish or frogs swimming close to the surface. These water spouts can then carry away the raptured creatures and deposit them several miles away. Sometimes while still alive! In 1930 an eight-inch turtle fell from the sky during a storm in Mississippi.

The Bible teaches that when Jesus returns the saved will be caught up to meet the Lord in the air. But many Christians misunderstand how this will happen. Unlike the popular notion that Christians will be raptured before Christ returns, the Bible teaches that when Jesus comes and the dead in Christ rise, "Then we who are alive and remain shall be caught up together with them in the clouds to meet the Lord in the air" (1 Thessalonians 4:17).

"And there will be signs in the sun, in the moon, and in the stars; and on the earth distress of nations, with perplexity, the sea and the waves roaring" (Luke 21:25).

Tsunamis are among the most destructive of natural disasters. This is due in part to the fact that much of the world's population lives within a mile of the ocean. Tsunamis are sometimes called tidal waves, but they really have nothing to do with the tide. They are actually seismic sea waves caused by earthquakes, undersea landslides, volcanic eruptions, or even asteroids striking the ocean that results in a sudden colossal movement of the sea water.

Tsunamis can look like great, massive, towering waves or appear as quickly rising monster tides that surge in without warning. Out in the deep ocean a tsunami wave can travel at speeds over 500 mph. That's as fast as a jet plane! These killer waves may be only a foot high in the deep ocean, and might not even be noticed by boats in the area, but as they reach shallow water the waves grow slower and taller, some to over 100 feet high!

Perhaps thousands of tsunamis occur all the time—the majority in the Pacific Ocean—but most are too small to even notice. But every few years, some seismic event will produce a large tsunami wave that kills thousands of people. The famous volcanic explosion of Krakatoa on August 27, 1883, generated terrifying tsunami waves that were up to 151 feet in height. These waves destroyed 295 towns and villages in Western Java and Southern Sumatra, and over 36,000 people were drowned.

The largest tsunami wave ever recorded in modern times was in Lituya Bay, Alaska, in 1958 and is described as a mega-tsunami. It was caused by a massive landslide triggered by an 8.3 magnitude earthquake. When the wave rushed across the bay it ran up the valley walls to a height of 1,720 feet.

In the Gospel of Luke, Jesus said one of the signs of the end will be "distress of nations, with perplexity, the sea and the waves roaring" (Luke 21:25). Natural disasters are increasing, signaling Earth's grand finale. This could be a frightening scenario, but we don't need to be afraid. In the words of Psalm 46, "God is our refuge and strength," even if the mountains fall into the sea. As long as we have Jesus, we are safe.

March 11 THE HAMMER ORCHID

"Beware of false prophets, who come to you in sheep's clothing, but inwardly they are ravenous wolves" (Matthew 7:15).

Most plants and flowers must pollinate to survive, so the Lord has devised many ingenious ways to help them exchange these particles of life. God has created many flower species that pretend to have food that insects want, emitting the scents of things like coconut or even rotting meat to attract them.

Some orchids, however, to achieve pollination, appear to offer insects the promise of marriage. Parts of the flower have been designed to resemble the female versions of certain insects, and the imitation is often astounding. Take, for example, the Australian hammer orchid which has taken advantage of a mating ritual of the Thynnid wasp.

The lower lip of the hammer orchid's flower mimics the female wasp resting on a twig, looking upward, waiting for a male flying by to spot her. Even to the human eye, it almost perfectly resembles the plump, wingless female Thynnid wasp, complete with a shiny head and furry body. The orchid even releases an enticing female wasp pheromone. That's a chemical copy of the same sexy perfume the female wasp wears when she's ready for marriage. Amazing! Poised at the end of an arm just above this alluring decoy are sticky bags filled with pollen.

A male Thynnid wasp flying by, lured by the imitation scent, will grab the decoy and try to fly off with "her" in his grasp. As he takes off, however, his momentum flips him and his flowery pretender up and over, right into the sticky pollen sacks. After realizing his mistake, he releases the decoy—and flies off, only to be fooled again by another hammer orchid, which he now pollinates with the pollen he picked up on his previous bad date. In the process, the wasp transfers pollen from flower to flower.

When real female Thynnid wasps are around, males will invariably choose a live one over the impostor. For this reason God conveniently designed these orchids to bloom in the brief period several weeks before female wasps emerge from underground, giving the flower a temporary advantage when male wasps are flying but females are not yet available.

Mimicry in nature is truly remarkable, even humorous, but wolves in sheep's clothes is no laughing matter. Jesus warned us that false prophets will come to deceive us before the Second Coming. They will look like the "real thing," but to the Christian who has carefully studied the Bible, we may detect and turn away from the lures of the devil.

"Then it happened, as they continued on and talked, that suddenly a chariot of fire appeared with horses of fire, and separated the two of them; and Elijah went up by a whirlwind into heaven" (2 Kings 2:11).

The United States has the dubious honor of having more tornadoes each year than every other country on the planet combined. These frightening storms can result in record numbers of injuries and deaths. One of the deadliest outbreaks ever seen was in April 1974. During a single 24-hour period, a record 148 tornadoes tore through the Midwest, killing more than three hundred people and injuring more than six thousand.

The worst tornadoes, classified as F5, are capable of tremendous destruction with wind speeds of 250 mph or more. In the spring of 1999, a massive F5 tornado stayed on the ground near Oklahoma City for one hour and 25 minutes, killing 41 people, destroying thousands of homes and vehicles, and racking up approximately one billion dollars of damages. Researchers clocked the wind at 318 mph, which is the fastest surface wind ever recorded on Earth.

Tornadoes have been known to transport a thousand-pound bale of hay over 5 miles, drive a piece of straw through a 2x4 piece of wood, imbed a plastic music record halfway into a telephone pole, and leave a semi-truck dangling from a tree. On April 24, 1990, a 100-yard-wide tornado touched down in Barton County, Kansas, lifting 88 train cars off the tracks and stacking them three to four cars high. Tornadoes have also done some bizarre things like putting cows in treetops. An unusual incident occurred in 1957 in Thomasville, Alabama: thousands of small fish, frogs, and crayfish fell from the sky. A tornado had pulled up lake water some miles away, and as the winds lost strength, the little animals rained down across the countryside.

In the Bible, God's judgment is sometime pictured as a tornado: "Behold, a whirlwind of the Lord has gone forth in fury—a violent whirlwind! It will fall violently on the head of the wicked" (Jeremiah 23:19). But God's people don't need to fear! "When the whirlwind passes by, the wicked *is* no *more*, but the righteous *has* an everlasting foundation" (Proverbs 10:25). In fact, one of God's righteous, Elijah, even rode a tornado to heaven!

March 13 EARTHQUAKES

"And there will be great earthquakes in various places ..." (Luke 21:11).

Earthquakes conjure up terrifying images of the ground rocking and rolling as if moved by some diabolical forces from the abyss. Unlike tornadoes or hurricanes, earthquakes usually strike without warning. In North America when we hear the word earthquake we typically think of Los Angeles, San Francisco, or maybe Alaska. But there have even been major earthquakes recorded in Boston, Charleston, South Carolina, and even Long Island.

Surprisingly, some of the greatest potential for a powerful North American earthquake is not on the Pacific or Atlantic Coast but rather the states around mid-America. The granddaddy of great earthquakes occurred between 1811 and 1812 on the New Madrid Fault (halfway between St. Louis and Memphis, beneath the Mississippi). These earthquakes shook the entire United States, affecting the topography of the North American continent more than any other earthquakes in recorded history. Judging from their effects, they were of a magnitude of 7.5 or higher. They were felt over the entire United States east of the Rockies. The shock was so massive, large areas sank into the earth, new lakes were formed, 150,000 acres of forests were destroyed, and the Mississippi River ran backwards, permanently changing its course. Many houses at New Madrid were thrown down. One source notes, "Houses, gardens, and fields were swallowed up." Fatalities and damage were low, because back then the area was sparsely settled. But in the last 200 years those same areas have become heavily populated.

For years geologists have not been wondering "if" but "when" the big one will hit! Earthquake forecasting is a science to determine the time, location, and magnitude of a future earthquake, especially the next big one in a specific region. Scientists believe there is a significant probability for major earthquakes to hit certain epicenters, causing catastrophic loss of life and property damage in the billions. But the science of prediction is still unreliable. That is why, for decades now, several North America cities have been looking down the barrel of a loaded seismic canon, *hoping* for another day of grace.

Jesus said just before His coming there would be earthquakes in different places. Such natural disasters continue to point us to the importance of being ready for Christ's soon return.

"The LORD on high is mightier than the noise of many waters, than the mighty waves of the sea" (Psalm 93:4).

In 1874, Methodists in Swan Quarter, North Carolina, decided to construct a permanent church building. The homeless Christians found what they believed was the ideal site for their church, a perfect lot in the heart of town on its highest ground. But when they approached the owner of the lot, Sam Sadler, he did not want to waste his prime real estate for a church. Even after their offer was increased, Sadler flatly refused to sell the land.

Soon after, the Methodists accepted a gift of land a half mile away on some low-lying property. The members cheerfully began building a modest but sturdy structure on brick piers. Then something miraculous occurred that has been confirmed by scores of witnesses. On September 17, 1876, right after they dedicated the small church, a powerful hurricane began to brew. Rain fell and the wind blew until the rising water lifted the little Methodist Church from its foundation and began to carry it like Noah's ark up the street. People awoke the next morning to witness an amazing sight—the entire church was floating down Oyster Creek Road.

A few good Samaritans saw the drifting church and tried to tie it off with ropes, but it broke its moorings and continued its journey as though it had a mind of its own. It went straight down the road to a corner, bumped into a general store, then took a sharp right turn and headed down that road for about two city blocks until it reached the corner of what is now Church Street. Then it took another turn to the left, crossed the Carawan Canal, and stopped.

The little church had settled exactly in the center of the property the members had originally requested for their house of worship, the parcel Sam Sadler had refused to sell for a church. After seeing the mighty work of Providence, Mr. Sadler, with trembling hands, gave the title deed for the land to the Methodist pastor. When the church was dedicated, it was called "Providence." Today, a sign stands in front of the Providence Church, reminding visitors this was the church "Moved by the Hand of God."

Just as God guided that floating church, He guides His people and His church today. "The LORD is your keeper ..." (Psalm 121:5). He will carry us through any flood of trouble or persecution that we face.

March 15 ICEBERGS

"And because lawlessness will abound, the love of many will grow cold" (Matthew 24:12).

On March 21, 2000, one of the largest icebergs ever seen broke free from the Antarctic's Ross Ice Shelf. An image, taken from a polar satellite 435 miles up, alerted scientists and mariners to the iceberg's birth. It is one of the largest ever seen at 183 miles long and 23 miles wide, with a surface area of 4,250 square miles. The biggest iceberg ever recorded was 208 miles long and 60 miles wide, a total of 12,000 square miles. That's larger than the country of Belgium. Even more amazing, it was spotted floating in the South Pacific. It's astounding how far from the Polar regions icebergs can wander. Icebergs from the Arctic north have reached as far south as the island of Bermuda, a journey of 2,500 miles. One iceberg from the Antarctic has reached almost as far north as Rio de Janeiro, a journey of 3,440 miles.

The tallest iceberg ever recorded was 550 feet high. That's as tall as a 50-story building! But remember that only 10 percent of an iceberg's mass is above water, meaning the bulk of this titan could have reached 4,000 feet deep. I have also read there is so much ice stored on the continent of Antarctica, that if you could cut it into huge ice cubes one mile thick you would end up with 6 million cubes. Should all of that ice melt, it would raise the sea level over the entire world by 260 feet. Ice on Antarctica is so heavy that over the years it has pushed the continent itself down several hundred feet.

Jesus warned us in the last days, because lawlessness will abound, the love of many will grow cold. How can we have our hearts warmed and our first loved rekindled in a spiritually cold world? Perhaps it is found in the words of John the Baptist: "I indeed baptize you with water; but One mightier than I is coming, whose sandal strap I am not worthy to loose. He will baptize you with the Holy Spirit and fire" (Luke 3:16).

When we invite Christ into our hearts and are filled with the Holy Spirit, there is a warming of our lives from within that will melt away the cold clutches of sin on our hearts. Then we will have purpose and not float aimlessly like a drifting iceberg.

"Therefore, as through one man's offense judgment came to all men, resulting in condemnation, even so through one Man's righteous act the free gift came to all men, resulting in justification of life" (Romans 5:18, 19).

The vanilla bean is the fruit of a unique species of fragrant orchid that is native to the rainforests of Mexico and Central America. Indigenous natives discovered that when the tasteless and odorless vanilla bean is dried by months of tropical heat and humidity, it produced a rich taste and aroma. Vanilla is the only orchid known to bear edible fruit.

Since the vanilla orchid only flowers for one day each year, it must be pollinated by hand. Then the vanilla bean takes approximately six months to mature, growing up to eight inches long. The beans must also be harvested by hand, just as the tip of the pod begins to split but before the entire pod splits. Next, harvested beans are immersed in a hot water bath, then put into wooden boxes and covered with blankets, where they will "sweat" for 24 to 72 hours. This begins the enzymatic change that produces vanillin. Afterward, the beans are placed on blankets and dried in the sun for three to four weeks. To complete the curing process, the beans are then stored in closed boxes for five or six months. The cured beans, now wrinkled and chocolate colored, are graded by length, appearance, and moisture content. The longest beans with the least splitting and blemishes bring the highest price. To make vanilla extract, the beans are tied in bundles, weighed, chopped, and percolated in large stainless steel containers, much like coffee percolators. After being aged for several weeks, the extract is bottled and shipped to stores. You can understand why vanilla is one of the most expensive flavorings in the world to produce!

Today vanilla beans are grown primarily in Madagascar and Indonesia. The precious extract is by far the world's most popular flavor and is used in ice cream, puddings, cakes, chocolates, baked goods, syrups, candies, liqueurs, tobacco, soft drinks, and even perfumes.

Salvation is the most expensive commodity in the universe, provided for by the "precious blood of Christ" (1 Peter 1:19). But, by the grace of God, it is free for the asking! Let's not waste a single drop.

March 17 THE REAL SAINT PATRICK

"This fellow persuades men to worship God contrary to the law" (Acts 18:13).

Typically on March 17, people all over the world join the Irish to celebrate Saint Patrick's Day. Cities like New York and Boston have large parades baptized in shamrocks, leprechauns, and the color green. Chicago will even dye its river green. Sadly there is far more myth than fact taught about this great man of God called Saint Patrick.

For starters, this patron saint of Ireland was not even Irish, but English. St. Patrick, whose real name was Maewyn Succat, was born in Roman Britain, around A.D. 389. He was captured by raiders when he was about 16 and conveyed to Ireland, where he was sold as a slave to care for pigs and sheep. While in captivity, like the prodigal son, he surrendered his heart to Christ. After six years he escaped slavery and returned back to his homeland. But a few years later he distinctly heard God call him to return to Ireland as a missionary to convert his former captors to Christianity. After he became a minister he took on the name Patrick, or Patricus, which means father of the people.

A popular legend has it that St. Patrick drove all the snakes from Ireland. It's true that, aside from zoos and pets, there are no snakes on the Emerald Isle. That's because there never were any snakes in Ireland. This has more to do with the island's 700-foot chalky cliffs on Ireland's west coast more than any miracles performed by St. Patrick. This tale may have arisen as a metaphor of his single-handed effort to drive the idol-worshiping Druid cult out of Ireland.

Saint Patrick was not technically a saint because the Catholic Church never canonized him. Even though they built hundreds of churches that bear his name, Patrick was not even a Roman Catholic. He operated as an independent Christian and self-supporting missionary. March 17th is not even St. Patrick's birthday but rather the day the old missionary died in his beloved Ireland. He had set free the land which once enslaved him.

It's amazing how many fables have become connected with the work of this great missionary. But this is not the first time this has happened. The apostle Paul was accused repeatedly of things that were distortions of his true work. While in Corinth, Luke writes, "When Gallio was proconsul of Achaia, the Jews with one accord rose up against Paul and brought him to the judgment seat, saying, 'This fellow persuades men to worship God contrary to the law'" (Acts 18:12, 13). God's people will continue to be misunderstood until Jesus comes.

March 18

"For you were bought at a price; therefore glorify God in your body and in your spirit, which are God's" (1 Corinthians 6:20).

The Dead Sea in Israel is one of the most unusual spots on the planet. At 1,312 feet below sea level, it's the lowest water surface on Earth. The Dead Sea receives over 6 million tons of water every day from the Jordan River alone, but even though it has no outlet the water level never rises. The old geographers used to think there was an enormous chasm in the bottom of the Dead Sea, and that its water poured itself down into the center of the earth. But Lieutenant Lynch of the United States Navy sounded every part of the Dead Sea and disproved that theory.

The sea bed is 47 miles long and an average of 9 miles wide. Therefore, evaporation in that seething desert basin exceeds the input, making the Dead Sea seven times as salty as the ocean. Because of its high mineral content, no one can ever sink or drown while bathing there. It was said that Vespasian, the ancient Roman commander, heard of this fact. He tested it by ordering slaves to be thrown into the sea with their hands and feet tied. The slaves floated.

The high concentration of minerals also makes the Dead Sea one of the most valuable spots on Earth. Among the precious minerals in the Dead Sea is potash. Often used for explosives, potash is also a potent fertilizer. It has been estimated that the Dead Sea has enough potash to provide the entire world's fertilizer needs for 2,000 years.

This body of water contains an estimated 22 billion tons of magnesium chloride, 12 billion tons of common salt, six billion tons of calcium chloride, two billion tons of potassium chloride, and one billion tons of magnesium bromide. The value of these chemicals comes to the staggering figure of $1,270,000,000,000. All the goods exported from Israel are nothing in comparison with the enormous mineral wealth in the Dead Sea.

Who would dream that a place that is so outwardly lifeless could be so valuable? Perhaps you have also underestimated your worth before God. Scripture tells us, "... you were not redeemed with corruptible things, like silver or gold ... but with the precious blood of Christ ..." (1 Peter 1:18, 19). In this way, God has placed immeasurable value on each one of us.

March 19 OCEAN SOUNDS

"Let the heavens rejoice, and let the earth be glad; let the sea roar, and all its fullness ..." (Psalm 96:11).

There is more noise in the ocean than merely the lapping of waves or bubbling fish. Humans cannot hear many ocean sounds when underwater because a pocket of air in the outer ear blocks them. But when using an underwater microphone you will discover that the ocean is full of amazing sounds. Dolphins chatter, triggerfish grate their teeth together, sea horses rub their heads against their backs.

Among the loudest creatures of the deep is a finger-size shrimp with an oversize claw resembling a boxing glove. The pistol shrimp (or alpheid shrimp) snaps shut a specialized claw to create a cavitation wave that generates noise like gunshots in excess of 200 decibels. This sea creature blasts bubbles at over 60 mph, producing a sharp cracking sound and a temperature comparable to that of the sun. The sound will not only scare off enemies but is capable of killing small fish. In fact, when colonies of the pistol shrimp snap their claws, the cacophony is so intense that submarines can take advantage of it to hide from sonar.

However, the greatest noise makers in the ocean are whales. The song of the humpback whale consists of vast roars, deep bellows, and groans interspersed with interesting sighs, chirps, and squawks. And the songs go on for 10 minutes or more. Once completed, the whale will repeat it again and again for hours. Each year the song tunes change somewhat, as the whales seem to experiment with different arrangements.

The largest creature in the world is of course the blue whale. It has the biggest lungs and makes the most noise. Blasts of 188 decibels have been reported, making the blue whale much louder than a jet, which reaches only 140 decibels! This extraordinarily earsplitting whistle can be heard for hundreds of miles underwater. Theoretical calculations once predicted that the loudest whale sounds might be transmitted across an entire ocean.

Some people think the second coming of Jesus is going to be a quiet event, yet the Bible teaches it is connected with a tremendous noise that will be heard across land and sea. "But the day of the Lord will come as a thief in the night, in which the heavens will pass away with a great noise" (2 Peter 3:10). The sound will surpass the greatest decibels Earth has ever experienced. Will you be listening for Jesus' coming?

"It is like a mustard seed which, when it is sown on the ground, is smaller than all the seeds on earth; but when it is sown, it grows up and becomes greater than all herbs, and shoots out large branches, so that the birds of the air may nest under its shade" (Mark 4:31, 32).

Corn is the most abundant crop grown in the U.S., more than twice that of any other. It is also one of the most versatile of all plants. Corn is used to make everything from flour, syrup, starch, oil, livestock feed, paint, soap, linoleum, nylon, antibiotics, lipstick, gasoline, and much more.

But when corn was first planted in the Americas it was nothing like the robust specimens we see blanketing the plains today. The plants were only about three feet tall, and the small uneven ears had scattered kernels. In order to improve their crop, farmers would look for the largest ears of corn with the most kernels to use as seed for the next year. Then in the early 1900s, botanists discovered they could combine the best qualities of different varieties of corn to develop hybrids. To produce these hybrids, different varieties of corn would be planted in adjacent rows. The tassels of the first variety would be removed, preventing it from releasing its pollen. The second variety, its tassels intact, would then pollinate both rows. The ears that grew from the stalk of the first variety would have the hybrid seeds. They found that this simple act resulted in higher yields and healthier plants. They called it "hybrid vigor."

Today most of the corn grown in the U.S. Corn Belt is hybrid and reaches about eight feet tall. But some varieties can grow to over 20 feet! In a way, the hybrid crosses are like the biblical mustard seed—something great from humble origins. The kingdom of God operates on the same principle. Jesus didn't choose the wealthy and powerful to be His disciples—He worked with humble fishermen. Yet the message that took root in the hearts of those unsophisticated Galileans eventually spread to every nation.

Do you ever feel insignificant? Take heart! "For you see your calling, brethren, that not many wise according to the flesh, not many mighty, not many noble, are called ... God has chosen the weak things of the world to put to shame the things which are mighty ... that, as it is written, 'He who glories, let him glory in the LORD'" (1 Corinthians 1:26, 27, 31).

THE AMAZON

"There is a river whose streams shall make glad the city of God ..." (Psalm 46:4).

The Amazon is undoubtedly the greatest river in the world by many measures. For starters, the volume of water it carries to the sea equals approximately 20 percent of all the freshwater discharge into the oceans in the world (one-fifth). In one second it pours 60 million gallons into the Atlantic. The drainage basin of the Amazon River and its many tributaries covers 2,720,000 square miles. It is also the longest river in the world at over 4,220 miles long. During the rainy season sections of the massive river can be up to 24 miles wide. The mouth of the Amazon River pushes so much water into the Atlantic Ocean that even after traveling more than 100 miles out to sea you can still dip fresh water out of the ocean. In fact, the volume of water surging from the Amazon River is greater than the next eight largest rivers in the world combined, and three times the flow of all rivers in the United States.

The Amazon River is home to many other "extremes" of the natural world. Of course it provides residence to the world's biggest snake, the anaconda, and the world's most ferocious fish, the piranha. Catfish that live here have all the room they want to grow as big as nature will allow. Some have been captured weighing over 200 pounds! The largest freshwater fish in the world, the arapaima, lives in the waters of the Amazon River. They have been found to reach 15 feet in length and can weigh up to 440 pounds. There are over 2,000 known species of fish that live in the Amazon, and more are being discovered all the time. More than 4,000 species of butterflies have been identified there.

Just as the Amazon is a river teeming with life, the Bible speaks of a river of life that flows from the throne of God. Ezekiel describes a future picture of nature that also speaks of a great river. "And it shall be that every living thing that moves, wherever the rivers go, will live. There will be a very great multitude of fish, because these waters go there; for they will be healed, and everything will live wherever the river goes" (Ezekiel 47:9). Someday I want to stand in that river, don't you?

"Consider the lilies, how they grow: they neither toil nor spin; and yet I say to you, even Solomon in all his glory was not arrayed like one of these" (Luke 12:27).

Orchids are truly amazing flowers! They represent the largest family of flowering plants in the world and come in a kaleidoscope of diversity. There are about 25,000 species of orchids. That's four times as many species as mammals, and twice as many as birds. Orchids grow on six continents in almost every habitat ranging from deserts to swamps, alpine pastures to polar tundra, but most species are found in the wet tropical forests. If you like vanilla, you actually like orchids. The vanilla stick is simply the fermented and blackened pod of an orchid found in Mexico.

Like many plants, orchids need outside help to pollinate and reproduce. Because few orchids offer nectar or edible pollen, they must resort to a broad array of very creative aromatic, visual, or tactile tricks to attract potential pollinators. Some orchid petals imitate bees or butterflies; other can look like lizards, frogs, or even hummingbirds. Others mimic male bees in flight, hoping to incite territorial combat that will result in pollination.

The flowers may produce attractive odors to lure bees with sweet promise by copying the appearance and scent of nectar-producing flowers, while others, as in the case of a Dracula orchid, attract gnats or flies by producing an array of nasty smells like fungus, rotten meat, or even dirty diapers.

Some orchids promise shelter, with petals in the shape of insect burrows. The bugs crawl in for protection and come out with pollen. Certain orchids accomplish pollination by mimicking the appearance, scent, and even the feel of a particular female bee. When a male bee jostles the orchid's column, two yellow sacs packed with pollen are stuck to his back with quick-drying glue. Then there's the catasetum (kat-uh-see-tum) orchids, which slingshot a sticky pollen-loaded bundle on any hapless insect that bumps the trigger.

Obviously, these flowers don't see or hear, and they're unaware of their own colors and patterns. Mindless flowers could never develop this astounding arsenal of pollinating methods by themselves. It took the hand of an intelligent Creator-God who loves and cares for all of His creations. In the words of Psalm 104:24: "O Lord, how manifold are Your works! In wisdom You have made them all."

March 23 BANANAS

"In the middle of its street, and on either side of the river, was the tree of life, which bore twelve fruits ..." (Revelation 22:2).

Bananas are a fruity miracle. They are colorful, nutritious, not to mention the amusing shape is easy to hold, peel, and eat. Bananas also contain three natural sugars—sucrose, fructose, and glucose—combined with a healthy dose of fiber. When a hungry person eats a banana they receive an almost instant and sustained boost of vigor. Research has proven that just two bananas provide enough energy for a strenuous 90-minute workout. This is why bananas are the favorite fruit of Olympic athletes. In fact, compared to an apple, a banana has four times the protein, twice the carbohydrate, three times the phosphorus, five times the vitamin A and iron, and twice the other minerals. It is also rich in potassium and is one of most affordable fruits around. So maybe it's time to change that well-known proverb to "A banana a day keeps the doctor away!"

Studies have shown that bananas can also help overcome or prevent a substantial array of illnesses and conditions ranging from depression, heartburn, and anemia, to stroke and morning sickness. Around the world different parts of the banana plant are used for clothing, paper, and tableware, and the skin of the banana is used to heal everything from insect bites to warts. Indeed, the banana appears almost perfectly designed for human consumption and distribution. It is difficult to conceive of a more practical blueprint for the ideal fruit.

Have you noticed the banana has no seeds? Amazingly the banana is a mutant; it is the result of the cross pollination of two almost inedible Asian fruits. The banana is a freakish genetic amalgamation; one that has survived through the centuries due to the sustained intervention of diligent humans. These fragile fruits can only be cloned from suckering shoots and cuttings taken from the underground stem of existing plants. Over time, Arab traders carried the new wonder fruit to Africa, and Spanish conquistadors brought them to the Americas.

So if you have ever pictured Adam and Eve savoring bananas in the Garden of Eden you better think again. Bananas only happen through man participating with God's creation. This is also true regarding the fruit of the Spirit. "I am the vine, you are the branches. He who abides in Me, and I in him, bears much fruit; for without Me you can do nothing" (John 15:5). I wonder what types of fruit will be on the tree of life in heaven.

"... Do you not know that a little leaven leavens the whole lump? Therefore purge out the old leaven, that you may be a new lump, since you truly are unleavened. For indeed Christ, our Passover, was sacrificed for us. Therefore let us keep the feast, not with old leaven, nor with the leaven of malice and wickedness, but with the unleavened bread of sincerity and truth" (1 Corinthians 5:6-8).

Living beneath the Strawberry Mountain Wilderness in eastern Oregon, researchers have discovered the largest living organism on Earth. A single fungus living three feet underground is estimated to cover over 2,200 acres. The small mushrooms visible above ground are only the tip of the iceberg. Officially known as *Armillaria ostoyae*, or the honey mushroom, the fungus is 3.5 miles across and takes up space equivalent to 1,665 football fields. Based on its speed of growth, experts estimate that this "Methuselah mushroom" is over 2,400 years old, but it could be much older.

Scientists discovered the fungus when they noticed large groves of trees dying in that region of the forest. When foresters cut into an infected tree they would find spreading white tentacles, called rhizomorphs. These filaments draw moisture and nutrients from the trees' roots to feed the fungus. The honey mushroom can eventually sap enough water and carbohydrates from the roots to kill the trees. Researchers collected samples of the fungus from a widespread area and grew them together on petri dishes. Instead of forming barrier lines, the samples simply grew together. In addition, the researchers analyzed the DNA of the samples, establishing that they were all from the same massive organism. This makes the honey mushroom one humongous fungus! Experts say that at this point there is no way to get rid of the mushroom—it is just too big. Now consider this monster mushroom started from a single spore too small to see without a microscope!

The Bible teaches that immorality is a lot like this humongous fungus. Paul told the Corinthian church to root out the immoral influences in their church because "a little leaven leavens the whole lump" (1 Corinthians 5:6). A little sin in the life works like yeast in bread or like the spores of a mushroom—it spreads. The best way to deal with sin is to root it out before it becomes entrenched. As we yield our hearts to the Holy Spirit, He will convict us of sin, root it out of our lives, and exchange it for righteousness.

March 25 DIAMONDS

"The Lord their God will save them in that day, as the flock of His people. For they shall be like the jewels of a crown ..." (Zechariah 9:16).

Diamonds are the hardest natural material known to mankind. Their hardness has been legendary since antiquity and is the reason for its name coming from the ancient Greek word *adamas* for "invincible." Approximately 130 million carats are mined annually, with a value of nearly $9 billion. About 220,000 pounds of manmade diamonds are synthesized every year. Diamond formation requires exposure of carbon materials to very high pressure. Diamonds can also form in other natural events. For example, very small diamonds, known as microdiamonds, have been found in craters caused by a meteorite impact.

The biggest earthly diamond is the 530-carat Star of Africa, one of the British crown jewels. That was, at least until August 28, 2007, when a diamond mine in South Africa announced it found a diamond believed to be twice the size of the former record holder. The uncut diamond is expected to sell for up to $30 million. But it still may not be the biggest. Some astronomers believe they have actually found the biggest known diamond in the universe up in the sky directly above Australia. According to American astronomers at the Harvard-Smithsonian Center for Astrophysics, a white dwarf star in the constellation of Centaurus, next to the Southern Cross, has been found to have a 2,000-mile-wide solid core of crystallized carbon, or in other words, a diamond. It weighs 2.27 thousand trillion trillion tons—that's 10 billion trillion trillion carats, or a one followed by 34 zeroes. "It's the mother of all diamonds," said astronomer Travis Metcalfe, who led the team of researchers that studied the star.

God loves jewels and will decorate the New Jerusalem with many precious stones that surpass anything we've ever seen on Earth. When we think of the Lord's creation in the heavens, it doesn't seem impossible that every gate in the city of God is highly unique. "The twelve gates were twelve pearls: each individual gate was of one pearl. And the street of the city was pure gold, like transparent glass" (Revelation 21:21). I look forward to walking on that street someday.

"And I also say to you that you are Peter, and on this rock I will build My church, and the gates of Hades shall not prevail against it" (Matthew 16:18).

First recorded about 100 years ago, the mysterious Sailing Stones of Death Valley have been a documented fact for decades. Within the famous California desert is a dry lakebed called the Racetrack Playa that measures about 2.5 miles long and one mile wide. Scattered across the mosaic of cracked clay on the flat lakebed are hundred of stones in varying sizes. No big deal, right? The amazing thing is that many of these stones have long tracks behind them where they have obviously moved.

Now you need to picture that some of the sliding stones weigh hundreds of pounds. Additionally, some of these trails left by the roaming rocks are hundreds of yards long. Some stones make straight tracks, others make oval or 90 degree turns, while still others create wavy-shaped trails. How can a stone that weighs more than 500 pounds drag itself across flat ground? For nearly a century many geologists have studied and mapped the drifting stones in Death Valley, and it has become quite a puzzle. As the years proceed, each stone takes its own different path. Some of the mysterious migrating stones even slide uphill.

It seems now there is a plausible theory that has solved the amazing mystery. Occasionally, winter rains will fill the lake with a foot or so of water that freezes. As the edges of the shallow lake thaw, the giant floating ice pancake in the middle can get pushed around by the hurricane-force winds that are common in this valley. Rocks captured in this layer of ice are pushed along with the frozen mass, gouging trails in the slick clay below. Of course when the ice melts all you see are the rocks and the trails. Still, no one has ever seen the rocks move, nor does anyone know how fast they go.

Jesus said He was going to build His church on an immovable rock. Matthew provides a play on the Greek words in this crucial quotation from Jesus: "You are petros [a small throwable stone], and on this petra [the feminine form of petros, which indicates an immovable ledge of rock] I will build My church." Peter is addressed and told that his confession is the petra upon which Jesus will build His church. With that rock as our foundation, we cannot be moved.

March 27 THE BINGHAM CANYON MINE

"Again, the kingdom of heaven is like treasure hidden in a field, which a man found and hid; and for joy over it he goes and sells all that he has and buys that field" (Matthew 13:44).

The Bingham Canyon Mine is the largest manmade excavation on Earth. The sprawling open pit mine, located about 14 miles southwest of Salt Lake City, has a colossal crater that is more than 2.5 miles wide, three quarters of a mile deep and covers over 1,900 acres. Because of its breathtaking and awesome magnitude the Bingham Canyon Mine is one of only two manmade objects on Earth that can be seen by astronauts from outer space—the other is the Great Wall of China!

Employing 1,400 people, Bingham Canyon Mine has been in constant use since 1906, and has also proven to be one of the world's most productive mines, removing 450,000 tons of material from the mine daily. As of 2009, ore from the mine has yielded more than 18 million tons of copper, 24 million ounces of gold, 195 million ounces of silver, and 850 million pounds of molybdenum. The gold and silver are impurities removed from the copper during refining. The value of the resources extracted from the Bingham Canyon Mine is greater than the Comstock Lode, Klondike bonanza, and California gold rush mining all combined.

The mountain of minerals and copper ore were first discovered in 1848 by pioneering Mormon brothers, Sanford and Thomas Bingham, who grazed cattle and horses there. But sadly they never received a penny for the amazing discovery that bears their name. When they reported their find to Mormon leader Brigham Young, he advised them against staking a claim and urged them to focus instead on the ranch settlements.

Jesus compared the kingdom of heaven with a treasure found in a field. Some people have treasure right beneath their feet but don't do anything about it! But when the gospel treasure is presented to us, the precious truths of God's plan of salvation for our lives, we should do everything within our power to take hold of that fortune. We should "stake a claim" and not settle for anything less.

"And whatever you ask in My name, that I will do, that the Father may be glorified in the Son. If you ask anything in My name, I will do it" (John 14:13, 14).

In the spring of 1921, a small group of British soldiers patrolling the Sinai Peninsula became completely lost in a terrible sandstorm. Wandering in the blistering desert, they soon ran out of water. Facing death from thirst, they decided to dig in the sand, hoping to create a well. As this effort proved fruitless, one of the men suddenly remembered the passage in the Bible where Moses struck the desert rock, and God brought forth water for the children of Israel. He reminded his companions they were in the same Sinai Desert and pointed to a rock outcropping nearby. Why not, he asked, try to find water just as Moses had done? The men were desperate enough to try anything, so they went to the rock and started to swing at the ledge with a small pick. Then, as they frantically struck out, a miracle occurred—a dribble of clear, sweet water came out of the face of the rock. The rock was actually soft limestone, and part of it covered a hidden spring. This steady trickle of water kept the men alive until they were rescued.

Have you ever wondered if God still answers prayer today like He did in the Bible? Countless times, modern men and women of faith have testified that He does! But the best part is that we don't need to rely on the testimonies of others. God is delighted when we try it out for ourselves. Like a good parent, God loves giving "good things to those who ask Him!" (Matthew 7:11). The first step is learning to abide in Christ: "If you abide in Me, and My words abide in you, you will ask what you desire, and it shall be done for you" (John 15:7). As we abide in Christ, our hearts are changed, and often, our prayers are changed too. When we're in Christ, "all the promises of God in Him are Yes, and in Him Amen, to the glory of God through us" (2 Corinthians 1:20).

March 29 AMAZING BAMBOO

"All flesh is as grass, and all the glory of man as the flower of the grass" (1 Peter 1:24).

Did you know a member of the grass family is considered to be the fastest-growing plant in the world? It is a member of the true grass family known as Poaceae (po-se-i), also known as Bambuseae. Better known as bamboo, these tall stalks are actually the largest members of the grass family. In the warmer climates of Asia they are capable of growing as much as 39 inches per day! How would you like to keep that grass mowed? Bamboo grows so fast that, if you stand in one of these bamboo forests on a sunny day, you can actually hear the plants growing. Some plants grow 98 feet tall.

Bamboo has economic and cultural significance to South Asia, Southeast Asia, and East Asia. There are around 1,500 different species of bamboo in the world that come in several different colors—such as black, green, gold, gray, red, yellow, and powder blue. The bamboo plant is also extremely versatile with an extraordinary range of uses, and can be made into many things like baskets, bicycle frames, bird cages, blinds, boats, bridges, brushes, buckets, canoes, carts, charcoal, chopsticks, clothing, cooking utensils, diapers, fans, fences, firewood, fishing rods, food steamers, furniture, garden tools, handicrafts, hats, incense, musical instruments, paper, particle board, pens, pipes, roofing, scaffold, tableware, toilets, toothpicks, toys, umbrellas, and walking sticks! In fact, during WWII in the South Pacific, the U.S. Navy even used bamboo to reinforce concrete. That is pretty incredible when you remember that bamboo is just gigantic grass.

When the apostle Peter compared mankind with the Bible, he used grass as an illustration. "All flesh is as grass, and all the glory of man as the flower of the grass. The grass withers, and its flower falls away, but the word of the Lord endures forever" (1 Peter 1:24, 25). The glory of man's accomplishments fades into insignificance when compared with God's glory. Our corruptible works will someday disappear, but the incorruptible fruit of God's Word will grow and last for eternity. That's a lot longer than the lifetime of bamboo.

"But as it is written: 'Eye has not seen, nor ear heard, nor have entered into the heart of man the things which God has prepared for those who love Him.' But God has revealed them to us through His Spirit. For the Spirit searches all things, yes, the deep things of God" (1 Corinthians 2:9, 10).

In many ways the ocean represents the last frontier on Earth. Seventy-five percent of the world's surface and ninety-seven percent of the water on the planet is found in the oceans. Less than one percent of the world's water is fresh, and most of that is contained in glaciers and ice caps.

The average depth of the oceans is about 2.5 miles, the deepest point being in the Mariana Trench, 6.8 miles down. By way of comparison, Mount Everest is only 5.5 miles high. The pressure at the deepest part of the ocean is over eight tons per square inch.

Earth's longest mountain range is the mid-ocean ridge system, which stretches over 40,000 miles around the globe, winding from the Arctic Ocean to the Atlantic, skirting Africa, Asia, and Australia, and crossing the Pacific to the west coast of North America. It is four times longer than the Andes, Rockies, and Himalayas combined.

Ninety percent of all volcanic activity occurs in the oceans. In 1993, scientists located the largest known concentration of active volcanoes on the sea floor in the South Pacific. This area, the size of New York State, hosts 1,133 volcanic cones and sea mounts. Two or three could erupt at any moment.

The highest tides in the world are at the Bay of Fundy, which separates New Brunswick from Nova Scotia. At some times of the year, the difference between high and low tide is 53 feet 6 inches, the equivalent of a three-story building.

The sea is also brimming with amazing life. Even though fishermen harvest over four million tons each year from bays and oceans, biologists estimate that approximately 2,500,000 marine species have yet to be discovered and described.

The Bible tells us there is another world soon to be discovered by those who love God that far exceeds anything we can imagine. "Nevertheless we ... look for the new heavens and a new earth in which righteousness dwells" (2 Peter 3:13). The same God who formed our marvelous ocean and its spectacular inhabitants will give to His children the beautiful earth made new!

STRANGLER FIGS

"And some seed fell among thorns; and the thorns grew up and choked it, and it yielded no crop" (Mark 4:7).

The tropical banyan fig tree is sometimes known as a strangler fig because of its unusual growth habits. Tiny, sticky seeds are deposited by a bird high in the branches of another tree. The aggressive sprouts grow quickly and begin sending roots down over the trunk of the host tree, seeking out the rich soil below. Once they have found the ground and anchored themselves, the strangler fig roots rapidly thicken. Where the fig roots cross each other they fuse together, creating a lattice around the host tree's trunk. As the roots grow thicker, they compete with the host tree for sunlight and nutrients from the soil. Soon, they squeeze the trunk of its host, cutting off its flow of sap. Gradually, the host tree starves as the banyan tree monopolizes its sunlight, water, and nutrients. Eventually, the host tree dies and rots away, leaving a hollow center with the fig standing in its place.

Some banyan trees put down "aerial roots"—roots that dangle from the branches until they reach the ground and become a second trunk for the same tree. One particular tree in India, called The Great Banyan, is listed in the 1985 Guinness Book of World Records as the world's largest tree. It is more than 250 years old and covers an area of four acres. Its 3,300 aerial roots make it appear more like a forest than a single tree. In the 1920s, its original trunk decayed and was removed, but the additional trunks continue to supply all the nutrients it needs.

At first, the sticky seeds of sin can appear small and harmless. But when tolerated, its tentacles will quickly grow. Soon the Christian's spiritual life begins to starve, and additional sins begin to take root. Eventually, the Christian is choked to death. In the parable of the sower, Jesus instructed His disciples that the thorns that choked the good seed were the "cares of this world, the deceitfulness of riches, and the desires for other things" so that the word of God sown in the person's heart becomes unfruitful (Mark 4:19). Are the cares of this world choking the word of God from your heart?

Famous People

"So David went on and became great, and the Lord God of hosts was with him."
2 Samuel 5:10

April 1

PROLIFIC POSTERITY

"But the children of Israel were fruitful and increased abundantly, multiplied and grew exceedingly mighty; and the land was filled with them" (Exodus 1:7).

Rachel Krishevsky truly believed the commandment to "be fruitful and multiply." When the 99-year-old great-grandmother passed away in Jerusalem, September 2009, she left behind children, grandchildren, great-grandchildren, and even great-great-grandchildren. Rachel got married to her cousin Yitzhak in 1929, just before turning 19. The couple brought seven sons and four daughters into the world. Within the ultra-orthodox Jewish community, large families are seen as a blessing. Her 11 offspring evidently adopted her outlook, and between them they produced 150 children of their own.

These 150 grandchildren continued the commitment to be fruitful and multiply and grew themselves to more than 1,000 children. From here, Rachel's posterity continued to multiply further, and she was blessed with a few hundred great-great-grandchildren. Due to their large numbers, the family is not precisely sure how many descendants there are. The grandchildren estimate there are at least 1,400 people since almost all of Rachel's family were prolific. Her grandchildren say, "Grandma was a God-fearing woman who knew the entire book of Psalms by heart, and participated in all the family gatherings. Up until she was 97 she knew all of her descendants by name."

This makes it much easier to understand how 70 Hebrews could grow into a nation of over two million while living in Egypt for 200 years. The Bible teaches that children are to be a blessing from God. "Happy is the man who has his quiver full of them ..." (Psalm 127:5). The children of Israel took God's command seriously, to "be fruitful and multiply," which is mentioned at least nine times in Genesis alone. Even in the face of persecution, families grew in Egypt. "But the more they afflicted them, the more they multiplied and grew. And they were in dread of the children of Israel" (Exodus 1:12).

In the same way that God's people in the Old Testament grew in number, so also they grew during times of persecution in the New Testament age and beyond. Luke writes during the time Saul persecuted the church, "Therefore those who were scattered went everywhere preaching the word" (Acts 8:4). It is amazing that sometimes it takes difficult times for the gospel to be spread and God's church to grow. But the Lord is faithful and promises that when we abide in Jesus, we will be fruitful and multiply spiritually!

"Now therefore, please be careful not to drink wine or similar drink, and not to eat anything unclean. For behold, you shall conceive and bear a son. And no razor shall come upon his head, for the child shall be a Nazirite to God from the womb; and he shall begin to deliver Israel out of the hand of the Philistines" (Judges 13:4, 5).

On Monday, January 10, 2010, a minivan struck and killed a man crossing a Brooklyn street. This was especially tragic because this was no ordinary man. Joe Rollino would have been 105 on March 19, and according to friends he looked younger than 80 and was the model of health. A World War II veteran with three Purple Hearts, Rollino got his start in the 1920s at the Coney Island carnival, where he was billed as the "Strongest Man in the World." At the height of his career, he stood about 5 feet 5 inches tall and weighed about 150 pounds. Pound for pound, Joe Rollino was one of the strongest men in modern times. He lifted 475 pounds with his teeth and moved 3,200 pounds with his back. But he was most proud of his finger strength—he once lifted 635 pounds with a single finger. At Rollino's 103rd birthday party, a friend gave him a quarter, and Rollino bent it between his fingers—then apologized because he used to be able to do it with a dime!

Rollino was an avid exerciser. He walked 5 miles every morning, rain or shine. He swam in the freezing Atlantic every day for eight years, even during a stormy six-degree day in January 1974. Rollino was also a boxer. In a 2008 interview, 103-year-old Rollino said that he was simply born strong: "Fighters would hit me in the jaw, and I'd just look at them. You couldn't knock me out," he said.

Did I mention that Joe Rollino didn't drink or smoke and was a lifelong vegetarian? If it weren't for the car accident, this strong man might have become one of the oldest men in modern times as well. The Bible also makes a connection between a strong man and a unique diet: Samson followed the Nazirite custom of abstaining from alcohol and unclean foods. Would you like to live to be a healthy 100 years old? Anything is possible when we follow God's health principles.

April 3 SAVED BY SHIPWRECK

"From the Jews five times I received forty stripes minus one. Three times I was beaten with rods; once I was stoned; three times I was shipwrecked; a night and a day I have been in the deep" (2 Corinthians 11:24, 25).

Unsinkable Violet Jessop experienced and survived an almost unbelievable array of events. Violet was born in 1887 to Irish parents who had immigrated to Argentina. In 1903 she sailed to England and fell in love with the sea. At 21, Violet became a stewardess for the White Star Lines, which was building a trio of the world's largest luxury ocean liners. The three sister ships were *Olympic*, *Britannic*, and *Titanic*. Violet first served on the *Olympic*, which she loved. But in 1911 the ship violently collided with the British warship *HMS Hawke*. Considering the damage, it was a miracle neither vessel sank.

The following year she joined the crew on the newest ship, *Titanic*. Violet was asleep when *Titanic* hit the iceberg. On deck, she saw passengers calmly strolling about. But soon women clung to their husbands as the crew tried to force them into lifeboats with their children. At this point, a ship's officer handed Violet a misplaced baby and ordered her into boat 16 to show other women it was safe. From the water she witnessed all the terrors of the *Titanic* sinking. After being rescued by the ship *Carpathia*, the baby was reunited with its mother.

During the First World War, Violet served in 1916 as a nurse with the British Red Cross. Incredibly, she was aboard the *Britannic*, which had been converted into a hospital ship, when it struck a mine and sank in the Aegean Sea. Violet grabbed her toothbrush before rushing from her cabin; it was the one thing she remembered missing most following the sinking of the *Titanic*. As *Britannic* was quickly going down, she was forced to jump. "I leapt into the water but was sucked under the ship's keel which struck my head." She attributed her survival to her thick auburn hair that padded the blow. At the war's end, Violet rejoined the White Star Line and again served aboard the *Olympic*. This Christian woman survived 42 years at sea, three historic shipwrecks, and two world wars. Violet retired to gardening in Suffolk, England, where she lived till age 84.

The Bible also speaks of someone who experienced three shipwrecks—the apostle Paul. Both Paul and Violet miraculously survived their ordeals, due to the grace of God. Have you put your life safely into God's hands today?

"Then we who are alive and remain shall be caught up together with them in the clouds to meet the Lord in the air. And thus we shall always be with the Lord" (1 Thessalonians 4:17).

Who would spend $20 million for a one-week vacation? Sixty-year-old Dennis Tito did with no regrets. In fact, you could say his vacation was literally "out of this world" after he became the first private citizen to visit the International Space Station. Dennis started his career as a space scientist, designing flight paths in the 1960s for three historic Mars missions. He then worked at NASA's Jet Propulsion Laboratory in Pasadena for five years. He left to set up a private finance company, Wilshire Associates, where he made his fortune. But Dennis never lost his love for the heavens.

On April 28, 2001, after years of negotiations and red tape, Dennis Tito was chauffeured by two cosmonauts in their Soyuz TM-32 spacecraft to the International Space Station. Tito spent 7 days, 22 hours, 4 minutes in space and orbited Earth 128 times, making him the first private citizen to purchase a trip into space. (I wonder if he booked his vacation on the Orbitz website?) Some reports say Tito paid $20 million for his trip, becoming the world's first space tourist. While in space Dennis performed several scientific experiments that he said would be useful for his company and business. Dennis was sorry his vacation could only last a week. Since Tito's historic vacation in space he has testified before several government agencies in the U.S. on "Commercial Human Spaceflight."

Did you know the Bible teaches it is now possible for you to book a journey through space that will last for eons? The good news is that the travel arrangements are already paid in full. In speaking of the assurance of the return of Christ to take us to heaven, Paul writes, "Now He who has prepared us for this very thing is God, who also has given us the Spirit as a guarantee" (2 Corinthians 5:5).

There is a ticket for the ultimate spaceflight to heaven. It has been paid for by the blood of Jesus Christ. It can be yours if you will accept it.

April 5 A SHOOTING STAR

"Beloved, do not believe every spirit, but test the spirits, whether they are of God; because many false prophets have gone out into the world" (1 John 4:1).

Phoebe Ann Moses was born August 13, 1860, in a log cabin on the Ohio frontier. Because of poverty and hardship, eight-year-old Phoebe began helping support her widowed mother and seven siblings by hunting. She soon discovered that she was a marvelous shot. By age 15 she had sold enough game to pay off the mortgage on her mother's farm and was enough of a local celebrity that she was invited to Cincinnati to enter a shooting contest with a traveling show marksman. Not only did she win the match with Frank Butler by one point, but she also won his heart and they married a year later.

For several years the Butlers performed together—and Phoebe adopted the stage name "Annie Oakley." In 1885 the couple joined the legendary Buffalo Bill in his Wild West Show. For the next 17 years, Annie Oakley was the show's star attraction with her marvelous shooting feats. Barely 5 feet tall, she was billed as "Little Sure Shot." In a single day, she used a .22 caliber rifle to shoot 4,472 of 5,000 small glass balls tossed in midair. With the razor thin edge of a playing card facing her at 90 feet, Annie could cut the card with one bullet and then puncture it with five or six more shots before it hit the ground. Her sharp shooting won her many awards and captivated audiences worldwide, including several heads of state in Europe. She even knocked the ashes off a cigarette held by the German Kaiser Wilhelm II!

Annie Oakley was the first American female superstar, and she remained a remarkable shot into her sixties. Even after a train accident that caused temporary paralysis and five spinal operations, and a car accident that left her wearing a steel leg brace for over a year, Annie was still setting records. Today, her name remains synonymous with precision marksmanship.

Friends, the Bible teaches that true prophets will also have consistent accuracy in their predictions. John warns us that we must test those claiming to be God's prophets—and one important test is whether or not their predictions come true! "As for the prophet who prophesies of peace, when the word of the prophet comes to pass, the prophet will be known as one whom the Lord has truly sent" (Jeremiah 28:9).

"And I will give him a white stone, and on the stone a new name written which no one knows except him who receives it" (Revelation 2:17).

Most of us have heard of the Nobel Peace Prize, but do you know the strange details that led to the forming of this prestigious award? Alfred Nobel was born in 1833 in Stockholm, Sweden. After receiving a first-class education in Russia the family returned to Sweden, where he and his brothers worked as chemical engineers.

Alfred Nobel did not invent nitroglycerin but was first to produce it commercially. In 1863 he developed a detonator for nitroglycerin using a strong shock rather than heat. But nitroglycerin in its fluid state is very volatile. Several explosions in his laboratory proved this, including one in 1864 in which his brother Emil and several others were killed. Recognizing this danger, Nobel moved his experimentation to a barge anchored on a lake outside Stockholm.

After much experimenting he eventually invented dynamite, also known as "Nobel's Safety Powder." This new material was made from a combination of nitroglycerin absorbed by a porous clay substance and was five times as powerful as gunpowder. This provided an easily handled, solid yet malleable explosive. Mining, railroad building, and other construction became much safer, more efficient, and cheaper. But military leaders also realized the value of dynamite for demolition and destruction. This deadly use of his creation greatly troubled the "Lord of Dynamite," who was a pacifist and strongly opposed the wartime uses of his inventions.

In 1895 a newspaper confused the death of Nobel's older brother with Alfred, and published Alfred Nobel's obituary before he had actually died. Nobel was horrified to read that he was remembered as the man who created the explosives that caused so much death and carnage. Perhaps to alleviate his conscience, and to improve his legacy, upon his death his will provided that the bulk of his vast fortune go to a fund that would award prizes annually for advancements in physics, chemistry, medicine, literature, and peace. Alfred was also a great entrepreneur. Over the years he founded 90 factories and laboratories in more than 20 countries, and he held 355 patents.

Few people read their obituary before their death, and fewer still get a chance to change their reputation. But because of the matchless gift and sacrifice of Jesus we can have a new name.

April 7

ONE CUP OF WATER

"For whoever gives you a cup of water to drink in My name, because you belong to Christ, assuredly, I say to you, he will be no means lose his reward" (Mark 9:41).

Kofi Annan, the former United Nations Secretary-General, was the founder of the Global AIDS and Health Fund to support developing countries in their struggle to care for hurting people. He was born on April 8, 1938, and currently serves as a Ghanaian diplomat. In his effort to raise global awareness on how people live in the world, he has presented incredible statistics from the United Nations Human Development Report. These numbers really put into perspective how we live in America!

- Four percent of the 225 richest men's wealth could provide for the entire globe: basic education, basic health care, adequate food, clean water, and safe sewers.
- Americans spend $8 billion a year on cosmetics—$2 billion more than the estimated total needed to provide basic education for everyone in the world.
- Americans each consume an average of 260 pounds of meat a year. In Bangladesh, the average is 6.5 pounds.
- The world's 225 richest individuals, of whom 60 are Americans, have a combined wealth of over $1 trillion—equal to the annual income of the poorest 47 percent of the entire world's population.
- Europeans spend $11 billion a year on ice cream—$2 billion more than the estimated annual total needed to provide clean water and safe sewers for the world's population.
- The three richest people in the world have assets that exceed the combined gross domestic product of the 48 least-developed countries.
- The richest fifth of the world's people consumes 86 percent of all goods and services, while the poorest fifth consumes just 1.3 percent. Indeed, the richest fifth consumes 45 percent of all meat and fish, 58 percent of all energy used, 84 percent of all paper, has 74 percent of all telephone lines, and owns 87 percent of all vehicles.

Annan encourages us to not look at faceless statistics, but think of the condition of how many people in our world truly live. When we consider the world's consumption bill of $24 trillion a year, the numbers seem overwhelming. Yet, in God's eyes, even a cup of cold water given to a thirsty child is not beneath His notice.

"Now in the fourth watch of the night Jesus went to them, walking on the sea" (Matthew 14:25).

Ida Lewis was the daughter of a lighthouse keeper in Newport, Rhode Island. When her father, Captain Hosea Lewis, suffered a paralyzing stroke, Ida and her mother assumed all the responsibilities of the Lime Rock Lighthouse. Ida was unafraid of the water and became known as the best swimmer in Newport. Besides tending the light, she rowed her younger brothers and sisters 200 yards from the small rock island to school and back each day. She was frequently seen rowing about the vast bay on errands in all kinds of weather.

Ida's rowing skills, strength, and courage came into play many times during her life. She conducted her first rescue when she was 16. With her station lifeboat, she rowed out and saved four young men unable to swim, who nearly drowned when their sailboat capsized. The boys were ashamed to be rescued by a slight young girl. In 1866, when she was 24, she rescued a drunken soldier in a disabled boat, towing him to shore. In 1867 she saved three workers from a swamped boat; they had gone after their employer's prize sheep that had jumped into the harbor. After rescuing the men, Ida returned to save the sheep.

On March 12, 1869, she performed her most famous rescue. During a blizzard, Ida was sick with a terrible cold when her mother saw a boat overturn in the freezing waves. Ida ran out into the churning icy water in her stocking feet and rowed a boat out to save them. She rescued three soldiers; a young boy drowned. This brave feat placed her on the cover of *Harper's Magazine*, and she became a national heroine.

Ida received fan mail from the rich and famous; even President Ulysses S. Grant visited her. She also received some marriage proposals. New York gave her a mahogany rowboat with red velvet cushions, gold braid around the gunwales, and gold-plated oarlocks. The boat was named "The Rescue." Over the 50 years Ida tended the lighthouse, this small woman rescued at least eighteen persons from the cold and often treacherous waters off Lime Rock. Unofficially, the number was much higher. When she died in 1911, every ship bell in Newport tolled all night.

You know, the Bible says Jesus crossed a stormy sea to rescue a boat in distress. Our Keeper is always willing to come to our rescue when we call to Him for help.

April 9 A MODERN JONAH

"And while the crowds were thickly gathered together, He began to say, 'This is an evil generation. It seeks a sign, and no sign will be given to it except the sign of Jonah the prophet'" (Luke 11:29).

In 1891, a whaling ship off the Falkland Islands spotted a huge 80-foot sperm whale. Two longboats were quickly launched to hunt the monster. Closing in, the crew harpooned the whale, which quickly dove down away from the boat. Suddenly, the whale resurfaced right under the first longboat, breaking it and throwing its men into the air. As the whale disappeared again, the remaining longboat rescued the survivors—but two men were missing and presumed drowned.

Soon, the dead whale floated to the surface, and the crewmen began their grisly job, removing its blubber. By midnight the task was still unfinished, and the sailors went to bed. In the morning, as they resumed their work, the unexpected happened: something in the stomach was moving spasmodically. Thinking it might be a giant squid, they cut the stomach open. Inside was one of the missing sailors, James Bartley, doubled up and unconscious.

As Bartley recovered over the next few weeks, he recalled being hit by the whale's tail and then encompassed by great darkness. He felt he was slipping along a smooth passage that seemed to carry him forward. His hands touched a slimy substance, which seemed to shrink from his touch. He could breathe the stifling air, but the heat was terrible. The next thing he remembered, he was waking up in the captain's cabin. Except for the fact that his face, neck, and hands had been bleached white, Bartley survived the belly of a whale! Understandably, Bartley left whaling and spent his remaining years working as a cobbler. When he was buried, his tombstone featured these words: "James Bartley—1870-1909...A modern Jonah."

When people in Jesus' day asked for a sign, He said the "sign of Jonah" was the only sign that would be given. When Jonah preached in Nineveh, his "back to life" experience with the whale likely gave credence to his message. Similarly, Jesus' resurrection is evidence of His divinity. But sadly, for many the sign of Jonah isn't enough—not only do they disbelieve the Jonah account, but they deny the resurrection as well. We're left with a choice: we can join the "evil generation" in disbelief, or the Ninevites in believing and repenting. Is the sign of Jonah enough for you?

"Take heed that you do not do your charitable deeds before men, to be seen by them. Otherwise you have no reward from your Father in heaven" (Matthew 6:1).

What do Herb Alpert, Mel Gibson, and Jami Gertz have in common, besides being famous celebrities? According to "The Giving Back Fund," a non-profit organization that tracks philanthropic giving worldwide, Jami Gertz and her husband, Anthony Ressler, topped the list by giving $10,569,002 to the Ressler-Gertz Foundation. Herb Alpert donated $9.1 million to the Herb Alpert Foundation, which focuses on the arts, compassion, and well being. And Mel Gibson signed a check for $6.8 million to help a foundation support the Holy Family Church.

Of course, most celebrities want their names associated with good causes. It's great PR. The more good they do for others, the more the public will appreciate them. Many accuse celebrities of promoting themselves this way, but it's also true that charities use celebrities to promote their work as well. So is this a virtuous cycle or a vicious cycle? After Christopher Reeve became paralyzed, his collaboration with the American Paralysis Association caused its revenue in the next three years double to $5 million. In fact, they changed their association's name to the Christopher Reeve Foundation.

Some of the others who made the top 30 list of celebrities contributing to non-profit organizations also include George Lucas (director, producer, writer), Nora Roberts (writer), Ndamukong Suh (NFL player), Lance Berkman and his wife, Cara (MLB player), Meryl Streep and her husband Donald Gummer (actress), and Jerry Seinfeld (comedian). Not all donations are what you might consider worthy causes. Hugh Hefner made the list for donating $900,000 to a trust for public land to save the iconic Hollywood sign from being plowed under in order to make room for four luxury homes!

Jesus said, "But when you do a charitable deed, do not let your left hand know what your right hand is doing, that your charitable deed may be in secret; and your Father who sees in secret will Himself reward you openly" (Matthew 6:3, 4). The purpose of giving big gifts is not to lift up ourselves, but to touch people's lives. Someday, God will publish a philanthropic list of people who gave much. That's the list I want to make!

JOHN FLYNN

"For so the Lord has commanded us: 'I have set you as a light to the Gentiles, that you should be for salvation to the ends of the earth'" (Acts 13:47).

In 1912, a Presbyterian minister named John Flynn established the Australian Inland Mission. He wanted to help the people of the Outback with spiritual, social, and medical needs. But the desperate need for emergency medical care was made clear to Flynn when he heard about the extreme case of a ranch hand with a spear embedded in his chest. The man was carried in a hammock slung between two horses for 400 miles, then to a station where he waited two weeks for a train that carried him 600 miles to a hospital in Adelaide.

At the time, there were only two doctors available for a region nearly 2 million square kilometers in size. When people in this area became ill or were injured, they were usually on their own. As a resident of the Outback himself, Flynn sympathized and wanted to do something to help provide a "mantle of safety" for people who made their homes in the bush, but what could he do to lessen the isolation of those living so far from civilization?

A letter from a pilot in 1917 convinced Flynn that aviation could provide the answer to that need. Over the next decade, Flynn gradually gathered support and the funds needed to launch the flying medical service. In 1928, the Aerial Medical Service—later known as the Flying Doctor Service—began making flights to assist those in need. During the first year, the little bi-plane named "Victory" made 50 flights, and 225 patients were treated. Soon two-way radios were available in many Outback locations, making medical assistance much more readily available. As a result of John Flynn's determined effort and God's blessing, this service has saved many lives over the years.

Jesus also provided care for those who were cut off from civilization, people who were isolated from others because of disease and sin. He reached out to touch lepers, demoniacs, and many others, offering healing and salvation to any person who was willing to receive it. By relieving their physical ailments, he opened their hearts to His love and truth. He asks us, as His disciples, to continue His work of providing physical and spiritual healing, bringing "salvation to the ends of the earth."

"You are my hiding place and my shield; I hope in Your word" (Psalm 119:114).

Sam Houston was a colorful and bold 19th-century American statesman, politician, and soldier. The seventh governor of Texas, he is known best for helping bring Texas into the United States. Though married three times, his third wife, Margaret Moffette Lea of Alabama, gave birth to eight children, the first of whom was Sam Houston Jr.

Sam Houston Jr. was born in 1843. He began service in the confederacy in 1861. On April 7, 1862, at the famous Civil War battle of Shiloh, Sam Houston Jr., son of the famous Texan, was struck in the back by a bullet. He was knocked to the ground and would likely have died had it not been for his mother's Bible, which he carried in his knapsack. Ripping through the pages, the lead ball stopped directly over the 70th Psalm, which reads, "You are my help and my deliverer" (verse 5).

After the war Sam studied in Independence and then went to medical school in Pennsylvania and became a doctor. But he later gave up his practice for writing. He married Lucy Anderson, and the couple had three children. Years later, after his wife died, Sam became discouraged and went to live with his sister Margaret. After eight years he passed away at the age of 51.

Sam Houston Jr. was literally saved by the Word of God. The Bible he carried actually stopped a bullet. Did you know we are being attacked by an enemy who wants to cut us down? The weapons he uses are not your typical guns and knives. The spiritual warfare of Satan is subtle and meant to destroy us forever. But the Lord has provided armor that we may put on and stand safe.

"Put on the whole armor of God that you may be able to stand against the wiles of the devil. For we do not wrestle against flesh and blood, but against principalities, against powers, against the rulers of the darkness of this age, against the spiritual hosts of wickedness in heavenly places. Therefore take up the whole armor of God, that you may be able to withstand in the evil day, and having done all, to stand" (Ephesians 6:10-13). When the "fiery darts" of the devil come shooting your way, hold up the "shield of faith" (verse 16) and extinguish them for good!

April 13

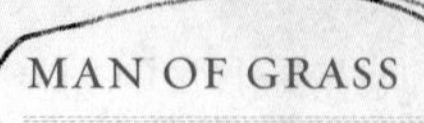

MAN OF GRASS

"Whatever your hand finds to do, do it with your might; for there is no work or device or knowledge or wisdom in the grave where you are going" (Ecclesiastes 9:10).

David Douglas was only 26 years old in 1825 when he sailed along the west coast of the United States and up the Columbia River. The young botanist from London was on a quest. Since a boy he had been obsessed with plants, and by the age of 21 he was appointed to the Royal Botanical Gardens in Scotland. Now, five years later, he was to examine the plant life of the New World.

As the ship approached land, one particular tree captivated David. As he reported later, "So pleased was I that I could scarcely see anything but it." He couldn't wait to see the tree up close, and when he did, he pronounced it "one of the most striking and truly graceful objects in nature." It was only fitting that this famous tree would later bear his name, as it does to this day—the Douglas fir.

David spent the next two years exploring the Northwest, finding new plants and shipping over 200 species back to England. His collecting adventures took him 12,000 miles on foot, horseback, and canoe. William Hooker, one of the world's leading botanists, described him as a man of "great activity, undaunted courage ... and energetic zeal." The Native Americans were immensely impressed with David's endurance, but they questioned his sanity. They called him "Man of Grass" because he would hike from first dawn to dusk collecting plants that he couldn't even eat.

On his 1829 trip to North America, David Douglas made a discovery that eventually changed the history of the New World. While collecting plants in California, he pulled a plant from the ground that contained many flecks of gold in the soil clinging to the roots. But as David packed the plant for shipment he saw only the plant. That's how gold was first discovered in California in 1831—not by loggers in Sutter Creek, but by the botanists in London who unpacked the shipment of plants from Douglas and saw the gold on the roots.

David Douglas had only one purpose in life. Nothing—not even gold—could distract him from his mission. That is the sort of focused and energetic zeal that God wants from us today!

"I will praise You, for I am fearfully and wonderfully made" (Psalm 139:14).

As a child and teenager, Jack experienced very poor health. Addicted to sugar and junk food, his volatile moods would frequently swing between suicide and homicide. The murderous behavior was usually directed towards his older brother, who he once nearly killed with an ax, and another time with a big butcher knife. Jack described himself as short and skinny with pimples. He was constantly bullied by the other kids at school.

When he was 15, Jack's mother, a Bible Christian, insisted he come with her to hear a nutritionist, Paul Bragg, speak on diet, health, and exercise. At the conclusion of his talk Mr. Bragg did backflips across the platform to punctuate his lecture. It was a life-changing experience. Jack instantly gave up junk food and began to focus on altering his diet and exercise habits. The transformation was so complete by the time Jack graduated high school he was offered several sports scholarships. Jack passed up a future in sports, instead dedicating the next 80 years to teaching others how to care for their bodies.

Thousands today speak of Jack LaLanne as "The Godfather of Fitness." Jack LaLanne firmly supported a vegetarian diet and blamed overly processed foods for many health problems. LaLanne always practiced what he preached, working out two hours a day. To promote healthful living in 1984, he fought strong winds and currents as he swam 1.5 miles while towing 70 boats with 70 people across the Long Beach Harbor. And he did this when he was 70 years old and while handcuffed and shackled! Jack's motto was "Be happy you are alive! Get up in the morning and say, 'Thank God I'm here again.'"

Some people think the Bible is just a spiritual book, but you would be surprised to see how much it says about practical health. David wrote, "I will praise You, for I am fearfully and wonderfully made" (Psalms 139:14). With proper self-discipline and maintenance these biological temples can provide 80-plus years of service, but if we neglect proper care of our bodies, happiness will elude us.

April 15 EATING LIKE A BIRD

"Foods for the stomach and the stomach for foods, but God will destroy both it and them. Now the body is not for sexual immorality but for the Lord, and the Lord for the body" (1 Corinthians 6:13).

You have probably heard the expression before: "he [or she] eats like a bird." Well, you might think again before using this phrase to describe a petite eater. A study of bird eating habits has exploded the popular idea that all birds have tiny appetites. For example, it showed the average parakeet eats nearly 100 times its own weight annually in seed, cuttlebone, gravel, and water. Because the parakeet weighs only about 3 ounces, this means that it consumes about eight pounds of food a year. To eat at the same rate, a man would have to devour some 16,000 pounds of food annually instead of his normal consumption of 1,300 pounds. Daily "bird rations" for a man would consist of about 45 pounds of food. An average hummingbird eats half its weight in sugar each day. Just imagine if a 100-pound woman ate 50 pounds of sugar a day. (On second thought ... let's not imagine that.)

Of course, there are always those exceptions of people who, at times, can even eat more than a bird. Take, for example, the famous athlete Milo of Crotona, a giant of a man who lived in ancient Greece. Milo was a top wrestler, crowned six times at the Olympic Games for wrestling, and was famous throughout the civilized world for his feats of strength—such as carrying an ox on his shoulders through the stadium at Olympia. This powerful man seemed always hungry, and devoured everything in sight. Once, when he was unusually hungry, he outdid himself and captured the world's record for big eating. Milo managed to polish off a whole calf weighing 150 pounds in one day.

Unfortunately, modern medical research indicates more and more people are eating like birds. Harmful high-fat and high-calorie diets reign in most households. But Scripture tells us the "drunkard and the glutton will come to poverty ..." (Proverbs 23:21), and gives this caution: "Or do you not know that your body is the temple of the Holy Spirit who is in you, whom you have from God, and you are not your own?" (1 Corinthians 6:19). Ultimately, we are responsible to God for the way we treat our bodies. "Eating like a bird" is something we should all try to avoid!

"But there is a God in heaven who reveals secrets ... " (Daniel 2:28).

It is nearly impossible to discuss the Renaissance without mentioning Leonardo da Vinci. Few, if any, men have been born whose intellect could match the genius of this Florentine man. Leonardo's artworks, like the "Mona Lisa," are remarkable for their harmony, soft light, and sharpness of observation. Not only was Leonardo an outstanding artist, but a universal genius in science, architecture, and engineering. His interests were so broad and numerous that it boggles the mind. He observed everything from the properties of herbs to the movements of the heavens.

A century before Galileo, Leonardo was able to find new fundamental knowledge about timekeeping and to connect it with machines, designing clocks that operated by weights, sand, and water. In the fields of anatomy, botany, zoology, geology, hydrology, aerology, optics, and mechanics, he was far ahead of his time. He designed everything from fortifications, weapons, and engines of war, to beautiful gardens, castles, churches, canals, and multi-tier roads. In fact, he wrote a book on the anatomy of horses. He loved all animals and trained them with great kindness and patience. Often, when passing a market where live birds were sold, he would let them out of their cages and then pay the vendor the price. A vegetarian, Leonardo wrote, "I have from an early age renounced the use of meat, and the time will come when men such as I look upon the murder of animals as they now look upon the murder of men."

Leonardo da Vinci was so brilliant one observer noted that he could write a letter with one hand and draw with the other simultaneously! Many know Leonardo da Vinci invented the scissors, but his other ideas were often far ahead of his time and only realized centuries after his death, such as the tank, the helicopter, and the parachute. In fact, in 1999 some Englishmen built a parachute according to Leonardo's indications and tried it out: it worked perfectly. Looking back on his drawings and designs it almost seems as if he could see into the future.

This naturally makes us wonder, can a man know the future? Not of his own accord. When Daniel spoke to King Nebuchadnezzar about the God of heaven, he explained how only the Lord "reveals deep and secret things; He knows what is in the darkness, and light dwells with Him" (Daniel 2:22). Man can know the future, but only through the gifts of God.

April 17 HUMBLE AMBITIONS

"For what profit is it to a man if he gains the whole world, and loses his own soul? Or what will a man give in exchange for his soul?" (Matthew 16:26).

Howard Hughes was born in Humble, Texas, on Christmas Eve, 1905. But, as a young man, his ambitions were anything but humble. He wanted to be a top film producer, a top aviator, and the richest man alive—and he managed all three! Starting in his early 20s, he produced several award-winning films and dated a string of Hollywood stars. As an aviator, he set several speed records in planes that he helped design. He also helped design and build the world's largest flying boat, the *HL-4 Hercules*, which was nicknamed the "Spruce Goose" (though it was actually built of birch). Hughes also became incredibly wealthy. At various points in his life, he owned a tool company, a motion picture studio, a medical research institute, gambling casinos, vast amounts of real estate and hotels in Las Vegas, several airlines, and an aircraft company.

Hughes was living life in the fast lane until 1946; while test flying a prototype, he crashed and nearly died. While recuperating, Howard Hughes became dependent on pain relievers. Over time, his behavior became increasingly more erratic. He became an eccentric recluse: for one four-month stretch he stayed in the darkened room of a screening studio, eating nothing but chocolate bars, chicken, and milk, and obsessively watching movies.

By 1966, at the age of 60, he was the world's wealthiest man, but he lived in constant fear of contagious disease. His employees had to wash their hands frequently and wear white gloves. He would use tissues to pick up items, and burned his clothing, fearing he'd had some contact with germs. Towards the end of his life, he was injecting codeine daily. His hygiene rapidly declined: he rarely bathed or brushed his teeth and allowed his nails to grow grotesquely long. His once-strapping 6-foot-4-inch frame shrank to barely 90 pounds. While flying to a hospital in Houston in 1976, he died of kidney failure. The FBI insisted on taking fingerprints to confirm that this pitiful shell of a man was indeed the legendary Howard Hughes.

In Matthew, Jesus asks what a man really wins if he gains the entire world but loses his soul. Hughes' life is a sad reminder that the only true way to live is to die to self and humbly follow Christ.

"Take heed and beware of covetousness, for one's life does not consist in the abundance of the things he possesses" (Luke 12:15).

Luxury took on new dimensions when Saudi billionaire Prince Al Waleed Bin Talal signed a deal to buy the world's first and largest privately owned Airbus 380 aircraft. Prince Waleed, billed as the 13th richest person in the world, emerged from his personal 747 to purchase the new A-380. The end-to-end double-decker behemoth has twice the space of the 747. The Saudi Arabian business tycoon plans to have the corporate jet converted into a virtual "flying palace" with private suites, board room, theater, and much more. It incorporates all of the most modern amenities to ensure maximum comfort and luxury. In keeping with the Middle Eastern custom, the design is expected to create separate living areas within the aircraft for men, women, and staff. The deal is valued at $319 million before any of the customizing interior work is done.

Al Waleed already owns a 282-foot yacht called the *Kingdom 5KR*, which he bought from Donald Trump for $40 million. He has ordered a 550-foot yacht worth $500 million and will name it *New Kingdom 5KR*. He travels between his private jets and yachts by driving one of his 38 cars. The most recent automobile the Saudi prince purchased is a totally diamond-clad Mercedes SL550. This bejeweled car is worth a whopping $4.8 million! If you can't afford to put this on your shopping list, don't worry. The prince will allow admirers to touch the royal car for a mere $1,000 per person.

Prince Al Waleed Bin Talal is founder, CEO, and 95 percent owner of Kingdom Holding Company, and in 2012 his personal wealth was estimated at $18 billion. The *Arabian Business* magazine places him as the most influential Arab in the entire world. He is sometimes called the "Arabian Warren Buffet." He has invested in Citibank, Citicorp, AOL, Apple Inc., MCI Inc., Motorola, Fox News, the Four Seasons hotel chain, the Plaza Hotel in New York, and even Euro Disney.

When someone asked Jesus to be an arbitrator in an inheritance dispute, Christ warned him about the trappings of desiring wealth. He then told a story about a rich man who felt secure in his wealth and did not know he would soon lose his life. "Fool! This night your soul will be required of you; then whose will those things be which you have provided?" (Luke 12:20). Christ admonishes, "So is he who lays up treasure for himself, and is not rich toward God" (verse 21). Investing in God's "Kingdom" is the best thing you can do with your wealth!

BILTMORE ESTATE

"Let not your heart be troubled; you believe in God, believe also in Me. In My Father's house are many mansions; if it were not so, I would have told you. I go to prepare a place for you. And if I go and prepare a place for you, I will come again and receive you to Myself; that where I am, there you may be also" (John 14:1-3).

In 1888, George Washington Vanderbilt, 26 years old at the time, visited the Smoky Mountains of North Carolina with his mother. He loved the scenery and climate so much that he decided to build a summer house in the area. However, this would be no ordinary summer house. George's idea was to replicate the working estates of Europe.

His "summer house," completed in 1895, contained 250 rooms and was 175,000 square feet. The dining room table alone could seat 64 guests. Intending that the estate be self-supporting, George set up forestry programs, poultry farms, cattle farms, hog farms, and a dairy. The estate included its own village and even a church.

In 1898, while in Paris, George married a young lady by the name of Edith. In 1912, he and Edith booked passage on the *Titanic* but canceled due to a premonition of Edith's mother. It was too late, however, for them to get their servant and baggage off the ship; both were lost when the *Titanic* sank.

George spent more than his annual income for the upkeep of his colossal house, and began to deplete his once-enormous inheritance. Some of the rooms of this house were never fully completed. After his unexpected death in 1912, George's widow, Edith, sold much of the land around the estate to the United States Forest Service at $5 an acre until only 12,500 acres were left from the original 125,000. In 1963, the estate was designated a National Historic Landmark, and today it is still the largest home in the United States.

Friends, how would you like to live in a mansion? Jesus is preparing the best of living conditions for those who love Him—greater than any home ever built on this earth. We can't even begin to imagine how beautiful it will be. Best of all, we will be with our Lord, never to be separated. Are you ready? He has a mansion for you.

"With long life I will satisfy him, And show him My salvation" (Psalm 91:16).

Nola Ochs was born November 22, 1911, and is an American college graduate. Nothing seems amazing about this—until you learn that she graduated from Fort Hays State University in Kansas on May 14, 2007. When you put the math together, you will discover that she received her degree at the age of 95, making her a Guinness World Record holder as the world's oldest college graduate! She graduated alongside her granddaughter, Alexandra Ochs, who was 21 years old at the time. Nola earned a general studies degree with an emphasis in history. Governor Kathleen Sebelius presented her diploma.

Nola somehow got sidetracked in life from completing studies she began in 1930. Seventy-seven years later she went back to school and completed her bachelor's degree. But wait! After taking time to help with the family's wheat harvest, Nola started pursuing her master's degree in liberal studies in August 2007. She received her master's on May 15, 2010, making her the oldest recipient of a master's degree at age 98!

Nola once told a news reporter, while she was back in school, that when she graduated she wanted to be a storyteller on a cruise ship. After graduation, Princess Cruises hired her to be a guest lecturer on a nine-day Caribbean cruise. She took her granddaughter along. Nola commented, "I've led a long, interesting life. We went through the dust storms. We had some difficult times in our marriage, financially. But it's been the Lord's will that I've lived this long life, and I thank Him kindly for it." She is especially proud to be the matriarch of a family that has included four sons, 13 grandchildren, and 15 great-grandchildren.

David's famous Psalm 91, which describes the safety of abiding in the presence of God, teaches us to honor God. "Because you have made the Lord, who is my refuge, even the Most High, your dwelling place,no evil shall befall you" (Psalm 91:9, 10). Though difficulties have come into the life of Nola, she has honored the Lord for her long life. That is the best graduation present anyone could wish for!

BRAINWASHED

"For God has not given us a spirit of fear, but of power and of love and of a sound mind" (2 Timothy 1:7).

On February 4, 1974, 19-year-old Patricia Hearst was kidnapped from her Berkeley, California, apartment by a violent urban guerrilla group called the Symbionese Liberation Army, or the SLA. Efforts were made to swap Hearst for jailed SLA members, but when that failed, the SLA asked that Patricia's family give $70 worth of food to every needy person in California. Patricia Hearst comes from a very wealthy family. She is the granddaughter of the publishing giant William Randolph Hearst and great-granddaughter of millionaire George Hearst.

After her father immediately gave $6 million worth of food to needy people in the Bay Area, the SLA still refused to release Patricia (since the food was supposedly of a poor quality). Then on April 3, 1974, Patricia Hearst announced on an audiotape that she had joined the SLA and took on the name "Tania." Can you imagine her father's shock and heartache when, after two months in captivity and giving out $6 million dollars, she decided to stay with her captors?

She later assisted the SLA in a bank robbery and was captured with other SLA members. During her trial she was interviewed by psychologists who believe she was brainwashed and exhibited classic symptoms of Stockholm Syndrome. Patricia was still found guilty and sentenced to 35 years' imprisonment. Her sentence was later commuted to seven years and later commuted again by President Jimmy Carter. On February 1, 1979, she was released and later given a full pardon by President Bill Clinton.

While being held, her kidnappers brainwashed her into thinking she was better off with them. Can you imagine how our heavenly Father must feel when we neglect to accept the freedom of eternal life and mansions He is offering us? Especially after sending his only son Jesus as the ransom to die for our sins?

"How shall we escape if we neglect so great a salvation, which at the first began to be spoken by the Lord, and was confirmed to us by those who heard Him, God also bearing witness both with signs and wonders, with various miracles, and gifts of the Holy Spirit?" (Hebrews 2:3, 4).

"Do not give what is holy to the dogs ..." (Matthew 7:6).

Billionaire and New York City real estate investor Leona Helmsley was a flamboyant personality with a reputation for tyrannical behavior. She earned the nickname "Queen of Mean" for her apparently heartless and vindictive behavior with employees and contractors. When convicted of federal income tax evasion and other crimes in 1989, Helmsley's fate was sealed when a former housekeeper testified during the trial that she had heard Leona once say, "We don't pay taxes. Only the little people pay taxes." The saying followed her for the rest of her life.

But when it came to her beloved dog, a Maltese called Trouble, the Queen of Mean was all heart. When Leona Helmsley died on August 20, 2007, she left $12 million of her estimated $8 billion estate for the upkeep of her eight-year-old pooch, even as two of her grandchildren got nothing. *Fortune Magazine* awarded this decision with 3rd place in their 2007 "101 Dumbest Moments in Business." The court eventually reduced the dog's inheritance to $2 million, saying it was more than adequate. Eleven-year-old Trouble lives in Florida with his caretaker in Helmsley's Sandcastle Hotel. Trouble's caretaker stated that the $2 million will pay for the dog's maintenance for more than 10 years—providing $100,000 for full-time security, $8,000 for grooming, and $1,200 for food. The caretaker is paid $60,000 a year for a guardian fee.

In 2012, Americans spent $52 billion on their pets—more than the gross domestic product of most of the world's countries. That's almost double the amount shelled out on pets a decade earlier. Food costs were $20 billion alone, and $4 billion went to grooming. About 62 percent of all households in the U.S. own pets (which is actually down from when surveys were first conducted in 1988).

God obviously loves animals and created pets for our enjoyment. The Lord even notices when a small sparrow falls to the ground (Matthew 10:29). But Jesus also said, "Do not give what is holy to the dogs; nor cast your pearls before swine, lest they trample them under their feet, and turn and tear you in pieces" (Matthew 7:6). Dogs and pigs were considered unclean scavengers in the Bible and are used to illustrate how we should carefully use our resources. It would be good to think about how we leave our inheritances. Are we remembering to be rich toward God?

SIMON BOLIVAR

"And having been set free from sin, you became slaves of righteousness" (Romans 6:18).

Simon Bolivar was South America's greatest general. He is known as "the great liberator" because his victories against Spain won independence for Venezuela, Panama, Colombia, Ecuador, Peru, and a country that bears his name, Bolivia.

In 1824, after Bolivar helped Peru win its freedom from Spain, the great general called for a convention to draft a constitution for the new country. After the convention, a delegation approached Simon Bolivar and asked him to become their first president. He gracefully declined, saying that he felt someone else deserved the honor more than he. But the people still wanted to do something special for Bolivar to show their appreciation for all he had done to free them from the oppression of Spain. So they offered him a gift of a million pesos, a fabulous fortune in those days.

Bolivar thoughtfully accepted the gift and then asked how many slaves there were in Peru. He was told that there were about 3,000. "And how much does a slave sell for?" he wanted to know. "About 350 pesos for an able-bodied man," was the answer. "Then," said Bolivar, "I will add whatever is necessary to this million pesos you have given me, and I will buy all the slaves in Peru and set them free." He added, "It makes no sense to free a nation unless all its citizens enjoy freedom as well."

The Bible teaches that Jesus came into the world to set captives free. Near the beginning of His earthly ministry, Jesus attended the synagogue in Nazareth on the Sabbath day and read from Isaiah's prophecy about Himself: "The Spirit of the LORD is upon Me, because He has anointed Me to preach the gospel to the poor; he has sent Me to heal the brokenhearted, to proclaim liberty to the captives and recovery of sight to the blind, to set at liberty those who are oppressed; to proclaim the acceptable year of the LORD" (Luke 4:18, 19).

On another occasion, when the Jewish leaders claimed that they were in bondage to no one, Jesus explained that "whoever commits sin is a slave of sin" (John 8:34). But He assured the people, "Therefore if the Son makes you free, you shall be free indeed" (verse 36). There is true freedom in Christ alone.

Are you truly free?

"Can a woman forget her nursing child, and not have compassion on the son of her womb? Surely they may forget, yet I will not forget you" (Isaiah 49:15).

One cold winter in South Wales, a mother was traveling cross-country with her young babe and was caught in a blinding blizzard. The following day, upon learning she never reached her destination, a group of men went out searching for her. They soon spotted a large mound of snow in the road that she was known to have traveled. They quickly swept away the white powder and found the frozen body of the barely dressed woman.

In her arms was a bundle of clothing, which they unwrapped to reveal her baby—alive. In the struggle of the snowstorm, the woman had taken off most of her clothing and wrapped it around the little boy to keep him alive. She knew that she would perish, but that the baby might survive. The baby was David Lloyd George, who lived on to become the celebrated prime minister of Britain during World War I. One of the reasons he achieved such greatness is that he never forgot about his mother's love and sacrifice.

God has infused into mothers the instinct to protect their offspring even at the peril of their own lives. The Creator has pre-wired this sacrificial nature not just into human mothers, but also in the animal kingdom. In the mountains of Northern California, we have a lot of black bears that are generally harmless. On the few occasions when black bears have attacked humans, it's usually because someone came between a mother and her cubs. Once a car was ripped apart by a mother bear because her cub was trapped inside when a well-meaning camper tried to take it home with him.

As the Bible says, "I will meet them like a bear deprived of her cubs; I will tear open their rib cage ..." (Hosea 13:8). There is a deep quality in the heart of a mother that describes God. The Lord was willing to give up all of heaven to redeem His children. Nothing would be withheld between the saving love of God. Not even the life of God's only begotten Son.

April 25 A SHRUNKEN MUMMY

"For what will it profit a man if he gains the whole world, and loses his own soul? Or what will a man give in exchange for his soul?" (Mark 8:36, 37).

John D. Rockefeller Sr. was strong and husky when small. He was raised a devout Christian but was determined early in life to earn money and drove himself to the limit. At age 33 he earned his first million dollars. At age 43 he controlled Standard Oil, the biggest company in the world. At age 53 he was the richest man on Earth and the world's only billionaire.

Then he developed a sickness called "alopecia," where the hair of his head dropped off, and his eyelashes and eyebrows disappeared. He became deeply depressed over his appearance, compounded by his constant stress, and looked like a shrunken mummy. His weekly income was one million dollars, but he digested only milk and crackers. He was so hated in Pennsylvania that he had to have bodyguards day and night. He could not sleep; he stopped smiling and enjoyed nothing in life.

The doctors predicted he would not live more than a year. Gleefully anticipating his demise, the newspapers had written his obituary in advance. Those sleepless nights set him thinking. A Christian friend told him if he did not begin to share his mounting wealth it would crush him like an avalanche. He realized with a new light that he "could not take one dime into the next world." Money was not everything.

The next morning found him a new man. He began to help churches with his amassed wealth; the poor and needy were not overlooked. He established the Rockefeller Foundation, which funded medical research that led to the discovery of penicillin and other wonder drugs. John D. began to sleep well, eat, and enjoy life. The doctors had predicted he would not live over age 54. He died at age 98.

God understands the power of our thinking. When we focus on ourselves, we will become the most miserable of all people. But when we live to give, health will come into our lives. "A merry heart does good, like medicine, but a broken spirit dries the bones" (Proverbs 17:22). Solomon, once the wealthiest man in the world, wrote this Bible verse. John D. Rockefeller discovered its truth.

"Surely blessing I will bless you, and multiplying I will multiply you" (Hebrews 6:14).

Perhaps the strangest human computer ever is Charles Grandemange of France. He was born in 1835—a one-pound baby without arms or legs. But he was endowed with a prodigious brain. At age 14 he toured Europe in demonstration of his calculating ability. He lived in a wooden box only one foot wide, but he could multiply two 100-digit numbers by one another within 30 seconds. He could divide a 23-digit figure by another and find the remainder at one glance. He was billed as the most lightning of all lightning calculators. It seems as if his misfortune resulted in the extraordinary development of mathematical skills.

More recently, Scott Flansburg of San Diego, California, has been dubbed "The Human Calculator" by Regis Philbin. This American mental calculator was entered into the Guinness Book of World Records in 2001 for his speed in mental calculation. Scott first realized his calculating skills at age nine and began solving his math teacher's questions without writing down the calculations. He began keeping a running tally of groceries being purchased by his family at the store and giving his father an exact amount before the cashier rang up the total.

Flansburg has the ability to add, subtract, multiply, divide, and find square and cube roots in his head almost instantly. His calculations are always accurate. He is an advocate for raising math standards and has appeared on television shows. He has also written a couple of books to help children and adults increase their math skills.

The ability to calculate and store numbers in your head is an admirable quality. But there is nothing like storing God's Word in your mind. David wrote, "Your word I have hidden in my heart, that I might not sin against You" (Psalm 119:11). To help Abraham understand the great power of God, the Lord had him do some math. "Then He brought him outside and said, 'Look now toward heaven, and count the stars if you are able to number them.' And He said to him, 'So shall your descendants be'" (Genesis 15:5). When we give our minds to the Lord, He promises to multiply our blessings. You can count on it!

April 27

ALI HAFED

"My son, if you receive my words, and treasure my commands within you, so that you incline your ear to wisdom, and apply your heart to understanding; yes, if you cry out for discernment, and lift up your voice for understanding, if you seek her as silver, and search for her as for hidden treasures ..." (Proverbs 2:1-4).

Ali Hafed was a prosperous Persian farmer living in India who owned a large and beautiful section of land with orchards, streams, and fertile fields. He was a happy and contented man until one day a Buddhist priest came to visit and told him tales of other farmers who'd become tremendously wealthy from discovering diamonds.

After hearing this, Ali Hafed became obsessed with thoughts and dreams of finding diamonds. Eventually, he sold his farm, left his family with relatives, and began searching for diamonds. Ali Hafed spent the rest of his life wandering the African continent, then Europe, in search of these elusive gleaming jewels. Finally worn out and penniless, in a fit of despondency he threw himself into the Bay of Barcelona in Spain and drowned.

Meanwhile, the man who had bought Ali Hafed's farm happened to be passing a small stream on the property when suddenly his eye caught a bright sparkle of blue and red light from the stream bottom. He bent down and picked up a good-sized crystalline stone. He took it home and put it on his mantel as an interesting curiosity. Several weeks later a visitor spotted the stone, looked closely at it, weighed it in his hand and nearly fainted. He asked the farmer if he knew what he'd found. When the farmer said he thought it was a piece of crystal, the visitor told him that he'd probably found one of the largest diamonds ever discovered. The skeptical farmer said that his stream was full of such stones. Not as large as the one on the mantel, but they were sprinkled generously along the stream bottom.

The farm that Ali Hafed had sold to go in search of diamonds turned out to be the Golconda Mines of India, for years the most productive diamond mine in the world, providing some of the largest diamonds in the English and Russian crown jewels. Ali Hafed had owned acres of diamonds but had sold his prosperous farm for practically nothing in order to look for diamonds elsewhere.

Real happiness is much closer than most people think. To find the greatest treasure, you need to look no further than the Word of God.

"Then He spoke many things to them in parables, saying, 'Behold, a sower went out to sow'" (Matthew 13:3).

Most Americans have heard of the legend of Johnny Appleseed, who went about the frontier with a kettle on his head, scattering apple seeds. But unlike Pecos Bill and Paul Bunyan, there really was a Johnny Appleseed. To begin with, his real name was John Chapman and he lived between 1775 and 1845. John had an extraordinary love for apples and wanted everybody to enjoy its fruit. He came from Philadelphia with apple seeds he collected and then planted them throughout the Ohio River Valley.

Johnny roamed the wild countryside with a vigilant eye, looking for a suitable place where young apple trees could flourish—by a spring or on the side of a hill with rich soil. With a hopeful prayer he would gently push those little seeds into the earth and pat the ground, then build a brush fence to protect the saplings before moving on to the next promising place to start a nursery. Every fall he'd return to the cider presses in Pennsylvania, where he selected good seeds from the discarded apple pressings that he carefully washed, dried, and bagged for planting the following spring.

As the orchards grew he would sell or trade the young trees to the thousands of new farmers that were settling the land. Even though he lived on the frontier he ate no meat, but he carried a stewpot or kettle with him. In this he could gather nuts or berries in season, carry water, boil potatoes, or cook ground cornmeal. He has been pictured wearing a pot on his head, but more likely he kept it tied to the top of his backpack.

John Chapman never married, but he was a deeply religious man who loved people and especially children. As the settlers moved into the wilderness, his lonely nights were fewer because he was a welcomed guest at every cabin. Many a night he would hold them all enthralled with his stories of the wild woods or read to them from the Bible he carried. As a result of practicing his favorite hobby for about 50 years, this one man provided mountains of apples to feed thousands of people for several generations!

The apostle Paul was sort of like Johnny Appleseed. When we read of his accounts in the book of Acts, Paul went far and wide to plant churches. I have often wondered what the world would be like if every Christian felt that same compelling desire to spread God's seeds of truth.

April 29 LIVINGSTONE'S BODY

"Then he [Jacob] charged them and said to them: 'I am to be gathered to my people; bury me with my fathers ...'" (Genesis 49:29).

Dr. David Livingstone was one of the most popular national heroes in the late 19th-century Britain. He was not only a missionary to Africa, but a scientific investigator, explorer, reformer, and anti-slavery crusader. He was especially known for his obsession with finding the source of the Nile River by penetrating the unknown (to Europeans) heart of Africa.

When the famous missionary and explorer died in 1873, his loyal friends Chuma and Susi buried his heart under a tree in Africa as he had requested. They then embalmed his body by filling it with salt and leaving it to dry in the sun for 14 days, then wrapping it in cloth. Next they enclosed the body in the bark of an Mvula tree, over which they sewed heavy sailcloth. This package was then tied to a long pole so that two men could carry it, along with Livingstone's important papers.

His two friends then started on a dangerous and epic 11-month, 1,000-mile journey to Zanzibar. When they arrived in February of 1874 they gave the body to the amazed officers of the British Consul. When the body arrived in England on April 15, there was some disbelief regarding the identity of the remains. However, upon examination of the left arm, they saw the awful scar from a lion attack Livingstone had survived. At that point all doubt disappeared.

On April 18, 1874, virtually all of London came to a standstill as the remains of David Livingstone were buried in Westminster Abbey. At his funeral, along with kings and dignitaries, were his children, along with his friends Susi, Henry Stanley, and the aged Robert Moffat, who had first called Livingstone to Africa 40 years earlier.

Did you know the Bible tells how another body remained embalmed over a period of 200 years and was carried by hand for more than 1,000 miles before it was buried? Joshua very carefully followed the request made by Joseph many years before when Israel returned to Canaan. "The bones of Joseph, which the children of Israel had brought up out of Egypt, they buried at Shechem, in the plot of ground which Jacob had bought from the sons of Hamor ... " (Joshua 24:32).

Someday, all who sleep in the grave waiting for Christ's return will awake to everlasting life. There will be no more separations, no more diseases that kill, and no more death.

"For the LORD is right, and all His work is done in truth" (Psalm 33:4).

America's premier showman is famous for saying, "There's a sucker born every minute." But in reality, Barnum never made the cynical statement. Here's the story:

In upstate New York, George Hull and his cousin William Newell plotted to bamboozle the public. They had a sculptor in Chicago carve a fake giant prehistoric man from a three-thousand pound hunk of gypsum. Then they arranged for well drillers to "accidentally" find the fake fossil of this 10-foot-tall man they had buried on their farm. Their Cardiff Giant, as it became known, became a popular attraction. Crowds paid fifty cents to see the supposed petrified remains. The carving looked so authentic that scientists argued whether the Cardiff Giant was a real petrified man or a prehistoric statue. Newell sold the giant to a banker, David Hannum, who displayed it in Syracuse, now charging a dollar per person to see it, a fantastic amount in 1869.

Meanwhile, P. T. Barnum was looking for a new exhibit for his American Museum in Manhattan. His museum was famous for such oddities as the White Whale, the Fiji Mermaid (which was really just the upper half of a monkey attached to the stuffed lower half of a fish), the famous dwarf "General Tom Thumb," and the original Siamese twins, Chang and Eng.

Barnum offered Hannum $60,000 for the Cardiff Giant. When Hannum refused, the ever-resourceful Barnum just made a copy, claiming it was the original. Angry, Hannum applied for a court order to stop Barnum. The judge ruled that both men had fake giants, reasoning that a forgery of a fraud was no crime.

It was the disgruntled banker David Hannum who was quoted when he saw the crowds lining up to see Barnum's copy of his scam: "There's a sucker born every minute." That's how the quote became associated with Barnum.

With all the swindles, scams, and cons in the world today, people everywhere are wondering if there is anywhere they can go for dependable truth. The Bible proclaims, "And the truth of the LORD endures forever" and "The entirety of Your word is truth" (Psalm 117:2; 119:160). Jesus assures us He is "the way, the truth, and the life" (John 14:6), and John testifies that "grace and truth came through Jesus Christ" (John 1:17). God and His Word are the one unfailing Source of truth.

Birds & Insects

"He shall cover you with His feathers,
And under His wings you shall take refuge;
His truth shall be your shield and buckler."
Psalm 91:4

THE IMPOSTERS

"And no wonder! For Satan transforms himself into an angel of light. Therefore it is no great thing if his ministers also transform themselves into ministers of righteousness, whose end will be according to their works" (2 Corinthians 11:14, 15).

The common cuckoo bird is known as a "brood parasite." A brood parasite is a bird that will trick another bird into raising its young. For example, the female cuckoo will spy on the nest of a small bird, such as a reed warbler. At the appropriate moment, the cuckoo hen flies down to the reed warbler's nest, pushes one of the eggs out of the nest, lays an egg, and flies off. The whole process is achieved in only about 10 seconds. Amazingly, the cuckoo egg very closely resembles the eggs of their chosen host. The dedicated reed warblers unwittingly incubate, feed, and raise the young imposter, usually at the expense of their own genuine young. A cuckoo may visit as many as 50 different nests in a breeding season, each time leaving one of its own eggs for others to hatch and care for.

The cuckoo chick typically hatches before the natural ones and then commences to push the other eggs out of the little nest. One of the tragedies of nature is when you see a pair of reed warblers working themselves to death to satisfy the voracious hunger of a fat cuckoo chick that might be three times their size. Meanwhile, if the other eggs have managed to hatch, the starving little warbler chicks are usually pushed out of the nest by the cuckoo chick!

Many people do not realize that the devil, like the cuckoo bird, has laid an egg in the Christian church that has been hatched, adopted, and fed until it has grown bigger than life. The Bible says Satan's ministers can "transform themselves into ministers of righteousness" (2 Corinthians 11:15). And Jesus warned about "false prophets, who come to you in sheep's clothing, but inwardly they are ravenous wolves" (Matthew 7:15).

That's one reason it's so important that we avoid trusting in other humans, no matter how "good" they seem. Even a person of good intentions may lead you in the wrong direction. Prominent leaders can err, and have often failed to live up to what is right. In the words of the old hymn—"*I dare not trust the sweetest frame, but wholly lean on Jesus' name.*" Only God is worthy of our complete and total trust.

"The spider skillfully grasps with its hands, and it is in kings' palaces" (Proverbs 30:28).

The goliath bird-eating spider, found in the jungles of Suriname and French Guiana, is (by mass) the largest spider in the world. This monster arachnid belongs to the tarantula family. It was named by explorers who witnessed one eating a hummingbird.

So how big are they? In 1965, a male specimen was collected that had a leg span over 11 inches! That's the size of a dinner plate! In addition, these amazing tarantulas also hold the record for the longest-lived spiders. One female specimen lived for an estimated 27 years. This same family of spiders holds the record for the heaviest spider. Another female collected in Suriname weighed a whopping 4.3 ounces. She was also sporting fangs 1 inch long. With creatures like this crawling around, you can understand why many people fear spiders more than death!

The goliath bird-eating spider is pretty harmless to humans, as are most species of tarantulas. They do carry venom in their fangs and have been occasionally known to bite people when threatened, but the venom just causes swelling and mild pain, something like a wasp sting. Most of the time, if a tarantula is forced to bite a human in self-defense they don't even inject venom—it's what is known as a "dry bite."

Strangely, the goliath bird-eating spider can do the most damage to people from the back side. Their abdomens are covered with twisted fiberglass-like hairs filled with microscopic hooks. If forced to defend itself, the tarantula may flick these fine vexing hairs off their tail section with their hind legs. The fuzzy hairs can become embedded in the flesh of anything close by and are extremely irritating to skin. They are especially troublesome if they get into delicate mucous membranes around eyes and mouth. So while most people are worried about the giant fangs in the front, it is really the little hairs in the back that do the most harm.

The Bible teaches the devil also does more damage through the little invisible things. Just as a spider can be found anywhere, even in the palace of a king, so the devil does not limit his work to certain places. Though we cannot see Satan, he roams everywhere on our planet. "And the LORD said to Satan, 'From where do you come?' So Satan answered the LORD and said, 'From going to and fro on the earth, and from walking back and forth on it'" (Job 1:7).

KEEPING WARM IN THE COLD

"And because lawlessness will abound, the love of many will grow cold" (Matthew 24:12).

The emperor penguin begins its life in the intense cold of an Antarctic winter. In March or April, the majestic penguins travel from the feeding grounds on the sea to the Antarctic ice pack. The journey can be as long as 60 to 100 miles, and they make their way by walking and sometimes sliding on their bellies. Arriving at a place that is as desolate as any on Earth, they stop and the female lays one egg. Her energy depleted, she delicately transfers the egg onto the male's feet. He quickly covers it with a fold of his fat, feathery fur to keep it warm. The female then returns to the sea to feed for the next two months.

For the next 64 days, during the severe South Pole winter, the males must fast as they incubate their eggs. The ice is so cold that if an egg is dropped, the chick will quickly die. In addition, winds can reach up to 120 miles per hour. In order to survive, the male penguins huddle in clusters of about 100 and take turns in the center. Soon after the babies hatch, the females return. During their absence, the males may have lost between 20 and 40 pounds.

While the female penguins feed the chicks by regurgitating food they've stored, the males return to the ocean to feed. For the next month and a half, the parent penguins will alternate making the long trek to the sea and caring for the chick. When the chicks are old enough, they will form a tight huddle of their own, while both parents forage for food and return frequently to feed their chick. By summer, the chicks are old enough to leave the breeding grounds and travel to the sea themselves.

Emperor penguins demonstrate some of the most patient devotion and warm love for their young of any creatures, and they do this in the coldest conditions on Earth, where temperatures may drop as low as 85 degrees below zero! The Bible says that in the last days "lawlessness will abound" and "the love of many will grow cold" (Matthew 24:12). But, as the emperor penguins demonstrate, it's possible to keep your love warm in a cold world! And for those who do, the rewards are outstanding: "He who endures to the end shall be saved" (Matthew 24:12).

"And these you shall regard as an abomination among the birds; they shall not be eaten, they are an abomination: the eagle, the vulture, the buzzard ..." (Leviticus 11:13).

Vultures have long been perceived as abominable creatures because of their repulsive feeding habits, but we are now beginning to better understand the important role these scavenging birds fulfill by "cleaning up" dead animals from our forests, fields, and roads. In fact, the Latin name for the turkey vulture is *Cathartes aura,* which means cleansing wind. It is true they eat dead carrion, but most people don't know 50 percent of their diet consists of vegetation.

The vulture does its best to keep itself clean. Observations have shown that each bird spends from two to three hours a day preening itself. Also, they will bathe in water whenever they can, submerse, shake, and scrub for half an hour. Then they walk up on the bank and hold their wings out to the sun to dry.

Vultures can fly up to 200 miles a day, but they are also homebodies. Some families of vultures have been known to use the same roost for 100 years or more. For years the vulture has been classified as a bird of prey along with hawks, owls, and eagles. But in 1994, due to DNA analysis and other studies on anatomy, physiology, and behavior, the vulture has been reclassified and placed in the stork family.

The largest flying bird on Earth is a vulture, the Andean condor, with a wingspread of up to 12 feet. But the turkey vulture is probably the most graceful soaring bird in the world, reaching heights of 20,000 feet. Turkey vultures also have an extraordinary sense of smell, having the largest olfactory system of all birds. They have been known to smell carrion from over a mile away, which is very unique in the bird world. Most American vultures are voiceless birds, but they have very keen eyesight. It is believed they are able to spot a three-foot carcass from four miles away on the open plains. And when they find it, they will circle above it to notify their friends so they can enjoy their abominable picnic lunch together!

Jesus warned us that impostors would come to deceive us about the Second Coming. "For just as the lightning comes from the east and flashes even to the west, so will the coming of the Son of Man be. Wherever the corpse is, there the vultures will gather" (Matthew 24:27, 28 NASB). The living and true Christ will be seen by all when He comes, not just by a few bird watchers.

May 5 MAKING SPIDER SILK

"O LORD, how manifold are Your works! In wisdom You have made them all" (Psalm 104:24).

One of the most amazing materials in nature is the light, flexible, yet incredibly strong compound spiders use to catch unsuspecting insects. It's spider silk. Pound for pound, the threads produced by these little arachnids can hold more weight than the most sophisticated manufactured materials. The silk in a spider web is an extremely strong substance that has a tensile strength of 300,000 pounds per square inch and is both stronger and lighter than compounds based on steel.

For a long time people have known about the impressive properties of spider silk, and some have dreamed of being able to create it, perhaps the way that the ancient Chinese learned to produce silk from silkworms. But unlike the gentle silkworm, spiders are aggressive, territorial, and not easily domesticated. Up until now all attempts to synthesize spider silk have failed, but a new venture involving gene-splicing is showing considerable promise.

A Canadian company, Nexia Biotechnologies, appears on the verge of manufacturing a substance similar to spider silk through a surprising method, using the milk of goats. Researchers put the spider silk gene into milk animals, since there are close anatomical similarities between the silk-producing glands of spiders and the milk-producing glands of these mammals. The scientists spliced the spider silk gene into cells taken from the mammary glands of goats. The silk genes worked with amazing efficiency in the mammary cells, and Nexia scientists were soon producing high-quality spider silk.

Now the challenge will be to mass breed these transgenic goats and extract the pure silk protein from the milk and spin it into fabric. If the new stock of genetically altered goats produce as expected, Nexia will have the beginnings of a spider-silk dairy. The product, called "BioSteel," may soon be used for a variety of applications, from medical sutures to artificial tendons or ligaments. It could be used to create lighter and stronger bulletproof vests, and even for the coatings of space stations to protect them from micro-meteorites.

It's interesting to consider how many of man's inventions have been plagiarized from the amazing creatures God has designed. The most amazing fact is that many people think all these wonders of nature have evolved by chance!

"I am the resurrection and the life. He who believes in Me, though he may die, he shall live" (John 11:25).

Living on New Zealand's North Island is a very large cricket-like insect with thorny legs called the tree weta. These giant flightless bugs typically live in holes in trees and eat lichens, flowers, seeds, and fruit. Some species grow four inches long and are as heavy as a cell phone. But don't reach for them if they vibrate; they can deliver a very painful bite with their powerful mandibles and also inflict irritating scratches with their bacteria-laced spiny legs.

The menacing physical appearance of the weta makes these giant thorny bugs scary enough, but when you mix that with their zombie-like ability to revive from death, well, you have one spooky bug. Of course the weta does not really return from the dead, but they do sometimes "play dead." When threatened it might lie still for a short time on its back, with legs splayed and claws exposed, and jaws wide open ready to scratch and bite. Another way wetas seem to cheat death is when they revive after being frozen alive for months. In the winter their bodies might be covered with frost at times in temperatures as low as minus 10 degrees C (14 degrees F). They are able to put themselves in a type of suspended animation because their haemolymph blood contains special antifreeze that prevents ice from forming in their cells.

Wetas can only pretend to rise from the dead, but the Bible says a day is coming when all will be resurrected. "Do not marvel at this; for the hour is coming in which all who are in the graves will hear His voice and come forth; those who have done good, to the resurrection of life, and those who have done evil, to the resurrection of condemnation" (John 5:28, 29). Christ rose from the dead and holds the keys of death. He offers to each of us the gift of the resurrection and everlasting life. Some Christians are Christian in name only. They are like the frozen wetas that need to be thawed and resurrected!

THE WISE ANT

"Go to the ant, you sluggard! Consider her ways and be wise, which, having no captain, overseer or ruler, provides her supplies in the summer, and gathers her food in the harvest" (Proverbs 6:6-8).

Ants are the most numerous creatures on Earth. It has been estimated that the combined weight of the world's ants is greater than the combined weight of all humans on the planet. We also admire ants for their ability to pull 30 times, and lift 50 times, their own weight. That would be equivalent to you or me out-pulling a Clydesdale or lifting an elephant. Ants understand team work too! If necessary, they will make their bodies into ladders to climb on, or rafts to float on.

Ants are also among the most organized insects. Some ant species herd aphids like domestic livestock. The ants and aphids are engaged in a symbiotic relationship in which each benefits from the other. On the one hand, the ants actually care for the aphids and protect them from ladybugs. In exchange, the ants receive nutritious "honeydew" excreted by the aphids. The ants tap the aphids with their antennae to let them know they would like some honeydew sap. Then they carry the "honey" back to the nest to feed others. While tending their flock, the ants may redistribute the aphids on the host plant to prevent local overcrowding. Before winter, these ants will even carry off aphid eggs to start a new herd of aphids in the spring.

Some ants are also farmers. Leafcutter ants from the tropical forests of Central and South America live in huge underground colonies, ruled by a single queen, that may contain as many as 8 million ants. The largest workers leave the nest and go out foraging for leaves and petals. They collect the leaves by cutting them with their sharp jaws into small pieces. They then carry the pieces back home. But they don't eat the leaves. Instead, these resourceful insects use them to grow their own food! Back at the nest, smaller worker ants chew the leaves into tiny pieces to form large compost heaps. This compost grows the fungus on which they feed. These fungus gardens deep underground are carefully tended by tiny gardener ants.

The Bible says, "Go to the ant, you sluggard! Consider her ways and be wise" (Proverbs 6:6). When we study God's creation, even the lowly ant can inspire us and give us wisdom.

"And it will be that you shall drink from the brook, and I have commanded the ravens to feed you there" (1 Kings 17:4).

We don't usually think of birds as being smart creatures. After all, that's where we get the expression "bird brain." But crows and ravens, both from the *Corvidae* family, are an exception. Researchers believe their clever, fun-loving, and witty behavior ranks crows and ravens with the intelligence of dogs and even chimps. Found just about everywhere in the world except South America, crows and ravens adapt well to almost any environment. Their omnivorous diet helps them thrive in cities and suburban areas in close association with humans.

Crows demonstrate a sophisticated social behavior, playing tricks on each other and fabricating tools to get food. One crow was videotaped using leverage to bend a straight piece of wire into a hook. He then used the hook to fish a bucket of food from a deep tube. No other animal—not even a chimp—has ever spontaneously solved a problem like this. Crows have a highly developed system of communication that is passed on from one generation to another. Different clans of crows seem to speak with different dialects. Just like parrots, they can mimic the sounds of other animals and even the human voice. Crows can even be trained to "speak."

The world's oldest crow, named Tata, died in July 2006. As a fledgling, Tata was blown from her nest in a Long Island cemetery during a fierce thunderstorm. The baby crow with a broken wing was adopted by a local family. That was back in 1947. Tata never did learn to fly, but that might be one reason she lived 59 years. Ravens are 30 percent bigger than crows and also have among the largest brains of any bird. They typically live about 15 years in the wild, although life spans of up to 40 years have been recorded.

Did you know the Bible talks about ravens? The first bird ever mentioned in the Bible was a raven. The Bible says of Noah after the flood, "Then he sent out a raven, which kept going to and fro until the waters had dried up from the earth" (Genesis 8:7). And Jesus told us we could learn from this wise bird: "Consider the ravens, for they neither sow nor reap, which have neither storehouse nor barn; and God feeds them. Of how much more value are you than the birds?" (Luke 12:24).

UNDER HIS WINGS

"He who dwells in the secret place of the Most High shall abide under the shadow of the Almighty. ... Surely He shall deliver you from the snare of the fowler and from the perilous pestilence. He shall cover you with His feathers, and under His wings you shall take refuge" (Psalm 91:1, 3, 4).

In the spring of 1977 in northern Wisconsin, several ornithologists were making an aerial survey of bald eagle nests. As they flew over one particular nest, they noticed something in the nest that didn't look right, and they guessed that it might be a dead adult eagle.

The next day the men visited the same nest from the ground to determine what had happened. When they arrived, two adult eagles began flying around and scolding, and it was obvious that there was at least one young bird alive in the nest. Now the men were really confused—if what they saw was really a dead eagle, why were there now two living adults scolding them? Climbing the tree to get a closer look, they found an eagle that had been dead for about a month, yet a very healthy chick about five weeks old was sitting in the nest. How could this have happened?

Upon further investigation, the men discovered that lightning had struck the tree: large limbs from the tree were strewn around on the ground, and there were burn marks near the nest. The men surmised that the lightning strike had killed the mother, but by some miracle the young bird had survived. Perhaps the mother was still incubating the egg when the storm hit, or perhaps, during the fury of the storm, the mother stretched out her wings to protect her newly hatched chick. Either way, it was apparent that soon after her death, the father had been able to recruit another mate to help with the very demanding task of feeding a growing eagle.

What a perfect example of the love that Jesus has for us! The Bible, describing Jacob's experience in the wilderness, says that the Lord led Jacob just like an eagle spreads its wings over its young (Deuteronomy 32:11). Just as God saved Jacob, He will save us: when we deserved death for our sins, Jesus was willing to spread His protective wings and take our death to save us.

"The Spirit of God has made me, and the breath of the Almighty gives me life" (Job 33:4).

In Europe, Asia, and parts of Africa lives a curious little spider that has its home under the water. The female water spider (also known as the diving bell spider) spins a tiny web in the shape of a bell, attaching it to stems of water weeds and plants just below the surface of a freshwater pond. All spiders need to breathe air, so the water spider takes its air along like a skin diver.

On the surface she traps tiny bubbles in the hairs of her body, then hurries home and brushes them off, releasing them under her web. The spider makes many trips to bring back air bubbles for her underwater bubble nest. The waterproof web becomes inflated with trapped air and makes a perfect diving bell where she lives, eats, and lays her eggs. If the fresh air is used up, the water spider returns to the surface to breathe and collect more fresh air bubbles for her home. Living below, and yet breathing the air from above, this little spider is constantly surrounded by water yet remains perfectly dry!

The water spider illustrates how Christians may be in the world but not of the world. No matter how much water surrounds the water spider, it still is able to breathe air because it takes a bubble of air with it wherever it goes. How can the Christian live with a constant connection to heaven while living in this sinful world? Through prayer. Like the breath of the soul, we can pray to Jesus no matter what our surroundings. Prayer is just as necessary to our spiritual life as oxygen is to our physical life.

I long for the day when we will be in heaven, but even now we may breathe the air of heaven through prayer. Jesus knows we are in the world, but we do not need to be "of" this world. "I do not pray that You should take them out of the world, but that You should keep them from the evil one. They are not of the world, just as I am not of the world" (John 17:15, 16). We can continue to "breathe" in the world as long as we keep our connection with God.

THE LIFE BELT

"Charm is deceitful and beauty is passing, but a woman who fears the LORD, she shall be praised" (Proverbs 31:30).

On a hot August night in 1942, the U.S. and Japanese were preparing to engage in the deadly naval battle of Savo Island for possession of Guadalcanal. Young Elgin Staples, Signalman 3rd Class on the USS *Astoria*, was awakened from an exhausted sleep by a loud explosion. Jumping to his feet, with his heart pounding, he grabbed his life belt and strapped it on.

Staples survived the first hail of enemy shells and was tending to the wounded when a gun turret exploded and he was blown overboard, plummeting 30 feet into the dark, shark-infested waters. Wounded in his leg and shoulder by shrapnel, he was kept afloat by his narrow life belt that he managed to activate. For four agonizing hours he drifted in the open sea as large, dark creatures brushed against his legs.

During the terrifying hours that passed, he thought about his mother and knew she was praying for him. At sunrise Staples was rescued by a passing destroyer and promptly returned to the floundering *Astoria*. But his ship was badly crippled and began to sink. Staples, still wearing the same life belt, forced himself to leap back into the sea. This time he was picked up by the USS *President Jackson* and evacuated to safety. On board the transport ship, Staples closely examined the life belt that had saved him. It was manufactured by Firestone Rubber Company and bore a unique registration number. He felt impressed to keep it as a souvenir.

On home leave, Staples told his story to his mother. He was surprised to learn she had taken a wartime job at the Firestone plant in Akron, Ohio. Curious, he grabbed the deflated life belt from his duffel bag and asked about the purpose of the number on the belt. She replied that the company made many thousands of life belts but insisted each one be examined and given a unique number by the inspector. When she looked up from the belt, her eyes were open wide with surprise. In a barely audible voice she said, "Son, I'm an inspector at Firestone and this is my inspector number!"

Just as his mother's life belt buoyed up the young sailor physically, her prayers buoyed up his spirit during his ordeal. A God-fearing, praying mother is a tremendous blessing from God. If you have a Christian mother, that's something to thank Him for.

"Then He brought him outside and said, 'Look now toward heaven, and count the stars if you are able to number them.' And He said to him, 'So shall your descendants be'" (Genesis 15:5).

The largest known cooperative organism living on Earth is a single "supercolony" of ants that stretches more than 3,700 miles! Scientists say the vast colony of Argentine ants extends from the northwest of Italy, tracing around the Mediterranean coasts of France, and rounding Spain up to Portugal—a distance wider than the entire United States!

Argentine ants were first introduced to Italy about 90 years ago. It is believed they hitched a ride across the ocean on a freighter carrying South American fruit or plants. After landing, they quickly became established in the ideal habitat. With plentiful food and few natural enemies, they spread like a plague.

A team of researchers captured about 5,000 ants from 33 separate nests in Italy, France, Spain, and Portugal and transported the insects back to a laboratory. Once in the lab, the scientists arranged ant fights—pitting ants against one another from among the 33 nests. Argentine ants will normally be friendly and cooperate with ants from their own colony, but fight fiercely with other types of ants or members of other colonies. Over the span of a year, the scientists arranged more than 1,000 ant fights. What they discovered was that ants from 30 of the nests were closely related and refused to fight one another! Even ants from opposite ends of the supercolony were able to recognize each other and cooperate.

Amazingly, large colonies have developed in California, Japan, and other parts of the world that are related to the supercolony in Europe. When scientists put ants from large colonies in North America and Asia with the European ants, the ants acted as though they were old friends; they were cooperative and non-aggressive. There are millions of nests comprising the enormous ant colony in Europe, and it is estimated to contain at least ten times as many ants as the number of stars in the Milky Way.

Did you know that in the Bible, God promised that His people would grow beyond the number of the stars? The promise was made to Abraham, and God is still in the process of fulfilling that promise. His Word says, "And if you are Christ's, then you are Abraham's seed, and heirs according to the promise" (Galatians 3:29). By accepting Jesus, you become part of His great supercolony!

May 13 KIWIS

"But ye are a chosen generation, a royal priesthood, an holy nation, a peculiar people ..." (1 Peter 2:9).

One of the strangest creatures in the world is a flightless bird found only in New Zealand called the kiwi. The kiwi is the smallest member of the ratite family, which includes the ostrich and emus. It is unique in several respects. For one thing, it is the only bird in the world that has its nostrils at the end of its beak, which is about one third of the body length. The kiwi literally sniffs out its food by plunging its long beak below the surface. They also have excellent hearing that can even detect a worm wiggling underground.

Kiwis live as monogamous couples, with the bigger female dominating the male, who may do most of the incubating of the eggs. And the eggs are huge. The female kiwi has one of the largest egg-to-body weight ratios of any bird. The mature egg averages 20 percent of the female's body weight, compared to two percent for an ostrich! A five-pound kiwi lays an egg that weighs just over a pound, a record in the bird kingdom. That would be like a 100-pound woman giving birth to a 20-pound baby. And the eggs take an exceedingly long time to hatch, up to 80 days, whereas a chicken egg only takes 21 days.

Kiwis are often confused for mammals. For one thing, it has wings but cannot fly. Its loose feathers have a hairlike appearance. Its long whiskers, plus the fact that it burrows in the ground, all contribute to the confusion. Some think it strange that New Zealanders like to call themselves "Kiwis" and have made the image of this bizarre bird a national emblem on their money, stamps, and coins.

The Bible teaches that Christians are called to be a peculiar people. But does that mean that we are commanded to be wacky or weird? Of course not. It means we are special to the Lord. "Now therefore, if ye will obey my voice indeed, and keep my covenant, then ye shall be a peculiar treasure unto me above all people: for all the earth is mine" (Exodus 19:5). To those outside the family circle we might seem strange, but to the Lord we are uniquely loved, just like the kiwi!

"By the word of truth, by the power of God, by the armor of righteousness on the right hand and on the left" (2 Corinthians 6:7).

There are over 300,000 different species of beetles in the world, but among them the bombardier beetle has been created with one of the most incredible defense systems in the natural world. Whenever threatened by an enemy attack from ants, frogs, or spiders, this spirited little beetle shoots a jet of boiling chemicals and irritating, foul-smelling gases at its attacker. This toxic spray explodes from two tail pipes on the tip of its abdomen, right into the face of the unfortunate aggressor.

With some bombardier beetles you can actually hear the explosion as a loud popping, which is a result of rapid firing. This rapid-fire action is called "pulse combustion" and jets the boiling liquid out at over 500 pulses per second and 212 degrees Fahrenheit! In addition, the beetle can rotate the end of its abdomen 270 degrees in any direction like a tiny cannon and hit the target with extreme accuracy.

Scientists and chemists have studied the bombardier beetle and learned that he makes his explosive by mixing together two very volatile chemicals—hydroquinone and hydrogen peroxide. In addition to these two chemicals, this clever little beetle adds another type of chemical known as an inhibitor. The inhibitor enables the beetle to store the chemicals indefinitely without blowing itself up. Whenever our beetle friend is approached by a predator, he squirts the stored chemicals into the two combustion tubes and, at the same moment, he adds another chemical—an anti-inhibitor. This knocks out the inhibitor, and a violent explosion occurs, scorching the poor attacker. But somehow the beetle is not bothered by the heat and irritation that comes from its own spray.

It is preposterous to believe that such a marvelous and complex mechanism could have evolved piecemeal over millions of years. This would require thousands of generations of these little beetles blowing themselves to pieces until finally they mastered their explosive gift.

Did you know those who mix prayer and Bible study can expect explosive power? The Bible says, "For the word of God is living and powerful ..." (Hebrews 4:12). And the Lord promises those who love Him, "He shall call upon Me, and I will answer him" (Psalm 91:15). Wouldn't you like to be answered by the God of the universe, and experience the power of His Word in your life today?

May 15 LOYAL GEESE

"Greater love has no one than this, than to lay down one's life for his friends" (John 15:13).

We see them coming in the fall and leaving in early spring, flying along in a "V" formation. The awesome migration of geese offers a number of inspiring lessons of sacrifice and teamwork. For one thing, as each bird flaps its wings, it creates uplift for the bird immediately following. By flying in V formation the whole flock adds at least 71 percent greater flying range than if each bird flew on its own. When a goose falls out of formation, it suddenly feels the drag and resistance of trying to go it alone ... and quickly gets back in to take advantage of the lifting power of the bird in front.

Even though they weigh between 20-25 pounds, geese can fly about as high as any bird. A Himalayan mountain climber at 16,000 feet was rather amazed when a flock of geese flew northward about two miles over his head, honking as they went. At 7,000 feet a man has a hard time talking while running, but those geese were probably flying at 27,000 feet, and even calling while they traveled at this tremendous height. Canada Geese can reach speeds of up to 60 mph during their flights. They can fly for up to 16 hours without rest.

Geese are also very loyal. When a goose gets sick or is wounded by gunshot and falls out of formation, two other geese follow it down to lend help and protection. They stay with the fallen goose until it is able to fly or until it dies. Geese mate for life, which averages about 20 years, and will stay together during all seasons. They are also excellent parents. They will sacrificially place themselves between any perceived threat and their young. Domesticated geese also make good "watchdogs," hissing and honking loudly when strangers come around. There are many accounts of how the family goose laid its life down to save a child from a venomous snake or rabid dog.

In describing the power of the gospel to change our lives, the apostle Paul speaks of Christ laying down His life for us. "I have been crucified with Christ; it is no longer I who live, but Christ lives in me; and the life which I now live in the flesh I live by faith in the Son of God, who loved me and gave Himself for me" (Galatians 2:20). Study the life and death of Christ and behold Jesus' expression of love for you, a love more loyal than geese.

"Answer me speedily, O LORD; my spirit fails! Do not hide Your face from me, lest I be like those who go down into the pit" (Psalm 143:7).

The record for the fastest flying insect is that of a male horsefly. Horseflies mate in a surprising way—the male catches the female midair and they both drop to the ground while mating. One entomologist reports that he was able to get a male horsefly to chase a plastic pellet from his air rifle. Amazingly, the fly caught and dropped to the ground with the pellet, which was going at least 90 miles an hour!

Another notable insect is the small, dull-colored moth called the dark sword-grass or black cutworm moth. With a wingspan of just five centimeters, this moth usually has airspeeds of five to eight mph, but when riding the winds of a cold front it has been known to sustain ground speeds of up to 70 mph.

The fastest moving land insects are Australian tiger beetles. These beetles, named after tigers because of their impressive jaws and hunting style, are incredibly fast relative to their body size. One species of this beetle, the *Cicindela hudsoni*, has the fastest absolute speed for a land insect—a whopping 5.57 mph, or 120 body lengths per second. In human terms, that would be nearly 520 mph—or the cruising speed of a jet! But another species of Australian tiger beetle, the *Cicindela eburneola*, has the fastest relative land speed—these beetles can move 171 body lengths per second, or 4.16 mph. This would be equivalent to a 6-foot-tall human running nearly 720 mph. In other words, a human running the corresponding speed of these beetles would almost break the sound barrier!

While these record-breaking bugs are certainly speedy, God really holds the speed record. In the Psalms, David often prayed for God to answer him "speedily"—sometimes because he was in danger, but also when he wanted God's "tender mercies" for his "former iniquities" (Psalm 79:8). When it comes to forgiving a repentant sinner, we can be sure that the following promise holds true: "Before they call, I will answer; and while they are still speaking, I will hear" (Isaiah 65:24).

THE HONEY CRISIS

"What is sweeter than honey?" (Judges 14:18).

To produce about 1 pound of honey, bees must make 25,000 trips between their hive and the flowers from which they gather precious nectar. Furthermore, that same pound of honey contains the essence of about two million flowers! In the process of making this honey, bees provide a crucial service to nature—pollination. Albert Einstein once remarked that "If bees were to disappear, man would only have a few years to live." This statement is especially sobering when you consider the recent decimating plague among U.S. bee colonies called colony collapse disorder (CCD).

Just before the beginning of 2007, beekeepers from all over North America began reporting colonies of their bees dying off in unprecedented numbers. Twenty-four U.S. states reported honeybees vanishing at an alarming rate, leaving beekeepers struggling for survival and farmers worried about pollination of their crops. The mysterious disappearance of bees ranges from 30 to 70 percent in some states. Blooming orchards that used to roar with buzzing bees are now strangely silent. One California beekeeper said, "I have never seen anything like it. Box after box after box is just empty. There's nobody home."

Experts are exploring several theories to explain the losses from CCD. These include viruses, mites, pesticide contamination and, strangely enough, poor bee nutrition. The mysterious colony collapse disorder highlights the fundamental role that honeybees play in the natural chain of God's economy, providing fruit and vegetables. Honeybee pollination contributes more than $14 billion worth of North American harvests each year. A broad assortment of crops like apples, peaches, avocados, soybeans, pears, pumpkins, cucumbers, cherries, kiwis, raspberries, blackberries, strawberries, and many more, depend on honey bee pollination. Some have suggested that if all honeybees suddenly died off, it would bring their vital work of pollination to an end. This environmental breakdown could easily cause an agricultural and economic chain reaction leading to a financial collapse and possibly a national famine.

Who would have guessed the work of these little creatures was so important! Maybe that's why the Bible has so much to say about honey! David writes about God's law: "How sweet are Your words to my taste, sweeter than honey to my mouth!" (Psalm 119:103). And Solomon says, "Pleasant words are like a honeycomb, sweetness to the soul and health to the bones" (Proverbs 16:24).

"And the dragon was enraged with the woman, and he went to make war with the rest of her offspring, who keep the commandments of God and have the testimony of Jesus Christ" (Revelation 12:17).

Passenger pigeons were once the most numerous birds in North America and possibly on Earth. The elegant birds had a slate-blue head, gray back, and a wine-red breast. The eye was scarlet with a short, slender black bill. Long-tailed, graceful, and fast, these pigeons could reach flight speeds of 60 to 70 mph. But they were not fast enough to escape annihilation.

Early settlers recorded massive flocks a mile wide and up to 300 miles long. These clouds of birds were so dense they darkened the sky for days as the immense flock passed overhead, one tier above the other. They were so thickly packed that a single shot from a shotgun could bring down 30 or 40 birds. Population estimates from the 19th century ranged from three to five billion birds.

Then began probably the most severe example of mass wildlife slaughter in history. The young chicks were regarded as a great delicacy, and the adults were killed for their feathers as well as their meat. Commercial hunters harvested tens of thousands of individuals daily, shipping them by boxcar-loads to markets in the East. In 1855, about 300,000 pigeons a year were being sent to New York restaurants. During 1874, Michigan sent over 3,000,000 birds east.

By the late 1880s, passenger pigeon flocks, which once numbered in the millions, contained no more than a few hundred birds. By the 1900s, no wild passenger pigeons could be found. From 1909 to 1912, the American Ornithologists' Union offered $1,500 to anyone finding a nest, but these efforts were futile. The last passenger pigeon, named Martha, died alone at the Cincinnati Zoo on September 1, 1914. Who could have dreamed that within a few decades the most plentiful birds would be reduced to zero?

The book of Revelation teaches that in the last days an all-out effort will be made to annihilate God's people. The image of the beast will "cause as many as would not worship the image of the beast to be killed" (Revelation 13:15). But Jesus said, "... My friends, do not be afraid of those who kill the body, and after that have no more that they can do" (Luke 12:4). Jesus alone holds the keys to our existence. He will destroy death and give His people everlasting life.

May 19 GIRL-SNATCHING EAGLE

"You have seen what I did to the Egyptians, and how I bore you on eagle's wings and brought you to Myself" (Exodus 19:4).

Great birds of prey have always filled man with admiration, and even fear. There are many legends regarding stories of large birds snatching and flying off with large creatures, such as sheep, or calves, but most of these accounts are purely fiction. The largest raptors, vultures, are primarily carrion feeders and don't have the ability for great feats of lifting. So man has generally blamed the great eagles, like the common golden eagle, for most stories.

The largest golden eagle on record measured 41 inches in length, weighed 20 pounds, and had a wingspan of 8 feet. The maximum load for the average golden eagle is usually only about 8 to 10 pounds. But when birds have been disturbed at a kill and need to make an emergency exit they seem to be able to haul greater loads.

Most tales of children being carried off by eagles have been scoffed at by ornithologists, but there is at least one case that apparently has been fully authenticated. In 1932, a four-year-old girl from the island of Leka, Norway, was playing in the yard of her parents' farmhouse. Suddenly a huge white-tailed sea eagle, a relative of the golden eagle, swooped down, grabbed her by her dress, and carried her off. The enormous bird tried to carry the girl (who was apparently small for her age) back to its nest 800 feet up the side of a mountain more than a mile away. But the effort was too great and the poor child was dropped on a narrow ledge about 50 feet from the nest.

One theory explaining the incident is that the bird had the advantage of the powerful up-current of air coming off the ocean. A search party organized by the desperate parents pinpointed the eagle soaring above the nest, and the girl was found in an unconscious state. Except for some scratches and bruises she was unharmed. The fortunate girl, Svanhild Hansen, grew up happily and kept the little dress she wore that frightful day, with the holes made by the eagle's talons.

It's hard to imagine that eagle wings could carry a little girl, but did you know that the Bible teaches that a grown woman was carried by eagle wings? "But the woman was given two wings of a great eagle, that she might fly into the wilderness to her place, where she is nourished for a time and times and half a time, from the presence of the serpent" (Revelation 12:14).

"The ants are a people not strong, yet they prepare their food in the summer" (Proverbs 30:25).

Perhaps you have heard of the famous parasol (or "leafcutter") ants that make gardens and raise their own crops. These amazing creatures are called "parasol" ants because they are often seen walking in processions, each one holding a piece of green leaf above its head! These bits of green leaf are not for food, but are taken to their nests and made into a compost soil. These ants are actually farmers. They deliberately sow, prune, fertilize, weed, harvest, and store a fungus crop as carefully as any gardener tends his vegetables.

There are ants living in Texas that clear a "field" of 1 or 2 square yards and then plant rice. They lay out the rice in beds with pathways running among the plants and keep their rice fields carefully weeded. When the rice seeds ripen the ants harvest them, remove the husks, and store the kernels for food. Later the ants with very large jaws crack the seeds and crush the kernels into meal for the rest of the ants. If the rice gets damp and is in danger of spoiling, certain ants have the sole responsibility of carrying the damp grain out into the sunshine for drying.

Another species of Mediterranean ant goes even further in producing its food from farmed seeds. These ants carefully take dried seeds out in the rain until they start to sprout. At that point, they kill the sprout and dry the seeds in the sunshine again. When the seeds are dry, the ants take them down into the kitchen where workers crush and chew them into a dough-like substance. They form the dough into cookie-shaped patties and then take the patties back out to bake in the sun. When the ant biscuits are baked, the ants store them in the nest again.

No wonder Solomon wrote, "Go to the ant, you sluggard! Consider her ways and be wise, which, having no captain, overseer or ruler, provides her supplies in the summer, and gathers her food in the harvest" (Proverbs 6:6-8). The same God who enables the tiny ant to prepare for its needs also gave us the intelligence to prepare for ours.

THE ELEPHANT BIRD

"So the great dragon was cast out, that serpent of old, called the Devil and Satan, who deceives the whole world; he was cast to the earth, and his angels were cast out with him" (Revelation 12:9).

Around the 1600s, early Arabian and Indian explorers began returning from the coast of east Africa with accounts of birds that were twice as tall as a man and three times as big as an ostrich. Naturally, their stories were scoffed at ... until they brought evidence: eggs up to three feet in circumference! They were the eggs of an *Aepyornis*—a giant flightless bird found only on the island of Madagascar. Today the *Aepyornis* is better known as the elephant bird because of the stories Marco Polo told of a bird so strong that it could lift an elephant.

Though now extinct, the elephant bird was the largest bird that has ever lived. Scientists estimate that it stood 11 feet tall and weighed 900 pounds. By comparison, an exceptionally large ostrich might reach 9 feet and 300 pounds. By the time the French settled in Madagascar in the 1640s, the elephant bird had already become very rare. The last sighting of a live elephant bird was in 1649. The natives' histories on Madagascar describe the elephant bird as a shy, peaceful giant. It was likely driven to extinction by people raiding its nests for the extraordinary eggs. In fact, its eggs were even bigger than the largest dinosaur eggs. One of the largest intact specimens is 35 inches in circumference around its long axis, and probably had a capacity of more than two gallons. Some biologists have calculated that these eggs were as large as a functional egg possibly could be, meaning the eggs of the extinct elephant birds were the largest single cells to have ever existed on Earth.

Many people thought the elephant bird was just a myth until they saw the undeniable evidence. Unfortunately, in spite of the obvious biblical evidence, some people still think that the devil is a mythical beast with goat hooves and a forked tail. But the Bible makes it clear that the devil is real—and a formidable foe. Peter describes him as a "roaring lion, seeking whom he may devour" (1 Peter 5:8). Yet the devil can be resisted! Peter also warns us to be watchful, vigilant, and steadfast in our faith and promises that eventually "the God of all grace" will "perfect, establish, strengthen, and settle" us (1 Peter 5:9, 10).

"He will cover you with his feathers, and under his wings you will find refuge" (Psalm 91:4).

After a forest fire in Yellowstone Park, a National Geographic photographer joined some forest rangers on their trek up a mountain to assess the inferno's damage. As they hiked through the burnt forest, the photographer found a scorched bird literally petrified in ashes, perched statuesquely on the ground at the base of a tree. Somewhat curious of the eerie sight, he gently struck at the bird with his boot. When he did, three tiny chicks scurried out from under their dead mother's wings.

The loving mother, keenly aware of impending disaster, had led her offspring to the base of the tree and had gathered them under her wings, instinctively knowing that the toxic smoke would rise. She could have flown to safety but refused to abandon her chicks. When the blaze arrived and the heat scorched her small body, the mother remained steadfast. Because she was willing to die, those under the cover of her wings would live.

The mother bird's instinct to protect her young at the cost of her own life describes a quality infrequently found among humans. During the shootings in the Aurora, Colorado, movie theater this last year, some people ran for their lives, leaving their own children behind. But others threw themselves over their family at the cost of their own lives. It reminds me of the Bible verse: "By this we know love, because He laid down His life for us. And we also ought to lay down our lives for the brethren" (1 John 3:16).

Jesus did not hesitate to give His life for a world soon to be enveloped in an unquenchable forest fire. Christ wept out the words, "O Jerusalem, Jerusalem, the one who kills the prophets and stones those who are sent to her! How often I wanted to gather your children together, as a hen gathers her chicks under her wings, but you were not willing!" (Matthew 23:37). Our Savior stretched out His arms over us, to shield us from the penalty of sin. Christ died in order that we might live.

The picture of a mother hen quietly sitting over her cute brood of little peeping chicks makes us smile. But the picture of Calvary is like the bird that died in the fire at Yellowstone, with outstretched wings, faithful unto death.

GARDEN GUARDIANS

"The angel of the LORD encamps all around those who fear Him, and delivers them" (Psalm 34:7)

Ladybugs are one of the most valuable natural forms of pest control on Earth. Farmers of the Middle Ages believed that the ladybug could work miracles for their crops, so they named the little beetle "Our Lady" or the "Bug of Our Lady," after the Virgin Mary. Other names for the ladybug include ladybird, lady beetle, and lady fly, but over time this was shortened to the simple modern name, ladybug. (Naturally, not all ladybugs are ladies; there are boy ladybugs too.)

There are more than 4,000 different kinds of ladybugs in the world; 300 varieties live in North America. Besides the familiar red with black spots coloration, they also come in pink, white, brown, metallic blue, and yellow, and one beautiful species is black with red spots—exactly the opposite coloration of the common type.

These hardy little beetles beat their wings 85 times a second when flying and can live for weeks without eating, and when insects are scarce they can switch from eating insects to eating pollen. Another reason ladybugs survive so well is their ability to emit a foul-smelling and bitter-tasting chemical from their leg sockets when attacked by a predator. So birds generally avoid them. A female ladybug can lay up to 1,000 eggs in her lifetime. In winter, ladybugs gather in huge groups to hibernate under sticks, bark, and even rocks. In California, 750 million ladybugs were discovered hibernating together in one group.

Ladybugs have even ventured into space. In 1999, four ladybugs were sent into space as part of an experiment on NASA's space shuttle. Upon completion of the mission, it was determined that the ladybugs survived very well in space and even ate aphids while in zero gravity.

Because of ladybugs' efficiency in the garden, farmers praise them for healthy crops. They are the good bugs that fight the bad bugs, eating billions and billions of aphids, scale insects, and mealy bugs every year. Gardeners even buy boxes of ladybugs to protect their gardens from pests.

Did you know the Bible teaches that God will send angels to protect those who trust in Him? Psalm 91 says, "For He shall give His angels charge over you, to keep you in all your ways" (verse 11). These heavenly guardians are sent by God to watch over and encourage us continuously.

"For false christs and false prophets will rise and show great signs and wonders to deceive, if possible, even the elect" (Matthew 24:24).

Black skimmers are graceful black and white gull-like birds. They get the name "skimmer" because the birds love to fly just above the surface of the water, with their lower bill skimming through the water for fish. Skimmers have elliptical-shaped eye pupils that allow them to tolerate the bright sun on the sand or shell surfaces where they love to rest and nest.

In 1968 a flock of 38 black skimmers decided to set up housekeeping on a large Dow Chemical parking lot made of oyster shells. The Texas chemical company was pleased to host the birds, hoping it would improve their environmental public image. Then one day someone removed the shells from the parking lot and the colony of black skimmers moved elsewhere. Removing the bird's habitat caused a great deal of negative publicity for the chemical company, so Dow immediately ordered that the oyster shell parking lot be restored.

But the skimmers didn't return. Dow consulted a wildlife expert who recommended placing a pair of plastic decoys on the shell surface. It worked! Soon, a few live skimmers noticed what appeared to be two of their own kind enjoying this new real estate, so they joined them. Eventually the lot was again covered with nesting skimmers. When left to themselves skimmers will always face away from the wind. But when the decoys were placed with their head facing into the wind, the real skimmers copied them. And when the decoys were placed very close together and off by themselves, the real skimmers began their nesting rituals.

The Bible teaches that in the last days many will be led astray by false christs and false prophets. How can we tell the difference? We will not be deceived if we know the real from the fake. That comes from studying the Bible very carefully. When we are daily in the Word of God looking at Jesus, we will know the true from the false. Paul's advice to Timothy sums it up well: "But evil men and impostors will grow worse and worse, deceiving and being deceived. But you must continue in the things which you have learned and been assured of, knowing from whom you have learned them" (2 Timothy 3:13, 14).

PART OF A COLONY

"For in fact the body is not one member but many" (1 Corinthians 12:14).

Ants are the most numerous creatures on Earth. Their combined weight is greater than the combined weight of all humans on the planet, and makes up one-tenth of the world's total animal tissue. Strong in relation to their size, ants can carry 10 to 20 times their body weight and work in teams to move extremely heavy things. If a man could run as fast for his size as an ant can, he could run the speed of a racehorse.

These little creatures have the largest brain among insects in proportion to their size. Their little mushroom-shaped brains have about 250,000 brain cells, which function similar to the gray-matter of human brains. A human brain has 10,000 million cells, so in theory a colony of 40,000 ants has collectively the same size brain as a human. How does it feel to know you are as smart as a hill of ants? Extremely social, ants also share these activities with humans:

- **LIVESTOCK FARMING**—herding aphids like sheep and "milking" them for nectar-like food
- **CULTIVATION**—growing and storing underground gardens for food
- **CHILDCARE**—tenderly feeding their young and providing intensive nursery care, all the while maintaining careful climate control of 77 degrees F for developing ants
- **EDUCATION**—teaching younger ants the tricks of the trade
- **CIVIC DUTIES**—working together and organizing massive group projects
- **MILITARY FORCES**—raising an army of specialized soldier ants to ward off other insects, animals, and any attacking enemies
- **EARTH MOVING**—moving little mountains every day
- **ENGINEERING**—tunneling from two directions and meeting exactly midway
- **FLOOD CONTROL**—incorporating water traps to keep out rain
- **COMMUNICATIONS**—have a complex tactile and chemical communication system
- **CAREER SPECIALIZATION**—learning new careers like cleaning, foraging, caring for the young, or guarding

But as intelligent and resourceful as they are, ants cannot survive alone. They can only exist and thrive as part of a colony. Likewise, the Bible teaches that Christians will only thrive as part of a church family. It is God's plan that we should care for one another.

"Remember the Sabbath day, to keep it holy" (Exodus 20:8).

If you have ever been to Arlington National Cemetery you have probably seen a sharp-looking sentinel guarding the Tomb of the Unknown Soldier. Every detail performed by this honor guard is flawlessly executed and meaningful. During his march by the tomb, the guard takes 21 steps, turns 90 degrees to face the tomb, pauses 21 seconds, turns another 90 degrees to face back down the mat, and pauses 21 seconds. These pauses allude to the 21-gun salute, the highest military honor.

For a soldier to apply to guard the tomb, he must be in superb physical condition and between 5'10" and 6'4" tall. Less than 20 percent of the soldiers who try out for this duty are accepted for training, and only a fraction of them become guards. Off-duty time is spent training and memorizing the notable people resting in Arlington National Cemetery and where they are interred. Every guard spends up to five hours a day making sure his uniform is impeccable. After serving for several months and passing a proficiency test and written test, the guard is given a Tomb Guard Badge that is worn on his uniform pocket. There have only been about 525 awarded, making it one of the least awarded Army badges, second only to the Astronaut Badge. Recipients are held to a high standard and must not do anything that brings dishonor upon the tomb. Only nine badges have been revoked.

The guards, which are changed every 30 minutes in summer and every hour in winter, have been patrolling the tomb 24 hours a day, 365 days a year continuously since April 6, 1948. They are so dedicated that their duty is performed in all types of weather. For them, guarding the tomb is not just an assignment–it is the highest honor that can be afforded to a serviceperson. Every year on Memorial Day, thousands of visitors to Arlington National Cemetery behold the awesome loyalty of these silent sentinels guarding the tomb.

Did you know the Bible teaches that God has a memorial to be remembered? The fourth commandment explains: "For in six days the LORD made the heavens and the earth, the sea, and all that is in them, and rested the seventh day. Therefore the LORD blessed the Sabbath day and hallowed it" (Exodus 20:11). Each week we memorialize God's creative power and honor Him as our Creator by keeping His Sabbath holy.

HUMMINGBIRDS

"[W]hile I was speaking in prayer, the man Gabriel ... being caused to fly swiftly, reached me about the time of the evening offering" (Daniel 9:21).

There are over 300 kinds of hummingbirds in the world, which come in every color of the rainbow. The smallest is the bee hummingbird from Cuba—the smallest bird in the world. It is only two inches long and weighs less than a dime at .07 ounces. The largest is the giant hummingbird that can reach a whopping eight inches in length.

Even though hummingbirds are small in size, they have enormous appetites. Hummingbirds feed often and must consume more than their body weight in food each day. (I would have to eat more than 160 pounds of food a day to do that!) In order to obtain enough nectar, they feed every 10 or 15 minutes from dawn until dusk. Hummingbirds consume between four and seven calories a day. That may not seem like much, but if humans (who normally eat 3,500 calories a day) had the metabolism of a hummingbird, they would have to consume approximately 155,000 calories a day! The hummingbird's copious need for calories is because of their extremely high heart rate and metabolism.

Hummingbirds are not very social animals, which is why you never see them flying in flocks. In fact, males and females live apart until breeding season. After mating, the female is on her own to build the nest and raise her young. The females usually lay one or two very tiny eggs about the size of a pinto bean. When they hatch out, these tiny babies are very vulnerable to predators, including large insects!

When it comes to flying, nobody does it better than a hummingbird. Like a helicopter, it can go up, down, sideways, backwards, and even upside down! This is because most of its wing is made of hand bones instead of arm bones like other birds. The ruby-throated hummingbird, for example, is reported to have a wing rate of 70 beats per second, or 4,200 per minute. Hummingbirds are such good fliers that most of them never walk more than two inches, and they can terrorize birds 10 times their own size with their acrobatic skill. Hummingbirds are also amazing hunters of insects, frequently plucking mosquitoes, gnats, and fruit flies right out of the air while hovering.

Did you know that the Bible teaches that angels do not travel at the speed of sound or even at the speed of light but rather at the speed of thought? The angel Gabriel came to Daniel from heaven while he was still praying!

"Then I saw another angel flying in the midst of heaven, having the everlasting gospel to preach to those who dwell on the earth—to every nation, tribe, tongue, and people—saying with a loud voice, 'Fear God and give glory to Him, for the hour of His judgment has come; and worship Him who made heaven and earth, the sea and springs of water'" (Revelation 14:6, 7).

Cicadas are a small insect with a big voice. They live all over the world in temperate to tropical climates, and they especially love to sing during the hotter hours of the day. Male cicadas have loud noisemakers called tymbals on the sides of their abdomens, which are essentially a corrugated membrane. Unlike crickets, which rub their legs together to make noise, the cicadas contract and release the internal tymbal muscles to produce an ear-splitting clicking sound as the thin membrane buckles in and out. The interior of the male abdomen is largely hollow, which serves to greatly amplify the sound.

While a jet flying overhead or a jackhammer is about 110 decibels, the sound of some cicadas can be as loud as 120 decibels, which makes them the loudest of all insects. In fact, if a cicada were to sound right next to your ear, it could cause permanent hearing loss! Of course, the intent of these ear-splitting sounds is usually to attract and court a mate.

Did you know the Bible says that just before the Lord returns there will be a series of loud messages that will reach all around the world? Frequently called the three angels' messages, these comunications are intended to do what the cicada's song should do: attract a mate—a bride. The first angel has the "everlasting gospel" to preach to everyone on Earth, and stresses giving glory to God and worshiping Him as Creator. The second angel warns that Babylon, or false worship, has fallen. The third angel gives a very explicit warning of the danger of worshiping the beast.

Will you respond to His invitation? "Let us be glad and rejoice and give Him glory, for the marriage of the Lamb has come, and His wife has made herself ready" (Revelation 19:7). Nothing could be better than being part of the bride of Christ!

PERFECT EYESIGHT

"My eyes are ever toward the LORD, for He shall pluck my feet out of the net" (Psalm 25:15).

Penguins have an almost perfectly streamlined body profile that's ideal for chasing fish. In fact, the penguin has the most hydrodynamic body shape ever gauged. A swimming chinstrap penguin seven inches wide slices through the water with less resistance than a quarter-sized pebble. These sleek bodies also help penguins snag prey and escape predators like leopard seals and killer whales. Not only are penguins able to swim faster than a man can run, their efficient shape enables them to travel long distances. Emperor penguins, for instance, have been known to cover almost 1,000 miles on foraging trips that last up to a month, swimming more than 40 miles per day. Not bad for a bird!

Penguins also have other features that make them highly capable fishers. Their tongues are armed with sharp, backward-facing barbs that help prevent prey from escaping. Penguins are also world-class divers. In the 1970s, dive recording devices attached to emperor penguins revealed the penguins were shown to be diving to depths of at least 1,755 feet in search of food. That's astonishing when you consider that is much deeper than a nuclear submarine likes to cruise. It's a mystery how these birds survive at such depths. At 1,200 feet, for instance, the birds are being compressed by 40 times the pressure they feel at the surface.

Penguin's eyes are another marvel. Their pupils can adjust much more than a cat, dilating from a pinhole to the size of a quarter. This enables sharp vision in both the pitch-black depths and at the blinding bright Antarctic surface. This is also an amazing accomplishment, since air and water demand very different kinds of sight. But penguins apparently make the switch smoothly by using fine eye muscles to bend and warp the lens in their eyes to correct for differences between air and water vision. Penguins can even see into the ultraviolet range of the electromagnetic spectrum.

The Bible teaches that a Christian must be able to maintain spiritual vision with their eyes on heaven while still living in the dark world below. Moses warned the Israelites, "Only take heed to yourself, and diligently keep yourself, lest you forget the things your eyes have seen, and lest they depart from your heart all the days of your life. And teach them to your children and your grandchildren" (Deuteronomy 4:9). We will keep our vision clear in the world when we keep our eyes on Christ and the ways He has led us.

"You lust and do not have. You murder and covet and cannot obtain. You fight and war. Yet you do not have because you do not ask. You ask and do not receive, because you ask amiss, that you may spend it on your pleasures" (James 4:2, 3).

Locust swarms have been plaguing mankind for thousands of years. Every continent except Antarctica has been decimated at one time or other by various species of these marauding mobs of grasshoppers. In Africa, a single swarm of desert locusts may contain as many as 18 billion insects, which normally live between three and six months. This adds up to 50,000 tons of locusts that can eat their own weight in vegetation every day. These swarms can cause countries huge losses of agricultural revenue, and may even lead to famine. During plagues, locusts may spread over an enormous area of some 25 million square miles, and travel as much as 120 miles in a day.

In the book of Joel, chapter 2, the prophet describes a plague of locusts: "... a day of clouds and thick darkness, like the morning clouds spread over the mountains. A people come, great and strong ... The land is like the Garden of Eden before them, and behind them a desolate wilderness; surely nothing shall escape them" (verses 2, 3).

So what causes a locust swarm? Normally grasshoppers are harmless and prefer to be alone. However, they occasionally undergo a radical, Jekyll-and-Hyde personality change called gregarization. Researchers discovered that under certain ideal conditions, extraordinary percentages of grasshoppers hatch and congregate in huge numbers, looking for food. The presence of other grasshoppers (could we call it peer pressure?) turns the solitary grasshoppers into gregarious locusts. While the sight and smell of other locusts do play a role in gregarization, the most important stimulus is physical jostling of their leg hairs with other grasshoppers. This apparently incites the swarm behavior, and they travel enormous distances and invade new areas, constantly in search of food, food, and more food.

The Bible teaches that people can also become constant consumers because of peer pressure. James says that humans murder, fight, and war to get what they want. But greed can consume the consumer! "So are the ways of everyone who is greedy for gain; it takes away the life of its owners" (Proverbs 1:19). If we ask Him with the right motives, God is happy to provide the things we need.

BABY GLUE GUNS

"Now you are the body of Christ, and members individually" (1 Corinthians 12:27).

I'm sure if these amazing little creatures were human that child labor laws would never allow these insects to work like they do. Weaver ants in Northern Australia have discovered that babies make good glue guns. Through an amazing orchestra of organization these ants, also known as green tree ants, make their homes out of living leaves. To achieve this, several worker ants will form chains with their bodies to pull leaves together. In the meantime, other ants climb up the tree trunk, carrying their children in their mandibles. These baby ants are actually little grub-like larvae, which they borrow from another existing nest.

Arriving at the construction site, these ants give their babies a gentle squeeze and then point them toward the leaves. Out of the baby comes a glue-like silk. Back and forth they swing their babies across the junction, which basically spot-welds the leaves together. It looks as if a white, silken network is holding the leaves in place. When the building project is finished the ants move into their new football-sized leaf nests. In spite of working the baby ants right out of the cradle, the larvae still manage to develop into healthy adult ants. Through total cooperation of young and old, the weaver ants are able to build a network of sturdy homes.

The social relationship of weaver ants can teach us about the cooperation God designs us to have in our homes and churches. Paul explained, "For as the body is one and has many members, but all the members of that one body, being many, are one body, so also is Christ" (1 Corinthians 12:12). Just as there are different types of weaver ants in a colony (queen, workers, foragers, and even larvae) to help it survive, so God has given different gifts in the church for its success. All parts of the body are important.

"But now indeed there are many members, yet one body. And the eye cannot say to the hand, 'I have no need of you'; nor again the head to the feet, 'I have no need of you'" (verses 20, 21). Like weaver ants, we would be much further ahead in the health of our churches and families if we valued every single member, even the babies!

SCIENCE

"So Solomon answered all her questions;
there was nothing so difficult for the king
that he could not explain it to her."
1 Kings 10:3

LOOKING FOR LIFE

"By the word of the LORD the heavens were made, and all the host of them by the breath of His mouth" (Psalm 33:6).

Mars is fascinating, and people have been captivated by the sight of the red planet since ancient times. The early observers knew it as a "wandering star." By the early 1600s, the telescope had been invented and opened the way to visual exploration of Mars. Galileo discovered that Mars had phases during which it was not completely round. Other observers noted the polar caps and other surface features. Not until the 1970s did a space vehicle successfully land on Mars. The first images sent back were sadly lacking in details.

Curiosity, the current Mars rover, landed on the red planet in 2012 to collect data as part of the Mars Science Laboratory Project. The rover contains recent advancements in technology from Russia, Spain, and the United States and truly is a laboratory on wheels. It is about the size of an SUV and is powered by a radioisotope generator which makes energy from radioactive decay. Strong and agile, it has the ability to crawl over obstacles as high as 25 inches. It uses a seven-foot robotic arm to help carry out experiments.

This rover contains an array of powerful tools. A gas chromatograph, a mass spectrometer, and laser spectrometer compare the different isotopes—variations of elements—found on Mars. Curiosity also has a camera with high definition video capability, a scoop, a drill, and sieving and portioning mechanisms for collecting soil and crushed rock. It uses an X-ray diffraction and fluorescence instrument to identify the types of minerals that are collected.

Curiosity's goal is to explore the region of Gale Crater for about two years. One of the main purposes of its mission is to assess whether the conditions there are, or were, favorable to supporting microbial life.

It's natural for humans to be curious. While there is a place for exploration, it seems that mankind is eager to look in all the wrong places to discover the origin of our planet and the life on it. The Bible states the truth very plainly: "Let all the earth fear the LORD; let all the inhabitants of the world stand in awe of Him. For He spoke, and it was done; He commanded, and it stood fast" (Psalm 33:8, 9). God made everything by His word. Our all-powerful God is the originator of all that exists.

"For thus says the High and Lofty One who inhabits eternity, whose name is Holy: 'I dwell in the high and holy place, with him who has a contrite and humble spirit'" (Isaiah 57:15).

What's the tallest mountain the world? Everyone knows that it is Mount Everest, reaching a height of 29,035 feet. But where do you start measuring Everest? At sea level. So, what if the base of a mountain can be clearly measured and followed below sea level? Then you just might have a mountain on Earth that is taller than Everest. That's why some people would call the dormant volcano Mauna Kea (on the Big Island of Hawaii) the tallest mountain in the world.

Mauna Kea stands 13,796 feet above sea level and is the highest peak in Hawaii. Yet most of this mountain is found below sea level. If measured from its base in the ocean, the total height would rise to 33,500 feet, significantly taller than Everest by 4,465 feet! It probably won't rise any higher since it last erupted about 4,600 years ago. The USGS has marked the Volcanic-Alert Level for this mountain as "Normal."

The mountain is known for having not only a high altitude, but a dry environment combined with a stable airflow. So, it is one of the best places in the world to observe the heavens. In fact, 13 telescopes funded by 11 countries sit on top of Mauna Kea—which makes many people upset about disrupting the "sacred landscape" of this special mountain. In Hawaiian mythology, the peak of Mauna Kea is one of the most sacred spots on the island and is only to be visited by high-ranking tribal chiefs.

It kind of reminds me of the time God called Moses to the top of Mount Sinai. The Lord wanted to meet with Moses and give Him the sacred law. Later, when God thundered the law to the entire nation of Israel, nobody was to even touch the mountain or they would die. "But Moses said to the Lord, 'The people cannot come up to Mount Sinai; for You warned us, saying, 'Set bounds around the mountain and consecrate it'" (Exodus 19:23).

The Lord has given us instructions on how to approach Him. Because God is holy and pure and we are sinful, it is in humility that we are to come before the Lord. We bow low to Him who is on high.

LIKE LIGHTNING

"For as the lightning comes from the east and flashes to the west, so also will the coming of the Son of Man be" (Matthew 24:27).

Very few natural phenomenon's are as impressive as lightning—and it's more common than you might think. Every day 44,000 lightning storms occur worldwide with lightning striking the earth 6,000 times a minute. The idea that lightning never strikes the same place twice is a complete myth. For example, the top of the Empire State Building averages over 20 hits per year. While most lightning occurs during thunderstorms, lightning can also be sparked by volcanic eruptions, intense forest fires, hurricanes, and even snowstorms! The average lightning stroke is three to four miles long, and it can raise the temperature of the immediately surrounding air to 50,000 degrees Fahrenheit. That's hotter than the surface of the sun!

Lightning enthusiasts have given names to several varieties of lightning with special characteristics. A "positive giant" is a lightning strike that hits the ground up to 20 miles away from the thunderstorm. They are often called "a bolt from the blue" because they seem to strike from a clear sky. Originating from the top of the storm cloud, they are especially destructive, with several times the energy of a typical lightning strike. "Crawlers" are a rare and beautiful form of lightning that seems to crawl along the horizon as it zaps from cloud to cloud. Radar has detected crawlers that are 75 miles long!

To estimate your distance from a lightning strike, count the number of seconds between when you see the lightning flash and hear the thunder. Each five second interval is roughly equivalent to one mile in distance. On average, thunder can only be heard over a distance of five or six miles, but at night lightning can be seen 100 miles away.

Perhaps this visibility is why Jesus compared His second coming to a strike of lightning. While we can't set a time for His coming, we'll certainly see it when it happens! Like a lightning storm on a divine scale, it will be an event with incomparable beauty and power. While it is wise to take shelter during earthly lightning storms, the Bible teaches that only the wicked will try to hide from Jesus' coming—the righteous will be anxious to watch the show. That's one display I don't want to miss!

"Jesus said to her, 'I am the resurrection and the life. He who believes in Me, though he may die, he shall live'" (John 11:25).

Evidence continues to mount that the mystery of life can only be explained by intelligent miraculous intervention. In the mid-1800s, when Charles Darwin wrote his theory of evolution, many scientists believed in something called "spontaneous generation." This is the belief that living things, like maggots, can spontaneously arise from non-living material. Many people believed this because they had observed worms and flies apparently springing forth from lifeless material like decaying meat or fruit.

In 1859, the great scientist Louis Pasteur proved the absurdity of spontaneous generation. He demonstrated when the decaying material was insulated from flies and insects, no larva ever appeared. Now more than ever, modern science confirms that life is extremely complex and can only arise from pre-existing life. This is why the best efforts of evolution scientists have not been able to produce a single cell of life even in the controlled environments of expensive high-tech laboratories.

Now with the marvels of 21st-century microscopes, scientists understand that even the simplest and smallest organism is, in effect, a virtual factory containing thousands of exquisitely designed pieces of intricate molecular machinery, far more complicated than the International Space Station. In fact, each microscopic cell is as functionally complex as a small city at rush hour! Now as we delve deeper into the cellular world, science reveals a virtual Lilliputian world of enormous complexity that has pushed the theory of evolution to a breaking point. It is likely that if Charles Darwin was alive today and could see a single cell magnified 50,000 times through electron micrographs, he would utterly renounce his theory as foolishness.

Because it is increasingly obvious there is no scientific explanation for the origin of life on Earth, evolutionists are now playing the alien card. In other words, they are saying life was introduced on our planet by a comet or meteor or by some alien visitors. Of course that creates an out-of-this-world argument that makes it virtually impossible to disprove their fantasy.

In spite of the staggering mountain of evidence that only a miracle could produce life, the modern world refuses to accept the Bible account of Jesus' resurrection. But not only did Jesus have a resurrection, He *is* the Resurrection! Jesus is the Author of life, the Source of life both now and eternally.

June 5 GECKO'S FEET

"...and the two shall become one flesh. This is a great mystery..." (Ephesians 5:31, 32).

Geckos are small, insect-eating lizards that have an almost miraculous ability to scurry up walls and stick to ceilings. Aristotle noted the amazing climbing abilities of geckos in the fourth century B.C. and scientists have wondering ever since how the noisy little creatures could walk up smooth surfaces or even upside down on a polished glass ceiling. They knew it was not suction and they also realized, without any glands on their feet, that geckos cannot produce their own sticky glue.

A team of researchers from the University of California, Berkeley, now think they have solved the riddle. It appears to come from a weak magnetic attraction that molecules have for one another when they are brought very, very close together. Scientists looked at the feet of a gecko through a microscope, which revealed about two million densely packed, fine hairs, or "setae," on each toe. The end of each seta is further subdivided into hundreds to thousands of structures called spatulae. These billion spatulae, which look like broccoli on the tips of the hairs, produce electrical attractions that are pressed so close to a surface they electrically glue the animals down.

The team of biologists and engineers calculated that the combined powerful adhesive force of all the tiny hairs lining the gecko's toes is 10 times greater than the maximum force needed to pull a gecko off the wall. The gecko hairs have also been shown to be self-cleaning, unlike any other known adhesive. The geckos have developed an amazing way of walking with these six million dry adhesive foot-hairs on each foot. They scamper up walls and across ceilings, roll these hairs onto the surface and then peel them off again just like tape, all within a fraction of a second. The attraction of the weak electrical forces allows the gecko to stick to virtually any surface—even polished glass. It has been estimated that if our feet had the same "sticking power" of a gecko foot, each foot could hold about 90 pounds to a glass ceiling.

Man continues to search for better glues, but the Bible speaks of glue that will hold a man and woman together for life. Regarding entering into the sacred marriage covenant, God says, "Therefore a man shall leave his father and mother and be joined [cleave] to his wife, and they shall become one flesh" (Genesis 2:24). With so many marriages falling apart these days, we need to put God back into our relationships to provide the sticking power to stay together.

"Now when He had said these things, He cried with a loud voice, 'Lazarus, come forth!' And he who had died came out bound hand and foot with graveclothes, and his face was wrapped with a cloth. Jesus said to them, 'Loose him, and let him go'" (John 11:43, 44).

We all know that when humans and other mammals freeze, it results in frostbite or death, but God has given some species of snakes and frogs, which live in very cold climates, the ability to survive being frozen! This capacity is not fully understood but is achieved by two possible mechanisms. One is called "freezing tolerance" where the body is able to survive freezing and the destructive ice formation in tissue cells followed by thawing. This is very rare. The other more common condition is "freeze avoidance" or "supercooling." In this process, the body contains substances such as glycerol which acts like a natural antifreeze and prevents ice formation in tissue cells.

For instance, below frozen lakes and ponds, painted turtles can stay submerged and motionless for as long as three months, but they never actually freeze. It's still a mystery how they can survive in this state of suspended animation for so long with zero blood oxygen! Humans, by contrast, begin to suffer irreversible nerve damage if oxygen to the brain is cut off for more than four minutes. Freezing will kill many cold-blooded species. But there are some amphibians and reptiles that hibernate at or near the soil surface where temperatures can drop substantially below the freezing point of their body fluids. These creatures have the amazing ability to endure the freezing of water in extracellular body compartments. In fact, among some frogs, as much as 65% of their total body water may be converted to ice. In this state, they can survive days or weeks of sub-zero conditions. When the spring thaw comes, the spark of life activates their muscles and they appear to return to life as if resurrected.

Since God can design cells that survive freezing, it's easier to believe He can order the molecules of a dead body to be reconstituted. Millions find it difficult to believe in the resurrection. But if you know the power of God in your own life, if you have experienced His re-creative power in your heart, you will be convinced that He truly is the giver of life.

BIOLUMINESCENCE

"You are the light of the world" (Matthew 5:14).

Bioluminescence is an amazing phenomenon in which a chemical reaction in living organisms produces light, without any appreciable heat. This cool light, usually green or blue, results from a chemical reaction involving specialized phosphorus-containing molecules in the organisms. Bioluminescence is found in creatures ranging from the common firefly and glow worm, to some species of bacteria, algae, and fungi. This built-in lighting system can also be found in many invertebrate animals like squid, jellyfish, worms, and crustaceans. In fact, in the dim mid-water, or twilight region of the ocean (between 200 to 1,000 yards deep), 90 percent of all animals, including shrimp, produce light.

This organic light is produced in some ways like the popular luminous glow-sticks. When a glow-stick is snapped, two chemicals mix, react, and create a third substance that gives off light. Marine organisms do essentially the same thing within special organs or cells. One substance, luciferin, is mixed with an enzyme, luciferase, and a new molecule is formed that gives off that glowing blue-green light. Science has barely touched the surface when it comes to replicating this efficient light production. Bioluminescence is used for a large variety of reasons. Some deep-sea fish are equipped with fleshy organs that produce luminescence to which prey is attracted. The flashes emitted by male and female fireflies are used as species-specific signals for mating. It is also an obvious form of communication between species in a dark environment. Light can also be used to repel predators.

The sophisticated squid can control when light is produced, and even its color and intensity. But most sea creatures, like the microscopic drifting algae, have simple light producing systems that are stimulated by water movement. This is what causes the glow in the wake of a large ship passing through the water. During blackout conditions in war, more than one lost pilot has found his way back to the aircraft carrier by following the green glow behind the moving ship.

God's church can be like a moving ship, creating a trail of light to lead others to heaven. Even our own lives should glow with light to attract others to Jesus. "Let your light so shine before men, that they may see your good works and glorify your Father in heaven" (Matthew 5:16).

June 8

"The statutes of the LORD are right, rejoicing the heart; the commandment of the LORD is pure, enlightening the eyes ... sweeter also than honey and the honeycomb" (Psalm 19:8-10).

Have you ever wondered why God called the Promised Land the "land flowing with milk and honey" (Exodus 3:8)? Milk and honey are the classic odd couple for several reasons. Milk is a perfect culture for disease. Left in the open air without being pasteurized or homogenized, milk will instantly begin to separate, spoil, and breed bacteria. On the other hand, honey is the only food that doesn't spoil. It can be used as a food preservative, and it will last practically forever by itself. In fact, crystallized honey that was thousands of years old was found in the pyramids, and it was reconstituted after heating. (I'm sure it tasted a little moldy!) Honey placed on an open wound will help to protect the wound, while milk will promote infection. One is produced by insects and the other by mammals. Milk and honey are also two animal products that can be eaten without killing the creatures from which they come.

Though it is not ideal, a person can live a long time on a diet of whole milk and natural honey with the pollen. However, because of their rich nature, God never intended that either milk or honey become a staple in man's diet; they were considered a treat that should be eaten sparingly. King Solomon counseled, "Have you found honey? Eat only as much as you need, lest you be filled with it and vomit" (Proverbs 25:16).

So why does God use the phrase "milk and honey" over twenty different times as a slogan for the Promised Land? In the Bible, milk and honey are symbols for the sweet, rich truth of God's Word. Isaiah, in the prophecy of the virgin birth, said that Immanuel would eat "Curds and honey ... that He may know to refuse the evil and choose the good" (Isaiah 7:15). The writer of Hebrews compared the "first principles" of God to milk and those who are still "unskilled in the word of righteousness" to babies (Hebrew 5:12-13). Of course, the Psalmist compared God's law to honey, saying God's commandments are even sweeter! Would you like a sweet treat? Dig into God's Word!

STRUNG OUT

"God thunders marvelously with His voice; He does great things which we cannot comprehend" (Job 37:5).

About 600 years before Christ, a Greek natural philosopher named Democritus (*dem-ok-rittus*) said that everything in the world was made up of very tiny particles so small that you couldn't see them with the naked eye. These tiny particles were arranged in various configurations that created the myriad of different things which we can see, such as animals, minerals, vegetables, and even air and water. These particles were so small that they could not be broken down into anything smaller. That's why he named them "atoms," from a Greek word *átomos* that means "uncuttable."

Of course, 2,500 years later that atomic theory became the foundation for all modern physics. And, yes, atoms are indeed small, so small that a mere drop of water contains billions of them. Today scientists understand that atoms are made up of even smaller parts: a nucleus, which is composed of protons and neutrons, and an electron, which spins around the nucleus. To give you a perspective of how small an atomic nucleus is, if an atom were the size of a football stadium, the nucleus would be the size of a marble. Then scientists realized that neutrons and protons were made of even smaller entities, called quarks.

But wait, there's more. Now they theorize that even quarks are made of smaller particles, called strings. How small is a string? *A string is to the size of a proton, as a proton is to the size of our solar system!* Strings are so small it would take a proton smasher a million billion times stronger than any we have now in order to smash the proton hard enough to get to the strings. And, what's more, some scientists now think that these strings might be made of something even smaller.

No wonder the Bible says: "O the depth of the riches both of the wisdom and knowledge of God! How unsearchable are His judgments and His ways past finding out!" (Romans 11:33). There is no question but that little things do matter.

"But to you who fear My name the Sun of Righteousness shall arise with healing in His wings; and you shall go out and grow fat like stall-fed calves" (Malachi 4:2).

Back in 1981, in the blazing desert near Barstow, California, the U. S. Department of Energy finished building what is called a "solar power tower." It looked something like an ocean lighthouse in the middle of a barren desert surrounded by a flock of mirrors. "Solar One," as it was called, was a pilot project constructed to generate electricity using the sun's power. The tower was surrounded by 1,818 dedicated mirrors called heliostats that tracked the sun all day long. Their purpose was to reflect the sunlight to one common focal point—redirecting the equivalent of 600 suns to a target at the top of the tower. This hot spot became superheated, creating steam from water that turned an electric generator and produced 10 megawatts of power every day. In 2007, the U.S. Department of Energy completed a solar-powered unit in Boulder City, Nevada which can produce 64 megawatts of power each day, or about 134,000,000 kilowatt hours per year.

This reminds me of an amazing event recorded by ancient Greek and Roman historians that has been much disputed by modern scholars. They claim that during the siege of Syracuse in 212 B.C., Archimedes, the famous ancient Greek inventor, constructed a sophisticated weapon. Through carefully arranging a combination of mirrors, he focused the magnified light of the sun to burn up an entire Roman fleet. Whenever an enemy warship came within the range of a bow shot, he directed the intense light at the vessel until it ignited. Because highly flammable pitch was used to seal the boats, they were quickly consumed. This incredible event in history has never been disproved, but many have put it to the test.

Recently, a team from MIT tried to recreate the famous "Archimedes Death Ray." With a series of mirrors carefully arranged, they were successful at starting a fire on a ship 75 feet away. Perhaps we should give more credit to ancient technology. After all, someone had to be pretty ingenious to build the pyramids.

The Bible teaches us that Jesus is the Sun of Righteousness, and every Christian is to reflect that light in this dark world. The power generated can save souls!

FLAT EARTH SOCIETY

"Then the Pharisees and Sadducees came, and testing Him asked that He would show them a sign from heaven" (Matthew 16:1).

Have you ever heard of the Flat Earth Society? Even after the launch of thousands of satellites, dozens of manned spaceflights—including multiple trips to the moon, and thousands of ships that have sailed around the globe—there are still educated people who believe the earth is flat. Despite all of the evidence to the contrary, they have their heads firmly planted in the sand and refuse to accept the earth is a sphere.

The International Flat Earth Society, begun in 1956, even has an official logo, showing our planet as flat as a dinner plate. Yes, they're serious. The world model used by the society holds that people live on a disc with the North Pole at the center and a 150-foot high wall of ice at the outer edge. They use the United Nations symbol as evidence for their views. The numbers of members have grown and waned over the years under different presidents of the society.

In one newsletter the aim of the society is stated: "To carefully observe, think freely, rediscover forgotten fact and oppose theoretical dogmatic assumptions. To help establish the United States ... of the world on this flat earth. Replace the science religion with SANITY." Much of the society's early literature focused on interpreting the Bible literally to show the earth is flat. Some headlines from the 70s in the newsletter include: "Whole World Deceived ... Except the Very Elect," "Australia Not Down Under," "The Earth Has No Motion," and "Science Insults Your Intelligence."

The society also took the position that the Apollo Moon landings were a hoax, staged by Hollywood and based on a script by Arthur C. Clarke. Someone once said, "A person convinced against their will is of the same opinion still." So, how much evidence does it take to change a person's mind?

Jesus was regularly confronted with leaders in His day asking Him to prove Himself. "Then some of the scribes and Pharisees answered, saying, 'Teacher, we want to see a sign from You'" (Matthew 12:38). Christ had already shown many signs and miracles. The Scriptures clearly validated His divinity. The bottom line was that nothing would convince these skeptics. They had already made up their minds.

"Oh, send out Your light and Your truth! Let them lead me; let them bring me to Your holy hill and to Your tabernacle" (Psalm 43:3).

No words are adequate to describe the magnificent splendor of the natural phenomenon known as the Aurora Borealis. This spectacular display is also called the Northern or Southern Lights because it is seen predominantly around the polar regions of the earth. The luminous marvel may appear in colors of red, green, yellow, blue, and violet as well as in a variety of forms, such as patches of light, streamers, arcs, rays, or even shimmering draperies.

The Northern Lights have been described since ancient times and are even mentioned in the Old Testament, but only recently have we discovered what causes them. The sun gives off high-energy-charged particles or ions that speed through space at over 500 miles per second. When this stream of plasma, or solar wind, strikes the earth's magnetic field, it is channeled toward the polar regions. When these electrically-charged particles collide with the oxygen and nitrogen atoms in the ionosphere, they start to glow. Oxygen atoms give off a green or brownish-red color, while nitrogen atoms emit blue or red. These may combine to form other colors. This is much the same way that electrons passing through the gases in a neon tube make a neon sign light up. So these spectacular auroras are really God's neon lights.

The brightest auroras seem to coincide with periods of the greatest sunspot activity and with magnetic solar storms. It has been estimated that these solar winds can generate up to 100,000 megawatts of electricity in a three-hour exhibition. Scientists are still studying the solar winds, hoping someday the energy of the auroras might be used for practical purposes. Unfortunately, these intense displays also cause interference with power lines, radio and television broadcasts, and satellite communications.

It is also true that most of the dazzling lights of Earth interrupt our communication with God. It's easy to allow the things of this life to distract us from our relationship with Him. The Bible tells us, "... all that is in the world—the lust of the flesh, the lust of the eyes, and the pride of life—is not of the Father but is of the world" (1 John 2:16). Those dazzling lights can hypnotize, unless we keep our eyes focused on the pure light of Jesus.

SOLAR STORM

"Now the whole world had one language and one speech" (Genesis 11:1).

On September 1, 1859, the Carrington Super Flare, the largest solar flare in modern history, struck the earth, causing the most powerful geomagnetic storm ever recorded. It caused the Northern Lights (Aurora Borealis) to shine so powerfully they were visible around the world, even from the Caribbean Islands. They were so bright over the Rockies that gold miners thought it was morning and got up to prepare breakfast!

Between August 28 and September 2, 1859 many sunspots and solar flares were observed in the sun. British astronomer Richard Carrington observed an unusually large flare just before noon on September 1. This storm, also called the 1859 Solar Superstorm, caused the failure of telegraph lines across Europe and North America. Some operators even received a shock from the incident. Telegraph pylons literally threw sparks and telegraph paper sometimes started on fire. There were some systems that continued to send and receive messages though disconnected from power. By and large, the communication system on which millions depended was fried.

A geomagnetic storm caused by a solar flare temporarily affects the earth's magnetosphere. Ice core samples from Greenland have shown that this phenomenon takes place about once every 500 years. Less severe storms have occurred in 1921 and 1960 and caused widespread radio disruption. In the fall of 2003, there were 17 major solar flares observed that resulted in an extreme radio blackout. It severely damaged a Japanese satellite and the WAAS system of the Federal Aviation Administration was offline for about 30 hours because of the storm. It is believed if a solar flare like the 1859 storm hit the world today it would suddenly wipe out the Internet and modern communications on a global scale.

The Bible says this would not be the first time international communications broke down through a heavenly phenomenon. Some years after Noah's flood, mankind began to migrate to a plain and build a tower "to make a name for ourselves" (Genesis 11:4). "They directly rebelled against God's instructions, and the Lord came down ..." and "confused their language" (v. 7) so they could not communicate. People were then scattered abroad and the Tower of Babel was never completed.

What towers of rebellion do we erect that cut off our communication with heaven?

"As a father pities his children, so the LORD pities those who fear Him" (Psalm 103:13).

Some of the most devoted fathers are found in the animal kingdom. Giant South African bullfrogs are so protective of their young they have been known to attack lions and elephants while defending tadpoles. Strangely enough, an ocean catfish is also a devoted father. He carries the eggs of his young in his mouth until they are ready to be born, which may take up to several weeks. During that time, he can't eat a thing!

Another devoted father is the lumpsucker fish. The lumpsucker gets its name from its pelvic fins, which form a "sucker" that helps the fish attach itself to rocks. Found in the cold Arctic and North Atlantic Oceans, the lumpsucker must reproduce in the warmer water near the shore. The female lays her eggs in a tide pool, and the father lumpsucker attaches to the rocks in order to stay behind and guard the eggs while the tide is out. Staying behind in the shallow water is dangerous, however, since it exposes the father fish to gulls and other predators.

Male seahorses are so devoted that they are pregnant instead of the female: the female places her eggs into the male's special pouch, where he fertilizes them and carries them for the next several weeks. He even develops a large, pregnant belly as the little seahorses grow. After two to four weeks of pregnancy, the father gives birth to an average of 100 to 200 young.

The red fox is also a wonderful father. Immediately after the birth of his litter, he works to provide the nursing mother with food. But, once the pups are three months old, it's time for them to learn to find food for themselves. Fox fathers have been observed burying food near the den in order to teach their pups to forage. One biologist observed a male fox playing an ambush game with his pups, as if to teach them how to escape from the predatory coyotes.

The devotion of these animal fathers to their young is just a small reflection of our Heavenly Father's devotion to His children. He loved us so much that He gave Jesus to die in our place, and now He calls all of us His sons and daughters: "Behold what manner of love the Father has bestowed on us, that we should be called children of God!" (1 John 3:1).

BOMB WITH FATHER'S NAME

"Fear not, for I have redeemed you; I have called you by your name; you are Mine" (Isaiah 43:1).

During the Second World War, a couple of young American GI's, stationed in Australia, were driving their jeep along an airfield when a Japanese squadron came over intent on bombing everything around the military target. Hearing the planes approach, the young airmen jumped out of their jeep, and dove for cover into a nearby ditch. Within seconds, one of the Japanese planes dropped a bomb that made a direct hit and destroyed the Jeep they were driving.

After the attack was over, the two young men crawled out of the ditch, shaken but unharmed, and walked over to inspect the damage. Poking around the smoldering Jeep, they found a large piece of shrapnel from the bomb wedged into the seat where the driver had been sitting. Picking it up, they saw clearly stenciled on the metal shard the name "Ray Ewing." The GI who had been driving the Jeep gave a gasp of astonishment. His name was Curtis Ewing, and his father's name was Ray Ewing. How did that piece of bomb shrapnel with his father's name get there?

Before the war, Ray Ewing sold his old Plymouth as scrap. He previously had stenciled his name on the engine block. The car, like other steel and iron junk discarded by Americans, found its way to Japan, a major market for old metal at the time. After the war began, all this steel went into weapons. The shrapnel that struck his seat evidently came from the Plymouth and literally had his father's name on it!

The Bible speaks of God's people having the Heavenly Father's name on them—obviously not in the form of a destructive bomb, but as a seal of His love and protection. John writes about this when he says, "Then I saw another angel ascending from the east, having the seal of the living God. And he cried with a loud voice to the four angels to whom it was granted to harm the earth and the sea, saying, 'Do not harm the earth, the sea, or the trees till we have sealed the servants of our God on their foreheads'" (Revelation 7:2, 3). The devil has a bomb with your name on it to destroy you. But God wants to mark you with His name and save you forever.

"No weapon formed against you shall prosper" (Isaiah 54:17).

Electronic metal detectors stationed at airports and government buildings which check for concealed weapons are not exactly new. Centuries ago one of the royal palaces in Chang-an, the ancient Chinese capital now known as Sian, had gates made of lodestone. Now lodestone is a powerful natural magnet also known as magnetite, which is a crystallized iron mineral with a black metallic luster. There are different theories on how lodestone becomes magnetized. One idea is that the strong magnetic fields surrounding lightning bolts change magnetite since lodestones are mostly found at the surface of our planet and are not buried deep in the earth.

Who discovered the magnetic properties of lodestone? The Greek philosopher Thales of Miletus makes a reference to lodestone in the 6th century. However, the American astronomer John Carlson found an artifact in Central America that indicates that the Olmec people may have used geomagnetic lodestone in compasses earlier than 1,000 B.C. The earliest Chinese literary reference to lodestone is found in the 4th century B.C. in a book called *Book of the Devil Valley Master*—not a work I'm interested in reading!

Why were the gates of the Chang-an royal palaces made of lodestone? If a would-be assassin came through these palace gates with a concealed dagger, the lodestone would pull at the hidden iron weapon like an invisible hand. Then the startled criminal would instinctively reach for the weapon. There were trained guards stationed by the magic gate who were carefully watching every movement, who would then spring forward and search the suspect. Because the superstitious people believed the ruler had special powers to read their hearts, few ever entertained thoughts of murder.

The Bible describes the gates of heaven (the New Jerusalem) to be very special. There are 12 gates, each made with a single pearl (Revelation 21:21). These gates will never be shut since there is no night in heaven (v. 25). But more than that, nothing will enter those gates that will put heaven at risk. "But there shall by no means enter it anything that defiles, or causes an abomination or a lie, but only those who are written in the Lamb's Book of Life" (v. 27). God has created His own security detector system to keep the entire Universe safe. And the Lord doesn't need lodestone to help!

FROM RED TO WHITE

"'Come now, and let us reason together,' says the LORD, 'Though your sins are like scarlet, they shall be as white as snow; though they are red like crimson, they shall be as wool'" (Isaiah 1:18).

Among the ancient Aztecs, red dye was considered more valuable than gold. That's because to acquire this bright red colorant it required the labor of hundreds of subjects to comb the desert in search of its source—the tiny female cochineal beetle. A pound of this rare extract required about a million insects. (Equally amazing, back in the days of the Roman Empire, a pound of royal purple dye required four million mollusks.)

After the arrival of Cortez in the 1500s, the Spaniards traded for the dried remains of this insect as a colorant that dyed items a bright crimson. This red cochineal dye was stronger than anything ever before known—and created a brilliant color that no one could duplicate.

Soon after its discovery, Europeans used it for fabrics, especially wool, and in handicrafts, rugs, and tapestries, in addition to using it as a food coloring. In the years that followed, Michelangelo used it in paintings, and the British and the Canadians used it for their red coats. It is thought that the first U.S. flag made by Betsy Ross had cochineal red stripes.

Today, less expensive synthetic dyes have replaced it, but it is still used as a natural, FDA- approved coloring for food, drugs, and cosmetics. In fact, strange as it may sound, some brands of fruit juice use this red bug as a colorant. The story of cochineal red gets even more fascinating. The Spanish traders never told the Europeans of its insect origin. Because the little beetles looked so much like seeds, they were traded as grain. For almost 300 years, the Spaniards perpetuated the notion that "dyed in the grain" was their special process for this permanent crimson dye that never faded. And that's where we get the English term "ingrained."

Did you know the Bible teaches that you can wash red stains with red blood and get white? God wants to wash away the crimson stains of our sins with the precious blood of Jesus and make our hearts "as white as snow." His Word promises, "But if we walk in the light as He is in the light, we have fellowship with one another, and the blood of Jesus Christ His Son cleanses us from all sin" (1 John 1:7).

"Then I stood on the sand of the sea. And I saw a beast rising up out of the sea, having seven heads and ten horns, and on his horns ten crowns, and on his heads a blasphemous name" (Revelation 13:1).

For many people just saying the number "666" conjures up ominous images of secret occult ceremonies and the evil powers mentioned in Bible prophecy. Others have refused phone numbers, license plates, and credit cards containing the numbers 666 because of their fearful superstitions. There is even a very long word describing this phobia. It's known as hexakosioihexekontahexaphobia.

Highway 666 running from Gallup, New Mexico to Monticello, Utah was nicknamed the "Devil's Highway" because of the Scripture that identifies that number with the beast of Revelation. This satanic connotation, combined with an unusually high fatality rate, convinced some people the highway was cursed. The problem was compounded because Satanists were chronically stealing the highway signs as souvenirs. So in 2003 the U.S. Highway Department decided to re-number Highway 666 as U.S. Route 491.

We don't have to be afraid of the number 666. It is the natural number sequentially following 665 and preceding 667. Nevertheless, mathematically 666 is a very unique number. It is an abundant number. It is the sum of the first 36 natural numbers (1 + 2 + 3 + 4 up to 36 = 666). Yes, that means if you add up all 36 numbers on a roulette wheel the resulting total is "666". While going to the casino will cost you dearly, you will not automatically receive the mark of the beast. The number 666 is also a triangular number since 36 is both square and triangular, 12 + 12 + 12 = 36. And of course 222 times three is 666.

The number 666 is also the sum of the squares of the first seven prime numbers (i.e. 22 + 32 + 52 + 72 + 112 + 132 + 172 = 666). If you add up the first six Roman numerals, IVXLCD, the total is, you guessed it, 666. Even organic molecules are based on carbon-12, with 6 protons and 6 neutrons in the nucleus, surrounded by 6 electrons.

With all this in mind it makes one wonder why the book of Revelation says, "Here is wisdom. Let him who has understanding calculate the number of the beast, for it is the number of a man: His number is 666" (Revelation 13:18). It obviously helps us to identify a power that is against God.

JOSEPH LISTER

"He who touches the dead body of anyone shall be unclean seven days. He shall purify himself with the water on the third day and on the seventh day; then he will be clean" (Numbers 19:11, 12).

One hundred and forty years ago, almost 50 percent of the patients undergoing major surgery died from infection due largely to the filthy conditions. Doctors were bewildered why 80 percent more women died giving birth in hospitals compared to those who had their babies at home. Back then, doctors wore bloody aprons and went from patient to patient without washing their hands or instruments. Patients with minor wounds often died from infection or blood poisoning transmitted by the doctor.

In the 1860s, a deeply religious English surgeon, Joseph Lister, was disturbed about the staggering number of patients dying from infection. He read in the Bible where God told the Israelites to wash after contact with the sick or a dead body. Based on this and Louis Pasteur's discoveries, Lister recognized germs as the likely source of infection. He suggested surgeons dress cleanly, wash their hands, and sterilize instruments before operating. He insisted that the operating room be kept clean. He also developed a method for preventing infection during an operation by treating wounds with an antiseptic.

At first Lister was regarded as eccentric, and nurses resented the extra work caused by his obsession with cleanliness. Then there was a period of significant mocking and resistance from his peers. Lister, a shy but determined man, was firm in his purpose. He humbly believed he was directed and inspired by God in this endeavor. In spite of all the opposition that he faced, he never gave up.

As the mocking went on, everyone began to notice a change. The deaths from blood poisoning, infection, and gangrene were greatly reduced in Joseph Lister's hospital ward in Glasgow. Eventually, British and American hospitals saw the benefits and gradually adopted the sterile procedures promoted by Dr. Lister. Before he died, Lister's services to medicine were recognized and he was awarded a knighthood. Louis Pasteur described Lister as one of the greatest men of the 19th century.

It's amazing how the world has been transformed by applying the simple rules of sanitation found in the Bible. But did you know there are many other biblical secrets of health the world is neglecting? The God who formed us knows the principles of caring for the bodies He has given us. He lovingly shares that wisdom with us in His Word.

"And if you are Christ's, then you are Abraham's seed, and heirs according to the promise" (Galatians 3:29).

For as long as anyone can remember the Lemba tribe in Zimbabwe, South Africa has claimed to descend from Hebrew ancestors. The Lemba people look like regular Africans but have some very Jewish customs. For example they abstain from eating pork and other unclean foods. They are monotheistic, keep the Sabbath, and shun idolatry. They wear yarmulke-like caps and prayer shawls. They conduct religious animal sacrifice, and mark their gravestones with a Star of David. They even circumcise their male children, which is uncommon in Zimbabwe.

For years people laughed at the Lemba claims of Jewish heritage. But now, according to a recent BBC report, the legend has been backed up by science. British scientists have succeeded in proving the 80,000 member tribe in Zimbabwe descended from Jewish ancestors. The scientists conducted DNA tests on a large sample of the Lemba people, which confirmed Semitic origins dating back more than 2,600 years. In fact, members of the priestly clan of the Lemba were discovered to have a unique genetic element only found among the Jewish priestly line known as Cohen. In addition, the report says the Lemba have a sacred prayer language that combines Hebrew and Arabic.

So how did their Jewish ancestors get there? The tribe's oral tradition says that centuries ago a small group of men fled the Holy Land, making a 3,000 mile journey from Israel to southern Africa. They carried with them a replica of the Ark and took African wives along the way. This story does coincide with the disappearance of the real Ark around 586 B.C., just before Nebuchadnezzar's destruction of the Jewish temple. Despite their "Jewish roots," many of the tribe people are now Christians. One Lemba pastor explained, "Christianity is my religion and Judaism is my culture."

Finding a genetic connection with Jewish ancestors is fun and interesting but will not guarantee you an automatic ticket to heaven. Paul, the Apostle to the Gentiles, explained to the Roman Christians, "Or is He the God of the Jews only? Is He not also the God of the Gentiles? Yes, of the Gentiles also, since there is one God who will justify the circumcised by faith and the uncircumcised through faith" (Romans 3:29, 30). We may all be God's children through faith.

MESSAGES FROM SPACE

"Then I saw another angel flying in the midst of heaven, having the everlasting gospel to preach to those who dwell on the earth—to every nation, tribe, tongue, and people" (Revelation 14:6).

Along the coastal plains of Puerto Rico is a giant aluminum "ear" that measures 1,000 feet across. Located 10 miles south of the coastal city of Arecibo, this enormous space-age radio telescope dish is aimed into the sky, listening. Built in 1963 by Cornell University at a cost of nine million dollars, the Arecibo Observatory dish is the largest curved focusing antenna on Earth. It also has the largest electromagnetic-wave gathering capacity.

The colossal collecting bowl was constructed inside a natural crater left by a huge sinkhole. The dish is made of nearly 40,000 aluminum panels, which are supported by steel cables. The vast antenna surface covers 18 acres—the same area as 26 football fields! Operated by the National Science Foundation, the facility requires a full-time staff of 140 people. Most of the staff are technicians and engineers, and nearly 30 are astronomers from all over the world.

When the huge telescope switches to a radar mode, it beams out a power signal of one million watts toward planets, moons, asteroids, and comets. The faint echo of the signal bouncing off the astronomical targets is collected by the huge dish and then amplified, allowing scientists to create scanner-like images and maps of the object. One of the other goals of this tremendous radio telescope is SETI—the Search for Extra-Terrestrial Intelligence. For over 45 years, radio astronomers at the Arecibo Observatory have been studying the radio signals emanating from the cosmos. Yet in nearly half a century of listening, SETI has not identified a single radio signal that seems to come from extra-terrestrial intelligence.

Nevertheless, messages have already come from space! In Revelation 14, we read of three angels flying through the sky, calling out in loud voices to the inhabitants of the earth. The word "angel" simply means "messenger," so these angels represent God's three-part message to the world at the end of time. Not only should these messages be carefully understood and heeded, but God's end-time church will have a part in spreading these messages. And once they are preached to "every nation," Jesus will return and take His children to their new home—where we won't need the Arecibo Observatory any longer!

"I know your works, that you are neither cold nor hot. I could wish you were cold or hot" (Revelation 3:15).

Our earth is filled with environmental extremes—high mountains, deep valleys, dripping wet jungles, burning dry deserts, and frozen tundra. People roam the world looking for the perfect climate that is ideal for vacation or retirement, where it not too hot or too cold. Since everyone talks about the weather you might be wondering, "Where are the hottest and coldest places on Earth?"

As for the hottest place, most people guess Death Valley in California. If you did you're a close second. On July 10, 1913 temperatures in Death Valley got up to 134 degrees F. But the highest temperature ever measured was recorded in Libya on Sept. 13, 1922 in 'Aziziya. It reached 136 degrees F and that was five feet above the ground in the shade! In fact, there's a good chance on the day this record-breaking temperature was recorded in 1922 there were other desert places that were even hotter, but most humans don't inhabit the hottest places on Earth so there are no weather stations or sensors to record the extreme temperatures.

So, where is the coldest place on Earth? If you guessed Antarctica you are right. In fact Antarctica is so cold that the warmest temperature ever recorded was only 58° F in Hope Bay. Strangely enough, Antarctica is also one of the driest places on Earth even though it is surrounded by one-third of the world's fresh water. Of course it's all frozen water. In case you are still wondering, the coldest temperature ever measured on Earth was on July 21, 1983 at the Vostok Station in Antarctica—they recorded minus 129 degrees F. Burr!

So what did Jesus mean when He said He would prefer we were spiritually hot or cold rather than lukewarm? Christ was so adamant about this that He said, "So then, because you are lukewarm, and neither cold nor hot, I will vomit you out of My mouth" (Revelation 3:16). That's pretty strong language.

Nothing seems to be more repulsive to God than lukewarm Christians, people who act and talk like they are followers of Christ, but do not live the life of Jesus. Not only do their lives represent a hypocritical façade, but they present this false life to the world, leading others astray. The Lord can work with a hot or cold Christian. But it is difficult to motivate the lukewarm, apathetic person who feels no need of change. For them, the temperature leading them to destruction is just right.

June 23

THE GREATEST PHYSICIAN

"He said to them, 'You will surely say this proverb to Me, "Physician, heal yourself!"'" (Luke 4:23).

Dr. Evan O'Neil Kane was the chief surgeon at Kane Summit Hospital in New York City. By the time he was 60, he had been practicing surgery for 37 years and was especially interested in anesthetics. Dr. Kane practiced back in the early part of the 20th century when the only kind of anesthetic used was general in nature, meaning the patient had to be completely knocked out. This often resulted in serious complications. Patients were sometimes left paralyzed and occasionally they died. Dr. Kane believed it was possible to operate on patients who only received a local anesthetic by simply numbing the smaller area that needed surgery. He wanted to somehow prove his point by finding a willing subject who would allow him try this procedure using local anesthetic. Finally he found a person who was agreeable to help him experiment.

The patient needed his appendix removed, so he was quickly scheduled for surgery. On Tuesday morning, February 15, 1921, the patient was prepared and rolled into the operating room. Kane had performed over 4,000 appendectomies so he easily performed the initial incision, and clamped the blood vessels while he located the appendix. He then skillfully removed it as he had done many times before. Through it all the patient only experienced minor pain. He recuperated quickly and was released from the hospital two days later.

Dr. Kane had proved his point. It was a milestone in medical history to demonstrate that a person could be operated on under local anesthetic while still awake. By the way, I should tell you that the surgeon and patient were one and the same. Dr. Kane operated on himself and removed his own appendix!

Perhaps you have heard the proverb, 'Physician, heal yourself!' Jesus spoke these words—and He did heal Himself! He told His disciples, "Therefore My Father loves Me, because I lay down My life that I may take it again. No one takes it from Me, but I lay it down of Myself. I have power to lay it down, and I have power to take it again. This command I have received from My Father" (John 10:17, 18). Jesus, the greatest Physician of all, laid down His life and took it again. He did this out of His intense love for us, to bring us healing.

"This is the message which we have heard from Him and declare to you, that God is light and in Him is no darkness at all" (1 John 1:5).

A "Black Hole" is a unique phenomenon in space caused by objects that are so concentrated, massive, and dense that their immense gravitational pull does not even allow light to escape. A star with a mass ten times the mass of the Sun would become a black hole if it were compressed to 60 miles or less in diameter.

To better understand, if you could throw a rock just hard enough to escape our planet's field of gravity that speed would be called the "escape velocity." Now imagine an object with a required escape velocity greater than the speed of light–which would be 186,000 miles per second. Since nothing can go faster than light, nothing could escape the object's gravitational pull. Even a beam of light would be pulled back and would be unable to escape a black hole!

The gravitational force is so strong in a black hole that laws of classical physics no longer apply, and astronomers must use Einstein's theory of relativity to explain the behavior of light and matter under such strong gravitational forces. By 1999 astronomers had found only about a dozen potential black holes in our observable universe. You might be wondering, what causes matter to become so concentrated as to produce a black hole? It occurs when a star dies and the core continues to collapse, forming this super mass that will not allow light to escape.

The Bible teaches us that when Lucifer fell he imploded like a fallen star and refused to allow the light of truth to escape his domain. Lucifer (whose name meant 'light bearer'), became Satan (whose name means 'enemy'). He lost his position of being the highest angel in heaven to become the lowest being on Earth.

Like a black hole that sucks light and creates darkness, Satan wants to pull us away from the bright truth of God's Word. But the Lord provides a gravitational pull through the love of Christ, giving us an escape velocity that redeems us from sin. "He has delivered us from the power of darkness and conveyed us into the kingdom of the Son of His love" (Colossians 1:13). Now, "You are all sons of light and sons of the day. We are not of the night nor of darkness" (1 Thessalonians 5:5).

TRADING THE TRUTH FOR A LIE

"Therefore God also gave them up to uncleanness, in the lusts of their hearts, to dishonor their bodies among themselves, who exchanged the truth of God for the lie, and worshiped and served the creature rather than the Creator, who is blessed forever. Amen" (Romans 1:24, 25).

The fourth-brightest object in the sky is Jupiter, which is two and a half times larger than all the other planets, satellites, asteroids, and comets of our solar system combined. Yet, in spite of Jupiter's immense size, it has the shortest day. Although it has a circumference of 280,000 miles, compared with Earth's 25,000, Jupiter manages to make one turn in nine hours and fifty-five minutes.

Jupiter's Great Red Spot, one of the planet's most recognizable features, is 25,000 miles wide. The spot may be the vortex of a hurricane that has been whirling for at least seven centuries. It rotates differently than the rest of Jupiter's atmosphere, and has a variable speed of rotation.

Jupiter doesn't have a solid surface but is composed mainly of the gases hydrogen and helium. This jumbo planet has over 60 known satellites, most of them small. Its four biggest moons—Ganymede, Io, Europa, and Callisto—are large enough that Galileo spotted them with his telescope in the early 17th century. Ganymede is the largest moon in our solar system, even surpassing Mercury in size. And Io is well known for its energetic volcanoes.

Although not as distinct as those of Saturn, Jupiter also has rings. The *Voyager I* space probe first observed these rings in 1979. These are believed to have formed, at least in part, from dust particles ejected from some of Jupiter's moons as a result of high-velocity impacts.

In Roman mythology, Jupiter (or Jove), was the ruler of the gods. Originally the god of the sky and king of heaven, Jupiter was worshiped as the god of rain, thunder, and lightning. As the protector of Rome, he was called Jupiter Optimus Maximus ("the best and greatest").

What was it that led the great civilizations like Rome and Greece to worship the creation instead of the Creator? The Bible records that they made all sorts of wrong choices in their lives. Since the true God would not approve of their self-destructive lifestyle, they invented gods who would allow them to live as they pleased—in lust and dishonor. Scripture sadly confirms that they traded the truth for a lie.

"For I know the thoughts that I think toward you, says the Lord, thoughts of peace and not of evil, to give you a future and a hope" (Jeremiah 29:11).

Sir Isaac Newton was one of the greatest scientists who ever lived. It was Newtonian physics that contributed most to man landing on the moon. More than any other scientist, Newton was responsible for laying the foundation for classical mechanics, optics, and even mathematics. As with many famous people, some of the stories about Newton have grown with time. For instance, Voltaire says that Newton was walking among his family's apple orchard when he saw an apple fall from a tree, giving him help in formulating the theory of universal gravitation. Newton says he was actually staring out a window in his house when he saw an apple fall from a tree.

Some other interesting details about his life: Isaac's mother remarried after his father's death and he so disliked his stepfather that he threatened, as a teenager, to burn their house down with them inside. His interest in school grew as a result of a conflict with a school bully who threatened young Isaac. He was smaller than the bully but decided to fight back and won. He then determined to beat the bully in scholastics as well. He later attended college and, because of the Great Plague, went home for a time while the school was closed down. It was during this two-year period that he developed his theories on calculus, optics, and the law of gravitation. In his later life he became interested in the interpretation of the Bible and even wrote on the prophecies of Daniel and Revelation.

What many don't know is that baby Isaac wasn't expected to live. He was born prematurely on Christmas Day in 1642. Isaac was named after his father, who died three months before he was born. He was so small his mother thought he might not survive. She said he was tiny and could fit into a quart mug jar!

There are many stories in Scripture of babies who almost didn't live. Perhaps the greatest is the life of Jesus. Herod was angry when the wise men from the East did not return from paying a visit to the Christ-child, and he later ordered that all the children less than two years of age in Bethlehem be slaughtered. But God intervened and Joseph was warned in a dream to escape to Egypt.

God had plans for Isaac Newton and he lived to be one of the greatest God-fearing scientists of all time.

HEAVENLY IMMUNITY

"Therefore, as through one man's offense judgment came to all men, resulting in condemnation, even so through one Man's righteous act the free gift came to all men, resulting in justification of life" (Romans 5:18).

Around the year 1927, in Ghana, West Africa, a blood specimen was taken from a native man named Asibi, who was very sick with yellow fever. From that blood sample, a strain of the yellow fever virus, now known as the Asibi strain, was identified. After years of testing and experimentation with monkeys, mice, and chick embryos, that mild strain of yellow fever was developed into a vaccine. Asibi recovered, but all the vaccine manufactured since 1927 derives from the original strain of virus obtained from this humble native. Carried down to the present day from one laboratory to another, through repeated cultures, and exponential multiplication, it has offered yellow fever immunity to millions of people around the world. Through the creative imagination of science, the blood of one man in West Africa has been made to prolong and improve life among the whole human race.

However, in order to receive a benefit from a vaccine, a person must personally take the vaccine shot. They can acknowledge the existence of the vaccine, understand how it works, rejoice in the marvel of its provision, and praise the man who provided it, but unless an individual actually receives it, it will be of no personal benefit.

Immunity from the penalty of sin works in a very similar manner. The blood of just one Man, Jesus, provides salvation to every person: "through one Man's righteous act the free gift came to all men, resulting in justification of life" (Romans 5:18). We can acknowledge that God exists, understand the finer points of doctrine, be amazed at God's provision, and praise Jesus for it, but unless we actually accept it by faith, it will do us no good. On the other hand, while vaccine supplies may at times run low, the grace of God is unlimited—everyone who asks for salvation can be sure of receiving it! Moreover, while it was infinitely expensive to obtain, it is provided free of cost: "being justified *freely* by His grace through the redemption that is in Christ Jesus" (Romans 3:24). In addition, the only side effect of God's vaccine is a new life in Christ! Won't you accept His heavenly immunity?

"My flesh longs for You in a dry and thirsty land where there is no water" (Psalm 63:1).

We've all heard about a person's "dry sense of humor" or a "dry and boring sermon" (of course, not at my church!), but what is the driest place on Earth? The Valley of the Moon (Valle de la Luna) in Chile probably qualifies as one of the greatest places of an extreme lack of moisture. Some areas of this desert have not received a single drop of rain in hundreds of years.

Located in the Atacama Desert of Chile, this strange land area has various stone and sand formations carved by wind and water. It actually has quite a variety of color, but most of it looks strangely like the surface of the moon. (Interestingly, the moon is one million times drier than the infamous Gobi Desert!) The Valley of the Moon has many dry lake beds with salt giving a white covering layer in many areas. It was declared a Nature Sanctuary in 1982 for its great natural beauty and strange lunar landscape. Scientists actually tested a prototype of a Mars rover in the valley. People actually enjoy traveling to visit this valley. Photographers capture its breathtaking views at dusk or in moonlight.

The Valley of the Moon is part of the greater Atacama Desert, which is known to be one of the harshest and driest regions on Earth. The whole desert area is located on the leeward side of the Chilean Coast Range, so very little water from the Pacific Ocean reaches the desert. The high Andes Mountains also block clouds which might bring rain from the Amazon Basin. The average rainfall in this area is 0.04 inches per year. Some weather stations in Atacama have never received rain. The Atacama is also the location of the 2010 Copiapo Mining Accident which trapped 33 miners 2,300 feet underground. They were successfully rescued after 69 days.

God's blessing on His people is compared to water on dry ground and on thirsty people. "For I will pour water on him who is thirsty, and floods on the dry ground; I will pour My Spirit on your descendents, and My blessing on your offspring" (Isaiah 44:3). Jesus fulfilled this promise when He came as the Water of Life. If you find your life dry and boring, it is time to ask for the drenching of God's Spirit on your heart.

NEUTRON STARS

"For we do not wrestle against flesh and blood, but against principalities, against powers, against the rulers of the darkness of this age, against spiritual hosts of wickedness in the heavenly places" (Ephesians 6:12).

Neutron stars are one of the mysterious wonders of the universe. They are created when an aging star swells to a red giant and explodes in a supernova, leaving behind a cooling core that forms into an ultra dense neutron star.

Earth rotates once every 24 hours, but neutron stars can rotate at fifty times per second, and their insides are hundreds of times hotter than the core of the Sun. A neutron star is so solid that one teaspoon of its material would contain more mass than 900 times the mass of the Great Pyramid of Giza. To put it another way, this density is approximately equivalent to the mass of the entire human population on Earth compressed to the size of a sugar cube. The resulting gravitational force of a neutron star is so powerful that if an object were to fall from a height of one yard it would instantly hit the surface, traveling at around 4,500,000 miles per hour.

When the largest stars explode in a supernova, they can implode and collapse till they form something even more dense than a neutron star—a black hole. The center of a black hole is called a singularity. It is believed at the center all its mass is squeezed into a single point where both time and space stop. Within a certain distance of the singularity, the gravitational pull is so strong that nothing—not even light—can escape.

Did you know the Bible speaks of another great star that imploded? Isaiah 14:12 says, "How you are fallen from heaven, O Lucifer, son of the morning! How you are cut down to the ground, you who weakened the nations!" And Revelation explains, "His tail drew a third of the stars of heaven and threw them to the earth" (Revelation 12:4). The devil and his angels gave in to sin and lost their place in heaven.

Sin is the blackest hole of all. It pulls us in, and we can't escape it in our own power. But Jesus has defeated sin, and it will lose its hold on us if we cling to our Savior.

"When I consider Your heavens, the work of Your fingers, the moon and the stars, which You have ordained, what is man that You are mindful of him..." (Psalm 8:3, 4).

For the better part of recorded history, Earth was thought to be the stationary center of the universe and the ancient wise men believed there were only 5,119 stars. The constellations were named and filled with colorful legends. Without a telescope the stars seemed to be just twinkling points of light that move across the night sky. Now we know when we look at the heavens that what we once thought were just single stars are often really a gigantic spiral of stars called galaxies.

A galaxy is like a colossal island in space made up of gas, dust, and millions of stars. On clear nights we see the spiral edge of our own galaxy called the Milky Way. Our Sun is just one small star in a pinwheel containing about a hundred billion blazing suns aligned in the form of a disk. And that's not counting the planets that could be orbiting around these stars. Recent research indicates that there are billions of galaxies in our universe.

A few years ago the Hubble Telescope took a picture of a small spot of sky near the Big Dipper. To give you a better idea of how big this area was, it was about the size of a dime held 75 feet away. In that tiny dot of sky scientists counted over 1,500 galaxies! Take that number times the volume of space in every direction and you would calculate that there are hundreds of billions of galaxies with billions of stars in each galaxy. Wow!

The distance of these galaxies are measured in light years. Keep in mind one light year is the distance you would travel if you could ride a beam of light 186,000 miles per second for 365 days. Our home, the Milky Way, is some 30,000 light-years across. That means you would have to travel the speed of light 30,000 years to cross just our galaxy! And you still wouldn't have even left our front yard. For example, if you wanted to visit the Andromeda Galaxy you would have to travel over the speed of light for over 2.4 million years.

When we consider the God who made all of this, we can only say, "How Great Thou Art!" It is almost inconceivable that the God who made the infinite cosmos wants to dwell with us. "What is man that You are mindful of him, and the son of man that You visit him?" (Psalm 8:4).

U.S. History

"Now all these things happened to them as examples, and they were written for our admonition, upon whom the ends of the ages have come."
1 Corinthians 10:11

"... seek, and you will find ..." (Matthew 7:7).

After Stan Caffy and his wife Linda married, as part of combining households, she urged him to clean out the garage. Stan, an admitted pack rat, was reluctant to part with a reprint of the Declaration of Independence he kept hanging in his shop. He bought the yellowed document about 10 years earlier at a yard sale for a couple of dollars. Linda won the clean-out-the-garage debate, and so in March 2006 she rolled up the old parchment and took it, along with an antique table, and donated them to a local thrift store.

Fast forward one year. Michael Sparks was visiting the Music City Thrift Shop in Nashville, where he bought a candle holder, a set of salt and pepper shakers, and a yellowed print of the Declaration of Independence. Sparks, a music equipment technician, also figured the document was a worthless modern reprint, so he paid the asking price of $2.48 and headed home.

After looking over the document for a few days, he wondered if it might be older than he thought. So he clicked around on the Internet to do some research and soon realized, based on a number of clues, he had purchased one of only 200 official copies of the Declaration of Independence! Copies of the original document were commissioned by John Quincy Adams in 1820, when he was secretary of state. They were printed by William Stone in 1823. Of those 200 early copies, only 35 had been found intact. Michael now had number 36.

It took a year for Sparks to have the print authenticated and preserved. Then he put it up for auction in Burlington, North Carolina. The bidding opened at $125,000 and climbed to the sale price of $477,650. Stan Caffey confessed he felt like the village idiot when he read in the paper the document he had hanging in his garage for 10 years was this rare copy of the Declaration of Independence.

This is not the only time a precious national document has been misplaced or unrealized. During the reign of King Josiah in Judah, a lost parchment was found. "Now when they brought out the money that was brought into the house of the LORD, Hilkiah the priest found the Book of the Law of the LORD given by Moses. Then Hilkiah answered and said to Shaphan the scribe, 'I have found the Book of the Law in the house of the LORD'" (2 Chronicles 34:14, 15). Finding this precious document brought about a national revival. Have you discovered the authentic truth in the Word lately?

"Stand fast therefore in the liberty by which Christ has made us free" (Galatians 5:1).

Perhaps no one name in American history is more associated with the Fourth of July than Thomas Jefferson, probably because he penned the immortal Declaration of Independence. Thomas Jefferson and the second president, John Adams, were good friends in their youth, but in later years political disagreements separated them. In fact, after John Adams left the White House to be replaced by Jefferson, they never saw each other again. They were eventually reconciled in the last 14 years of their lives, and they exchanged over 150 warm and affectionate letters.

John Adams died at the ripe age of 91, and his last words were, "Thomas Jefferson still lives." But had Jefferson known this, he would have said to Adams in his dry manor, "Wrong as usual." You see, at the age of 83, during his last hours in his home in Monticello, Virginia, Jefferson passed in and out of consciousness. In July 1826, just a few hours before Adams died surrounded by friends and family, Thomas Jefferson died. His final words were, "Is it the Fourth?" They said, "Yes." Then he breathed his last. Amazingly they both died on the same day, July 4th, which also happened to be the 50th anniversary of the Declaration of Independence. They were two of the last three surviving signers of that historic document.

Have you ever heard about the Day of Atonement? It was a lot like an independence day for the Jewish people. The annual occassion took place on the 10th day of the seventh month and was the most solemn day of the year for Jews. On this day all the sins of the preceding year were disposed of in the ceremony of the cleansing of the earthly sanctuary. It represented a day of cleansing from sin and reconciliation with God. Everyone was to "afflict their souls"—in other words, search their hearts and repent of all known sin. God instructed Moses, "For on that day the priest shall make atonement for you, to cleanse you, that you may be clean from all your sins before the Lord" (Leviticus 16:30). When we are cleansed from sin, we are set free from its power over us. It truly is a day of independence!

AS THE DAYS OF NOAH

"The earth also was corrupt before God, and the earth was filled with violence" (Genesis 6:11).

The American Civil War was over, and the *S.S. Sultana* was heading home, overloaded with recently liberated prisoners of war anxious to see their families. Even though the *Sultana* had a legal capacity to carry only 376 passengers, there were more than 2,300 people crammed on the sagging decks. With six times more passengers than she had been designed to carry, there was barely room for standing. To make matters worse, the *Sultana* had been neglecting proper maintenance.

These ominous factors came together during the homeward journey. At 2:00 a.m., three of the ship's four boilers exploded, destroying a good portion of the ship and sending hundreds of soldiers flying into the icy water. Some of the dazed men were able to cling to floating wreckage until other boats arrived to rescue them, but most were not so fortunate. Hot coals scattered by the blast caught the rest of the ship on fire, forcing many to choose between burning on the ship and drowning in the cold water.

When it was over, an estimated 1,600 of the 2,300 passengers perished, and many others were badly wounded. In fact, more people died in the *Sultana* disaster than the infamous *Titanic*. The *Sultana* might be listed as one of the greatest ocean disasters, except the *Sultana* never went to sea. It sank in the Mississippi River—only 150 yards from land. Moreover, news of this terrible steamboat tragedy was relegated to the newspapers' back pages: it was April 27, 1865, and the War Between the States was just ending. The recent assassination of Abraham Lincoln, the killing of John Wilkes Booth, and the deaths of more than 600,000 soldiers in America's bloodiest war filled the papers. Surrounded by violence, the nation had become desensitized to death. The deaths of 1,600 Union soldiers on their way home from Confederate prisons did not seem like front-page news.

Could we become numb to violence again? Jesus predicted that the end of time would be "as the days of Noah were" (Matthew 24:37). Though the earth will be filled with wickedness and violence, mankind will be preoccupied. But God's people will not be numb to the wickedness: they will "sigh and cry over all the abominations" (Ezekiel 9:4). May God grant us Christ's tender heart so that the wickedness and violence of the world will never become our normal!

"Which of the prophets did your fathers not persecute? And they killed those who foretold the coming of the Just One, of whom you now have become the betrayers and murderers" (Acts 7:52).

Assassinations of presidents are a tragedy for a nation. The injustice of one person changing the course of the country is felt by millions. People have wondered, "What if Lincoln had not died? Would the nation's Civil War wounds have healed faster?" Interestingly, four U.S. Presidents have been assassinated while in office (Lincoln, Garfield, McKinley, and Kennedy), but there have actually been at least a dozen failed assassination attempts on either sitting or past United States Presidents.

Did you know that President Harry Truman was almost assassinated while he temporarily was staying at the Blair House, while the White House was undergoing renovations? On November 1, 1950, two Puerto Rican nationalists, Griselio Torresola and Oscar Collazo, tried to shoot Truman from the street outside the residence. A White House policeman was mortally wounded, but Leslie Coffelt shot and killed Torresola before dying. Collazo was found guilty of murder and sentenced to death, but Truman commuted his sentence to life in prison. The president was actually taking a nap when he heard shooting and jumped up to look out his bedroom window to see what was happening.

Three years before Kennedy was killed in Dallas, Texas, the president-elect was almost a victim of an assassination plan by a retired postal worker. The family was vacationing in Florida in December 1960 when Richard Paul Pavlick loaded his car with dynamite. He intended to ram the president-elect's limousine. But when Pavlick saw Kennedy's wife and two children, he changed his mind. Secret Service agents, who had been investigating Pavlick's strange behavior, arrested him a couple days later.

The Bible actually records several instances of people being assassinated, often rulers or kings. For instance, Eglon (king of Moab) was assassinated by Ehud, a deliverer raised up by the Lord during the time of the Judges (see Judges 3:15-22). King Joash was assassinated by his servants (see 2 Kings 12:20). And Amnon was assassinated at the command of his brother Absalom (see 2 Samuel 13:28, 29). Of course, the greatest murder of a King was when the Jewish leaders unjustly condemned Christ to death on a cross.

THE BIG DISCOUNT

"For God will bring every work into judgment, including every secret thing, whether good or evil" (Ecclesiastes 12:14).

Shoplifting is a rampant problem in the United States, but can you imagine someone stealing from a charity event? Timothy Clark did just that. What's more, it was an event at a Walmart store in Maryland, attended by 50 police officers! He allegedly tried to steal over $500 in video game products while the law enforcement officers were holding a "Shop with a Cop" program for the community.

The store's security unit caught Clark cutting open and shoving video games and accessories into his shirt. They immediately contacted police who were ... right there! The suspect had no chance to run out the door since officers were all over the place. Authorities found 26 PlayStation and Xbox games, two controllers, and various other video game accessories. Strangely enough, the purpose of the charity event was to "build good relations between law enforcement and local youth."

Shoplifting, also called "boosting" and "five-finger discount," is one of the most common property crimes in the United States. Most shoplifters are amateurs, but there are those who make a living at it. Retailers say that on average they lose about 0.6 percent of their inventory to shoplifters. One figure says shoplifting costs businesses about $25 million a day. Some businesses use closed-circuit television to catch thieves. Others pay personnel to watch people, some using uniformed guards to discourage shoplifting activity.

The devil, in one sense, has shoplifted planet Earth. He has stolen the innocence, the purity, and the safety of our world when he successfully tempted Eve to eat the forbidden fruit, telling her, "You will not surely die" (Genesis 3:4). Shoplifters believe that they will not get caught and that there are no consequences to their actions. But the Bible teaches that God sees all. "And there is no creature hidden from His sight, but all things are naked and open to the eyes of Him to whom we must give account" (Hebrews 4:13). The Lord's surveillance system is without fault.

"Therefore I love thy commandments above gold; yea, above fine gold" (Psalm 119:127).

The United States Bullion Depository, located on the Fort Knox Army post site, is said to be the most impregnable vault on Earth. The virtual fortress is built out of granite, concrete, and steel, sealed behind a 22-ton door, protected by a 109,000-acre U.S. military base, and watched over day and night by Army units with tanks, heavy artillery, and Apache helicopter gunships at their disposal. It is ringed by fences and multiple alarms, and few people have been inside the highly classified Fort Knox bunker. The depository is a top-secret facility. Visitors are not permitted, and exceptions are not made. It is easy to see why the depository's nickname, Fort Knox, has become synonymous with total security and inspired expressions like "It's locked up tighter than Fort Knox."

The U.S. Mint says that the Fort Knox vault contains 147.2 million troy ounces of gold, stacked in bars measuring 7 inches long, 3 and 5/8 inches wide, and 1 and 3/4 inches thick. Each bar weighs approximately 400 ounces, or 27 and 1/2 pounds. In today's market that's about $238 billion. If all the pure gold were put in a single cube, it would measure 20.3 feet on a side. In total, the depository holds 2.5 percent of all the gold ever refined.

Since its construction in 1937, the treasures locked inside Fort Knox have included more than gold. During the uncertainties of World War II, other national treasures from Europe and the U.S. were also protected in the vault. These included the United States Constitution, the Declaration of Independence, the Gettysburg Address, the Magna Carta, and three volumes of the Gutenberg Bible. Yes, Bibles! Those priceless copies of the Scriptures may have been the most valuable bullion ever stored in Fort Knox.

How valuable are the Scriptures in your life? King David wrote that he loved God's commandments more than fine gold, while King Solomon said, "How much better to get wisdom than gold!" (Proverbs 16:16). If David, called a man after God's own heart, and Solomon, the wisest king in history, valued God's Word so highly, shouldn't we make it our top priority as well?

LIBRARY OF CONGRESS

"Sanctify them by Your truth. Your word is truth" (John 17:17).

According to Guinness World Records, the largest library in the world is none other than the U.S. Library of Congress, which contains more than 151.8 million items. The library, first built in 1800, is now housed in four separate buildings in Washington, D.C. (as well as the Packard Campus in Culpeper, Virginia), and contains 838 miles of bookshelves that currently hold over 34 million books. In addition to books, this mega library houses 3.3 million recordings, 13.4 million photographs, 5.4 million maps, 6.5 million pieces of sheet music, and 66.6 million manuscripts. To top things off, the inventory grows by approximately 10,000 new items each working day.

The library was originally housed in the United States Capitol for most of the 1800s. Unfortunately, many books were lost during the War of 1812 when the British troops set fire to the Capitol building. About 3,000 volumes were lost. A few years later Thomas Jefferson sold his entire personal collection of books to the library (6,487). After the Civil War a separate building was constructed. Even though the library is open to the public, you cannot check out a book unless you are a library employee, member of Congress, a Supreme Court Justice, or some other high-ranking government official.

One of the interesting collections in the Library of Congress is the "incunabula" books, which are books or pamphlets printed before the year 1501, of which 5,600 are housed. The Library of Congress actually houses one of three rare copies of the Gutenberg Bible (printed in 1455 on vellum). In spite of the massive variety of books found in the Library of Congress, only one book has always stayed on the top of bestseller lists– the Bible. Paul says, "All Scripture is given by inspiration of God ..." (2 Timothy 3:16). No other book housed in any library can compare with the Bible. Buildings and books may burn, but "You shall keep them [the words of the Lord], O Lord, You shall preserve them from this generation forever" (Psalm 12:7).

"Now the word of the LORD came to Jonah the son of Amittai, saying, 'Arise, go to Nineveh, that great city, and cry out against it; for their wickedness has come up before Me'" (Jonah 1:1).

Because there are so many pigeons in the world, we sometimes fail to appreciate these remarkable birds. Pigeons mate for life, make excellent parents, and have been known to live over 30 years! The racing pigeon is the marathon athlete of the air. It has the ability to beat its wings up to 10 times per second, and maintain a heart rate of 600 beats per minute for up to 16 hours without rest, while flying 50 to 60 mph! In addition, it can fly nearly straight up.

These skills have made homing pigeons a valuable communication tool for carrying messages in wartime. During WWII, 98 percent of pigeon missions were successful, often despite enemy fire. A famous WWI homing pigeon named Cher Ami delivered a vital message—the location of the famous Lost Battalion. The mission of that pigeon alone is credited with saving nearly 200 human lives! Cher Ami was awarded a medal for his heroic service. He died from his extensive battle wounds.

The French, Swiss, Israeli, and Chinese armies still use homing pigeons today because their messaging is not affected by electronic jamming. In the 17th century, King George of England decreed all pigeon droppings to be property of the Crown—and the lofts were policed to enforce the law! The reason? Pigeon manure was used in making gunpowder.

Advanced studies at the University of Montana and at Harvard have concluded: "Pound for pound, the pigeon is one of the smartest, most physically adept creatures in the animal kingdom." They have been taught to use tools and were found to retain hundreds of objects or images in their memory! Knowing this, the pharmaceutical industry in Australia employed pigeons trained to identify anomalies in pills on a moving conveyor. The birds did outstanding work, but authorities soon ended the practice, fearing backlash from the perception that pigeons were more efficient workers than people. And, of course, they would work for chicken feed!

Did you know there was a prophet in the Bible whose name was pigeon? Jonah's name means "dove" or "pigeon." Unlike the faithful homing pigeons, Jonah tried to flee from duty. God mercifully spared his life, and Jonah went on to preach God's message of warning, which saved an entire city from destruction.

LINCOLN AND KENNEDY

"[T]here is nothing new under the sun" (Ecclesiastes 1:9).

Have you ever noticed some uncanny similarities between Presidents Abraham Lincoln and John F. Kennedy?

Abraham Lincoln was elected to Congress in 1846.
John F. Kennedy was elected to Congress in 1946.
Lincoln was elected President in 1860.
Kennedy was elected President in 1960.
Lincoln's wife lost a child while living in the White House.
Kennedy's wife lost a child while living in the White House.
Lincoln had a secretary named Kennedy who urged him not to go to the theater.
Kennedy had a secretary named Lincoln who urged him not to go to Dallas.
Both Lincoln and Kennedy were shot in the back of the head in the presence of their wives.
Lincoln was shot in the Ford's Theatre.
Kennedy was shot in a Lincoln made by Ford.
The names Lincoln and Kennedy each contain seven letters.
Both Lincoln and Kennedy were killed on a Friday and were assassinated by Southerners.
Lincoln's assassin was known by three names, John Wilkes Booth, comprised of fifteen letters.
Kennedy's assassin was known by three names, Lee Harvey Oswald, comprised of fifteen letters.
Booth shot Lincoln in a theater and fled to a warehouse.
Oswald shot Kennedy from a warehouse and fled to a theater.
Both Oswald and Booth were killed before being brought to trial.
Lincoln's successor was Andrew Johnson, born in 1808.
Kennedy's successor was Lyndon Johnson, born in 1908.

Are these coincidences? Probably, but did you know that the Bible teaches that history does have a tendency to repeat itself? Solomon once wrote, "That which has been is what will be, that which is done is what will be done, and there is nothing new under the sun. Is there anything of which it may be said, 'See, this is new'? It has already been in ancient times before us" (Ecclesiastes 1:9, 10).

"And in that day His feet will stand on the Mount of Olives, which faces Jerusalem on the east. And the Mount of Olives shall be split in two, from east to west, making a very large valley; half of the mountain shall move toward the north and half of it toward the south" (Zechariah 14:4).

In the early afternoon on April 9, 1865, Wilmer McLean stood on the front porch of his two-story brick house. General Robert E. Lee arrived first on horseback that day, accompanied by Colonel Charles Marshall. Wil greeted the two Confederate officers and invited them into his parlor. At about 1:30 p.m., General Ulysses S. Grant arrived on horseback. Among his Union officers were Major General George Armstrong Custer, and Captain Robert Todd Lincoln, son of President Lincoln.

For about an hour and a half, General Lee and General Grant talked until they finally agreed on the terms of surrender for the Confederate Army of Northern Virginia, which, in effect, ended the long, bloody Civil War. While Lee and Grant were conferring, Wil McLean waited outside the house where, we can only surmise, he must have thought about the very strange hand of fate that brought this historic event to his home.

Meeting in Wil's home was especially unusual because, at the outset of the Civil War in 1861, Wil was a farmer living in northern Virginia with his family. The beginning of the war had struck very close to home. In fact, a cannon ball from the first battle landed in his kitchen. Concerned for the safety of his family, Wil moved them from the war zone to central Virginia and eventually bought a home at Appomattox Court House. The first battle of the Civil War, known as the First Battle of Bull Run, fought on July 21, 1861, took place on Wil McLean's farm. In one of the strangest and most unusual twists of fate, the Civil War started in Wilmer McLean's back yard in 1861 and ended in his parlor in 1865!

In similar fashion, the Bible teaches that the last spot that Jesus' feet touched the earth when He left—the Mount of Olives—will be the very spot He places them when He arrives with the New Jerusalem to establish His eternal kingdom of peace on this earth.

July 13

BIZARRE LAWS

"Oh, how I love Your law! It is my meditation all the day" (Psalm 119:97).

There are some pretty strange laws on the books of different states and cities in the United States. For instance, did you know it is against the law to:

- Doze off under a hair dryer in Florida.
- Play hopscotch on Sunday in Missouri.
- Hunt camels in Arizona.
- Insert a penny in your ear in Hawaii.
- Transport an ice cream cone in your pocket in Kentucky.
- Tie a giraffe to a telephone pole in Atlanta.
- Catch mice without a license in Cleveland.
- Whistle underwater in Vermont.
- Put a skunk in your boss's desk in Michigan.
- Bathe less than once a year in Kentucky.

And if those don't make you wonder, here are a few more interesting law facts. Did you know the Chico, California City Council enacted a ban on nuclear weapons, setting a $500 fine for anyone detonating one within city limits? Did you know there are about two million laws in the United States? If a man could review them at the rate of two a day, he could be qualified to act as a law-abiding citizen in about 6,000 years. In ancient Rome all the laws were ordered by Emperor Justinian to be compiled during the 6th century A.D. With 16 assistants, Tribonian came up with 2,000 volumes after three years.

Here's a final strange history fact on law. According to Robert Ripley, the French statesman Ferdinand Flocon was the only man who succeeded in making a poem out of the law. He took the whole French Civil Code, with its 2,281 articles, statues, annotations, and amendments, and converted them into an immaculate poem of 120,000 words—perfect in rhyme and meter. He did it ostensibly to make the many laws more palatable!

Someone once said the more lawless a people, the more laws they will need. Yet in 10 simple principles any child could learn, God was able to summarize the whole duty of man toward God and his neighbor. But how sad it is that many pastors are teaching the Ten Commandments still have too many laws. The Bible says, "For whoever shall keep the whole law, and yet stumble in one point, he is guilty of all" (James 2:10). Every commandment of God is important. None of them are bizarre or to be set aside.

"Then Moses stretched out his hand over the sea; and the Lord caused the sea to go back by a strong east wind all that night, and made the sea into dry land, and the waters were divided" (Exodus 14:21).

When people think of the London Bridge, they generally think of fog and cold, not cactus and sand! But today, the 140-year-old London Bridge resides in the middle of Lake Havasu City, Arizona. In 1963, chainsaw mogul and entrepreneur Robert McCulloch purchased 8.5 square miles of property in western Arizona and promised to develop it into Lake Havasu City. But McCulloch had a dilemma—how would he interest home buyers in relocating to a small town in the remote Arizona desert?

At the same time, the London Bridge was sinking into the clay of the Thames River. The famous bridge, built in 1831, was the victim of its own immense weight. London officials decided they'd have to replace the old bridge. Instead of simply tearing it down, they decided to sell it! In 1968, McCulloch purchased the bridge for $2.46 million—the highest price ever paid for an antique at that time.

Over the next three years, workers disassembled the five arches of the 1,000-foot-long and 50-foot-wide bridge in London. Each of the granite bricks were numbered to help with reassembly. Then, the granite bricks were shipped to America, where they were hauled to the brand new Lake Havasu City. The pieces were reassembled over land, and then a canal was dug out underneath, turning a peninsula into an island. The reconstruction cost an additional $7 million and the bridge was ready for business in 1971.

The unique purchase paid off for McCulloch. Pretty soon, tourists started showing up and eventually folks who came to see the bridge bought homes and decided to stay. Today, hundreds of thousands of people come every year to see the oddly placed landmark. By 2010 Lake Havasu City had grown to a respectable 52,000 residents.

Usually a bridge is built to cross a water barrier. In this case, a water barrier was dug in the desert to accommodate a multi-million-dollar bridge to nowhere! The Bible tells of a different sort of bridge in the desert. When the Israelites found themselves trapped by the Egyptian army on one side and the sea on the other, God miraculously created a dry-land bridge through the Red Sea. Truly, there is no dilemma too difficult for God!

July 15 A CUP OF WATER

"For whoever gives you a cup of water to drink in My name, because you belong to Christ, assuredly, I say to you, he will by no means lose his reward" (Mark 9:41).

After the first day of fierce fighting in the Civil War battle of Fredericksburg, hundreds of Union soldiers lay crying on the battlefield, wounded and bleeding. All through the night, and most of the next day, artillery fire prevented their relief. Yet all that time their agonized cries went up, "Water! Water!" Finally, a noble Southern sergeant, Richard Kirkland, rose above his love of life and told his General Kershaw, "I can't stand this any longer! Those poor souls out there have been praying and crying all night and all day, and it's more than I can bear! I ask your permission to go and give them water."

"But you know," said the general, "that as soon as you show yourself to the enemy, you will be shot."

"Yes, sir, I know it," he answered, "but to carry a little comfort to those poor dying men, I'm willing to run the risk!"

The general hesitated, but his heart was also touched with sympathy over the suffering soldiers. "Kirkland, it's sending you to your death, but I cannot oppose such a motive as yours. I hope God will protect you. Go."

So the brave soldier, furnished with a supply of water, stepped over the stone rampart and began his work of Christlike mercy. Wondering eyes watched as he knelt by the nearest sufferer, tenderly raised his head, and held the refreshing cup to his parched lips. Every soldier in the Union line understood his tender mission, and not a single shot was fired. For over an hour, one after another of the crying, wounded, and dying was given refreshing drink, had his cramped or mangled limbs straightened, his head cushioned on his knapsack, and was covered with his coat or blanket as tenderly as though by his own mother.

It's the same on life's great battlefield, where souls are crying and dying from the fearful effects of sin. They are thirsty for the water of life, with no one to reach out to them the refreshing draft they so crave, except the One who stepped over the ramparts of heaven and came down to risk His all. Christ, on the cross of Calvary, rescued them from their sins by giving to them "a fountain of water springing up into everlasting life" (John 4:14).

"[K]nowing that you were not redeemed with corruptible things ... but with the precious blood of Christ" (1 Peter 1:18, 19).

During World War II, a young Marine lay badly wounded in a military hospital on a South Pacific island. Shrapnel had ripped through his chest, and unless he received a series of blood transfusions at once the boy was doomed to die. But the type of blood required turned out to be very rare. No donors were immediately available and hope for saving the Marine was fading quickly.

Then a medic discovered a supply of the rare blood in a recent shipment from the United States. The transfusion was given and the marine lived. When he recovered, the grateful young man asked about the donor. She turned out to be a Boston woman, and he wrote to thank her for the gift of her life-saving blood. Then he wrote to his father in Kentucky and told him about his miraculous experience. His father recognized the donor's name. She was his long-lost sister and the Marine's own aunt! The wounded man had never known his aunt, but her donation of rare blood, which matched his, saved his life in the faraway Pacific.

Thousands of lives are saved every year because of blood donations. Every day someone needs blood that comes from donors. Only 3 out of 100 people in the United States have donated blood. The term "blood bank" was created to describe the collection and storage of blood donations to be used for transfusions. Careful guidelines and screening of blood lowers the risk of infection or incompatibility of different blood types. Blood doesn't simply go from a donor to a recipient without being carefully tracked, tested, processed, stored, and transported.

Did you know, friends, that there is a unique type of blood that is still saving thousands today? The Bible says, "But God demonstrates His own love toward us, in that while we were still sinners, Christ died for us. Much more then, having now been justified by His blood, we shall be saved from wrath through Him" (Romans 5:8, 9). The greatest blood donation was made by Jesus Christ when He shed His blood on Calvary to redeem us from sin.

DOORSTOP OF GOLD

"Jesus said to them, 'Have you never read in the Scriptures: "The stone which the builders rejected has become the chief cornerstone. This was the Lord's doing, and it is marvelous in our eyes"?'" (Matthew 21:42).

One Sunday in 1799, Conrad Reed, the 12-year-old son of a German immigrant, was playing hooky from church. While fishing with his siblings in a creek on his father's farm, he spotted an interesting object in the creek—"a yellow substance shining in the water"—and decided to lug it home. The 17-pound rock, about the shape and size of an iron, was actually a gold nugget. Because of its unusual weight, the family used the huge nugget as a doorstop for three years.

Then in 1802, Conrad's father, John Reed, took the nugget to a jeweler in Fayetteville, North Carolina. The jeweler told Reed that they had been tripping over a hunk of gold for the last three years and offered to refine it for him. When Reed returned, the jeweler had turned the 17-pound nugget into a gold bar six or eight inches long. The jeweler offered to buy it, allowing Reed to name the price. Still not realizing the value of the gold, Reed sold it to the jeweler for a mere $3.50. Of course, the gold was actually worth a thousand times that modest sum.

The Bible teaches that millions of others have tripped over a priceless gem as well, unaware of the riches within their reach. For example, Jewish tradition says that when Solomon's temple was built, the cornerstone, or capstone, was pushed aside unrecognized. When it was finally needed, the builders sent word to the masons asking for it, only to find it had already been delivered. When the chief priests and Jewish elders challenged Jesus' authority, He reminded them of this story: "The stone which the builders rejected has become the chief cornerstone" (Psalm 118:22). Though rejected by the Jewish leaders, Jesus is the cornerstone on which the Christian church was built—He is the only way to obtain salvation!

Thankfully, John Reed's story still has a happy ending—he eventually mined the rest of the creek bed on his farm and became a very wealthy man. When we recognize the riches of salvation that are available to us in Christ Jesus, our story can have a happy ending as well!

"Command those who are rich in this present age not to be haughty, nor to trust in uncertain riches but in the living God" (1 Timothy 6:17).

It's really a game of chance. Gambling is impacting more and more people all over the world. And it's winning at the expense of other people. It is addictive. It creates false hopes. And it violates principles of Christian stewardship. Families break down because of gambling, and society at large loses. It doesn't really generate income; it takes away income and gives it to a few winners who don't really need it.

In 1998, people in the U.S. lost $60 billion in legal gambling. This amount has increased every year for over two decades—often at double-digit rates. And there is no end in sight. The most amazing fact about gambling in America is that over the past 25 years the United States has been transformed from a nation in which legalized gambling was rare and limited, into one in which such activity is common and growing.

Today, all but two states have some form of legalized gambling. Lotteries have been established in 37 states (including the District of Columbia), with more states poised to follow. Indian casinos operate in every region of the country. From cruise ships to riverboats to western mining towns, gambling sites continue to proliferate. Internet and telephone gambling is legalized in more states, so an increasingly large share of the public can now place a bet without ever leaving home. Universally available, "round-the-clock" gambling may soon be a reality.

In Australia, the state of New South Wales has more than 10 percent of the poker machines in the whole world. It is not uncommon to see housewives playing the slot machine while shelling peas after their mid-morning shopping. Many problem gamblers have separated or divorced while others have committed suicide after losing heavily on the poker machine. The problem is that gambling now accounts for up to 10 percent of the income of many states. And who wants to kill the goose that lays golden eggs?

If you really want to "win big," don't gamble. Christians don't put their hope in money. Our hope is in the soon coming of our Lord, Jesus Christ. Make a sure choice with absolute results every time—choose to follow Christ. The payout is something you don't need to make a bet on.

A PLACE OF REFUGE

"Therefore He is also able to save to the uttermost those who come to God through Him, since He always lives to make intercession for them" (Hebrews 7:25).

On the Big Island of Hawaii there are ancient ruins of a village with a large oblong temple enclosure inside a huge L-shaped wall. The wall was constructed from thousands of lava rocks around 1550. It measures roughly 1,000 feet long by 700 feet wide. It is about 20 feet thick at the base and up to 20 feet high. This temple village was called Pu'uhonua, or the place of refuge. The massive wall separated the Pu'uhonua from the home of the chief.

In centuries past, even until the early 19th century, Hawaiians were forced to keep strict laws or pay a terrible penalty. They could not walk in the footsteps of a chief, touch any of his belongings, or get too close to him. There was even a law forbidding their shadows from touching the royal grounds. When a native Hawaiian committed *kapu* and broke one of the sacred laws, he was sentenced to death unless he fled to the place of refuge where the k*ahuna pule* or "big priest" lived. Once inside the walls, he or she was safe and protected from judgment. No one was allowed to harm the person who sought refuge there. Later, the "big priest" would perform a rite of purification for the guilty party. They could then be declared forgiven; they were once again innocent and were free to begin a new life.

Cities of refuge are mentioned in the Bible as well. God told Moses to "appoint cities to be cities of refuge for you, that the manslayer who kills any person accidentally may flee there. They shall be cities of refuge for you from the avenger" (Numbers 35:11, 12). People who had caused someone else's death by accident could run to a city of refuge and be protected while they awaited trial. No one was allowed to harm them as long as they stayed within the boundaries of the city of refuge.

Since we all incur guilt in our lives, we all need a place of refuge. That place is in the arms of Jesus. He says, "All that the Father gives Me will come to Me, and the one who comes to Me I will by no means cast out" (John 6:37). In Christ we receive refuge, forgiveness, and unending love.

"Cast out this bondwoman and her son; for the son of this bondwoman shall not be heir ..." (Genesis 21:10).

Distinguished scientist and chemist James Macie was born in France in 1765, the illegitimate son of a British duke. With Jim's father out of the picture, the boy's devoted mother, also a woman of wealth, returned to England with him to fight for her son's official acceptance. Because of the laws of 18th-century England, she barely managed to have Jim declared a British citizen. Because of his illegitimacy, James Macie's other basic rights were restricted at every turn. Perhaps what hurt Jim most was that he could never hold the title of his real father, the 1st Duke of Northumberland.

Knowing these restrictions as he grew up, Jim Macie determined to excel in other ways. In 1786, Jim graduated from Pembroke College with honors, and shortly thereafter launched himself upon a glowing scientific career. Many sophisticated experiments and published results later, Jim became a respected scientist. While his scientific colleagues, with less talent, would be knighted for their accomplishments, Jim was denied that honor simply because he was born illegitimate. It is no wonder that James Macie was hurt. He vowed never to marry, realizing that the stigma of a tarnished heritage would be passed to his children.

So, James Macie conceived of a plan that would serve as a final rejection of the country that had rejected him. When Jim passed away in 1829 he died a very wealthy man, with no heirs who could claim his vast fortune. In his will he sought revenge on England by leaving all of his money to a newly formed country that England called illegitimate—the United States of America. Jim had never even visited the United States. Yet by willing his fortune to us he disinherited England as it had disinherited him.

In his will he specified that his money was to be used for the foundation of an institute that would increase and diffuse knowledge among men and that would perpetuate his true family name that was denied him at birth—the name Smithson. And thus, the gift James Smithson gave us, which represents the torment of illegitimacy, is today our country's most magnificent storehouse of culture and scientific accomplishment. I expect you have heard of the Smithsonian Institution.

Did you know the United States is also mentioned in prophecy? "Then I saw another beast coming up out of the earth, and he had two horns like a lamb and spoke like a dragon" (Revelation 13:11).

POSTPONED BURIAL

"Then Joseph took an oath from the children of Israel, saying, 'God will surely visit you, and you shall carry up my bones from here'" (Genesis 50:25).

In 1803, John Colter was hired by Lewis and Clark to join them on their epic expedition because of his amazing ability to hunt wild game. One time, while trapping in an area inhabited by the Blackfoot Indians, Colter was captured. They stripped him and asked if he could run. He told the natives he was slower than a snail. Actually he was one of the fastest runners in the entire Kentucky region. The Blackfoot warriors signaled him to run for his life. He loped out slow for about 200 yards, and then broke into a hard sprint. After about two miles of running, there was only one brave still with him. Colter stopped so fast, the warrior almost tripped over him. He quickly dispatched the warrior and evaded the other Blackfoot.

Somewhere along the way to the trading post, he discovered the Yellowstone region. When he described the geysers and marvels he had seen, the other trappers teased him, calling the region "Colter's Hell." Incredibly, he escaped another capture and later returned to Missouri, where he married and settled down to farm. Colter was a neighbor to Daniel Boone. When the United States declared war on Great Britain in 1812, Colter enlisted and fought under Daniel Boone's son, Nathan.

Sadly, a year later he died from illness while serving his country. His remains were shipped back to Missouri. However, his wife was too poor to provide a proper burial, so she left him lying "in state" in their cabin and moved away to her brother's home. Amazingly, the body of this forgotten hero continued to lie in the remote cabin for the next 114 years, as the house slowly disintegrated around him.

This champion of the Lewis and Clark expedition and pioneer of Yellowstone was nearly lost to history until 1926, when the ruins of the cabin were discovered with his bones, as well as a leather pouch portraying his name. Afterward, his remains were gathered and buried with honors on a bluff in New Haven that overlooks the Missouri River.

Did you know the Bible talks about a hero that postponed burial for over 200 years after his death? Joseph made the children of Israel promise to carry his bones back to the Promised Land. His faith was rock solid that God would one day lead His people out of Egypt and take them on a cross-country expedition that would lead them home.

"Lord, how often shall my brother sin against me, and I forgive him?" (Matthew 18:21).

Did you know that in the 1800s, in the United States, you could be thrown in jail for not paying your debts? Unfortunately, those jailed not only had to pay back their debt, they also had to pay for their imprisonment! Many debtors died while serving time, unable to work or secure funds to get out. The Annapolis jail where many debtors were held was described as "a place of death and torment to many unfortunate people." In 1766 the same jail was described as "so filthy and nasty that it is exceedingly nauseating." Some prisoners were held under these conditions for debts as little as 50 cents.

One of our country's more important citizens, and a signer of the Declaration of Independence, landed in a debtors' prison—Robert Morris. He actually helped finance the American Revolution. In late 1776, George Washington called upon Morris to raise cash to fight the British. Washington had thousands of troops without clothing, food, guns, or ammunition. At the time there was no U.S. Treasury to turn to for help. The Continental Army was in a state of severe deprivation. Morris loaned $10,000 of his own money to the government, who used the cash for provisions for the desperate troops at Valley Forge. Those soldiers went on to win the Battle of Trenton and, in turn, changed the course of the war.

Indeed, Robert Morris became the chief financier of the American Revolution. In 1781 he was even appointed by Congress as the first superintendent of finance. Sadly, because of some bad land investments, he was arrested for debt in 1798 and confined to a prison in Philadelphia. Not until 1802, with the passage of the national bankruptcy law, was he liberated. It's hard to believe a man who lent money to George Washington to fight the Revolutionary War would later be cast into a debtors' prison by the country he helped to liberate!

Amazingly, Jesus tells a parable of a man who did something similar to a friend. When a king kindly released a servant who owed him a lot of money, this same servant turned around and demanded his friend pay him a couple of bucks or he would throw him into prison. When the king heard about this unforgiving servant, he was pretty upset. "And his master was angry, and delivered him to the torturers until he should pay all that was due to him" (Matthew 18:34). The story illustrates the generosity of God toward us and how we, in turn, should be forgiving toward others.

July 23 MIRACLE FUEL

"And my God shall supply all your need according to His riches in glory by Christ Jesus" (Philippians 4:19).

During World War II an American bomber ran out of gas over the Pacific and was forced to land on a Japanese-held island. Without fuel to get away, the crew knew they would be soon captured and resigned themselves to this looming fate. But the bomber was also carrying a chaplain. A firm believer, he refused to give up hope and prayed to God for deliverance. Though the crew respected his faith, they did not share his optimism. But the next day they changed their minds. Early that morning, just before dawn, one of the crew was awakened suddenly with a strong feeling that he should go down and walk on the beach. There he found, bobbing on the incoming waves, a huge drum of aviation gasoline. With a shout, the astonished airman awakened the rest of the amazed crew, who rushed down to the water, pulled the big drum ashore, and transferred the miraculous gift of gas to the stranded plane. Soon they were safely off the island, airborne to their not-too-distant base.

Later, the facts concerning the miraculous gasoline came to light. The drum had been part of a cargo of fuel that had been jettisoned from its barge following a Japanese attack. All the other drums had been lost, but this one had managed to float nearly 1,000 miles past 25 other islands to finally wash up at the very feet of the men who desperately needed that gasoline to save their lives.

God delights in miraculous rescues! He rescued the disciples from sinking in a storm on the Sea of Galilee by walking on water. He rescued Jonah from drowning by allowing a whale to swallow him. He rescued Daniel from a den of hungry lions by sending an angel to shut the lions' mouths. And he rescued Joseph from a lifetime of imprisonment by sending a pagan king a dream. Are you in a difficult situation? Paul counseled, "Be anxious for nothing, but in everything by prayer and supplication, with thanksgiving, let your requests be made known to God; and the peace of God, which surpasses all understanding, will guard your hearts and minds through Christ Jesus" (Philippians 4:6, 7). Perhaps God has a miraculous rescue planned for you!

"Go through the gates! Prepare the way for the people; build up, build up the highway!" (Isaiah 62:10).

After World War I, leaders in Washington became concerned about the state of the nation's roads. The automobile was still a relatively new invention, so most transcontinental travel depended on a few train tracks spanning the country. The U.S. War Department wanted to know if the nation's roads could handle coast-to-coast movements of Army units by road. As a test, the Transcontinental Motor Convoy—some 80 military vehicles and 280 soldiers—took an epic road trip from Washington, D.C. to California. The starting date was July 7, 1919.

Like the cavalry of old, Army scouts would ride in advance of the convoy to check out the conditions that lay just ahead, except they were mounted on Harley-Davidsons instead of horses. The convoy traveled over dirt roads, rutted paths, winding mountain trails, and shifting desert sands roughly along the route of present-day Interstate 80.

Many areas were nearly impassable, and the men often had to push or pull the heavy trucks along through the summer heat. The vehicles frequently broke down, got stuck in quicksand and mud, and sank when roads and bridges collapsed under them. In spite of the hardships, 62 days after it left Washington, D.C., the convoy reached San Francisco. It had covered 3,251 miles, averaging 58 miles a day at an average speed of 6 mph. The official report of the War Department concluded that the existing roads in the United States were "absolutely incapable of meeting the present-day traffic requirements."

One of the Army officers on the convoy was 28-year-old Lieutenant Colonel Dwight D. Eisenhower, who later said the roads they encountered "varied from average to non-existent." Eisenhower never forgot this grueling experience, and one of the most important things he did after becoming president was to create the interstate highway system. Construction began in 1956, and the entire interstate system now has a total length of 46,837 miles. It's the largest highway system in the world and the largest public works project in history.

Did you know the Bible speaks of an army of highway workers that will go before the Lord? "The voice of one crying in the wilderness: 'Prepare the way of the Lord; make straight in the desert a highway for our God'" (Isaiah 40:3). Not only did John the Baptist fulfill this prophecy, but we too may help make straight roads that guide others to heaven.

TRAFFIC SIGNALS

"Nor do they light a lamp and put it under a basket, but on a lampstand, and it gives light to all who are in the house" (Matthew 5:15).

Until the end of the 19th century, traffic in large cities was mainly uncontrolled chaos. Carriages and wagons dashed about in every direction, and the danger of frequent runaway horses added to the madness. Getting across a busy street could be a life-and-death challenge. In the 1860s, the NYPD formed the famous "Broadway Squad." These police officers were the largest in the department, with a minimum height of six feet, and their primary duty was simply to escort pedestrians safely across the bedlam of Broadway!

In the 1890s, the traffic pandemonium increased with the bicycle craze. This inspired Police Commissioner Theodore Roosevelt to organize a police bicycle squad, nicknamed the "Scorcher Squad," to control the bicycle speed-demons who were constantly breaking the 8 mph speed limit.

With the advent of automobiles there were even more problems when attempting to negotiate the thunderous maze of people, horses, carriages, bicycles, and autos on streets that were often unpaved, muddy, or dusty! The early cars frequently broke down, clogging the busy streets, and it was not uncommon to see traffic disputes settled by drivers "duking it out." It became apparent that some method to regulate traffic was an absolute necessity. Most cities had police directing traffic, which was among the most dangerous assignments. Scores were injured or killed, many died from illness through constant exposure to weather extremes, not to mention daily breathing the brew of dust, manure, and choking auto exhaust. Some cities tried a confusing system of train signals to regulate traffic. London even had gas-powered lamps that blew up.

Then in 1912, Lester Wire, a detective on the Salt Lake City police force, thought of the words of Jesus in Matthew 5:15: "Nor do they light a lamp and put it under a basket, but on a lampstand, and it gives light to all ..." This inspired Lester to invent one of the world's first electric traffic lights—a wooden box with red and green colored lights, up on a pole where cars could see it. Soon the idea spread to other cities, where it was improved and refined. Think of how many lives have been saved by this simple verse of Scripture!

"And another angel followed, saying, 'Babylon is fallen, is fallen, that great city ...'" (Revelation 14:8).

One of the most outstanding flights ever made by any war pigeon took place on October 18, 1943. On the day before the flight, the British 56th Infantry Division had requested air support to assist them in breaking the stubborn German defensive lines at the heavily fortified village of Calvi Vecchia, in Italy. However, soon after this message was sent, the British suddenly succeeded in making a surprise breakthrough. Without warning, the German resistance collapsed completely and the English troops overran the little town.

The British quickly realized that this unexpected victory would be disastrous for them unless they could get word through at once to call off the air support they had so recently requested. If not, they would certainly be massacred by their own planes, since they now occupied the very position they had asked to have bombed. It was at this point that they discovered they could not get word of their danger to the airfield. All communications had broken down in the hectic advance.

There was no choice now but to entrust their urgent message to one of the pigeons always kept on hand for just such an emergency. "G.I. Joe" was the pigeon chosen to carry this life-or-death message. Flying swiftly over the battle-torn land, the pigeon flew the 20 miles back to the U.S. air support base in 20 minutes, arriving just as the planes were warming up for takeoff on their mission to Calvi Vecchia. The successful completion of this historic flight saved the lives of more than 1,000 British soldiers.

After World War II, G.I. Joe was housed at the U.S. Army's Hall of Fame in New Jersey along with 24 other pigeon heroes. In November 1946, G.I. Joe was cited and awarded the Dickin Medal for gallantry by the Lord Mayor of London. In March of 1957, he was placed with the Detroit Zoological Gardens, where he died June 3, 1961, at the age of 18. G.I. Joe is the only bird or animal in the United States to receive such a high award for successfully carrying a life-saving message.

Did you know the Bible talks about a life-saving message carried by three angels? Of the first, the Bible says, "Then I saw another angel flying in the midst of heaven, having the everlasting gospel to preach to those who dwell on the earth ..." (Revelation 14:6). What greater message could there be than one that could save the whole world?

WHISTLIN' DIXIE

"And truly if they had called to mind that country from which they had come out, they would have had opportunity to return. But now they desire a better, that is, a heavenly country. Therefore God is not ashamed to be called their God, for He has prepared a city for them" (Hebrews 11:15, 16).

In 1859, Daniel Emmett, a New York minstrel man, wrote a catchy song that swept across the country. It was based on some words and music he had once heard slaves singing in the Carolinas. These slaves had sung of a happy place called "Dixieland," and so Emmett called his song "Dixie." It was an immediate success.

Later, during the Civil War, the stirring strains of "Dixie" became the official song of the Southern Confederacy. In fact, the word "Dixie" became a synonym for the Southern United States. But what Emmett and the Confederacy never knew was that the "Dixieland" which the slaves were singing so longingly about was not even in the South, but was actually in New York, just a short distance from where Emmett wrote his famous song.

As the story goes, years earlier a Dutch farmer in Manhattan tried to grow tobacco on the New York island. This was before the abolition of slavery in the North, so he brought in slaves from Africa to help him work the land, but his farm proved a failure. Reluctantly, he had to sell the slaves to a plantation in Charleston, and it was there in South Carolina that the word "Dixieland" was first used in song.

It is said that the Dutch farmer for whom the slaves worked in Manhattan had been a kind, jolly, and generous man, and the slaves often wished they could be back on his farm. So they would sing: "I wish I was in Dixieland" ... because the name of that kind Dutch farmer was Johann Dixie. So, ironically, the song "Dixieland" was originally not about sweet memories of the South but rather a farm in New York City.

Friends, did you know that when the Bible speaks of the patriarchs' yearning for a place in Canaan land, it has nothing to do with the nation of Israel? Anyone who lives for God and embraces His promises looks forward to a better land—His heavenly kingdom. His Word promises that "He has prepared a city" for those who love Him (Hebrews 11:16).

"Prepare the way of the Lord; make straight in the desert a highway for our God" (Isaiah 40:3).

What is the largest public works program since the pyramids in Egypt? It is probably the National Highway System in the United States. This project was named after President Dwight D. Eisenhower, who brought about its formation. Construction began in 1956 and was completed 35 years later. It has been extended over the years and now covers 47,182 miles. About 25 percent of vehicles on the road use the interstate system. The cost for construction has been estimated at $425 billion.

Several interesting milestones were reached during construction of this massive system. On October 17, 1974, Nebraska was the first state to complete all of its mainline interstate highways. On October 14, 1992, the original interstate highway system was completed with the opening of Interstate 70 through Glenwood Canyon in Colorado, which is an engineering marvel with a 12-mile section featuring 40 bridges and many tunnels, making it the most expensive rural highway per mile. Three states actually claim to be the first to lay pavement for the highway: Kansas, Missouri, and Pennsylvania.

President Eisenhower, who was lobbied by major U.S. automobile manufacturers, helped push forward the highway system. After his experience of crossing the country in the 1919 Army convoy on the Lincoln Highway, he was convinced of its value. An interesting urban legend still persists that one out of every five miles of the interstate highway system must be built straight and flat so as to be usable by aircraft during times of war. The highways were never designed to serve as airstrips. The longest interstate route is I-90 (3,020.54 miles) going from Seattle, Washington, to Boston, Massachusetts. Texas has the most interstate miles (3,233.45 miles). The entire highway system has a total of 14,750 interchanges, 55,512 bridges, and 82 tunnels.

Did you know a highway was to be created to welcome and introduce Jesus Christ to the world? When religious leaders came asking John the Baptist who he was, the prophet responded, "I am the voice of one crying in the wilderness: Make straight the way of the Lord" (John 1:23). As the forerunner of Jesus, the Baptist prepared people for the coming of the Messiah. The roadway John made ready was not with bulldozers and steamrollers, but through preaching that opened pathways in the hearts of people.

TREASURES OF DARKNESS

"I will give you the treasures of darkness and hidden riches of secret places, that you may know that I, the LORD, who call you by your name, am the God of Israel" (Isaiah 45:3).

In 1859, as the California gold rush began to fade, two miners, Pat McLaughlin and Peter O'Reilly, wandered into western Nevada and staked a claim at the head of Six Mile Canyon. When they found gold, another clever miner, Henry Comstock, claimed it was on his property, convincing them to give him a share of the stake. Soon fortune seekers everywhere heard the news and the surrounding hills were sprinkled with gold mines.

The biggest problem the miners faced was the sticky, bluish mud surrounding the gold. It stuck to their boots, picks, and shovels. They called it that "blasted blue stuff," and it made their gold mining a miserable business. But when the blue mud was tested, it was found to be some of the richest silver ore ever discovered, worth over $2,000 a ton—and that's in 1859! These miners had been knee-deep in one of the greatest single mineral strikes in history, and they didn't know it. The fabulous strike was the richest known silver deposit in the United States and became known as the Comstock Lode. But that's not all—the blue mud was about to change history.

By 1864, the staggering amounts of silver and gold coming out of the mine reached the attention of President Abe Lincoln. Lincoln needed the riches of the Comstock Lode to help win the Civil War, but he also needed the votes of another state to assure re-election. So even though Nevada was sparsely populated, the entire Nevada Constitution was telegraphed to Congress two weeks before the election. It was the longest telegraph message in history, taking two days to send and costing well over $4,000! But it worked, and so, because of the blue mud, Nevada became a state on October 31, 1864.

Sometimes, it is in the midst of trouble and trial that we discover the greatest riches. God says that there are "treasures" even in "darkness"—and who are we to argue with our Maker (Isaiah 45:3)? After all, we can have confidence that "all things work together for good to those who love God, to those who are the called according to His purpose" (Romans 8:28).

"You are of your father the devil ... When he speaks a lie, he speaks from his own resources, for he is a liar and the father of it" (John 8:44).

President Bill Clinton was once accused of renting out White House rooms in exchange for campaign contributions. That was nothing compared to Arthur Furguson's enterprise. He leased the entire building. Arthur Furguson was a dapper little Scotsman, always with immaculate dress and charming manner. He began his illustrious career in the roaring '20s as a small-time scam artist working the streets of London, but by the time he arrived in America in 1925 he was a con man without peer.

In one summer in London he managed to sell American tourists Nelson's Column in Trafalgar Square, with the lions, for $30,000; he sold Big Ben for a bargain price of $5,000; and accepted a $10,000 down payment for Buckingham Palace. While visiting Paris, he even managed to sell the Eiffel Tower for scrap at an unknown price to yet another American. At this point, Scotland Yard detectives were hot on his heels, so naturally Furguson boarded a ship for America.

Arthur Furguson had only been in Washington briefly when, posing as a government official, he managed to lease the White House to a cattle rancher for 99 years at a cost of $100,000 per year. Furguson told the believing rancher they were going to build a bigger residence for the president closer to the Capitol Building. Furguson convinced the rancher that income from tours of the old White House would bring a handsome profit. Naturally, the first $100,000 was due in advance. When the deal was consummated, Furguson quickly caught a train to New York City with a bag full of money, leaving it to the government officials to explain that the White House was not available for lease.

Did you know the Bible tells about an even bigger con artist who tried to sell the whole world? The Bible says, "Again, the devil took Him up on an exceedingly high mountain, and showed Him all the kingdoms of the world and their glory. And he said to Him, 'All these things I will give You if You will fall down and worship me.' Then Jesus said to him, 'Away with you, Satan! For it is written, "You shall worship the LORD your God, and Him only you shall serve."' Then the devil left Him, and behold, angels came and ministered to Him" (Matthew 4:8-11).

MODERN GHOST TOWN

"I beheld, and indeed the fruitful land was a wilderness, and all its cities were broken down ..." (Jeremiah 4:26).

How can a bustling U.S. city with more than 14,000 people turn into a deserted, apocalyptic ghost town? Located on the Kansas state line, Picher was Oklahoma's most northeastern city. Newspapers reported in 1913 that the town was born overnight after lead and zinc ore were discovered in abundance. Picher, named in 1918 after O. S. Picher, owner of the Picher Lead Company, had a population of 9,726, which by 1926 exploded to 14,252. Between 1917 and 1947 Picher produced more than $20 billion in ore and was one of the most productive lead mining fields in the U.S. Over 50 percent of the lead and zinc metal consumed in World War I came from the Picher mines. During the boom years more than 14,000 men worked in its mines, and another 4,000 worked in approximately 1,500 related businesses.

But the relentless exploitation of the land's resources could not hold out forever. As the mining decreased, the population also dwindled. By 1960 there were only 2,500 people living in Picher. Lead and zinc mining finally ceased in 1967, and water stopped being pumped from the mines. Soon the 1,400 mine shafts began to fill with water, contaminating local wells. Towering piles of mine waste covered 25,000 acres, and sinkholes developed everywhere. The U.S. Environmental Protection Agency arrived and began a monumental task trying to clean up 70 million tons of waste tailings, and 36 million tons of mill sand and sludge.

Then to top things off, on May 10, 2008, a one-mile-wide F4 tornado with 175 mph winds ripped through what was left of Picher. The tornado took the lives of eight people, injured at least 150, and leveled 114 homes. By September of 2009 Picher was officially closed as a city. Today Picher, Oklahoma, looks like a surreal ghost town hit by Armageddon. All that remains of the once bustling city with thousands of souls are the white mountains of toxic tailings, overgrown foundations, pits, and a few remaining buildings.

It sounds like the condition of the world during the millennium. Jeremiah describes the earth at this time. "I beheld the earth, and indeed it was without form, and void ... and there was no man, and all the birds of the heavens had fled. I beheld, and indeed the fruitful land was a wilderness, and all its cities were broken down at the presence of the LORD, By His fierce anger" (Jeremiah 4:23-26).

Where do you plan to be during the millennium?

Amazing Feats

"And Samson lay low till midnight; then he arose at midnight, took hold of the doors of the gate of the city and the two gateposts, pulled them up, bar and all, put them on his shoulders, and carried them to the top of the hill that faces Hebron."
Judges 16:3

THE LONGEST SERMON

"And seeing the multitudes, He went up on a mountain, and when He was seated His disciples came to Him. Then He opened His mouth and taught them ..." (Matthew 5:1, 2).

An Anglican vicar from Lancashire, England, has delivered a 28-hour, 45-minute sermon, breaking the world record for the longest unscripted speech. Chris Sterry, 46, began his marathon sermon June 29, 2001. He was not allowed to repeat himself, talk nonsense, or to pause for more than 10 seconds, but was permitted a 15-minute break every eight hours. Two referees who worked four-hour shifts were on hand to make sure rules were followed.

A former lecturer on the Old Testament, Sterry "talked his way into the Guinness Book of Records" when he took the first four books of the Bible as the text of his sermon. Before he began preaching, he stated, "As a former lecturer on the Old Testament I am looking forward to unlimited opportunity to talk about one of my great enthusiasms."

Sterry's sermon was broadcast live every 15 minutes on CNN throughout June 30. He says he undertook the challenge as a fund-raising effort for his church. There were more than 100 people in church when he broke the record. If it looked like he was about to drop off, people in the congregation would "heckle" (encourage) him to keep going. News reports do not indicate whether any of his parishioners also lasted the entire distance!

The Sermon on the Mount was Jesus' most famous and longest recorded sermon in the Gospels. Given when Christ appointed the twelve disciples, it was like an inaugural address that tells us about how the kingdom of heaven was to operate. The "sermon" was given from a mountain. Just as Moses proclaimed God's law from Mount Sinai, Jesus' proclamation from the "mount of blessing" affirmed the same law. What is recorded in the Gospels is probably an abbreviation of the greatest sermon ever given.

When is the last time you prayerfully read through Christ's Sermon on the Mount? Why not take time to read Matthew 5:1 to 8:1, or the shorter version found in Luke 6:17-49. And it won't take you 28 hours and 45 minutes!

"But this is the covenant that I will make with the house of Israel after those days, says the LORD: I will put My law in their minds, and write it on their hearts; and I will be their God, and they shall be My people" (Jeremiah 31:33).

Nearly everyone in the Western world has heard of "The Lord's Prayer." Even if they don't remember all the words, most people would certainly recognize it. Here it is, from Matthew 6:9-13 (KJV): "Our Father which art in heaven, Hallowed be thy name. Thy kingdom come, Thy will be done in earth, as it is in heaven. Give us this day our daily bread. And forgive us our debts, as we forgive our debtors. And lead us not into temptation, but deliver us from evil: For thine is the kingdom, and the power, and the glory, for ever. Amen."

In the late 1800s, a convicted forger named A. Schiller spent many years at the notorious Sing Sing prison in New York. One day the guards discovered he had died in his cell. Among his personal effects were seven straight pins, six silver and one gold. They were typical-size pins, yet something about them caught the attention of one of the guards, so he examined them more closely with a magnifying glass.

To everyone's amazement, under 500X magnification, they saw that Schiller had etched on the head of all seven pins the entire Lord's Prayer with 65 words and 254 letters. The surface measured only 47/1000 of an inch in diameter. That's pretty small. Of the seven pins, the prayer etched on the gold pin was flawless and a true masterpiece. No one is sure why there were seven. Perhaps he carried a silver one for each weekday and the gold one for the Sabbath.

Schiller had spent many years of his life placing the prayer on each pin, using a powerful magnifying glass and tools so small you couldn't see them with your naked eye. It is estimated that it took 1,863 separate strokes to etch out each prayer. Before his death, Schiller went blind, perhaps partly due to the incredible eyestrain of his astonishing artwork. Though he's long gone, the prayers on the pins remain.

Schiller etched a prayer on the head of a pin; the Bible tells us we should allow God to write His law in our own hearts. God promises to those who do so, "I will be their God, and they shall be My people."

August 3 CUBAN WINDSURFER

"Now in the fourth watch of the night Jesus went to them, walking on the sea" (Matthew 14:25).

In February 1994, a 21-year-old Cuban windsurfer waded ashore in the Florida Keys and asked for asylum. He told the amazed sheriff's deputies his story. The windsurfer, Eugenio Maderal Roman, had made the 110-mile trip across the open sea, looking for freedom. He had a childhood friend, Lester Moreno Perez, who had windsurfed to Florida in 1990 and worked as a computer programmer in Miami. Eugenio said he thought of following his friend but at the time decided it would be dangerous to attempt. Eugenio said he windsurfed almost daily in Cuba.

On this particular morning Eugenio set out, as he often had, from his girlfriend's house in Varadero about 1 p.m. and went for a spin around the beach resort. "I went surfing to catch some air and have a little fun." Then he was going to head over to his aunt's house. He began surfing that evening and when he caught a favorable northern breeze, on a whim and a prayer, he just kept going with freedom urging him on. "Something was calling me," he said. "When I saw water all around me, I just kept on going." He worked as a windsurfing instructor and made a pretty good wage, but said he was tired of Cuba's hardships.

Eugenio encountered friendly porpoises along the way, but he avoided resting in the dark waters that are also the frequent haunt of large sharks. He said he oriented himself by the sun and then by the North Star after nightfall. The young man made the epic trip from north Cuba to Marathon Key in about nine hours. The Coast Guard was not involved in the case because Mr. Maderal made it all the way to shore unassisted. Eugenio said he had wanted to come to the United States for a long time but didn't plan for it to happen this way. "If I'd thought about it twice," he said, "I wouldn't have done it."

The Bible teaches that one windy night long ago Jesus made a difficult trip across stormy waters to save his friends. More than that, He crossed an ocean of space to bring freedom to a world enslaved by sin. It was a risky journey, but Christ wanted to release us from the government of Satan and set us free. Jesus thought about it more than once. He didn't hesitate because of His great love for you.

"Then some of the Pharisees who were with Him heard these words, and said to Him, 'Are we blind also?' Jesus said to them, 'If you were blind, you would have no sin; but now you say, "We see." Therefore your sin remains'" (John 9:40, 41).

On November 8, 2008, Jim O'Neill, age 65, was flying alone in his Cessna at 5,500 feet over North Yorkshire, England, when he suddenly was unable to see his controls. Believing he was being blinded by the sunlight, O'Neill frantically radioed a mayday alert. Air traffic controllers did their best to guide him in to the nearest airfield, but when O'Neill was unable to see even the large runway, the controllers realized that it was not simply a matter of being dazzled by the sun.

Thankfully, a military training plane was already in the air nearby. Wing Commander Paul Gerrard, a chief flying instructor, flew within 300 feet of the stricken pilot and established radio contact. After reassuring O'Neill, Gerrard used a series of very carefully chosen words to guide him: "Turn left, a little right, reduce power, 10 percent flaps." The Royal Air Force pilot guided the disabled aircraft down towards an R.A.F. airfield, with O'Neill feeling for and finding the various controls from memory. The Cessna landed halfway down the runway at high speed, bounced twice, and finally stopped safely at the very end of the runway.

At the hospital, doctors discovered that O'Neill had suffered a stroke that put pressure on his optic nerve, rendering him blind. After medical treatment, most of Jim O'Neill's eyesight returned. The R.A.F. remarked that they are used to "shepherding" lost airplanes—but this was the only time they had shepherded a blind one!

Friends, it wasn't until the air traffic controllers realized the extent of O'Neill's blindness that they were able to help him effectively. Jesus told the Pharisees that if they recognized their blindness they could be helped, but because they claimed to see when they couldn't, their sin remained. We must recognize that without the Word of God to guide us, we are all flying blind! When we admit our need, God is ready to help us, and He promises to help each of us land safely: "I will instruct you and teach you in the way you should go; I will guide you with My eye" (Psalm 32:8).

August 5 DUTCHMAN'S ARK

"Make yourself an ark of gopherwood; make rooms in the ark, and cover it inside and outside with pitch" (Genesis 6:14).

Dutch creationist Johan Huibers had a dream that someday Holland would be flooded. That led to his building a replica of Noah's ark, complete with life-size animals. The seaworthy ark is only half the size of Noah's original, but it is still nearly 230 feet long, 45 feet high, and 30 feet wide. Life-size models of giraffes, elephants, lions, crocodiles, zebras, and bison are included in the ark's interior. Even with all the animals it still has room for a 50-seat theater, where the story of Noah's flood is retold. Eventually there will even be a petting zoo, with lambs, chickens, goats, and one camel. The total cost of the project was estimated to be around $1.2 million.

Johan also built the ark as testament to his literal belief in the Bible. He said, "This will speak very much to children, because it will give them something tangible to see that Noah's ark really existed." Assisted by his son, the 47-year-old contractor spent nearly two years building the ark by the water in Schagen, 30 miles north of Amsterdam.

As far as possible he has tried to remain true to the ark proportions described in the Bible, but Johan's ark is constructed with American cedar and Norwegian pine rather than "gopher wood." Biblical scholars are still not exactly sure what kind of wood that was. When the ark opened its doors in April 2007, visitors were stunned by its size. They think the Netherlands is probably the right place for an ark to be built. With all the talk of global warming, some fear Holland will be the first place flooded if the polar caps melt much faster. Johan's ark is a fully functional model and will even meet all the naval, fire, and animal rights regulations. Mr. Huibers plans to sail the ark through the interior waters around Holland. He's praying this colossal exhibit will help renew interest in Christianity in the Netherlands, which has dramatically fallen in the past 50 years.

So will there be another global flood before Jesus returns? After Noah left the ark when the flood waters receded, the Bible says, "Thus I establish My covenant with you: Never again shall all flesh be cut off by the waters of the flood; never again shall there be a flood to destroy the earth" (Genesis 9:11). We are assured our world will not be destroyed again by water. But the Lord has warned that someday the earth will be cleansed by fire.

"For thus says the High and Lofty One who inhabits eternity, whose name is Holy: 'I dwell in the high and holy place, with him who has a contrite and humble spirit, to revive the spirit of the humble, and to revive the heart of the contrite ones'" (Isaiah 57:15).

From the time baby boys first pull themselves up to walk, men seem to have a yearning to climb—trees, mountains, even tall buildings. Most of us learn a natural fear of dangerous heights, but some never develop that fear. Take, for example, George Polley, the first "human fly" in North America. He began his climbing career as a boy when, in 1910, an owner of a clothing store promised him a free suit if he would climb to the roof of the building. He succeeded.

In 1920, he climbed the Woolworth Building but was arrested for climbing without official permission. Nevertheless, George was soon in demand for his climbing skills. He was often invited to climb a building as part of the opening ceremonies of some new business. Sometimes he spiced up his performance by pretending to slip and drop from one windowsill to another. Over his short career, Polley climbed the walls of over 2,000 tall buildings. Tragically, George Polley died at the age of 29, not from a fall but due to a brain tumor.

Another remarkable building climber was George Willig, who on May 26, 1977, climbed the south tower of the World Trade Center without ropes or net. The mayor of New York City fined him $1.10, one penny for each of the 110 floors. Then there is the French Spiderman, Alain Robert, who climbs for publicity. He has scaled the Eiffel Tower, Sears Tower, and over 30 other skyscrapers, including New York's Empire State Building.

It makes one wonder if this urge to build and scale higher is one reason early man built the Tower of Babel. But there was an additional reason. The builders of the Tower of Babel turned away from their Maker. Proud and ambitious, they forgot to be humble before God. When they exalted themselves, God brought them down.

In contrast, Jesus, though He ruled the universe, "made Himself of no reputation, taking the form of a bondservant," and laying down His life. Because of that, "God also has highly exalted Him and given Him the name which is above every name, that at the name of Jesus every knee should bow" (Philippians 2:7, 9, 10). God rewards a humble heart.

August 7

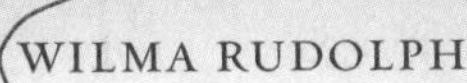

WILMA RUDOLPH

"Therefore we also, since we are surrounded by so great a cloud of witnesses, let us lay aside every weight ... and let us run with endurance the race that is set before us" (Hebrews 12:1).

Wilma Rudolph faced adversity from the very beginning. When she was born prematurely, the 20th of 22 children, she weighed only 4.5 pounds. By the time Wilma was 4 years old, she contracted double pneumonia and polio, which left her with a paralyzed left leg. Doctors said she'd never walk again without assistance. By the time she was 12 years old she had also survived scarlet fever, whooping cough, chicken pox, and measles.

But Wilma's simple faith in God and determination would not allow her to give up. At age nine she stunned her doctors when she removed the metal leg brace she had been dependent on and began to walk without it. By 13 she had developed a rhythmic walk, which doctors said was a miracle. That same year she decided to become a runner. She entered a race and came in last. For the next few years, every race she entered she came in last. Everyone told her to quit, but she kept on running.

Then one day she actually won a race. And then another ... and she won every race she entered from then on. In the 1960 Summer Olympic Games in Rome, Rudolph became the first American woman to win three gold medals during a single Olympic Game—all in track and field. The international coverage of the Olympics made her a hero around the world. She became known as "The Tornado." The Italians called her "The Black Gazelle," and the French nicknamed her "The Black Pearl." Eventually this little girl, who was told she would never walk again, went on to be known as the fastest woman on Earth. She never gave up!

The Bible says, "If you can believe, all things are possible to him who believes" (Mark 9:23). Rudolph was especially motivated to pay tribute to Jesse Owens, a star in the 1936 Summer Olympics held in Berlin, Germany. As Christians, we should be motivated by "looking unto Jesus, the author and finisher of our faith, who for the joy that was set before Him endured the cross ..." (Hebrews 12:2). Christ is the One who ran before us and gives us strength to stay the course unto the end.

"Let no one despise your youth, but be an example to the believers in word, in conduct, in love, in spirit, in faith, in purity" (1 Timothy 4:12).

During World War II, a young 21-year-old man entered an Air Force enlistment center and eagerly asked to join the service. He said his name was Kincaid, and he wanted to become a flyer. Passing the physical, he was accepted into the Air Force and, after training in the United States, he was assigned to a bomber squadron at the Benghazi Air Base in North Africa.

As a skillful gunner on a B-24 bomber, Kincaid soon ran up a terrific record, was decorated and promoted to sergeant. But then one day his best buddy was killed, and this so deeply affected Kincaid that the depressed young airman asked for a transfer. Because of his sterling record, the transfer was granted.

The flyer returned to the United States and immediately went to see his commanding officer. His name, he told the astonished officer, was not Kincaid, it was Fletcher, and he was not 21 years old as his military record stated, but only 16. He had been only 15 when he had enlisted the year before, lying then about both his name and his age. Tom Fletcher was the youngest combat flyer in Benghazi; at the age of 16 he was already a veteran. He had completed 35 combat missions, flying 300 hours. He had been given the Air Medal with one silver cluster and five bronze clusters, and had won the Distinguished Flying Cross.

Sometimes young people doubt that God can use them in His service because of their youth. Paul told young Timothy not to let anyone put him down because of his age. He advised him to study and to use the special gift God gave him to help others. He also told Timothy if he continued following the right path and doing good, he would become a powerful example to others and a soul-winner for God.

God loves to have young people in His service. The Bible says, "Remember now your Creator in the days of your youth, before the difficult days come, and the years draw near when you say, 'I have no pleasure in them'" (Ecclesiastes 12:1). Don't let lack of experience hold you back. God isn't looking for experienced disciples, just dedicated ones.

August 9 THUNDERCLOUD GLIDER

"Hold me up, and I shall be safe, and I shall observe Your statues continually" (Psalm 119:117).

On February 15, 2007, while practicing for the World Paraglider Championships, German Paraglider Ewa Wisnierska was sucked up 32,612 feet above sea level by a storm in New South Wales, Australia. Thirty-five-year-old Wisnierska flew underneath a massive thunder cloud and got lifted up to the altitude at which passenger jets fly. The temperature at that elevation is minus 50 degrees Fahrenheit and the oxygen is very thin. It's higher than Mount Everest.

Ewa soared up about 15 minutes traveling at 65 feet per second. She radioed her team leader at 13,123 feet and said, "I can't do anything. It's raining and hailing and I'm still climbing. I'm lost." She just remembered going up, with lightning around her in the cloud and being pummeled by hailstones the size of tennis balls. She passed out for more than 40 minutes while her paraglider flew on uncontrolled, sinking and lifting several times in the violent storm.

Ewa's ground team used her GPS and radio equipment to track and record her entire epic flight. When she woke, the glider was still flying on its own. Ewa saw her gloves were frozen and she didn't have the controls in her hands. She and her glider were covered in ice. Her clothes were frozen to her body. Incredibly, her glider kept flying perfectly in spite of the terrible battering. Despite the bitter cold, she still managed a perfect landing just near a farmhouse. She then curled up in the fetal position to restore her body heat.

Ewa suffered from severe frostbite and also had bruises all over her body from the hail stones. Her German teammates were overjoyed to hear she survived. Not even 747s fly through those storm cells. An event organizer said, "The chance of surviving what she has done is the equivalent of winning the lottery ten times in a row." Wisnierska said being in the bowels of a monster thundercloud was both frightening and amazing. "You can't imagine the power. You feel like nothing, like a leaf from a tree going up."

Did you know the Bible talks about someone who survived an incredible stormy journey going down to the bottom of the mountains? Jonah, from the belly of a whale, cried out to God: "I went down to the moorings of the mountains ... Yet You have brought up my life from the pit, O Lord, my God" (Jonah 2:6). Whether your life is brought to dangerous heights or depths, your cries to God will always be heard.

"[The devil] was a murderer from the beginning, and does not stand in the truth, because there is no truth in him. When he speaks a lie, he speaks from his own resources, for he is a liar and the father of it" (John 8:44).

In October 2002, Abraham Abdallah pled guilty to 12 counts of fraud while on trial for the largest identity theft operation in recent history. The 32-year-old busboy and high school dropout had attempted to steal the identities of Steven Spielberg, George Lucas, Oprah Winfrey, Ted Turner, and scores of other famous people whose names he got from a Forbes list of wealthy Americans. When he was caught, he had scores of sensitive personal information noted in his dog-eared copy of the Forbes 400 list—checking account numbers, account balances, social security numbers, cell phone numbers, and more. Abdallah started small: he would call the victim's bank, giving the clerk publicly available personal information, trying to convince the clerk he was the victim's financial adviser. With each call he would try to glean just a tiny bit of information—perhaps only an account balance. But hundreds of calls later, Abdallah had enough information to request account transfers from genuine accounts to fraudulent accounts he had created. By the end, he had access to $80 million dollars.

Abdallah had a second scheme: he used his connection with an employee of an online company to steal credit card numbers and would use those numbers to order merchandise, like a machine to make his own credit cards. At the time of his arrest, Abdallah had 800 fake credit cards and had stolen $78,000 worth of goods.

But Abdallah is far from the worst identity thief—the thief who has stolen the identity of the entire world and left us with an immeasurable debt. While God created mankind in His image, the devil has stolen that holy identity and left us sinners. He started small, but his lies eventually gave him access to the entire human race. Yet the devil will not be allowed to practice his thievery forever! The time will soon come when the devil will be "cast into the lake of fire and brimstone" (Revelation 20:10). And the debt of his victims? Praise be to God—Jesus has paid that debt!

August 11 HANG ON!

"But hold fast what you have till I come" (Revelation 2:25).

Back in 1987 on a commuter flight from Portland, Maine, to Boston, the pilot, Henry Dempsey, heard an unusual noise near the rear of the aircraft shortly after takeoff. When they reached about 4,000 feet Captain Dempsey turned the controls over to the co-pilot and went to the back of the 15-passenger turboprop to investigate the strange sound. As he reached the tail section the plane hit an air pocket, and Dempsey was bounced against the rear door. He quickly discovered the source of the mysterious noise. The rear door had been improperly latched prior to take-off and it flew open. Dempsey was instantly sucked out of the tiny Beechcraft 99.

The co-pilot heard the wind rushing through the cabin and saw the red light indicating an open door. It became obvious what had happened. He quickly radioed the nearest airport requesting permission for an emergency landing. He reported that the pilot had fallen out of the plane and asked a helicopter to search the area of the ocean over which they had been flying.

After the plane landed, the ground crew was astonished to find Dempsey alive, desperately clinging to the outdoor stair railing of the aircraft. Somehow when the stair door popped open and his upper body fell through the door he instinctively seized the handrail. Amazingly, for 10 minutes Dempsey endured the force of howling 200 mph winds, and when landing he barely kept his head from hitting the runway, which was only 12 inches away. According to news reports, Dempsey was holding on to the stair railing with such tenacity of force that it took the airport rescue team several minutes to pry his hands loose.

Jesus warned that difficult times will come for His people. "And you will be hated by all for My name's sake. But he who endures to the end will be saved" (Matthew 10:22). There are times of discouragement when it is tempting to give up or to let go. But when you consider the experience of Henry Dempsey, think of the alternatives. Remember, the harder you cling to Jesus, the tighter will be His grip on you!

"But he who endures to the end shall be saved" (Matthew 24:13).

In November 1942, a 25-year-old Chinese seaman named Poon Lim was working as a steward on a British merchant ship called the S.S. *Ben Lomond*. After leaving Capetown, the vessel was torpedoed by a German U-boat near South Africa's coast. As the ship sank, Poon Lim grabbed a life jacket and jumped overboard just as the ship's boilers exploded. Poon Lim floated around naked in the Atlantic for two hours, then spotted an empty life raft and pulled himself aboard.

That was the beginning of one of the most amazing sagas of survival at sea ever recorded. He was thankful for the meager supplies in the life boat—a canvas sail, chocolate, a bag of sugar, some flares, a jug of water, a tin of hard biscuits, and a flashlight. Seven days into his ordeal, he frantically tried to get the attention of a ship, but it just passed by. Then he spotted seven U.S. Navy patrol planes. He sent up flares, but they did not see him. A German U-boat spotted him, but chose to leave him to fate instead of rescuing (or killing) him.

Poon Lim could have given up and died, but instead decided to use his skills and limited supplies to stay alive. He rationed himself a biscuit and few mouthfuls of water a day. He made a fish hook from the flashlight spring, used hemp from the rope line, and a piece of biscuit for bait. When he caught a fish, he cut it with a tin-can knife and dried it. He swam daily to keep his muscles fit and body clean, while watching for sharks and staying tethered to the boat. He caught rainwater in a piece of canvas. When a storm spoiled his fish and fouled his water, Lim, barely alive, caught a bird and drank its blood to survive. Another time he hooked a 30-pound shark and ate the liver.

On April 5, 1943, when he staggered ashore in Brazil, he'd lost 20 pounds. Poon Lim survived a record 133 days alone on the Atlantic. He said, "I hope no one will ever have to break that record."

Jesus said, speaking of the last days, "He who endures to the end shall be saved" (Matthew 24:13). In our sin-plagued world, we face difficulties like waves of the sea. But if we cling to Jesus, He will keep us afloat through every trial and give us the strength to endure.

August 13 HIDING IN AN ATTIC

"And it was told Joshua, saying, 'The five kings have been found hidden in the cave at Makkedah'" (Joshua 10:17).

One of the most bizarre records for hiding out was made by a young Chinese foreign exchange student by the name of Cheng Guan Lim. He was studying engineering at the University of Michigan but was doing very badly in physics and math. If his studies did not improve, he would have to leave school, quit his job as janitor at Ann Arbor's First Methodist Church, and take the humiliating news of his academic failure back to his father, who was a schoolteacher in Singapore.

One day in October 1955, Cheng disappeared. His friends, including the Rev. Eugene Ransom, pastor of the church, called the police, but they found no clues. Cheng's Methodist friends had another mystery to ponder: strange bumping noises that came out of the deserted church at night. Early one morning, four years after Chang's disappearance, a pair of private detectives called in by Rev. Ransom, heard a trap door to the church attic slam. Together with police, they climbed up and swept their flashlights about the attic. And there, crouched above them in the rafters, was Cheng.

For four years the attic of the church had been his home. The bumping noises had been Cheng skipping rope to keep in shape. During the day he slept on padding from a pew. At night he walked around the church and helped himself to food from the kitchen. Physically, Cheng seemed unaffected by his hermit's existence. But as police hauled him off to the county jail, his four-year preoccupation with loss of face suddenly vanished. "I have been a coward," he said. "I'm glad I was found."

Instead of leaving him in jail, local businessmen started a fund to help him finish his education. The university permitted him to resume studies, and he eventually graduated in 1961 and later went on to earn his master's degree. Cheng eventually returned to Singapore.

Did you know that the Bible speaks of a time when Satan will be forced to live the life of a hermit? "Then I saw an angel coming down from heaven, having the key to the bottomless pit and a great chain in his hand. He laid hold of the dragon, that serpent of old, who is the Devil and Satan, and bound him for a thousand years" (Revelation 20:1, 2). Like the five enemy kings in the time of Joshua who were found hidden in a cave, Satan will someday be brought out and destroyed forever.

"Therefore, having been justified by faith, we have peace with God through our Lord Jesus Christ" (Romans 5:1).

Simeon the Stylite was born in A.D. 390 in northern Syria as it became part of the Byzantine Empire. Influenced by his deeply religious mother, he developed a strong zeal for Christianity. By the age of 13, he began to frequently fast from food. Before he was 16, Simeon entered a monastery and commenced a regimen of fasting and prayer so severe he was asked to leave. He then shut himself up for three years in a hut, fasting up to 40 days during Lent, seeking peace with God. But the hut was too comfortable, so Simeon moved to a rocky cliff in the desert and compelled himself to remain a prisoner within a narrow ledge.

Crowds of pilgrims, hearing of this holy hermit, invaded the desert to seek his counsel and prayers. All this attention left him little time for his own private devotions. This inspired him to adopt a new way of life. If he could not avoid the world horizontally, he now hoped to find peace by escaping it vertically. Simeon discovered an ancient pillar, 48 feet high, amongst some ruins. On top of this pillar, with the help of friends, he built a platform about twelve feet square. He lived many years perched on top of this pillar, exposed to the elements. He became known to history as Simeon the Stylite (the Latin word "stylus" means "pillar").

But the new pillar drew more pilgrims and curious sightseers. Simeon patiently allowed people to visit him every afternoon by means of a ladder. He wrote some letters we still possess today, in which he instructed disciples, and he sometimes preached about holy living to his visitors. After spending 37 years on his pillar, Simeon died at the age of 69. He inspired many imitators, and for the next century ascetics living on pillars, or stylites, were a common sight throughout the Byzantine East.

Today Simeon is commemorated as a saint in the Coptic Orthodox Church, but is it really necessary to be an aerial ascetic to find peace with God? The Bible makes it clear that we are justified by faith, enabling us to "have peace with God through our Lord Jesus Christ" (Romans 5:1). Only Jesus, the Prince of Peace, can bring reconciliation. We can never do anything to improve on what He has already done. We find peace with God by placing our faith in Jesus.

August 15 GOLDEN GATE JUMPER

"You shall not tempt the LORD your God" (Deuteronomy 6:16).

Have you ever heard your parents say, "If your friends told you to jump off a bridge, would you do it?" Apparently some do. On March 11, 2011, a California high school student visiting the Golden Gate Bridge on a morning field trip climbed over a railing and jumped. He was evidently urged on by a dare from fellow classmates. Miraculously the teenager survived the 220-foot plunge into San Francisco Bay that kills dozens of people each year. Landing on water after a 220-foot fall feels like landing on concrete after a 100-foot drop.

Most jumpers die a grisly death with massive internal injuries, broken bones, and skull fractures. Some die from internal bleeding, while others drown in the cold water. But amazingly the 17-year-old lived. A statement from his school said he suffered no severe injuries beyond bruising and tenderness. He was rescued by a surfer who paddled over and towed him ashore.

California Highway Patrol Officer Chris Rardin said, "It's a miracle in itself. The majority of folks do not survive this type of fall." Windsor Unified School District Superintendent Bill McDermott said he didn't think the teen was trying to commit suicide, but instead jumped after other students from the high school in Sonoma County dared him. Suddenly his shocked classmates saw the teen go over the railing.

Someone leaps off the iconic bridge an average of once every two weeks. In 2010, 32 jumpers died, most of those deaths suicides. About 98 percent of those plunges end up being fatal. The other 2 percent are seriously injured.

Did you know the Bible says the devil once dared the Savior to jump from a high precipice, but Jesus did not fall for the temptation? "Then the devil took Him up into the holy city, set Him on the pinnacle of the temple, and said to Him, 'If You are the Son of God, throw Yourself down. For it is written: "He shall give His angels charge over you," and, "In their hands they shall bear you up, lest you dash your foot against a stone."' Jesus said to him, 'It is written again, "You shall not tempt the LORD your God"'" (Matthew 4:5-7).

Don't ever fall for the taunting of the devil.

"And Enoch walked with God; and he was not, for God took him" (Genesis 5:24).

The average pair of feet take up to 8,000 steps a day, or about 2.5 million steps a year. Over a lifetime, the average person will walk approximately 115,000 miles! But some people walk much farther. In 1970, David Kunst, with his interest in adventure sparked by the moon landing the summer before, decided to walk around the world. Accompanied by his brother John and a pack mule named Willie Makeit, the 30-year-old Dave set out from Waseca, Minnesota, on June 20. Dave and John walked to New York, flew to Portugal, and then walked all the way to Iran.

Two years into their epic journey, Afghan bandits killed John and wounded David. Nevertheless, after four months of recuperation, David resumed the walk from the site of the shooting, this time accompanied by his brother Peter. Together they crossed India. But when it came time to fly to Australia, Peter needed to return home, so Dave continued on alone. While walking across the Australian desert, his mule died. But Dave would not give up. Providentially, Jenni Samuel, an Australian school teacher, volunteered to tow the mule's wagon with her car. So, on October 5, 1974, David Kunst walked back into Waseca, Minnesota, becoming the first person to have circled the land mass of the earth on foot. His historic 15,000-mile odyssey required four and a half years, 21 pairs of shoes, and three mules. The long walk earned Kunst an entry in the Guinness World Records and a spot on *Ripley's Believe it or Not*. It also earned him a bride—the same Jenni Samuel who towed his wagon across Australia!

Walking around the world is a feat that requires a lot of soul (pardon the pun), but there is a man who accomplished a greater feat—he walked all the way to heaven! The Bible says Enoch "walked with God." He knew God so well—through communion with Him and guided by Him so completely—that God simply took him to heaven early. While we may not be translated like Enoch, Jesus has extended an invitation to all of us to walk with Him: "As the Father loved Me, I also have loved you; abide in My love" (John 15:9). Won't you accept His invitation?

FREEZE-RESISTANT PEOPLE

"I could wish you were cold or hot" (Revelation 3:15).

Normally a person's core body temperature is around 97.8 degrees Fahrenheit. But when a person is exposed to cold for a prolonged period of time, hypothermia can set it. Once the body temperature hits 90 degrees, vital organs begin slowing down and death can come within minutes—but not for Wim Hof of the Netherlands. Wim, also known as the Iceman, possesses such a strong resistance to cold that scientists remain baffled how his body endures the freezing extremes that would kill most people.

For example, in January 1999 he traveled 100 miles north of the Arctic Circle to run a half marathon in his bare feet. Three years later, Wim earned a Guinness world record when he dove under the ice at the North Pole dressed only in a swimsuit. He held his breath for more than 6 minutes while swimming 265 feet under the ice, almost twice the length of an Olympic-size pool. Then Hof tried to scale Mount Everest in his shorts (but wasn't able to finish because of a foot injury).

Hof says he discovered his ability to withstand cold temperatures more than 20 years ago. A lot of scientists are working to figure out how the 49-year-old Dutchman is able to withstand freezing temperatures that could be fatal to the average person. Wim simply describes his ability as being able to use his brain to adjust his own thermostat. In 2008, in New York City, Wim broke his previous world record by staying immersed in ice up to the neck for 1 hour, 13 minutes, and 48 seconds with nothing on but a swimsuit! No one else out there seems able to compete with him. He just keeps breaking his own records.

In the Bible we are told it is better to be hot or cold than have our spiritual thermostat lukewarm. Jesus warns the church of Laodicea, a church that represents our present age, "I know your works, that you are neither cold nor hot. I could wish you were cold or hot. So then, because you are lukewarm, and neither cold nor hot, I will vomit you out of My mouth" (Revelation 3:15, 16). Why such strong language? These believers do not sense their need of the Holy Spirit. Living in a cold world, they will soon spiritually die and not even know it.

"... let us lay aside every weight, and the sin which so easily ensnares us, and let us run with endurance the race that is set before us, looking unto Jesus, the author and finisher of our faith ..." (Hebrews 12:1, 2).

On February 12, 1908, over 250,000 cheering spectators gathered in Times Square to witness the start of the longest automobile competition in history—a global race from New York to Paris. Six cars and their teams from France, Italy, Germany, and the United States would follow an ambitious course west across the U.S. to Seattle, cross the Pacific by ship to Japan, then through Russia, Germany, and finish in Paris.

The starting pistol was fired and off they went. The American car, built by the Thomas Motor Company, had a four-cylinder, 60-horsepower engine that could reach a maximum speed of 60 mph. The lead place was exchanged several times by the German, Italian, and American teams. This torturous race began in mid-winter back when there were few maintained roads, no snowplows, no 4WD, no radios, unreliable maps, and no regular gas stations or food stops. When possible they would follow railroad tracks, a bone-jarring experience. Sometimes they were lost for days and had to backtrack. Often, horses were hired to pull the cars through the deep Iowa snow or Siberian mud. Occasionally the teams even stopped to help rescue each other. On they pushed, and finally after 169 days and over 22,000 miles, on July 30, 1908, the American team arrived in Paris to win the race.

Of the six teams that started the grueling contest, only three arrived in Paris. Incredibly, the winning American driver, George Schuster, appeared in Times Square only to deliver the Thomas Flyer to the starting line. When the chosen mechanic withdrew at the last minute, George was asked to fill in as the team mechanic. On a whim he changed his clothes, climbed aboard, and made history. Before the race was over, George had become the driver and was the only original member of the American team to finish the historic race. George, who lived to 99, had also become the first person to drive across the United States during the winter in an automobile.

Did you know the Bible speaks of the Christian life as a great race? It encourages us to give this race everything we've got. And if we keep our eyes on Jesus, who is "the author and finisher of our faith," we can't lose!

"Then the Lord came down upon Mount Sinai, on the top of the mountain. And the Lord called Moses to the top of the mountain, and Moses went up" (Exodus 19:20).

Mountain climbing can be a dangerous business. In one 1996 Everest expedition eight climbers were killed and several others were stranded by a rogue storm. Some mountains are even more treacherous than Everest. The Annapurna peaks in the Himalaya range are among the world's most perilous mountains, with a fatality rate of more than 40 percent among those who attempt to scale them.

So why do people climb mountains? When British climber George Mallory was asked in 1924 why he wanted to climb Mount Everest, he responded "Because it's there." August of that year Mallory and his partner, Andrew Irvine, disappeared on the way to the summit. For 75 years he was missing, but in 1999 his body was discovered in remarkable condition at about 27,000-foot elevation. No one is quite sure whether or not he and his partner made it to the summit. We hope so.

Then there is Reinhold Messner, an Italian mountaineer from South Tyrol, who is often viewed as the greatest mountain climber of all time. He is renowned for making the first solo ascents of Mount Everest without supplemental oxygen and for being the first climber to ascend all 14 peaks over 8,000 meters or 26,000 feet above sea level. Of course Mount Everest, at 29,032 feet, is the highest peak in the world. The mountain was officially conquered on the morning of May 29, 1953, when Edmund Hillary and his Sherpa guide, Tenzing, reached the summit where they took a few pictures and buried a cross.

Did you know the Bible says in the last days every believer may have to become a mountain climber? "So when you see the 'abomination of desolation,' spoken of by Daniel the prophet, standing where it ought not (let the reader understand), then let those who are in Judea flee to the mountains" (Mark 13:14). God's people have often fled to the mountains for safety. When the armies of Titus destroyed Jerusalem, over one million people died and about 97,000 were taken captive. But during a break in the siege, all the Christians fled, as Christ directed, and not one of them died.

"Do you not know that those who run in a race all run, but one receives the prize? Run in such a way that you may obtain it. And everyone who competes for the prize is temperate in all things. Now they do it to obtain a perishable crown, but we for an imperishable crown" (1 Corinthians 9:24, 25).

Back in 1904, a mailman in Havana, Cuba, read in a newspaper that the Olympic Games that year would be held in St. Louis, Missouri. That's when the 5-foot-1-inch Felix Carvajal suddenly decided to run in the Olympics. Nearly penniless, and with no formal running experience or sponsor, Felix decided to pay his own way to the Games. After work he would go to Havana's Central Plaza and run in circles to draw a crowd. He would then announce his intention to claim a prize for the greater glory of Cuba. His appreciative audience donated enough money to help him enter the race and secure Felix's travel on a steamer bound for New Orleans.

However, the boat passage was expensive, and what little money Felix had left was stolen in New Orleans. Undaunted, Felix Carvajal walked, ran, and hitchhiked 700 miles to St. Louis, arriving moments before the marathon start. It was a 100-degree day, and Felix was wearing woolen trousers, heavy shoes, and a felt beret. The race was delayed while Felix's trousers were cut off to fashion a pair of running shorts. Then, with a bang, the 31 runners were on their way.

Amazingly, Felix kept pace easily, seemingly unconcerned over the prospects of victory, even chatting with bystanders. Felix hadn't eaten for more than two days, and there was only one water station on the more than 26 miles of dusty heat, so he picked a few apples from a nearby orchard. Alas, the green apples triggered wrenching stomach cramps, causing another unscheduled pit stop and precious minutes lost.

Incredibly, Felix still finished fourth among a field of the world's best runners. Hailed by the international press for his determination and amiable manner, he returned to Cuba a hero and resumed his mail route. We can't help but believe Felix would have won the 1904 Olympic marathon if he had been better prepared.

Are you prepared to win your spiritual race? The Bible says in order to be successful we should run like we mean it and be "temperate in all things." Keep in mind the prize—not a "perishable crown," but one that lasts forever!

AMAZON TREKKER

"Brethren, I do not count myself to have apprehended; but one thing I do, forgetting those things which are behind and reaching forward to those things which are ahead, I press toward the goal for the prize of the upward call of God in Christ Jesus" (Philippians 3:13, 14).

Someone said it couldn't be done, so Ed Stafford decided to do it. After leaving the military, the 34-year-old British army captain became bored with office life. So when someone told him no one had ever walked the length of the Amazon, he took it as a personal challenge. Ed began his trek on April 2, 2008, leaving the Pacific Ocean in Southern Peru. His friend and traveling companion, Luke Collyer, returned home after just three months. Along the way, he recruited Sanchez Rivera, a 31-year-old Peruvian forestry worker, and the two continued the journey together.

At first, Stafford guessed that his jungle trek would take around a year to complete, but he soon realized that was wishful thinking. Each step of the 4,200 miles brought a new battle. Stafford and Rivera contended with piranhas, giant anaconda snakes, whirlpools, flood currents, relentless rain, mosquitoes, and disease. They dodged 18-foot-long caiman crocodiles and endured many food shortages. They lived off piranha and palm hearts, with occasional stops for provisions at villages along the river. But the biggest threats were the territorial natives—mistreated for decades, the villagers were often distrustful and frequently violent. Nevertheless, for two and a half years, Stafford relentlessly trudged, swam, and climbed along the river bank, often needing to hack his path one step at a time with a machete.

Just one day shy of his destination, Stafford collapsed at the side of the road, his body so spent that he broke into a whole body rash. However, after a few hours of rest, he was back to his feet, pressing on. Fifty-three miles later, on August 9, 2010, an exuberant Ed Stafford ran into the Atlantic Ocean at Crispim Beach in northern Brazil. He is the first person to walk the entire length of the Amazon River, from the Pacific to the Atlantic.

Sometimes the Christian life can seem like a difficult and endless journey, but all things are possible with Christ. Paul encouraged the Romans with this thought: "The sufferings of this present time are not worthy to be compared with the glory which shall be revealed in us" (Romans 8:18). Let's press forward, friends, for our pilgrimage will soon be completed!

"But no man can tame the tongue. It is an unruly evil, full of deadly poison" (James 3:8).

Kanchana Ketkeaw made herself comfortable in the glass box where she lived for 32 days. She had a refrigerator, television, magazines, a small plant and 3,400 scorpions! On October 23, 2002, Kanchana emerged from the room, setting an unofficial world record for the longest stay in a room full of poisonous scorpions. She said, "It was like being in a room at home, only with thousands of little friends."

Living with scorpions was not unusual for the 30-year-old Thai entertainer. She has performed with the menacing little creatures daily as a tourist attraction, even putting them in her mouth as part of the routine. And Kanchana has been stung hundreds of times. She was stung nine times during the record-breaking stay in the 130-square-foot room. She was stung once when she got out of bed without looking at the floor. But Kanchana says the venom has little effect on her because of the immunity she has built up over seven years.

Some of the scorpions died in the glass chamber and new ones were added. Some even gave birth. She fed them a daily mixture of raw egg and ground pork. Her room at a resort town department store had a bed and a toilet guarded from the public eye by a curtain. Kanchana was allowed to leave her room for 15 minutes every eight hours to shower. She did have a difficult time getting to sleep because the mall, where her cubicle was set up, didn't close until late.

The previous world record was set the previous year by a Malaysian woman who endured 30 days with 2,700 scorpions. Before her record-breaking attempt was approved, Kanchana had to send a full report, including video footage and photos, to the Guinness World Records office in London. You can't help but wonder what would possess a young woman to willingly live with scorpions.

But thousands of young people are stung everyday by choosing to marry the wrong person. The Bible says, "Can two walk together, unless they are agreed?" (Amos 3:3). When choosing a marriage partner, it is important that you both follow God's Word or you may end up biting and devouring one another!

August 23 SHEEP FARMER ENDURANCE

"Therefore we also, since we are surrounded by so great a cloud of witnesses, let us lay aside every weight, and the sin which so easily ensnares us, and let us run with endurance the race that is set before us" (Hebrews 12:1).

In 1983, a 61-year-old sheep farmer named Cliff Young decided to participate in the world's toughest race, a 544-mile ultra-marathon from Melbourne to Sydney, Australia. When the 150 world-class athletes gathered at the starting line they were amused to see old Cliff enter the race wearing overalls with galoshes over his work boots.

As soon as the race started, the pros quickly left Cliff shuffling behind. Spectators were hoping someone would stop the crazy old man before he hurt himself, but he kept plodding along. Normally the contenders run about 18 hours and sleep 6 hours during the seven-day race. But no one told Cliff he was supposed to sleep! So while the other runners slept he kept running, gaining on the pack a little more each day. By the last night, he passed all of the world-class athletes. By the last day, he was way in front of them. Incredibly, not only did Cliff run the Melbourne to Sydney race at age 61 without dying, he won first place, breaking the race record by 9 hours and becoming a national hero!

When asked how he could run all night, Cliff said. "See, I grew up on a farm where we couldn't afford horses, and whenever the storms would roll in, I'd have to go out on foot and round up the sheep. We had 2,000 head, and sometimes I would have to run those sheep for two or three days nonstop." Throughout the race, he just imagined he was chasing sheep. When Cliff was awarded the first prize of $10,000, he said he didn't know there was a prize and insisted they split it among the other lead runners. The nation fell in love with the 61-year-old vegetarian who came out of nowhere to defeat the world's best long-distance runners.

Cliff Young, because of his upbringing, had incredible endurance. The Bible says we also must have endurance for "the race that is set before us." But where do we get the strength and stamina we need? The Psalms tell us that God is "He who gives strength and power to His people," and "It is God who arms me with strength" (Psalm 68:35; 18:32). The strength and endurance we need come only from Him.

"And truly if they had called to mind that country from which they had come out, they would have had opportunity to return" (Hebrews 11:15).

In the spring of 1927 a young woman named Lillian Alling, who was living in New York City, became very homesick and decided to return to her family in Russia. After two unhappy years among the teeming people, this peasant girl knew life in the noisy city was not for her. Lillian was unable to save enough to afford passage across the Atlantic by boat, but all she could think about was going home. So, this young slip of a woman about 25 years old chose to walk the 12,000 miles to Russia!

Very timid, Lillian refused to accept rides from strangers, so supplied with hand-drawn maps, an iron rod for protection, and a few dollars she began her epic journey on foot. Averaging 30 to 40 miles a day, the frail girl passed through Chicago and on to Winnipeg. Keep in mind, back in 1927 there were no roads in the Northwest, and, except for the odd trading post or telegraph station, there was nothing but an unbroken stretch of the world's toughest terrain and wilderness.

When asked where she was heading her firm reply was, "I am going to Russia. Please do not stop me." When she reached Vancouver, her ragged condition and lack of provisions caused great concern among the locals. To prevent her from continuing on, she was arrested for vagrancy and thrown in jail.

When spring arrived, Lillian resumed her daunting quest. Across the Yukon and Alaska, telegraph station operators kept track of her progress. Lillian arrived in Nome in July 1929 wearing a different type of men's shoe on each foot. Soon after leaving Nome, Lillian was last seen rowing a boat from Cape Prince of Wales across the 36 miles of the Bering Strait to Siberia. There is one report of a man who claimed he saw a woman on the Siberian coast in the fall of 1930, explaining to an astonished policeman she'd walked all the way from New York.

We marvel at Lillian Alling's incredible determination to get to her home in Russia, yet so many are indifferent about reaching the home Jesus has prepared for them in heaven. The heroes of faith knew of a better country and exercised faith in making a journey to that place prepared by God. "But now they desire a better, that is, a heavenly country. Therefore God is not ashamed to be called their God, for He has prepared a city for them" (Hebrews 11:16). Are you willing to make the journey?

August 25 FLYING LAWN CHAIR

Great peace have those who love Your law, and nothing causes them to stumble" (Psalm 119:165).

In July of 2007, Kent Couch settled down in his lawn chair with some snacks, a BB gun, and a parachute. Attached to his chair were 105 extra-large helium balloons. With a satellite phone, an altimeter, and a handheld GPS in his pocket, Couch headed up into the Oregon sky.

Nearly nine hours later, the 47-year-old gas station owner came back to earth in a farmer's field near Union, Oregon, about 200 miles from home. Couch said, "Every kid holding a helium balloon thinks about it. I don't know about girls, but I think most guys look up in the sky and wish they could ride on a cloud. When you're lying in the grass on a summer day, and you see the clouds, you wish you could jump on them. This is as close as you can come to jumping on them."

This was actually Couch's second flight. In September 2007 he got off the ground for six hours. When he used a BB gun to pop the balloons, he began to descend too quickly and had to parachute to safety. Couch's wife, Susan, called him crazy but added: "It's never been a dull moment since I married him."

This time Kent was better prepared to control his decent. Attached to the chair he had several plastic bags holding five gallons of water each to act as ballast. After lifting off from Bend, Oregon, at 6:06 a.m., he drifted east at about 25 mph. Couch said he could hear cattle and children below, and he said he even passed through some clouds. "It was beautiful–beautiful," he told reporters. Around 3:00 p.m. he popped enough balloons to set the craft down in Union, which caused quite a stir. Kent remarked about his flight, "The best thing is the peace, the serenity."

It seems people everywhere are looking for peace and serenity, but do you need helium balloons to find it? The Bible says that those who love God's law will have great peace. And Jesus promises His followers, "Peace I leave with you, My peace I give to you; not as the world gives do I give to you. Let not your heart be troubled, neither let it be afraid" (John 14:27). If we are obedient to Jesus and trust in Him, we will receive the peace of God in our hearts.

"But he who endures to the end shall be saved" (Matthew 24:13).

The man who holds the most Olympic world records in swimming is Michael Phelps. Nicknamed the "Baltimore Bullet" and the "Flying Fish," he is the most decorated Olympian of all time with 22 medals. Michael is a four-time Olympian and has also won 33 World Champs LCM medals. In fact, in the 2012 Summer Olympics in London, Phelps won four gold medals and two silver medals, making him the most successful athlete of the Games for the third Olympics in a row! Phelps started the Michael Phelps Foundation to raise awareness on the sport of swimming and also to promote healthier lifestyles.

But one of the greatest triumphs of endurance is held by Benoit Lecomte, who was the first person to swim across the Atlantic Ocean without a kickboard! On July 16, 1998, he set out from Cape Cod with eight wet suits, a snorkel, and some flippers. He was guided across the ocean by three French sailors on a 40-foot sailboat. The boat also suspended a large cage with an electronic force field over Benoit to protect him from sharks. He did, however, still encounter sea turtles, dolphins, and jellyfish. And for five days he was followed by a great white shark!

Lecomte swam six to eight hours a day through 3,736 nautical miles of relentless waves. He stopped for equipment repairs and to rest for one week in the Azores Islands. Seventy-two days after beginning his epic trip he swam ashore, exhausted but heroic, in France. Lecomte is now considering swimming across the Pacific Ocean from Japan to California. What would ever make a man swim across an ocean? Love. When Benoit's father died of colon cancer in 1992, it spurred him to do something extraordinary to raise awareness and money for cancer research.

The Bible says someone else crossed an ocean of space for the same reason. Paul challenges us to have the same mindset as Christ. "Let this mind be in you which was also in Christ Jesus, who, being in the form of God, did not consider it robbery to be equal with God, but made Himself of no reputation, taking the form of a bondservant, and coming in the likeness of men" (Philippians 2:5-7). Christ participated in an event that took His life. He carried His cause to the limit to save us.

MARATHON RUNNER

"... let us run with endurance the race that is set before us" (Hebrews 12:1).

In September in 490 B.C., Darius the Persian king sent an army of 25,000 to crush an army of 10,000 Athenian troops fighting for liberty. The Greek general, aware that his army was greatly outnumbered, sent Pheidippides [fi-dip-i-deez], one of the fastest runners in Greece, to carry the urgent request to Sparta asking for reinforcements. Pheidippides covered the 147 miles in a day and a night. The Spartans agreed to come following the full moon.

After eating a small meal, and with no sleep, Pheidippides ran with the message all the way back to Athens, again in 24 hours. Almost immediately after arriving, poor Pheidippides had to then march with the army to the plain of Marathon, where they engaged in a fierce but triumphant battle against the Persians. As soon as the fight was over he then ran the 23 miles back to Athens. Upon reaching the Athenian marketplace Pheidippides shouted, "Victory, victory!" and then fell dead. Some think it was the 23-mile marathon that killed Pheidippides. It was more likely the lack of sleep, lack of food, the infantry battle, and over 300 miles of cross-country running in four days that killed him.

The first Greek marathon runner has nothing on Dean Karnazes. *Men's Fitness Magazine* says, "Dean might just be the fittest man in the world" (March 2006). Dean has traveled the country, speaking and running ultra-marathons to promote the importance of physical exercise and good diet. He recently ran 50 marathons in all 50 states in 50 consecutive days, finishing with the New York City Marathon. As a finale to his incredible achievement, he then ran back from New York City to St. Louis, Missouri, covering nearly 1,300 miles along the way.

A lover of the outdoors, Dean has pushed his body and mind to inconceivable limits. Among his many accomplishments, he has run a 135-mile ultra-marathon across Death Valley in 120-degree-Fahrenheit temperatures, and a marathon to the South Pole in minus 40 degrees Fahrenheit.

Did you know the Bible tells about a prophet that fled 40 days and 40 nights, covering over 1,000 miles on only one meal? "And the angel of the Lord came back the second time, and touched him, and said, 'Arise and eat, because the journey is too great for you.' So he arose, and ate and drank; and he went in the strength of that food forty days and forty nights as far as Horeb, the mountain of God" (1 Kings 19:7, 8).

"It was right that we should make merry and be glad, for your brother was dead and is alive again, and was lost and is found" (Luke 15:32).

On October 5, 2010, three teenage boys from the remote South Pacific island of Atafu made a reckless decision. Without consulting their parents, the three cousins decided to attempt a journey across 50 miles of open ocean in a 12-foot aluminum boat to visit some girls from a neighboring island. They never made it. After weeks of searching, the two 15-year-olds and a 14-year-old were given up for dead. Hundreds gathered with their families to grieve and eulogize them in a memorial service. Then, 50 days after the boys set out, a tuna boat was headed back to New Zealand by a route they didn't usually take when they spotted the boys waving frantically from their tiny vessel. Their craft had drifted nearly 800 miles to a desolate part of the Pacific Ocean northeast of Fiji. The boys were dehydrated, exhausted, and anemic, with second-degree sunburns and fungal infections, but they were alive.

The boys told reporters that they had begun their journey in a drunken haze and soon passed out in the bottom of the boat. When they awoke, they had drifted out of sight of land. Eventually, they ran out of gas for their outboard motor. All their provisions—just 20 coconuts and a mayonnaise jar full of water—were gone within the first six days. After that, they told their rescuers, they survived by catching rain water on a tarp and eating the few raw fish that happened to wash into their boat. Once, they caught a sea bird that landed on their boat, which they also ate raw. Their rescue came just in time: medical staff said they wouldn't have lasted another week.

The father of one of the boys told reporters that the entire village was so excited that they were crying, singing, hugging, and shouting the good news to each other in the streets. According to the Bible, a similar scene takes place in the streets of heaven each time one sinner repents! Jesus tells us that "there is joy in the presence of the angels of God over one sinner who repents" (Luke 15:7). And when we finally reach our heavenly home, God will do just what the father of the prodigal son did—bring out the best He has to celebrate our arrival!

HENRY "BOX" BROWN

"Therefore if the Son makes you free, you shall be free indeed" (John 8:36).

Henry "Box" Brown was born as a slave in Virginia about 1815. He worked for years in a tobacco factory in Richmond. But when his owner suddenly sold Henry's wife and three children to a new owner in another state, Henry determined to escape. In 1848 he persuaded a couple friends to build him a wooden box three feet long and two feet wide. After writing "This Side Up" on the outside of the box, Henry squeezed inside and had two friends mail the box from North Carolina to abolitionists in Philadelphia through the Adams Express Company for $86.

Brown's box traveled by wagon, then railroad, steamboat, wagon again, another railroad, ferry, railroad, and finally delivery wagon. The journey lasted over 27 hours. Henry had a little water and ventilation holes, but despite the box's label, workers handled it roughly, and several time he was put upside down. Nevertheless Henry always remained still and gave no indication that he was inside the box. After the long, cramped journey Henry Brown made it to freedom. One of those present when the box was opened remembered his first words: "How do you do, gentlemen?" He then sang a psalm from the Bible chosen for this moment of liberation.

Henry dedicated the rest of his life to helping liberate other slaves and became a well-known speaker for the Anti-Slavery Society. He published two versions of his autobiography and later toured Britain for 10 years conducting a performance on slavery in America. At one time he was criticized by the abolitionist Fredrick Douglass, who wished Brown hadn't shared so many details about his escape that may have helped others escape.

Did you know the Bible speaks of someone else who escaped slavery in a small container? "Jesus answered them, 'Most assuredly, I say to you, whoever commits sin is a slave of sin'" (John 8:34). But was Christ a slave of sin? "For He made Him who knew no sin to be sin for us, that we might become the righteousness of God in Him" (2 Corinthians 5:21). Jesus took sin upon Himself and received the penalty of death. But the grave "box" could not hold Him. "I am He who lives, and was dead, and behold, I am alive forevermore. Amen. And I have the keys of Hades and of Death" (Revelation 1:18).

If you are locked in the box of sin, Christ can set you free.

"Whatever your hand finds to do, do it with your might; for there is no work or device or knowledge or wisdom in the grave where you are going" (Ecclesiastes 9:10).

Roz Savage is an intrepid ocean rower and environmental advocate, but the first half of Roz's life was anything but adventurous. In 2001, the 34-year-old Brit was a management consultant and investment banker working every day in an office cubical. That year, while on a train trip, she thoughtfully wrote out two possible obituaries for her life—the one she was currently living and the one she really wanted to live. So Roz made a gutsy decision to give up her steady income and big house in the suburbs.

In 2003, she took part in an expedition that discovered Inca ruins in the Andean cloud forests near Machu Picchu. Next she ran in the London and New York marathons, finishing in the top two percent. Roz had done some rowing while attending Oxford, so one day she decided to row across the Atlantic Ocean ... solo in a 23-foot rowboat, without a support vessel. Along the way all four oars broke, forcing her to row more than half the trip with patched-up oars. Her cooking stove failed after only 20 days, then her navigation equipment and music player went bad. She managed to maintain her daily weblog right up until day 80, when her satellite phone failed, leaving only her position transponder to indicate by her movement that she was still alive. On March 14, 2006, after 103 days of rowing, she completed the Atlantic crossing.

In 2008, she became the first woman to row solo from California to Hawaii. In 2009, she rowed from Hawaii to Tarawa in the Kiribati Islands. Then in June 2010, Roz Savage, 42, rowed her boat from Kiribati to Madang in Papua, New Guinea, becoming the first woman to row solo across the Pacific. So far she has rowed over 11,000 miles, taken 3.5 million oar strokes, and spent over a year of her life at sea.

The Bible says, "Whatever your hand finds to do, do it with your might" (Ecclesiastes 9:10). Since our time on Earth is limited, we should strive to accomplish all we can, especially in spiritual matters. Jesus said, "I must work the works of Him who sent Me while it is day; the night is coming when no one can work" (John 9:4). How important it is to make God and His work the first priority of our lives!

HIGH ADVENTURE

"No one has ascended to heaven but He who came down from heaven, that is, the Son of Man who is in heaven" (John 3:13).

Few people have had more high adventure with balloons than Joseph Kittinger. In 1950, Kittinger joined the U.S. Air Force and quickly got into experimental aviation. In 1953 he joined a unique mission called Project Manhigh. This venture used high-altitude balloons to study if humans were capable of going into space. On June 2, 1957, Kittinger made his first high-altitude ascent. It took him up to 96,760 feet in a pressurized suit, nearly out of Earth's atmosphere, for almost seven hours. After this flight, Kittinger transferred to Project Excelsior (meaning "ever upward"). For this assignment, those who went up took the fastest route down—by jumping out of the balloon! In 1959, Kittinger jumped from a balloon 74,700 feet high and set a record for the longest free-fall (55,500 feet).

On August 16, 1960, Kittinger made his most famous free-fall. He reached the altitude of 102,800 feet, where he stayed about 12 minutes—challenging at minus 94 degrees Fahrenheit! Then he jumped and fell towards Earth for almost five minutes before opening his main parachute. As he streaked toward the ground he reached 614 mph, approaching the sound barrier, and achieved the fastest speed by man through the atmosphere. In 1962, he spent over 18 hours in a Project Stargazer balloon at an altitude of 82,200 feet, researching the effects of high altitude on man and telescope.

Later, Kittinger flew 483 missions in Vietnam before being shot down and held as a POW for almost a year. A Christian, Kittinger was sustained by prayer. In 1983, Colonel Kittinger set a record for flying a balloon from Las Vegas to New York in less than 72 hours. To increase distance, he expended all available ballast and landed in only his underwear. A year later he became the first man to cross the Atlantic Ocean in a balloon, setting a record for the longest solo balloon flight at 83 hours and 40 minutes. As of this writing, Joseph Kittinger is still flying balloons in Orlando, Florida, and still holds many records, including the highest balloon ascent, fastest speed by man through the atmosphere, and more.

You have heard the expression "What goes up must come down." But the Bible teaches there is one Man who came down and went back up! In the highest adventure of all, when Jesus returns, all His children will be caught up with Him in the clouds!

Animals

"But now ask the beasts, and they will teach you;
And the birds of the air, and they will tell you"
Job 12:7

September 1 KANGAROO MILK

"For though by this time you ought to be teachers, you need someone to teach you again the first principles of the oracles of God; and you have come to need milk and not solid food. For everyone who partakes only of milk is unskilled in the word of righteousness, for he is a babe" (Hebrews 5:12, 13).

Kangaroos are among the most unique creatures on our planet. The word "kangaroo" stems from the Aboriginal word "gangurru" that was used to describe the grey kangaroo. Today the name kangaroo or "Roo" encompasses all species of kangaroos, wallabies, and wallaroos. The adult male kangaroo is called a buck, boomer, or jack. An adult female is a doe, flyer, or jill. Young kangaroos are joeys, and a group of kangaroos is a mob.

Fossils tell us Australia once had kangaroos 10 feet tall, weighing 500 pounds. Today the red kangaroo is the world's largest marsupial, at six feet and 200 pounds. In addition, they can run nearly 40 mph, bounding as far as 25 feet! Their strong tails are used for balance when hopping, or as fifth limbs when grazing. Oddly, kangaroos can't move backwards or move their hind legs independently on land. But when swimming, they can kick each leg separately. All kangaroos are herbivores, and those living in drier regions need little water. But these vegetarians can be deadly. The powerful hind legs with long, sharp toenails are a dangerous weapon. With one kick, kangaroos can disembowel opponents.

The doe kangaroo can mate and become pregnant directly after a joey is born, but the development of that pregnancy will be suspended until the first baby kangaroo is either lost or leaves the pouch. This means a female kangaroo can have three babies at the same time: an older joey living outside the pouch, a young one in the pouch, and an embryo on hold, awaiting birth. Then, amazingly, the doe will develop two different kinds of milk, one in each teat, to feed her two offspring—a high fat milk for the younger joey in the pouch, and a high-carbohydrate milk for the older joey. Eventually they must learn to live off solid food.

Did you know the Bible says some baby Christians never get weaned? Some who should be teaching others by now are still on infant formula—being bottle fed the simple basics of Christianity they should already know. If a baby doesn't grow, something is wrong. Likewise, the Christian life requires growth and moving on to the solid food in God's Word.

"One man of you shall chase a thousand, for the Lord your God is He who fights for you, as He promised you" (Joshua 23:10).

What can accelerate from 0 to 60 mph in three seconds? I'm not describing a car but an animal. The cheetah is the fastest land animal on Earth and has been clocked at speeds up to 75 mph in short bursts. This large cat lives in most of Africa and parts of the Middle East. It measures 30 inches tall at the shoulder and weighs between 110 and 140 pounds. The cheetah lives about 10-15 years and loves the open plains, where it mostly hunts for antelope.

We think of lions as majestic and leopards as ferocious, but the lean cheetah is elegant and graceful. It's been referred to as the "greyhound" of cats. It is smaller than its bigger cat sisters, but much faster. A cheetah is aerodynamically built for speed. It has long, slim, muscular legs that can spring instantly into action. A small, rounded head, long neck, deep chest, and flexible spine help as well. Interestingly, it has non-retractable claws (sort of like cleats) and special pads on its feet for superb traction. Even its long tail (about 28 inches) gives it extra balance in chasing game.

A cheetah will stalk its prey by getting as close as possible before bursting into full speed. It relies on tall grass to camouflage itself. As it comes close it will reach out and trip the animal (usually antelope) with its front paw and then grab it by the throat. Actually, only about half the chases are successful and only last for about 20-60 seconds. The cheetah eats its kill quickly since there are other bigger carnivores that will steal its food.

The Bible tells how King Saul chased David into the wilderness, seeking to destroy him. He writes, "When the wicked came against me to eat up my flesh, my enemies and foes, they stumbled and fell" (Psalm 27:2). Satan seeks to trip us while pursuing us, but like David, we can be confident in God's protection. The primary focus of this Psalm is finding refuge in the sanctuary. We too can find safety in the tabernacle of God when being chased by the devil. No matter how fast he runs, we will quickly find help in our time of need.

September 3 UNIQUELY YOU

"For You formed my inward parts; You covered me in my mother's womb. I will praise You, for I am fearfully and wonderfully made" (Psalm 139:13).

No doubt you've heard the American folk song that begins "Oh, give me a home where the buffalo roam, where the deer and the antelope play ..." Contrary to these well-known lyrics, North America doesn't have any antelope—but it does have the pronghorn. Although it is often called an antelope, the pronghorn is its own species, and they are unique in many ways.

If you ever see a pronghorn on the prairie, you can be sure it saw you first. Their exceptional eyes have a 320-degree field of vision and can pick up movement up to three miles away. Another defense mechanism is its speed. It can be argued that it is the fastest land mammal in the world. It can sprint 65 mph and can sustain a speed of 35 mph over rough terrain for miles! The African cheetah, often called the fastest land mammal, can sprint over 70 mph—but only in short spurts. Over a long distance, there is no other land mammal that can match the pronghorn's speed. In addition, when a herd of pronghorn must run, they do it in an oval-shaped formation, similar to a flock of birds. But while the pronghorn is a great runner, it is not a great jumper. When it encounters a fence, it ducks underneath!

Another unique feature of the pronghorn is its horn, which is neither an antler nor a true horn. True horns, like on a goat or cow, are made up of a living bone core surrounded by keratin. They are not shed annually and are often curved, but never branched. Antlers, on the other hand, are made of bone with a velvet coating, and they are shed annually and are branched. The horns of a pronghorn are a bit of both—they are made of bone surrounded by keratin like a true horn, but they are branched like an antler. In addition, the keratin covering is shed annually, which is something no other animal does.

God specializes in unique creations! Each species has its own quirks and oddities—and no person is just like another. God told Jeremiah, "Before I formed you in the womb I knew you ... I ordained you a prophet to the nations" (Jeremiah 1:5). Can you imagine God carefully shaping each of us in our mother's womb, giving each of us our own unique traits? Truly, we are His amazing creations!

September 4

"After these things I looked, and behold, a great multitude which no one could number, of all nations, tribes, peoples, and tongues, standing before the throne and before the Lamb, clothed with white robes, with palm branches in their hands" (Revelation 7:9).

Prairie dogs are highly social, curious, and playful creatures that live in large colonies or "towns." While prairie dogs are related to rodents, they are very intelligent and exhibit an elaborate communication system using about a dozen separate calls to send messages. These animals were once found across the plains west of the Mississippi ranging from Mexico to Canada. It is estimated that in the early 1800s, some 700 million acres of North American rangeland were inhabited by five billion prairie dogs.

When the Lewis and Clark expedition entered the Great Plains in 1804, they saw many animals unknown to Eastern settlers such as coyotes, antelope, and grizzly bears. In all, 122 animals were described in their journals, but most memorable was the prairie dog. When they first encountered a village of prairie dogs, the whole expedition team spent an entire day trying to flood prairie dogs out of their tunnels to ship specimens back to President Thomas Jefferson, but they only managed to capture one live prairie dog.

The next spring, this lone prairie dog was included in a shipment to President Jefferson. From North Dakota, that animal traveled down the Missouri River to St. Louis. From there, the furry cargo was put on another ship and sent down the Mississippi to New Orleans. There, another ship took the rodent through the Gulf of Mexico, around Florida, and up the coast to the Chesapeake Bay and on to Baltimore. Finally, after several months, this prairie dog arrived in Washington, D.C., still alive! Jefferson arrived in Washington six weeks later. Still, the animal was active and healthy when the president saw it on October 4, 1805. Jefferson sent the prairie dog to a natural history museum in Philadelphia's Independence Hall, where the animal lived out its days.

Today, because of habitat loss and devastating plagues, prairie dog populations have been reduced by 90 percent. It's hard to imagine at one time there was a single prairie dog colony in Texas covering 25,000 square miles. It contained an estimated 400 million animals.

Did you know the Word of God teaches that there will be an innumerable tribe of people saved in God's kingdom? Because of His immeasurable love and grace, heaven will be filled with multitudes of His grateful children.

ROTTEN EGGS, GARLIC, & BURNT RUBBER

"Dead flies putrefy the perfumer's ointment, and cause it to give off a foul odor; so does a little folly to one respected for wisdom and honor" (Ecclesiastes 10:1).

What's the first thing that comes to your mind when you hear the word "skunk"? It is probably the strong, foul odor used by these cute little striped black and white polecats to protect them from danger. Most animals and people are smart enough to stay clear of the scent glands used by skunks as a defensive weapon. Someone once described the odor as a mixture of rotten eggs, garlic, and burnt rubber. Because of muscles around these glands, skunks are pretty accurate in their aim at up to 10 feet away. People can easily smell this odor up to a mile away.

Actually, the skunk is reluctant to fire this weapon. It has enough to shoot five or six times, but then needs about 10 days to make another supply. Seeing the black and white stripes (or spots) is enough for most animals and people to stay clear. But if pressed, the skunk will still give warnings by hissing, stamping its feet, and raising its tail high before spraying. The stink is so strong it will even drive a bear away. But there is one predator of the skunk, the great horned owl, which, as you might guess, has a poor sense of smell!

Some states in the U.S. permit people to make pets out of skunks and have their scent glands removed. Most people come across skunks that are searching for food near garbage cans or trying to find cat or dog food in a garage. Because of their poor eyesight, skunks are often hit by cars on the road. Skunks also carry rabies, though it is more common in raccoons. (Almost all rabies cases in people come from dogs and bats.) Perhaps it is because their spray is enough to keep people away.

The Bible talks about the judgment of God against Judah when it turned away from the Lord. Especially condemning the luxury of these self-sufficient people, God lists jewels, clothing, and perfumes used by a haughty and proud people. Isaiah writes that the Lord will take away the perfume boxes. "Instead of a sweet smell there will be a stench" (Isaiah 3:23). A selfish life stinks. When we give our hearts to Jesus and live to bless others, it is a sweet smell to all around us.

"When you pass through the waters, I will be with you; and through the rivers ... " (Isaiah 43:2).

What animal has killed more people in Africa than any other? If you guessed the lion or crocodile you are wrong! It's the hippopotamus. When you see a hippo yawning and stretching open his giant mouth, it is not because he is lazy, tired, or bored. It is actually a threat gesture. The hippo shows off his long, thick, razor-sharp canine teeth to tell you "back away." They are fearlessly protective of their turf and have even been known to bite a small boat in half!

The name "hippopotamus" comes from two Greek words: "*hippo*" means horse and "*potamus*" means river. They live in the central and southern parts of Africa (and up along the Nile River). These big vegetarian creatures can weigh up to 4,000 pounds and love to live in rivers with deep water. They will eat grass, fallen fruit, and sometimes cultivated crops at night. They spend most of the day in the water. Hippos can grow to 17 feet long and 5 feet tall with a big mouth (over two feet across). They are the third largest animal in Africa, after the elephant and rhinoceros. And if you think this big animal is slow, hippos can easily outrun a human being and have been clocked at 19 mph for short distances.

We often think of someone who is courageous being as strong as a lion. But the Zulu warriors preferred to be compared to the hippopotamus. The bite of a hippo has actually been measured by scientists at 1,821 foot-pounds. The jaw hinge on a hippo is located so far back that it can open its mouth to almost 180 degrees. Those big teeth in the lower jaw can grow to 20 inches and are sharp. It's a good idea to stay clear of the hippo, which has been called the most aggressive creature in the world and certainly the most dangerous animal in Africa.

The Bible speaks about an aggressive animal with a large mouth that we should avoid. In describing the church, Christ, and Satan, John writes, "And the dragon stood before the woman who was ready to give birth, to devour her Child as soon as it was born" (Revelation 12:4). Later, this same dragon spewed water out of its mouth to try to carry the woman away and destroy her (verse 15.) The serpent, Satan, is depicted in the Bible as the most aggressive creature on Earth. But we are safe from his attacks when we stay close to Jesus.

September 7 STRIPED WONDER

"You shall hide them in the secret place of Your presence from the plots of man ... " (Psalm 31:20).

Are zebras black with white stripes or are they white with black stripes? We'll look at this in a moment. But first, let's consider where zebras come from. There are three species of zebras: the plains, the Grevy's, and the mountain zebra. They are all from the horse family and all from Africa. An old African tale is that the zebra was a white animal that got its stripes after fighting over a waterhole with a baboon and then falling into a fire. The fire sticks left scorch marks on the zebra, and hence its stripes.

Zebra stripes are not all the same. On the Grevy's zebra they are more numerous and do not extend to their bellies. The black and white pattern is a form of camouflage called "disruptive coloration," which breaks up the outline of their bodies. It helps them to hide in grass. (Lions are colorblind.) During the day it is not as noticeable. But at night the stripes help them to blend into the darkness when predators are hunting. The stripes can also confuse their distance from enemies. Another theory about their stripes is that when a herd of zebra are together, all these stripes can confuse a predator trying to pick out one lone zebra. They all seem to blend together into one large animal.

A zebra's shiny coat helps to dissipate heat, and some believe the stripes help it withstand the intense heat from the sun. But are zebras white animals with black stripes or vice versa? People used to believe they were white animals with black stripes because their underbellies are often white. But growing evidence indicates they are probably black animals with white stripes and bellies as additions.

The Bible says the devil is like a roaring lion seeking to devour us (1 Peter 5:8). Can the Lord protect us from this enemy and hide us, keeping us safe? David was pursued by an enemy, but God hid him and protected him. "For in the time of trouble He shall hide me in His pavilion; in the secret place of His tabernacle He shall hide me; He shall set me high upon a rock" (Psalm 27:5).

When Satan is pursuing you, the Lord will protect you. And you don't need stripes to hide from him!

"For by Him all things were created that are in heaven and that are on earth, visible and invisible, whether thrones or dominions or principalities or powers. All things were created through Him and for Him" (Colossians 1:16).

One of the strangest animals in the world is the long-beaked echidna [i-kid-na], or spiny anteater. Weighing about 20 pounds, this nocturnal creature is found mainly in the humid mountain forests of New Guinea and Indonesia. Interspersed with its brownish or black fur are sharp spines of varying lengths. The spines on its body can be erected and its arms and legs withdrawn for protection, much like a hedgehog. At the end of its long, down-curved, tubular snout is a very small mouth through which the long tongue can be rapidly extruded and retracted. It has no teeth in its mouth but compensates with rows of tooth-like spikes on the tongue. The echidna probes with its long beak in the muddy soil until it detects a worm or other invertebrates by their faint electrical current. The tongue then darts out, and the worm is hooked by the spikes and reeled in like a fish.

Even though it is technically a mammal, the female long-beaked echidna lays shell-covered eggs that are incubated and hatched outside the body of the mother like a reptile, but then carried and nursed in a small pouch like a marsupial. Perhaps its most remarkable feature is a large and complex brain with high intelligence, characteristics unexpected in the world's most reptile-like mammal. They also live a surprisingly long time, with one having been kept in the London Zoo for over 30 years, and another in the Berlin Zoo for 31 years.

Today, the long-beaked echidna is an endangered species. Some reasons for its decline appear to be loss of forest habitat to logging, mining, and farming, and traditional hunting. The oily meat of the echidna is relished by many of the people of New Guinea.

The spiny anteater is an enigma for evolutionists, because it looks like God assembled it from spare parts left over after He created all the other animals, and it stands in a class of its own. Despite the mass of media messages, the world did not evolve over multiplied millions of years. Scripture confirms the truth that God is the Creator, and that everything in heaven and on Earth was "created through Him and for Him."

September 9 EAT FOR STRENGTH

"Blessed are you, O land, when your king is the son of nobles, and your princes feast at the proper time—for strength and not for drunkenness!" (Ecclesiastes 10:16, 17).

Wolverines are found in isolated forests and mountains from Alaska to Siberia. Stocky and muscular with glossy brown hair and dull yellow stripes along its sides, the adult wolverine is about the size of a medium dog and looks like a cross between a small bear and a skunk. It has been known to give off a very strong, unpleasant odor, giving rise to the nicknames "skunk bear" and "nasty cat." Despite its name, the wolverine is not related to the wolf, but rather the weasel.

The wolverine can run up to 30 mph, climb trees, and swim. The wolverine is also remarkably strong for its modest size and, pound for pound, is considered one of the most ferocious mammals. It has been known to kill prey as large as elk and even moose. In addition, it can keep cougars, grizzlies, and wolves away from its kills. In spite of its ferocity, it is known to be very shy and is rarely seen.

The Latin name for the wolverine is *Gulo* and means "glutton." The wolverine lives up to its name. It will eat about anything it can find or kill. In addition to hunting, it will often find carrion left by other predators, and sometimes it even steals the catch of another predator. After gorging on pounds of meat, it will bury its leftovers. Then it further protects its hoard by spraying it with a stinky musk to keep other animals away. In their endless search for food, males may cover more than 240 square miles, traveling 40 miles a day to satisfy their voracious appetites. It would be safe to say the wolverine lives to eat.

There are also many humans who struggle with the same tendency! Some find it surprising that God cares about something as basic as our eating habits, but the Bible has much to say on the topic. Solomon warns that "the drunkard and the glutton will come to poverty," while Paul exhorts us to eat and drink "to the glory of God" (Proverbs 23:21; 1 Corinthians 10:31). We would all be much healthier if we followed the wise king's suggestion to eat for strength and not for gluttony!

"There I will make the horn of David grow ..." (Psalm 132:17).

Besides being a very large and strong animal, one of the most notable features about a rhinoceros is its horn (or horns). The name rhinoceros comes from two Greek words–*rhino*, meaning "nose," and *ceros*, meaning "horn." It is amazing that this mammal, which can weigh up to two tons and grow up to six feet tall, is a vegetarian. There are five different rhinos in the world. Two come from Africa (the black rhino and the white rhino) and three from southern Asia (the Indian rhino, the Sumatran rhino, and the Javan rhino). Rhinoceroses have very thick skin (1/2 inch to 2 inches) with folds that make them look like they have armored plating.

The best friend of a rhinoceros is the tick bird (or oxpecker). It eats ticks off the rhino, but is also a guard, making lots of noise when danger lurks close by. Rhinos are often thought of as ill-tempered, but probably have become more so in areas where they are constantly being disturbed. They do have poor eyesight but excellent hearing. When they attack, rhinos usually lower their heads, growl or grunt, and come charging at up to 30 mph, striking powerful blows with their horns–not somebody you want to get in the way of! Rhinos have only one enemy–humans. Unfortunately they have been hunted to almost near extinction. Even with strong laws, poachers still make a dent in the diminishing population because of rhinos' valuable and sought-after horns.

Does a rhino have one horn or two? It depends. The Javan and Indian rhinos have only one horn while the white, black, and Sumatran have two. The horn is actually made up of keratin, the same material as our fingernails and hair. Some people believe the horn has medicinal value when ground into powder. Armed park rangers in South Africa try to stop poachers, who can get up to $25,000 for a horn. In 2011, up to 448 rhinos were killed for their horns.

The Bible refers to horns in many different ways. In prophecy, horns stood for kings, kingdoms, or other powers. One such horn will play a role in the time of the end before Christ comes. That horn will be destructive. Daniel writes, "I was considering the horns, and there was another horn, a little one, coming up among them, before whom three of the first horns were plucked out by the roots. And there, in this horn, were eyes like the eyes of a man, and a mouth speaking pompous words" (Daniel 7:8).

September 11 SHIPS OF THE DESERT

"It is easier for a camel to go through the eye of a needle than for a rich man to enter the kingdom of God" (Mark 10:25).

Most people know that camels are very well adapted to sandy desert life. Their soft feet spread out so they won't sink into the sand. To protect their eyes from sand, they have two thick rows of eyelashes. They can see through a thin third eyelid during a sand storm. Camels can close their nostrils against blowing sand and have extra hair inside their ears to keep sand out. Contrary to popular myth, camels don't store more water than other animals, yet they can handle extreme dehydration much better, enabling them to go for days without needing a drink. Camels have been known to safely lose body water equivalent to 40 percent of their weight, a loss that would be lethal to any other animal. To make up for previous fluid loss, camels can take in very large amounts of water at one session, drinking up to 27 gallons of water in 10 minutes. Because of the wide swings in desert temperatures between night and day, the camel's system has the ability to endure very large fluctuations in body temperature (from 97.7 to 107.6 degrees Fahrenheit).

Before the Civil War, efforts were made to use camels for crossing U.S. deserts, but the experiment failed. Their soft-padded feet were unsuitable for much of the rocky southwestern terrain. They frightened horses and they were detested by their handlers, who were accustomed to more docile mules. In contrast, at about the same time, camels were introduced to Australia, where they flourished. Wild camels are now scattered through the arid interior of Australia and are estimated to number over 500,000. Camels and kangaroos live side by side. For centuries camels have been called "ships of the desert" because they resemble boats floating across a sea of sand and can travel up to 100 miles in a day, carrying loads as heavy as 1,000 pounds.

Keep this picture in mind when you consider Jesus' words: "It is easier for a camel to go through the eye of a needle than for a rich man to enter the kingdom of God" (Mark 10:25). Jesus also told a parable about a rich man who landed in Hades that has been greatly misunderstood. His point was that rich people who have no concern for others have their only reward in this life. Riches can easily distract us from the kingdom of God.

"Bow down your ear to me, deliver me speedily; be my rock of refuge, a fortress to save me" (Psalm 31:2).

Did you know a male rabbit is called a buck, a female is called a doe, and a baby rabbit is a kit (and several are kittens)? When a doe gives birth to a bunch of little bunnies it is called a litter. Interestingly, domestic rabbits are born without fur. A group of rabbits living in the wild is called a herd. Some can breed as early as three months old, which is why they can populate so rapidly. One of the largest litters of kittens ever born was 24!

Here are some other interesting facts about rabbits. Their teeth never stop growing. When they grind their teeth it can sound like they are purring like a cat. Rabbits do not have the ability to vomit (I hope you are not reading this during mealtime!). They are nearsighted animals. The world's heaviest rabbit was named Darius and weighed 50 pounds. Rabbits only sweat on the pads of their feet. A rabbit has five toenails on its front two paws and four toenails on its back two feet, making a total of 18 toenails per rabbit.

North America has the largest number of domesticated rabbits. There are over 45 recognized breeds of rabbits. Some rabbits are raised for their meat and others for their fur. Pet rabbits tend to live longer (8-10 years) than their friends in the wild. In England the third most popular pet (after dogs and cats) is the rabbit. They have very sensitive backbones and can be easily hurt if dropped. Rabbits can actually suffer from osteoporosis if they don't get enough exercise.

Some people believe that to carry around a rabbit's foot will bring them good luck, but the Bible teaches that life is not so much about chance as choice. Our destiny does not come from the roll of dice, but whether we choose to follow Jesus or the devil. When Joshua challenged the Israelites as they settled in Canaan, he said, "Choose for yourselves this day whom you will serve ... But as for me and my house, we will serve the LORD" (Joshua 24:15).

We don't need lucky charms like a rabbit's foot to protect us. We are safe when we choose to be in the hands of God.

September 13 CAT EYES

"Indeed, the darkness shall not hide from You, but the night shines as the day; the darkness and the light are both alike to You" (Psalm 139:12).

Cats are nocturnal animals and have a need to see well at night. Cats need only one-sixth of the light needed by people to see when it's dark. Plus, their eyes need to work well during the daytime. How do their eyes function so well in low light? The Lord has created some special abilities in the eyes of Puff and Snowball.

First of all, when the lights go down, the pupil of a cat's eye needs to open really wide to let more light inside. Our eyes have circular muscles that open and close our pupil, which limits just how much they can open. A cat's eye has a couple of muscles that open and close the pupil like a shutter, giving the eye a slit-like pupil when it's bright outside. In fact, the relative size of a cat's eye is bigger than a human's eye. It also has a more curved lens, which brings in more light and also gives it a greater ability to sharpen its focus on objects.

Did you ever notice that when you shine a light on a cat's eyes at night they seem to glow? That's because of the *tapetum lucidum*, which is like a mirror behind the retina reflecting more light back onto light-sensitive cells in the retina. This special "mirror" gives the cat's eyes the characteristic nighttime glow when they are caught in a beam of light. Another feature of a cat's eye is the type of light receptor cells on the retina. Cones are cells sensitive to high levels of light and are good with color detection. Rods are cells sensitive to low levels of light and are helpful with black and white detection. A cat has far more rods in its eyes than people. Even the location of the optic nerve on the back of the eye is positioned to help our feline friends see better movement at night.

God's vision is even better than that of a cat. The Lord can see you no matter where you are. When Abraham sent Hagar away, she cried out to God. The Angel of the Lord spoke to her, and she responded; "Then she called the name of the Lord who spoke to her, You-Are-the-God-Who-Sees; for she said, 'Have I also here seen Him who sees me?'" (Genesis 16:13). We have a God who sees very well, even in our darkest nights.

"The wolf and the lamb shall feed together, the lion shall eat straw like the ox ..." (Isaiah 65:25).

Little Tyke, a female African lion born and raised in America, lived her entire lifetime without ever eating meat. In fact, her owners, Georges and Margaret Westbeau, alarmed at the lioness's dislike of meat, went to great lengths to try to coax their unusual pet to develop a taste for it. They even advertised a cash reward for anyone who could devise a meat-containing formula that the lioness would like. The curator of a New York zoo advised the Westbeaus that putting a few drops of blood in the lioness's milk would help, but the lioness refused to drink the milk—even when only a single drop of blood had been added.

Meanwhile, Little Tyke continued to do extremely well on a daily diet of cooked grain, raw eggs, and milk. By four years of age she was fully grown and weighed 352 pounds. To condition her teeth and gums—as she refused to gnaw on bones—Little Tyke was given heavy rubber boots to chew on, which generally lasted about three weeks. The lioness not only survived on a vegetarian diet, she thrived. One of America's "most able zoo curators" apparently said that the lioness "was the best of her species he had ever viewed." As well as Little Tyke, the Westbeaus had sheep and cattle on their 100-acre ranch. Visitors to the ranch were often amazed to see a full-grown African lioness wandering peacefully among the sheep and cattle, and even chewing on succulent tall grass in the field.

Some of Little Tyke's favorite friends were Pinky the kitten, Becky the lamb, and Baby the fawn. The lamb especially liked the lioness and preferred Little Tyke's company above all the other animals on the Westbeaus' farm. She was once filmed by a TV crew to see how she would respond to chickens. To the surprise of the owners, they brought in four-day-old chicks. Little Tyke was gentle with them all.

Did you know that the Bible predicts that one day every lion on Earth will be vegetarian? "The wolf also shall lie down with the young goat, the calf and the young lion and the fatling together; and a little child shall lead them. The cow and the bear shall graze; their young ones shall lie down together; and the lion shall eat straw like the ox" (Isaiah 11:6, 7).

September 15 CLEVER HANS

"But Jesus, knowing their thoughts, said, 'Why do you think evil in your hearts?'" (Matthew 9:4).

In Germany around 1904, Wilhelm von Osten owned an extremely bright horse he named Clever Hans. He earned his name because, von Osten claimed, his horse could solve complex arithmetic problems, tapping out the answer with his hoof. Observers asserted that Hans could even read the instructions to a mathematics problem written on a chalkboard and then tap out the correct answer.

Hans never seemed to give the wrong answer. It appeared that the horse had the mathematical ability of a calculus professor. Skeptical researchers tested Hans, asking strangers to present the math problems. Nothing made a difference. Hans was even able to answer questions posed in foreign languages, questions whispered to him, even questions not asked at all but merely thought. Hans still came up with the correct answer. For a brief moment in history, Clever Hans had the German scientific community chasing its tail trying to explain the phenomenon. Many believed they had found a horse that was at least as intelligent as a human and possibly even brighter.

But along came a skeptical psychologist, Dr. Oskar Pfungst, who refused to believe the obvious. Through a series of tests, Dr. Pfungst proved that although Hans was able to provide correct answers, he was not solving the problems himself. The horse was exceptionally clever about observing people. Hans was carefully watching the person presenting him with a problem, slowly tapping his hoof until he noticed a slight flicker of behavior that told him it was time to stop tapping. His perception was so keen that he noticed slight reactions that humans could not see. He was so gifted that he could recognize the slightest change in the facial expression or body language of everyone he observed. Hans was better at reading the behavior of people than people are at reading the behavior of horses.

Some have wondered, "Do angels know what we are thinking by reading our minds or are they simply observing our body language?" The Bible teaches that only God can read our minds. "The Lord knows the thoughts of man, that they are futile" (Psalm 94:11). Perhaps angels can observe our body language better than human beings, but only God can see deeply into our inner thoughts. That's why even when we pray silently, the Lord can hear us.

"And take the helmet of salvation, and the sword of the Spirit, which is the word of God" (Ephesians 6:17).

Wood rats are nocturnal rodents that are native throughout North America. These social creatures eat seeds, fruits, roots, and vegetation, with a few bugs thrown in for added protein. They can grow up to 20 inches long, including their tail. Wood rats are also called pack rats because they have a curious habit of collecting an assortment of manmade material for their nests. They are especially fond of confiscating small, bright, shiny objects like tin, colored glass, shells, coins, and stones. Wood rats are also sometimes called trade rats because of the popular myth that when it takes something, it always leaves a replacement. In fact, what's really happening is that, while carrying one prize, the pack rat may spot another trophy that is more attractive, and so drops the first object to pick up the second.

Pack rats build large nests on rock ledges, in woods, and in fields. The bulky nests are generally made of sticks, twigs, and leaves and may be as much as four feet high. But these big nests make it nearly impossible for the wood rats that live in the open deserts to hide their homes from their enemies. As it turns out, God has given pack rats the wisdom to use the natural resources of the desert to overcome this problem. The pack rat covers its conspicuous nest with cactus plants; then, for additional protection, it places pieces of cactus spines all around the entrance to the nest. Amazingly, the little wood rat can scramble easily over and around the long, sharp spines of the cactus without being hurt. It is one of the few animals that can navigate safely between the thorns to feed on the juicy pads. But the coyote that tries to dig a wood rat out of its nest will be very sorry! The pack rat has prepared in advance and has little to fear from the wily coyote. His home is so well protected that it is almost as though it's a fortress defended by an army with drawn swords.

And just as God protects the wood rat in its desert home, we can be protected from the temptations of the enemy by collecting treasures of truth and surrounding ourselves with "the sword of the Spirit"! God's Word is our security.

September 17 A TALL STATEMENT

"Again the high priest asked Him ... 'Are You the Christ, the Son of the Blessed?' Jesus said, 'I am.'" (Mark 14:61).

Among the land animals, giraffes stand head and shoulders above the rest, towering up to 18 feet above the grasslands of Africa. Giraffes are herbivores, and their extended necks combined with an 18-inch-long tongue allow them to reach the tasty leaves high in the tall, thorny acacia trees. Although the giraffe's neck is about seven feet long, it contains the same number of vertebrae as a mouse (seven). Of course, each vertebra is greatly elongated.

The giraffe's circulatory system is specially adapted to its long neck. It has elastic blood vessels in the neck and head to handle changes in blood pressure due to head swings. This is why a giraffe's heart must weigh a whopping 24 pounds to pump the blood to such a high altitude!

The name "giraffe" probably comes from the Arabic word *zarafa*, which means "one who walks swiftly." With each step a giraffe travels about 15 feet. They are also fast runners and can reach speeds faster than a horse, over 35 mph. Though male giraffes will often "neck wrestle" to establish dominance, they are generally passive, non-territorial, and sociable. They live in loose, open herds grazing peacefully with zebra, wildebeest, and antelope.

Giraffes are the most vulnerable when drinking, because they must spread their front legs far apart in an awkward stance to get their heads low enough to reach the water. Fortunately giraffes can go without water even longer than a camel.

The first giraffe ever seen in the West was brought to Rome about 46 B.C. by none other than Julius Caesar. When giraffes first entered Rome, because they were as big as camels with spots like leopards they were thought to be the result a freakish breeding of the two animals. Although we know the giraffe is not a combination of these two animals, the scientific name *camelopardalis* stuck.

We may laugh at the gullible Romans who believed you could combine a camel with a leopard and get a giraffe, but a bigger question is: "How can someone be half God and half man?" The Jews thought this impossible. In fact, at Christ's trial the high priest was so angry after Jesus spoke about His divinity that he tore his clothes. "What further need do we have of witnesses? You have heard the blasphemy! What do you think?" (Mark 14:63, 64). They condemned Jesus to death.

What do you think of the Man who claimed to be God?

"Nevertheless these you shall not eat among those that chew the cud or those that have cloven hooves: the camel, because it chews the cud but does not have cloven hooves, is unclean to you" (Leviticus 11:4).

Armadillos are among the strangest of God's creatures. Like their cousins, the anteaters, armadillos have a very long, sticky tongue to slurp up bugs as quickly as possible. They are also equipped with strong claws to tear open ant nests and to dig a burrow 15 feet long in which to bear their young. Unlike other mammals, the female armadillo always bears four young, which are always the same sex. Some female armadillos have been known to give birth up to two years after they were captured! These "virgin births" are a result of the female's amazing ability to delay implantation of the fertilized egg.

Armadillos are good swimmers, but because their heavy shell makes them sink they must swallow air to become more buoyant. If necessary, they can hold their breath for up to six minutes, and can even travel underwater, walking along the bottom of streams and ponds like a lobster.

The nine-banded armadillo is 29 to 36 inches long including the tail; it usually weighs 8 to 17 pounds. Armadillos make timid pets, partly because they sleep an average of 18 hours per day and only come out at twilight or when it's very cloudy because their eyes are sensitive to light. But some still say they can be housebroken and make good pets.

Generally, armadillos struggle in their coexistence with man. The greatest cause of death is automobiles. But most armadillos seen dead on the road weren't hit by the wheels. They have a habit of jumping straight up into the air when they are frightened. This increases their mortality rate on the road. Unfortunately, armadillos are also ideal creatures for many types of medical research. Their low body temperature causes them to have a very weak immune system. Because of this trait they are used in leprosy research because they are the only animal besides humans that can get leprosy. In fact, some people have been known to contract leprosy from eating armadillos.

Perhaps this is one of the reasons the Bible says we shouldn't eat unclean animals. Many people mistakenly believe that Jesus abolished the health laws, but they were given for a purpose. There is a solid scientific basis behind each of these laws. God, who gave us life, wants to protect our health.

September 19 MAN'S BEST FRIEND

"And she said, 'Yes, Lord, yet even the little dogs eat the crumbs which fall from their masters' table'" (Matthew 15:27).

Man's best friend comes in all shapes and sizes. And some of the sizes are simply amazing! For instance, the world's heaviest as well as longest dog ever recorded was an English Mastiff named Zorba. In 1989, Zorba weighed 343 pounds. He stood 37 inches at the shoulder and was 8 feet, 3 inches long from nose to tail! Zorba is now deceased, but was eight years old when he set this world record.

The smallest dog in the world, in terms of length, is a female Chihuahua named Heaven Sent Brandy, who measured six inches long from the nose to the tip of the tail. Brandy set this record on January 31, 2005, and lives with her owner in Florida. On the other hand, the smallest dog in the world in terms of height is Boo Boo. This long-haired female Chihuahua measured 4 inches tall on May 12, 2007, and lives in Kentucky.

A Great Dane named George is officially the tallest dog on record. He stands at 43 inches tall from paw to shoulder and weighs 245 pounds. There was so much conflict over this record that Guinness officials sent a judge to Tucson, Arizona, to verify George's height. George eats about 110 pounds of food a month and sleeps in his own queen-sized bed.

The oldest dog that has been documented was an Australian cattle dog named Bluey. He was put to sleep at the age of 29 years and 5 months. Though some question whether Bluey, who died in 1939, truly was that old, another dog from Australia named Chilla is reputed to be the oldest dog in the world. In 1984, when Chilla died, he supposedly was 32 years old. In human years that would equal 224 years! The current oldest living dog is Max, a terrier from the United States who is 29-plus years old.

Dogs are known for their faithfulness, but the Bible tells us of a true Friend. "A man who has friends must himself be friendly, but there is a friend who sticks closer than a brother" (Proverbs 18:24). That friend is Jesus, who set a "universal record" when, as the Divine Son of God, He laid down His life for us. Now that's a record that will never be beat!

"Let all bitterness, wrath, anger, clamor, and evil speaking be put away from you, with all malice" (Ephesians 4:31).

Between 1883 and 1918, over 80,000 wolves were systematically slaughtered. By the early 1920s, wolves in the lower United States were all but completely wiped out. Near the end of the wolf extermination a lone wolf limped up to a ranch house in South Dakota. He had lost one of his toes in a trap. Wolves are social creatures, and because he had lost all his fellow wolves he seemed to be seeking human aid. Instead of help, he was met with a raised rifle and had to flee. From that day until his death in 1925, Old Dakota Three Toes waged a vicious one-wolf war on Harding County, South Dakota.

Measuring six feet and weighing over 80 pounds, Three Toes spent his remaining years killing ranchers' stock. In one three-month period he destroyed $6,700 worth of sheep, cattle, and even horses. This "renegade wolf" who had watched his species annihilated undertook seemingly wanton attacks on cattle and sheep, killing scores in a night out of what seemed sheer vengeance.

Whole communities marshaled their resources to kill this last of the Dakota wolves. Old Three Toes proved to be more intelligent than the 150 professional hunters who tracked him. He led riders down ravines that became too narrow for the horses, and through fields full of gopher holes where the horses could easily trip. He once hid in the body cavity of a dead horse. The old wolf ate only his own freshly killed prey to avoid poisoned bait. He was also especially good at springing traps.

Finally, the legendary old wolf was trapped by a state deputy predatory animal inspector who buried traps on a hill, then transplanted sagebrush beside them. The next day Three Toes, curious about the freshly dug earth round the bush, stepped into two of the traps. "Old Three-Toes," the last natural wolf in South Dakota, was killed in 1925. He had lived for nearly 20 years, twice as long as the average wolf, driven by vengeance.

Some people spend much of their lives driven by bitterness and anger until they self-destruct. Peter once rebuked a man named Simon who thought to buy the Holy Spirit for money. "Repent therefore of this your wickedness, and pray God if perhaps the thought of your heart may be forgiven you. For I see that you are poisoned by bitterness and bound by iniquity" (Acts 8:22, 23). In the end, vengeance will trap and destroy us.

September 21 SUPER SENSES

"Their idols are silver and gold, the work of men's hands. They have mouths, but they do not speak; eyes they have, but they do not see; they have ears, but they do not hear; noses they have, but they do not smell; they have hands, but they do not handle; feet they have, but they do not walk; nor do they mutter through their throat. Those who make them are like them; so is everyone who trusts in them" (Psalm 115:4-8).

The star-nosed mole is a weird and wonderful little creature that inhabits the low wetlands of eastern North America. Like other moles, it ekes out an existence by digging a network of narrow tunnels where it forages for insects, worms, and mollusks. Living in almost complete darkness, the star-nosed mole has poorly developed eyes and is virtually blind. To compensate, the Creator has given it a very sensitive star-shaped nose. Its nose surface is surrounded by a star of 22 fleshy finger-like "tendrils." These pink whiskers are covered with 25,000 ultra-sensitive receptors (six times more sensitive than the human hand). This makes the little mole's ugly nose the most sensitive organ in the entire animal kingdom.

By rapidly scanning back and forth, the mole can essentially see with his nose, mapping his tunnels and finding food. And boy is it fast! This organ enables the star-nosed mole to decide whether something is edible with astonishing speed, a mere eight milliseconds, and then bring that object into the mouth to swallow in only 120 milliseconds. It can locate and consume eight separate prey items in less than two seconds!

In fact, the mole's little brain processes the information at a speed that approaches the upper limit at which any nervous system is capable of functioning. This is why the star-nosed mole was recently entered in the Guinness Book of Records as the world's fastest forager! His amazing appendage even enables the mole to smell underwater, something previously thought impossible for mammals. The animals were filmed with high-speed cameras as they followed underwater scent trails that led to food. While foraging underwater they were found to exhale and inhale micro bubbles that contained odorant molecules.

Only a powerful and loving God can invest his creatures with such extraordinary senses. That's why it doesn't make any sense for people to worship idols with no senses. Senseless idols do nothing to help their worshipers, but God loves, forgives, and saves His followers.

"Truly, this only I have found: that God made man upright, but they have sought out many schemes" (Ecclesiastes 7:29).

Perhaps the greatest myth about gorillas is that they are violent creatures. Since they have been featured in monstrous films of fantasy, such as *King Kong*, we often think of them as aggressive and dangerous. They are actually gentle and will never attack a human unless provoked. Male "silverbacks," who are the troop leaders, have been observed carefully nurturing an orphaned baby gorilla. In spite of their size, they are shy, non-aggressive, and very calm animals.

Gorillas live in central Africa and are primarily grouped in to Eastern lowland and Western lowland gorillas. Males usually weigh between 300-500 pounds and have very muscular arms that are longer than their legs. A male gorilla can spread his arms eight feet across and is as strong as four to eight strong men. They "knuckle walk" using their long arms. They can grow to over six feet tall and don't usually stand upright. Adult female gorillas are about half the size of the males. An adult male becomes a silverback at about age 15, when he is fully grown and the hair on his back begins to turn silver colored.

Some scientists go to great lengths to show a connection between the gorilla and humans in order to demonstrate them as our closest ancestors. They show comparisons of DNA, the make-up of hands and feet, abilities to communicate and show expression, using tools, and even their blood types to connect us as relatives some 7 million years ago. Are these plant-eating gentle giants our next closest kin, along with chimpanzees?

The Bible says, "So God created man in His own image; in the image of God He created him; male and female He created them" (Genesis 1:27). If you take Genesis 1 at face value, there is no room for eons of evolutionary time to eventually produce people! "And God said, 'Let Us make man in Our image, according to Our likeness'" (verse 26).

Whose image and likeness do you most want to reflect?

September 23 THE BUMBLEBEE BAT

"I am left alone; and they seek to take my life" (1 Kings 19:14).

The smallest bat in the world also happens to be the smallest mammal in the world. The bumblebee bat is only about one inch long and lives in Thailand and Myanmar. It weighs about as much as a dime. It really is about the size of a large bumblebee. This reddish brown (or gray) little creature has no tail, but has a wingspan of about 6.5 inches. It is formally called Kitti's hog-nosed bat (you can guess why) and lives in limestone caves along rivers. Like many endangered animals, its habitat has been disturbed by mankind. It was mostly unknown to the world until 1974 when scientists were classifying bats in Thailand.

Like most bats, the bumblebee bat flies out of its roosting place at night to catch insects. Its activity is briefer, 20-30 minutes in the evening and then again before dawn, because short flights are easily interrupted by heavy rain or cold temperatures. Though very small, the bat's long wing tips allow it to hover like a hummingbird. Female bats give birth to one baby bat a year, and it takes about a year to raise their young. Since this takes so long, it makes these bats even more susceptible to extinction. Burning forests near these limestone caves has hampered their survival. Some indicate there may only be about 2,000 of these cute (can you call any bat cute?) little guys left.

Someone else was concerned about the number of God's prophets becoming extinct. Elijah felt all alone after he ran from Jezebel. While hiding in a cave, God called to this prophet who thought he was the last one left. Elijah said to God, "I have been very zealous for the LORD God of hosts; because the children of Israel have forsaken Your covenant, torn down Your altars, and killed Your prophets with the sword. I alone am left; and they seek to take my life" (1 Kings 19:14).

But Elijah was discouraged and blind to the truth. The Lord said to him, "Yet I have reserved seven thousand in Israel, all whose knees have not bowed to Baal, and every mouth that has not kissed him" (verse 18). Sometimes we may feel so alone that it seems we are almost extinct. But when the Lord opens our eyes, we will realize there is always a remnant that is faithful to Him. Are you part of God's endangered species?

"And you will seek Me and find Me, when you search for Me with all your heart" (Jeremiah 29:13).

The incredible sense of smell in a dog boggles the mind. Did you know that from a single drop of urine from an animal, a dog is able to determine its diet, health, sex, mental state, and whether it is friendly, dominant, or submissive? In fact, a dog's ability to pick up smell is so powerful that it can detect extremely diluted odors that not even the most sophisticated scientific instruments can measure. It can even discriminate different odors, making it impossible to cover up one odor with another. A dog can tell the difference.

God gave dogs an amazing sense of smell. The average dog has about 200 million scent receptors in its nose. (Humans have about 5 million scent receptors.) A dog also has about seven square meters of nasal membranes. (Humans have about half of a square meter.) When you walk into a room and say, "Something stinks in here," imagine what a dog would say! One dog expert explained that dogs see a 3-D image of odors in a much more detailed way than what people see with their eyes. A dog's world is all about smell. That's why they love the smell of their favorite blanket (or your favorite coat or sweater!). If a dog is hanging his nose out the window while you drive around town, he will know when you turn down your street because of the smell in the air.

Some dogs are professionally trained to use their nose to find substances like explosives, illegal drugs, or blood. Different from hunting dogs that search for game, or search dogs that search for missing people, detection dogs are often used to pick up specific items. In California, dogs have been trained to detect the quagga mussel on boats, since it is an invasive species. Some springer spaniels have been trained to detect bumblebee nests. And some have even been trained to find illegal cell phones in prison cells. So, if you need to find bed bugs, money, firearms, mold, or even termites, hire a dog!

The Bible says 50 men searched for three days to find Elijah when he went to heaven. They couldn't find him. Neither could Ahab find Elijah during the time of no rain. When Obadiah finally found him, he told Elijah, "There is no nation or kingdom where my master has not sent someone to hunt for you ... " (1 Kings 18:10). But God always knows where we are. He can sniff us out anywhere!

But have you searched for God yourself?

September 25 KOALA BEARS

"Then the kingdom of heaven shall be likened to ten virgins who took their lamps and went out to meet the bridegroom. Now five of them were wise, and five were foolish. Those who were foolish took their lamps and took no oil with them, but the wise took oil in their vessels with their lamps. But while the bridegroom was delayed, they all slumbered and slept" (Matthew 25:1-5).

The Australian koala bear certainly looks like a round, furry teddy bear, but the koala is actually a pouched marsupial related more to the kangaroo and the wombat; it really has no close relatives. Today these quiet and cute marsupials are Australia's premier icon, but until the late 1920s koalas were nearly hunted to extinction for their skin, with as many as 500,000 a month being exported. Thankfully, they are now protected and loved as one of Australia's most unique animals.

You might say koalas are "all thumbs" because each koala foot has three toes and two thumbs, helping it climb and cling to branches. The koala is also unique from other marsupials because its pouch opens at the bottom rather than the top. The young are born small, blind, and hairless. The baby crawls to its mother's pouch, where it suckles and grows for six months. Then the young koala climbs out onto its mother's back and she teaches it how to feed.

The koala spends almost all its time in eucalyptus trees and is an amazingly fussy eater. Of the more than 600 species of eucalyptus in Australia, it will only eat from 50. And it will pick through 20 leaves for every one it decides is good enough to eat. The eucalyptus leaves contain strong-smelling oils that act as a bug repellent, keeping the animal free from parasites. Unfortunately, they also make the koala smell like very strong cough syrup!

Because the eucalyptus is not very nutritious, adult koalas have to eat about 2.5 pounds a day, and they spend most of the day sleeping in the fork of a tree to conserve energy. In fact, a koala spends up to 18 hours a day—or three quarters of its life—asleep.

Did you know that Jesus warns that just before His coming most of the churches will be sleeping, due in part to bad nutrition? Friends, we need to feast on the Bread that came down from heaven. The Bible says, "If anyone eats of this bread, he will live forever" (John 6:51). Now that's good nutrition!

"Then I wished to know the truth about the fourth beast, which was different from all the others, exceedingly dreadful, with its teeth of iron and its nails of bronze, which devoured, broke in pieces, and trampled the residue with its feet ..." (Daniel 7:19).

The elephant is the largest land mammal left on Earth. Throughout history elephants have been revered, honored, and prized for their great size and strength. On the battlefield, soldiers with elephants have terrified and trampled enemies. Elephants also have been trained to carry heavy supplies through jungles and to haul huge logs from the forests where they once lived.

The most obvious characteristic of elephants, besides their massive size, is their trunk. An elephant's trunk is nothing more than an elongation of their nose and upper lip, but it is the most versatile of all mammalian creations. The trunk is composed of an estimated 150,000 muscles and is employed as a nose, arm, hand, and multipurpose tool to pull branches off trees, uproot grass, pluck fruit, and to place food in their mouths. The trunk is also used for smelling, trumpeting, drinking, greeting, or throwing dust for dust baths.

Elephant tusks are elongated upper incisors and are the largest and heaviest teeth of any living animal. The tusks are used for digging for roots and water, stripping the bark off trees for food, defense from predators, and fighting each other during mating season. Elephant tusks grow continuously throughout the elephant's life. They can grow as long as 10 feet and weigh as much as 150 pounds each. This ivory, also known as "white gold," was used at one time in the manufacture of piano keys, billiard balls, and other objects. Over the years hunters have slaughtered thousands of these magnificent animals just for their tusks. At the turn of the 20th century, elephants numbered from 5 million to 10 million, but widespread hunting and habitat destruction reduced their numbers to an estimated 600,000. Ivory poaching has almost driven elephants into extinction.

Did you know the Bible predicts that in the last days real Christians will be hunted because they obey God's commandments? "Therefore rejoice, O heavens, and you who dwell in them! Woe to the inhabitants of the earth and the sea! For the devil has come down to you, having great wrath, because he knows that he has a short time" (Revelation 12:12). There is only one thing more frightening than being charged by an angry elephant, and that is to have the devil come after you. But in Christ we can find refuge.

September 27 LIGERS AND GIANTS

"There were giants on the earth in those days, and also afterward, when the sons of God came in to the daughters of men and they bore children to them. Those were the mighty men who were of old, men of renown" (Genesis 6:4).

Most people know that when you cross a donkey stallion and a horse mare you get a mule. Or maybe you have even heard that you can cross a zebra with a donkey to get a zonkey. Yep, it's true! Or did you know the Sea Life Park in Hawaii has the world's only known whale-dolphin mix? It's called a wholphin. Crossbreeding between animals of the same species is rare in the wild but occurs more commonly in captivity, producing amazing results.

One of the most interesting mammal hybrids is a liger, the offspring of a lion father and tiger mother. Their unofficial scientific name is *Panthera leo/tigris*. Ligers share characteristics of both parents. Some look very lion-like, while others more strongly reveal their tiger heritage. The liger coat usually has the tan coloring of a lion, with tiger stripes running through it. The tiger mothers involved are usually the common orange color, but white tigers have been crossed with lions to produce white ligers. Even their roar is made up of both lion and tiger sounds. They usually roar like a lion and chuff like a tiger. A male liger may have a mane, typically much shorter than on the African lion. Ligers usually inherit a love of water, which comes from their tiger side of the family.

Hybrid animals often display what's known as "hybrid vigor." This means the offspring grow much larger and faster than either parent, and it appears that many hybrid pairings cause gigantism. This is why ligers are the largest cats in the world. They can stand 12 feet tall on their hind legs and weigh over 1,000 pounds! That's over half a ton, up to double the weight of a fully grown tiger. That's also a lot of kitty food. Fortunately, these cats have a gentle and easygoing disposition.

Did you know the Bible tells of a time when a race of giants roamed the land? They were hybrids of a sort. The Bible says the "sons of God"—descendants of faithful Adam—married the "daughters of men"—those from the line of rebellious Cain. This pairing produced "mighty men" and "giants." Unfortunately, things deteriorated rapidly after that, and humanity became so wicked that God sent the Flood to cleanse the world.

"[F]or this my son was dead and is alive again; he was lost and is found" (Luke 15:24).

There are no creatures on Earth quite like cats. Today there are about 100 distinct breeds of the domestic cat. Cats can hear ultrasound and are able to produce over one hundred vocal sounds, while dogs can only produce about ten. In spite of their keen vision, cats cannot see directly under their noses. This is why they cannot seem to find the tidbits on the floor after they eat. And just like fingerprints, every cat's nose pad has a unique pattern.

Cats are one of the sleepiest of all mammals. They spend between 14 to 16 hours each day sleeping. That means a seven-year-old cat has only been awake for two years of its life! And 30 percent of their waking hours are spent grooming themselves. A cat in South Wales named Lucy has become the oldest ever, living to 39 years old. That's the equivalent to 172 human years, more than double the average life expectancy. Neutering a cat extends its life span by two or three years.

Like birds, cats have an incredible homing ability that uses their biological clock, the angle of the sun, and the earth's magnetic field. A cat taken far from its home can somehow find its way back. Sixteen-year-old Shaun Philips and his father, Ken, lost their cat Silky about 200 miles north of Brisbane, Australia. That was in the summer of 1977. On March 28, 1978, Silky turned up at Mr. Philips' house in a suburb of Melbourne. According to his owner, "He was as thin as a wisp and stank to high heaven." Silky had traveled 1,472 miles to get home.

Have you ever felt like you've wandered too far from God to find your way back? Jacob felt that way one lonely night while running away from home to escape his brother's rage. He had deceived his father to get the birthright and was plagued with guilt. Did God still love him?

As he lay on the ground sleeping, God revealed Himself in a dream. Jacob saw a ladder stretching between heaven and Earth with angels going up and down. Notice these comforting words from God to Jacob: "Behold, I am with you and will keep you wherever you go, and will bring you back to this land; for I will not leave you until I have done what I have spoken to you" (Genesis 28:15).

God had not forgotten Jacob. No matter how far away you wander from the Lord, He can bring you back home.

September 29 A WEIRD CONGLOMERATION

"Then I wished to know the truth about the fourth beast, which was different from all the others ..." (Daniel 7:19).

The first time European naturalists saw this animal they were baffled. Some thought this beaver-like creature with a duck bill was a hoax and actually tried to cut the bill off with a pair of scissors. But the unusual egg-laying, beaver-tailed, otter-footed, venomous platypus of eastern Australia was for real! The strange mammal has become a symbol of Australia and is an emblem for the state of New South Wales.

The platypus lives near freshwater streams and lakes and is an excellent swimmer with webbed feet, fine fur (that keeps it dry and warm), and a beaver-like tail. On land the platypus actually walks on its knuckles and curls its webbed feet back. It usually sleeps most of the day and hunts at night in the water for shrimp, worms, mussels, and aquatic insects. It uses its rubbery and flexible bill to locate prey. It has hundreds of receptors that respond to touch and tiny electric currents made by prey when they move. Interestingly, it swims with its eyes, ears, and nose shut.

Predators of this strange creature include hawks, eagles, owls, and foxes. The platypus lives in a burrow, usually with two entrances. To protect itself, the male has a hollow spur on his hind ankle that is venomous. It can kill a small animal or incapacitate a human. In the early 1900s platypus were hunted for their fur. They are now protected and not listed as an endangered species.

Some people have stated that God must have had a sense of humor when creating the platypus. But there is actually another creature in the Bible that appears as a conglomeration of different animals. When Daniel the prophet first saw this beast he must have been as confused as scientists who first saw a platypus. But this creature was not some cute little animal. "After this I saw in the night visions, and behold, a fourth beast, dreadful and terrible, exceedingly strong. It had huge iron teeth; it was devouring, breaking in pieces, and trampling the residue with its feet. It was different from all the beasts that were before it ... " (Daniel 7:7).

This beast represented a kingdom that crushed other kingdoms and sought to destroy God's people. It rose in power and spoke blasphemous words against the Most High. Though it was subdued for a time, this power rose again and will play a role in the time of the end when God will finally slay this rebellious kingdom. This is one animal that we will all be glad becomes extinct!

"For I say, through the grace given me, to everyone who is among you, not to think of himself more highly than he ought to think" (Romans 12:3).

Giant anteaters are among the strangest animals God ever made. This largest of the anteater species lives in grasslands and open tropical forests of Central and South America. Covered with stiff, straw-like hair that grows up to 10 inches long on the tail, a full-grown creature weighs about 90 pounds and grows to be about 4 feet long (about the size of a German shepherd), and that's not including a puffy tail that adds an additional 3 feet. Giant anteaters have large, sharp, hook-like claws on each front foot. They walk on the back of their wrists to protect them. These claws are used to dig for food and for self-defense against jaguars and pumas, their natural enemies.

Anteaters are of course insectivores, eating mostly ants and termites, but will also eat other insects as long as they don't sting. At the end of the anteater's very long nose is a very small mouth, barely big enough to pass a pencil, but they are great at catching insects using their 2-foot-long sticky tongue, flicking it in and out up to 160 times each minute! The tongue has backward-pointing barbs that mash the captured insects against the hard pallet. Because they are toothless, most chewing occurs in the gizzard-like stomach, aided by ingested pebbles.

Though they have terrible eyesight, the giant anteater has excellent hearing and awakens at the slightest sound. They mark their territory with a gland on their hind end. The odor is so strong that some have nicknamed them "stinker of the forest." They have a keen sense of smell that can identify the species of ants and termites that are in the nest before they rip it open. Even though their sense of smell is 40 times more powerful than man's, they don't seem to be bothered by their own stink!

Some Christians seem to feel they have keen senses that can pick out sin in the lives of everyone around them. Jesus spoke to people who critically judge others when He said, "And why do you look at the speck in your brother's eye, but do not consider the plank in your own eye" (Matthew 7:3). Paul warned us, "Let nothing be done through selfish ambition or conceit, but in lowliness of mind let each esteem others better than himself" (Philippians 2:3). Sometimes we can be so proud that we are not bothered by our own stink!

Strange People

"... "O Lord God of our fathers, are You not God in heaven, and do You not rule over all the kingdoms of the nations, and in Your hand is there not power and might, so that no one is able to withstand You?"
2 Chronicles 20:6

October 1 THE FIRE STARTER

"For He does not afflict willingly, nor grieve the children of men" (Lamentations 3:33).

He may have been the worst serial arsonist in U.S. history. Between 1984 and 1991, federal agents believe that John Orr may have set as many as 2,000 fires in the Los Angeles area in which at least four people died. What makes this even more shocking is that John Orr was a fire captain and arson investigator for the Glendale California Fire Department. Orr trained at least 1,200 firefighters and solved many arson investigations. Orr was eventually caught, convicted, and is currently serving a life sentence in prison.

John Leonard Orr was also a novelist and wrote—you guessed it—about an arsonist he named Aaron Styles. Part of the investigation work uncovered almost perfect similarities between the novelist's fires and those taking place in Southern California. This "Fire Lover," as Joseph Wambaugh's bestselling true crime book on Orr refers to him, had very specific methods to starting fires. Using a timing device, Orr would bundle three matchsticks to a lit cigarette and wrap it in ruled yellow writing paper secured by a rubber band. He would also set fires in other areas, like small grassy hills, to draw firefighters away from his arsonist work.

Orr claims innocence. He believes he is the victim of a corrupt judicial system and defends his book by stating, "The character of Aaron Styles was a composite of arsonists I arrested." On June 25, 1998, he was convicted of four counts of first-degree murder from a 1984 hardware store fire. When asked to be sentenced to death, the jury deadlocked and the judge sentenced Orr to life plus 20 years in prison without the possibility of parole.

People trusted John Orr to stop fires when he was actually the one starting them. Some people look at God in the same way. They believe the Lord is cruelly feeding the fires of hell to eternally torture sinners. But how does the Bible describe God? "Say to them: 'As I live,' says the Lord God, 'I have no pleasure in the death of the wicked, but that the wicked turn from his way and live ... '" (Ezekiel 33:11). Our God is compassionate and has done everything possible to stop the fire that will someday consume all sin.

"Then He said to the disciple, 'Behold your mother!'" (John 19:26).

Anna Jarvis deeply loved her mother. Following her mother's death in 1905, Anna campaigned for years to have a national day dedicated to appreciating mothers. She thought it should be a time for sons and daughters to visit their mothers or write letters expressing their love. Finally, in 1914, Woodrow Wilson signed it into national observance, declaring the second Sunday in May as Mother's Day.

Strangely, years after she struggled to establish Mother's Day, Anna Jarvis then fought to abolish it. Jarvis had soured because of the way she felt commercial interests had eclipsed the real meaning of the day. She wanted Mother's Day "to be a day of sentiment, not profit." Beginning around 1920, she urged people to stop buying flowers and other gifts for their mothers. She referred to the florists, greeting card manufacturers, and candy makers as "charlatans, bandits, pirates, racketeers, kidnappers and termites that would undermine with their greed one of the finest, noblest and truest movements and celebrations." Jarvis became crushed and bitter, believing that greed had destroyed Mother's Day, the holiday she helped create.

Near the end of her life Jarvis was seen going door to door in Philadelphia, trying to collect signatures on a petition to rescind Mother's Day. In 1948, Anna Jarvis died poor, blind, and childless. Ironically, Jarvis would never know that during the closing days of her life it was the florist companies that anonymously paid for her care.

The Bible also warns about the danger of something sacred becoming over commercialized. "So they came to Jerusalem. Then Jesus went into the temple and began to drive out those who bought and sold in the temple, and overturned the tables of the money changers and the seats of those who sold doves. And He would not allow anyone to carry wares through the temple. Then He taught, saying to them, 'Is it not written, "My house shall be called a house of prayer for all nations"? But you have made it a "den of thieves."'" (Mark 11:15–17).

Obviously, we should honor our mothers, and perhaps Anna has a point about turning special days into commercialized celebrations without genuine and heartfelt expressions. May our worship of God never turn into "pretty sentiments."

October 3 FAKED OWN FUNERAL

"Sir, we remember, while He was still alive, how that deceiver said, 'After three days I will rise'" (Matthew 27:63).

A 45-year-old Bosnian named Amir Vehabovic wanted to find out how loyal his friends were (he obviously had his doubts), so he faked his own death and arranged his own funeral. Then Amir hid in the bushes to count the attendees. Only his mother turned up. Incensed, he sat down and wrote an angry letter to all 45 of his mates. "I paid a lot of money to get a fake death certificate and bribe undertakers to deliver an empty coffin," he wrote. "I really thought a lot more of you, my so-called friends, would turn up to pay your last respects. It just goes to show who you can really count on." There is no word on exactly what his former friends didn't like about him. Perhaps they found him a bit needy.

In another interesting story, a man supposedly died to protect his family from ... his death? That was the intention. Graham Cardwell was a dockmaster who supposedly disappeared in September 1998. Eight months later he was discovered. Someone asked him, "What were you thinking?" His response: "I thought I had cancer and wanted to spare my family." Cardwell had never even been to a doctor. His supposed sickness was "just a hunch."

Still another man faked a drowning when he went canoeing in March 2002, even though the weather was calm and a massive search for his body turned up nothing. Five years later the man, John Darwin, walked into a London police station and claimed to have no memory of the previous seven years. But his wife told on him when she explained that he showed up at their house to collect money from a life insurance policy. He had actually been living at home for three years. After her confession they were both arrested.

The chief priests and Pharisees had successfully carried out their plot to have Jesus crucified. But they were concerned that Christ's body might be stolen and the disciples would "claim" that the Lord rose from the dead. So, they sent a delegation to Pilate asking for the tomb to be guarded. But after three days Jesus rose from the dead. There was nothing fake about Christ's death. Even His enemies knew He was dead and wanted Him to stay dead. Jesus had other plans!

"For I am not ashamed of the gospel of Christ, for it is the power of God to salvation for everyone who believes, for the Jew first and also for the Greek" (Romans 1:16).

In 2005, cancer patient Georgia Hayes won a 2.2-billion-dollar judgment in a lawsuit against her former pharmacist, Robert R. Courtney. His crime: diluting her chemotherapy drugs with water. He did this to reap the profits from selling more of the expensive drug to other patients, but in the meantime his victim missed her best chance for a cure because she was not properly treated. The pharmacist admitted to watering down drugs for over a decade, affecting as many as 4,200 patients! The 48-year-old father of five children is now serving a 30-year sentence in prison!

This is not an isolated case. Sadly, drug counterfeiting has become an increasing problem in our society. The Food and Drug Administration checked out an average of five cases a year back in the 1990s, but now there are over 20 investigations a year. With more sophisticated technology, counterfeiters sometimes succeed in introducing counterfeit drugs into the system. For example, Procrit, which fights anemia and fatigue in cancer and AIDS patients, was counterfeited in 2002. Tap water that had not been sterilized was used to water down the original drug until it was only one-twentieth of its original strength. Not only was it weakened, it also posed a threat of infection from contaminated water. Epogen, a drug that is used to treat severe anemia, was also recently counterfeited. And there are others. These watered-down drugs could not be nearly as effective and did not help the patients who took them.

Likewise, some people water down the Water of Life. By teaching and preaching a "soft" or "cheap" gospel, they tamper with the medicine for people's souls. Just like the watered-down medications, a diluted gospel is dangerous to spiritual health. One form of a diluted gospel says it is okay to keep sinning, because God always forgives the sinner. Paul addresses this argument by saying, "Shall we continue in sin that grace may abound? Certainly not! How shall we who died to sin live any longer in it?" (Romans 6:1, 2). And Jesus said, "If you love Me, keep My commandments" (John 14:15).

The true, undiluted gospel of Jesus Christ is a call to obedience and discipleship.

SELLING THE MOON

"Eye has not seen, nor ear heard, nor have entered into the heart of man the things which God has prepared for those who love Him" (1 Corinthians 2:9).

In 1967, the United Nations signed the international Outer Space Treaty, which forbids any government from claiming the moon, or any part of space, as their territory. The treaty failed to mention anything about private individuals or corporations, so this left a loophole in international law as big as the expanse of space itself.

In 1980, Dennis Hope of Gardnerville, Nevada, sent letters to the United Nations, the United States government, and the government of the Soviet Union, informing them that he was officially claiming ownership of all planetary and lunar surfaces in our solar system (aside from Earth). He even gave them the opportunity to respond if they had objections, and as crazy as it sounds, he hasn't heard a word from any of them since.

So, for over 20 years Dennis Hope has been selling plots of acreage on the moon, Mars, and other heavenly bodies for a pretty reasonable price—about $20 an acre! And he's been pursuing this not just as a novelty sale but a serious real estate transaction (complete with covenants and bylaws that prevent the unsightly or trivial usage of the property). His sales are accelerating, and within a couple of years he anticipates he'll have a constituency in the millions—enough to put serious pressure on the U.N. and the U.S. to recognize the government of Luna.

In the meantime, Dennis Hope, now 55, continues to operate his company selling people "official" title to land on the moon, Mars, and Venus. Although others are in the same business, Hope has earned about $6.5 million since he began his heavenly real estate business. That averages out at $270,000 a year, selling land on planets he has never been to and that he does not possess. Very clever!

But did you know that the Bible teaches there is some heavenly real estate you can truly own? And the price is already paid! Before Jesus left this earth, He told His disciples, "I go to prepare a place for you. And if I go and prepare a place for you, I will come again and receive you to Myself; that where I am, there you may be also" (John 14:2, 3). I sure look forward to the heavenly real estate Jesus is planning for us, don't you?

"Cast your bread upon the waters, for you will find it after many days" (Ecclesiastes 11:1).

Joe Richardson of Buna, Texas, has a fish story that may be hard to swallow, but it's true. More than 20 years after losing his graduation ring from Universal Technical Institute while fishing in Lake Sam Rayburn, Richardson received a phone call to inform him that his ring had been found. It was not discovered on the lakeshore or an area pawnshop, but in the mouth of an 8.4-pound bass! The 41-year-old mechanic says he received a call the day after Thanksgiving 2008 from a fisherman who claimed he found the long-lost ring in the mouth of a large bass he had caught. At first Richardson thought the call was an old friend pulling a prank, but soon realized that it was real. His wife, Lisa, said, "He was in shock and couldn't believe it until he held the ring in his hand."

Three soldiers fishing during the holiday reeled in an 8-pound bass on the lake. When the fish started flopping around in the bed of the boat, the fishermen noticed a ring pop out of its mouth. Using mosquito spray and WD-40, the soldiers cleaned the grime off the ring. Eventually they were able to barely make out the name "Joe Richardson" etched on the inside of the band. Then, right there on the lake, one of the fishermen pulled out his iPhone and started searching the Internet for Joe Richardsons in the area. He made three other calls before reaching the right person. They later met Joe and Lisa at a Dairy Queen and presented the ring to its original owner. Lisa said, "This was like a miracle, and we wondered why God chose to perform a miracle in our lives." Joe, on the other hand, could not help but wonder how many fish the ring had been through in two decades.

Did you know the Bible talks about finding money in a fish's mouth? Jesus told Peter, "... go to the sea, cast in a hook, and take the fish that comes up first. And when you have opened its mouth, you will find a piece of money; take that and give it to them for Me and you" (Matthew 17:27). Joe received back his lost ring. God wants to give you back the life you lost to sin.

October 7 COMPULSIVE HOARDING

"For what will it profit a man if he gains the whole world, and loses his own soul?" (Mark 8:36).

Compulsive hoarding is a condition where a person habitually gathers or buys growing piles of useless possessions, and then seems powerless to discard anything. This expanding collection of junk can lead to unbearable living conditions that cause significant clutter and impairment to mobility within their home. Of course, this pathological collecting is a strain on relationships, but it can also interfere with basic living activities such as cooking, cleaning, showering, or sleeping.

For example, an eccentric loner in Britain hoarded so much junk and trash he had to burrow through it to get around his home. Then in January 2009 he evidently got lost in the maze of tunnels and died of thirst. This 74-year-old human mole, Gordon Stewart, had filled the rooms of his house clear up to the ceiling with years' worth of old newspapers, garbage, and clutter, making it impossible to walk around. Neighbors said Mr. Stewart's home had been accumulating rubbish for at least 10 years. Heaps of plastic bags could clearly be seen piled up against his front window, while broken furniture, computer parts, and even an old TV spilled over onto his front lawn. A car dating back to the 1950s stood in the garage, untouched for years as garbage accumulated around it.

Neighbors in Broughton, England, called authorities after failing to see him leave his house for several days. When police arrived, the stench from the garbage was so foul they brought in a police scuba diving team with breathing apparatus to search the dwelling. They crawled around through mountains of junk and garbage, searching the elaborate network of tunnels until they located Stewart's body. The compulsive hoarder is believed to have become disorientated inside the walls of rotting trash and unable to find a way out until he collapsed from dehydration.

The Bible says there is " ... A time to keep, and a time to throw away" (Ecclesiastes 3:6). We might roll our eyes at people who struggle with hoarding, but there is probably a touch of greed in everyone's heart. If insecurity drives us to find peace in collecting the things of this world, let us do a deep work of removing the clutter of such thinking and rest in Jesus.

"... and turning the cities of Sodom and Gomorrah into ashes, condemned them to destruction, making them an example to those who afterward would live ungodly; and delivered righteous Lot, who was oppressed by the filthy conduct of the wicked (for that righteous man, dwelling among them, tormented his righteous soul from day to day by seeing and hearing their lawless deeds)—then the Lord knows how to deliver the godly out of temptations and to reserve the unjust under punishment for the day of judgment ..." (2 Peter 2:6-9).

A 29-year-old engineer for Mitsubishi Heavy Industries, Tsutomu Yamaguchi, was on a business trip in Hiroshima, Japan, when the U.S. dropped the first atomic bomb. On the morning of August 6, 1945, Yamaguchi was stepping off a streetcar when the atomic device, nicknamed "Little Boy," detonated above Hiroshima. Yamaguchi said he was less than two miles away from ground zero when he saw the blinding flash of light. Then his eardrums ruptured and his upper torso was burned by the blast that followed. The explosion destroyed most of the city's buildings and killed 80,000 people. Yamaguchi spent a painful night in a bomb shelter and the following day returned to his hometown of Nagasaki, 200 miles away.

By August 9, Yamaguchi made his way to his Nagasaki office, where he told his boss about the terrible Hiroshima blast. This was precisely when the second bomb, known as "Fat Man," was dropped on Nagasaki, killing 70,000 people there. Yamaguchi said, "Suddenly the same white light filled the room. I thought the mushroom cloud had followed me from Hiroshima. I could have easily died on either of those days." Yamaguchi became the only official survivor of both atomic blasts to hit Japan in World War II.

Six days after the Nagasaki attack, Japan surrendered. Yamaguchi recovered from his wounds, went to work for the American occupation forces, became a teacher, and eventually returned to work at Mitsubishi. He was in good health for most of his life, said his daughter; despite the double radiation exposure, he lived to be 93 years old.

The Bible talks about other cities that were wiped out by fire from heaven, but the witnesses were not so fortunate. The people of Sodom and Gomorrah, having "given themselves over to sexual immorality and gone after strange flesh" (Jude 1:7), were completely destroyed. Sadly, they turned away from the only Source of life.

October 9 BURIED ALIVE

"Or do you not know that as many of us as were baptized into Christ Jesus were baptized into His death?" (Romans 6:3).

On September 29, 2000, a 46-year-old Romanian man from the small village of Braila was placed in his coffin. At the funeral home, grieving family and friends filed past the open casket to pay their last respects. However, before he could be buried, Ionel Olteanu sprang to life and walked back home. Neighbors were shocked to see Olteanu strolling the streets of the village. Doctors who had certified Olteanu as dead aren't sure what really happened. They speculate that he might have fallen into a temporary diabetic coma.

Did you know history is littered with frightening examples of people buried alive, accidentally and deliberately? In 1896, T. M. Montgomery, who supervised the moving of all the remains at the Fort Randall Cemetery, reported it seemed, "Nearly two percent of those exhumed appeared to be victims of suspended animation." On the island of Iona, in the 6th century, one of St. Columba's monks, Oran, was dug up the day after his burial and found to be alive. Legend has it when he told his fellows he had seen heaven and hell, he was promptly executed and re-interred on grounds of heresy.

In the late 16th century, the body of Matthew Wall was being borne to his grave in Braughing, England. One of the pallbearers tripped, causing the others to drop the coffin, thus reviving the dear departed. Wall lived on for several more years, dying in 1595. He celebrated his "resurrection" every year. And in the early 17th century, Marjorie Elphinstone died and was buried in Ardtannies, Scotland. When grave robbers attempted to steal the jewelry off her body, the deceased scared the daylights out of them by groaning. The terrified robbers fled for their lives, and Marjorie revived, walked home, and outlived her husband by six years.

The Bible addresses another kind of premature burial that happens more than you think. When the apostle Paul described the meaning of baptism, he wrote, "Therefore we were buried with Him through baptism into death, that just as Christ was raised from the dead by the glory of the Father, even so we also should walk in newness of life" (Romans 6:4). What dies in baptism? Paul says, " ... our old man was crucified with Him ... " (verse 6). When we are baptized without genuinely turning from our old and sinful way of life, it is as if we are being buried alive. This sinful nature needs to die "that we should no longer be slaves of sin" (ibid.). Have you been buried alive?

"And He said, 'Your name shall no longer be called Jacob, but Israel; for you have struggled with God and with men, and have prevailed'" (Genesis 32:28).

Many years ago in the little town of Woodleigh, England, Annie Grey grew up knowing she would one day marry the boy who lived next door, William Coltart. And Coltart knew he would marry Annie. But Will decided he should develop some financial security before settling down with a family, so off he went to Australia.

When Annie did not hear from him for several years, she concluded that his love for her had faded, and she married a very rich merchant in town, Jonathon Tong. Soon after this, Coltart returned and was heartbroken to find his Annie wedded to another. Nevertheless, he settled down in his hometown and never married. After several years Jonathon Tong died, and Coltart felt that then he could propose to Annie. But when Jonathon's will was read, it stated clearly that Annie was to be cut off without a penny if she married Coltart. Obviously, Annie's deceased husband sensed there were feelings between his wife and Coltart, who he did not think much of.

But Jonathon Tong's spiteful will proved useless. Unknown to the dead man, Coltart had legally changed his name to "John Temple" during the time that he lived in far-off Australia. The English court ultimately decided that Annie could marry "John Temple" and still keep her inheritance, despite her jealous husband's attempt to disinherit her if she married her childhood sweetheart.

Did you know the Bible says we are offered a new name, a loving relationship, along with a fabulous inheritance? In Jesus' message to the church in Pergamos, Christ promises, "He who has an ear, let him hear what the Spirit says to the churches. To him who overcomes I will give some of the hidden manna to eat. And I will give him a white stone, and on the stone a new name written which no one knows except him who receives it" (Revelation 2:17). In the Bible, a new name represents a new character. So, what is your name?

ODD LUCK OF TODD LINCOLN

"Behold, this day I am going the way of all the earth. And you know in all your hearts and in all your souls that not one thing has failed of all the good things which the LORD your God spoke concerning you. All have come to pass for you; not one word of them has failed" (Joshua 23:14).

Robert Todd Lincoln, son of Abraham Lincoln, seemed to have a life of close calls. For starters, Robert was the only one of four brothers to survive beyond the teenage years. Then, when Robert was about 20, he fell between a moving train and the station platform. A fast-thinking stranger seized Robert by the coat collar and pulled him back to the platform, saving his life. Robert quickly recognized the good Samaritan as the famous actor Edwin T. Booth. If that name sounds familiar it's because Edwin's infamous brother, John Wilkes Booth, assassinated Robert Lincoln's father one year later. He was not at the Ford Theater when his father was shot, but was present at his bedside when he died.

Later, Robert carved out his own political career and was rewarded with the Secretary of War post under President James Garfield. In 1881, only four months into his new position, Garfield invited Robert to join him on a trip to New Jersey. Before either man could step onto the train, Garfield was gunned down. A few years later Robert Lincoln was in Buffalo, New York, by invitation of President William McKinley. While at a speaking engagement, McKinley was shot twice by an assassin. Robert did not see the shooting but was in the room and heard the gunshots. McKinley died eight days later from his wounds.

Knowing he seemed to be bad luck for his presidential pals, Robert turned down just about every presidential invitation that came his way, saying, " ... there is a certain fatality about presidential functions when I am present." He made one exception, and he did attend the dedication of the Lincoln Memorial in 1922. President Warren G. Harding and former President William Howard Taft survived the occasion.

Few people have witnessed so many history-making events. But the Bible speaks of one or two. Joshua, who was appointed to leadership after Moses, saw astonishing events unfold during his lifetime. He led the children of Israel into the Promised Land and witnessed, many times over, the amazing fulfillment of God's promises. Let's take time to review these events and have our own faith strengthened.

"But I do not want you to be ignorant, brethren ... "
(1 Thessalonians 4:13).

In 1982, a 33-year-old truck driver in Los Angeles made national news. Abject boredom prompted Larry Walters to go out and buy 42, six-foot weather balloons, a huge tank of helium, and some rope. He figured on tying the balloons to his lawn chair, filling them with helium, and gracefully floating up a few hundred feet for an aerial view of the neighborhood. As his neighbors watched, Larry secured his lawn chair to the bumper of his Jeep, and one by one he filled the balloons with helium. Then he tied them to his lawn chair. Before liftoff he provided himself with a two-way radio, a parachute, some jugs of water, a couple of peanut butter and jelly sandwiches, and his BB gun to regulate his altitude by shooting out excess balloons.

When he was ready, he yelled, "Let's go!" and his neighbors cut the ropes. But he didn't slowly rise 100 feet. He shot straight up so fast that he lost his glasses, climbing over 1,000 feet per minute. At one point he climbed to over 15,000 feet! For several hours he drifted in the cold air over the Pacific, near the landing pattern of the LAX airport. Eventually, a pilot of a DC-10 reported that he had passed a man in a lawn chair with a gun, and the control tower told him to report in immediately upon landing. They thought the pilot may have been drinking.

Eventually airport officials sent up helicopters to rescue him. On the ground, Larry found himself surrounded by TV crews, the police, and fire and rescue squads. It was a major event. One of the reporters asked, "What in the world made you do this?" Larry thought about it for a moment and said, "A man can't just sit around." Larry Walters is right, you can't just sit around, but his casual calculations for his historic flight nearly got him killed.

The Bible teaches that when Jesus returns, the redeemed will be caught up to meet the Lord in the air. But many sincere Christians are in danger of being deceived because they have miscalculated the nature of this event. Paul did not want Christians to be confused about Christ's return and wrote that when Jesus returns, "Then we who are alive and remain shall be caught up together with them in the clouds to meet the Lord in the air" (1 Thessalonians 4:17). There will be no secret rapture ahead of time. The righteous will all rise together. And we won't need the assistance of helium or lawn chairs!

MARCHING OFF THE MAP

"For the Lord your God has blessed you in all the work of your hand. He knows your trudging through this great wilderness ... " (Deuteronomy 2:7).

When Alexander the Great was leading his victorious armies down through Asia Minor, the great leader came at last to the foothills of the mighty Himalayas, beyond which lay the Khyber Pass and India. As far as Alexander was concerned, he was standing at the end of the world. You see, up until that time no maps had been made of the vast territory before him. As far as he knew he was marching his soldiers off the map of the world!

Often when ancient mapmakers reached the edge of what had been charted, they drew a line and depicted dragons and monsters beyond. You can understand why this practice didn't exactly encourage exploration. One Roman commander in the first century had led his troops beyond the line on the map into "dragon territory." He sent a courier back to Rome with a straightforward message: "We have just marched off the map. Please send new orders."

In the same way, when Columbus first sailed west in search of a shortcut to the Indies, he knew he would be essentially sailing off the map into a region that mapmakers marked with sea monsters. Moreover, because of the unknown distance ahead, he loaded his ships with as many provisions as they could carry and set sail by faith across the trackless sea, believing God was urging him forward.

When we consider conditions in the world today, with the unprecedented change in every arena of life, it would seem we have reached a point in history where we are drifting off the map! But the good news is that nothing that happens takes God by surprise. All these things have been charted before in Bible prophecy. When Daniel was asked to interpret a strange dream of an ancient Babylonian king, he said, "But there is a God in heaven who reveals secrets, and He has made known to King Nebuchadnezzar what will be in the latter days" (Daniel 2:28).

Nothing is hidden from God's eyes, not even the ends of the earth. The past, present, and future are all before the Lord.

"For God so loved the world that He gave His only begotten Son, that whoever believes in Him should not perish but have everlasting life" (John 3:16).

One stormy night in 1910, a group of traveling musicians arrived at the city of Riga, on the Baltic Sea, to fulfill a concert engagement. The weather was so bad, however, that the conductor of the orchestra tried to persuade the manager of the hall to cancel the concert. He felt sure that no one would venture out on such a rainy night. The manager refused to cancel, but he did agree that if not even one listener turned up, the orchestra could leave early in order to catch the night boat bound for Helsinki, Finland.

When the musicians arrived at the concert hall they found only one person sitting in the audience—a stout old man who seemed to smile at everyone. Because of this one old man, the musicians were forced to play the entire concert and were unable to leave early to catch the boat. After the concert was over the old man continued sitting in his seat. Thinking he was asleep, an usher nudged his shoulder. Only then was it discovered that the old man was dead. The musicians had played the entire concert for a dead man. But, ironically, in doing this they had actually saved their own lives, for the boat they would have taken to Finland sank that very night with a complete loss of life.

The Bible also speaks of how the death of one man saved the lives of many. In Paul's great letter explaining salvation to the Romans, he writes, "Therefore, as through one man's offense judgment came to all men, resulting in condemnation, even so through one Man's righteous act the free gift came to all men, resulting in justification of life" (Romans 5:18). And what was the "righteous act"? "But God demonstrates His own love toward us, in that while we were still sinners, Christ died for us" (verse 8).

Through Adam's one act of disobedience, death came to us all. But because of Christ's life of perfect obedience—which led Him to die on the cross for our sins—life may come to us all! Have you accepted Jesus' gift of salvation?

THE EMPEROR OF THE UNITED STATES

"Who do men say that I, the Son of Man, am?" (Matthew 16:13).

Joshua Abraham Norton, or as he preferred to be called, His Imperial Majesty Norton I, proclaimed himself emperor of the United States and protector of Mexico in 1859. Although a pauper, he was fed in San Francisco's best restaurants for free. Although a madman, he had all his state proclamations published in San Francisco's newspapers. Though he was generally considered insane, or at least highly eccentric, the citizens of San Francisco (and the world at large) in the mid- to late-19th century celebrated his presence, his humor, and his deeds—among the most notorious being his "order" that the U.S. Congress be dissolved by force, and his decrees calling for a bridge to be built across San Francisco Bay.

Norton was born in England and spent most of his early life in South Africa. He came to San Francisco in 1849 after receiving a bequest of $40,000 from his father's estate. He initially worked as a businessman but lost his money investing in Peruvian rice. He left San Francisco but later returned, apparently mentally disturbed, when he began to proclaim himself emperor of the United States. People were humored by his statements (although it is interesting that, years after his death, a bridge was built across the San Francisco Bay).

On January 21, 1867, an overzealous police officer arrested His Majesty Norton I for a mental disorder and thereby created a major civic uproar. The police chief apologized to Norton and ordered him released. Several scathing newspaper editorials followed the arrest. All police officers began to salute Norton when he passed them on the street. Norton I was so beloved that 30,000 people turned out for his funeral in 1880.

We smile at Norton's visions of grandeur, but many other men throughout history have made bold claims. Virtually all major world religions can be traced to some founder or charismatic leader. But claims are meaningless unless they are true. Christ asked His disciples who people thought He was and then asked, "But who do you say that I am?" (Matthew 16:15). That is the critical question. I hope you answer like Peter, who said, "You are the Christ, the Son of the living God" (verse 16). If that statement comes deep from within your heart, it will probably not give you a free ticket into many restaurants, but it will guarantee you a place in God's kingdom.

"Knowing this, that our old man was crucified with Him, that the body of sin might be done away with, that we should no longer be slaves of sin. For he who has died has been freed from sin" (Romans 6:6, 7).

After his sister died in 1951, James Nelson Gernhart was outraged because relatives wanted to bury her with a low-budget funeral. At 75 and alone, "Old Jim," as he was known, wanted to make sure this didn't happen to him. He resolved that everybody in tiny Burlington, Colorado (population 2,200), would know that he was going out with more dignity. He would have his funeral *before* he died!

Some townsfolk didn't think Old Jim should have his funeral when he wasn't even dead. They refused to let him use the community center. Then the singers Jim had scheduled backed out. Undaunted, Old Jim rented the town armory and substituted records of his favorite hymns. In the next town he hired a pastor to officiate. Then he plunked down $3,600 of his savings for a solid copper casket—a lot of money back then. Using newspaper ads, Old Jim invited everyone in town to his funeral.

In spite of the objections, nearly half the town filed into the dimly lit room, sat solemnly down on folding chairs, and watched as a hearse rolled up to the door. Eighteen honorary pallbearers formed a double line while eight old friends carried in the casket. With a sad expression on his weather-beaten face, Old Jim walked behind the casket, hat in hand. The preacher began his text: "He that believeth in me though he be dead yet shall he live." Old Jim beamed, and tears gathered in his eyes when the recorded strains of "Beautiful Isle of Somewhere" floated out over the armory. The service continued for the next 55 minutes. Finally, the piano played "Rock of Ages." Old Jim wrote out a $100 check for the minister and marched cheerfully out. "Now I don't care what they do with me when I die," he said. "I've got myself fixed up real good."

I know this may sound odd, but did you know the Bible recommends you conduct your own funeral? To break free of the slavery to sin, our old self must be crucified, and the "body of sin" must be "done away with." In this way, the Bible says, " ... reckon yourselves to be dead indeed to sin, but alive to God in Christ Jesus our Lord" (Romans 6:11).

October 17 SIR JEFFREY HUDSON

"Now behold, there was a man named Zacchaeus who was a chief tax collector, and he was rich. And he sought to see who Jesus was, but could not because of the crowd, for he was of short stature" (Luke 19:2, 3).

Sir Jeffrey Hudson was born of common parents north of London in 1619. On his 7th birthday, Jeffrey was presented to the Duchess of Buckingham who, because of his small handicap, invited him to join her household in London. What was this little handicap? Jeffrey Hudson was extremely small! How small? Well ... a few months after he came to live with the duke and duchess, the couple invited the king of England, Charles, and his young French wife, Henrietta, to their home. The climax of the lavish banquet was when a pie was placed in front of the queen, and Jeffrey popped up from the crust, standing 18 inches tall and dressed in a miniature suit of armor. The queen was so delighted, the duke and duchess offered Hudson to her as a gift.

In the palace, Jeffrey became her companion and confidante. He was famous as the "queen's dwarf" and "Lord Minimus." Educated by the best tutors in England, Jeffrey's intellect grew, but not his stature. He learned to charm and entertain with his wit and courtly behavior. Because of Jeffrey's amazing and well proportioned smallness he was considered one of the "wonders of the age" and a "rarity of nature." He looked as though a perfectly proportioned 20-year-old man had been shrunk down to 18 inches in height.

In spite of his diminutive size he experienced an unusually exciting life. He fought with the Royalists in the English civil war as a captain, serving with enough valor to earn him the nickname of "Strenuous Jeffrey." After one too many insults because of his size, he shot and killed a full-grown man while dueling from horseback. For this he was banished to Paris. He was twice captured by pirates and spent 25 years as a slave in North Africa before being ransomed by England. Sir Jeffrey was briefly restored to the royal court. He died at the age of 63. From the lowest social strata he rose to the courts of kings and queens. Yet this little big man died alone.

Jesus once asked the question, "Which of you by worrying can add one cubit to his stature?" (Matthew 6:27). Of course, worry will not help us grow one inch. But Zacchaeus grew by climbing down from a tree and confessing his sin. In the eyes of Jesus, Zacchaeus stood tall.

"Then they brought to Him one who was deaf and had an impediment in his speech, and they begged Him to put His hand on him. And He took him aside from the multitude, and put His fingers in his ears, and He spat and touched his tongue. Then, looking up to heaven, He sighed, and said to him, 'Ephphatha, that is, 'Be opened.' Immediately his ears were opened, and the impediment of his tongue was loosed, and he spoke plainly" (Mark 7:32-35).

Many years ago the Swamp United Church of Christ in Ephrata, Pennsylvania, celebrated the appearance of a strange lightning bolt. According to Evangelical Press news service, it seems that when circuit-riding preacher John Waldschmidt died in 1786, his wife could no longer hear or speak. During a church service six years later, lightning struck the cemetery outside. Upon investigation, say church records, the shocked congregation discovered that the bolt had split Waldschmidt's tombstone in two—and that the widow was healed the same instant.

In 1911, Mrs. Jane Decker, a Connecticut resident who had been deaf since childhood, was cured of her deafness in a similar way. During a storm, a lightning bolt tore down through the roof of her house and shattered rafters, windows, and frames, stunning Mrs. Decker and her daughter. The 65-year-old woman had minor injuries and was sore for several days, but her hearing was restored.

A farmer in Falmouth, Maine, also experienced a lightning cure in 1980. He had been involved in an accident with a tractor trailer and had lost his sight and hearing. One stormy day he was out in the farmyard searching for his pet chicken, Tuck-Tuck, when lightning struck him and blew the hearing aids right out of his ears. After recovering himself, he made his way back into the house, his sight and hearing miraculously restored.

Another unusual restoration of hearing occurred in the summer of 2011. Robert Valderzak, a patient in a VA hospital, had suffered from severe hearing loss for several months after fracturing his skull. Then, after a 5.8 earthquake that shook him from his bed, his son spoke to him and he heard his voice. Valderzak considered it a miracle.

Most of us have probably never had an experience like these people had, but it's not hard to imagine their emotions as they realized their senses were restored. The people Jesus healed must have felt the same astonishment, joy, and gratitude to God.

October 19 STINGY HETTY

"Do not lay up for yourselves treasures on earth, where moth and rust destroy ..." (Matthew 6:19).

When young Ned Green broke his leg during the late 1800s, his mother, Hetty, did her best to treat it herself, thinking hospitals in New York City were far too expensive. But after a few days Ned's leg grew worse. Hetty sadly shook her head and realized that only a doctor could save her son. Knowing how much a private hospital charges for patient care, Hetty loaded her fever-racked son into an old carriage and began searching from one end of Manhattan to the other looking for a free clinic where the poor could be treated for little or no money. After continuing unsuccessful home treatments, she finally found a doctor who had to remove the gangrenous leg. The frustrated physician must have thought, "This poor boy will live out the rest of his life as an invalid because this poor woman couldn't afford basic medical attention!"

What the good doctor didn't know was that "Hetty," Henrietta Howland Green, was far from poor. At the time of her son's injury she was the world's richest woman—and probably the world's stingiest too. When she died a few years later, she was worth well over $100 million. That's more than $17 billion in today's money! Also known as the "witch of Wall Street," Hetty Howland was legendary for her eccentric penny-pinching. Not only was she willing to let her son lose his leg rather than pay some small medical expense, she never turned on the heat in her home nor used hot water. She wore one old black dress and bought broken cookies in bulk, because they were cheaper. She would travel thousands of miles to collect a debt of a few hundred dollars. I should add, years later, as Hetty watched her son hobble about on crutches, she finally bought him a cork leg. But it still makes you wonder how somebody with so much money could neglect the basic needs of their only son?

The Bible gives us insight into the hearts of many people when Jesus stated, "For where your treasure is, there your heart will be also" (Matthew 6:21). There is nothing wrong with obtaining wealth, but when we do not lay up treasures in heaven by honoring God and being generous toward others, we will end up hoarding the things of this world.

"With long life I will satisfy him, and show him My salvation" (Psalm 91:16).

Few people have lived as long and gallant a life, filled with so many amazing memories, as Sergeant Patrick Gass. Love of adventure carried young Patrick across the virgin continent with Lewis and Clark on their epic voyage of discovery. Sergeant Gass became the carpenter of the expedition and kept a diary during the entire adventure. Before he died in 1870, just before his 99th birthday, great cities had been built and untold wealth found in the land he had helped discover.

Born in Falling Springs, Pennsylvania, in 1771, before the Revolution, he lived to see this country grow from the original 13 colonies to 38 states. He voted at the election of 18 presidents who served during his lifetime, from Washington to Grant. He experienced four great wars—the Revolutionary, the War of 1812, the Mexican, and the Civil War (not to mention numerous Indian battles, fighting alongside greats like Davy Crockett and Daniel Boone). During the War of 1812 he fought with Andrew Jackson in some of the bloodiest battles of the campaign on the Canadian border.

At the age of 63 he decided to settle down as a farmer, so he married a girl of 20. She died 13 years later leaving him, at the age of 76, with five children to raise. When he was almost 90, he tried to enlist in the Army during the Civil War on the side of the North, but was gracefully turned down. What a man! I have thought how thrilling it would be to be able to interview Sergeant Gass and hear him tell of his century of adventures across the American frontier. It's hard to imagine the things he must have seen and experienced.

The Bible tells us it is impossible for us to imagine the wonders of the Promised Land God has prepared for those who love Him. "But as it is written: 'Eye has not seen, nor ear heard, nor have entered into the heart of man the things which God has prepared for those who love Him'" (1 Corinthians 2:9). Yet, we have been given a taste in the book of Revelation of what we will enjoy. And it will never be cut short by death (Revelation 21:4).

October 21 THE LADY WHO GREW BACKWARD

"... till we all come to the unity of the faith and of the knowledge of the Son of God, to a perfect man, to the measure of the stature of the fullness of Christ; that we should no longer be children ..." (Ephesians 4:13, 14).

The lady who grew backward was a woman who lived in Virginia some years ago. In the *Virginia Medical Monthly* her doctor told the story. She had grown normally, married, and had three children. Life was good until the husband and father died when the children were in high school. The mother doubled her devotion to the children. She changed her clothes to those of a girl of 20, and joined in her children's parties and fun.

In a few years the children noticed that as they grew older their mother was growing younger. Psychiatrists call it "personality regression," which means "a person walking backward." Usually such people stop going backward at a certain age. But not this woman. She slipped backward at the rate of one year for every three or four months of time that went forward. Although she was 61 years old she acted and talked like a 6-year-old. She was sent to a sanitarium, where she insisted on wearing short dresses, playing with toys, and babbling like a child.

Then she became like a three-year-old; she spilled her food, crawled on the floor, and cried "Mama." Backward still further to the age of one, she drank milk and curled up like a tiny baby. Finally, she went back over the line and died.

Spiritual regression is an even more serious disorder. Peter tells us to "grow in grace and knowledge of our Lord and Savior Jesus Christ" (2 Peter 3:18), but some Christians seem to slide backward in their growth. Moving forward is our best weapon against turning from God. And it happens through growing both in knowledge and grace. Not only do we need to study God's Word every day, seeking to understand more about the Lord, but we are to walk in grace.

The church isn't one giant nursery meant to pass out baby bottles and pacifiers to everyone who walks through its doors. It is a training ground for "growing up" (see Ephesians 4:15) into mature Christians who represent Jesus and are strong in faith.

"Now to Him who is able to keep you from stumbling, and to present you faultless before the presence of His glory with exceeding joy ... " (Jude 24).

On January 21, 2007, a Wisconsin man, Joshua S. Hanson, and two friends were in Minneapolis for a dart tournament. After a few hours out drinking they returned to their Hyatt Regency Hotel about 1:30 in the morning. They took an elevator to the 17th floor and were evidently horsing around. For some reason, 29-year-old Hanson ran from the elevator down a short hallway and apparently lost his balance and crashed through the large double-paned window. He tumbled down 16 floors and crashed into the awning of the hotel's main entrance overhang. Amazingly, he survived. His most serious injury was a broken leg. Minneapolis Police Lieutenant Dale Barsness said, "This man must have an angel on his shoulder."

The record for surviving the highest fall without a parachute is held by a Serbian woman, Vesna Vulović. On January 26, 1972, she was flying over the Czech Republic. Croat terrorists had placed a bomb onboard JAT Yugoslav Flight 364, on which Vulović was a flight attendant. The 22-year-old wasn't even supposed to be on that flight; her schedule had been mixed up with another flight attendant. The explosion tore the DC-9 to pieces, but Vulović survived. She remained strapped into her seat in the middle section of the plane that was right above the wings. The assembly spiraled down 33,000 feet then struck the snow-covered flank of a mountain. Her injuries included a fractured skull, two broken legs, and three broken vertebrae, one of which left her temporarily paralyzed from the waist down. She was also in a coma for 27 days. She regained the use of her legs after several months of surgeries. Vulović was the only survivor on the flight, and not only lived to tell about it, but continued working for JAT at a desk job following her full recovery. Vulović later became a national hero in Yugoslavia.

The Bible teaches that all men have morally fallen, but there is a way you can survive the fall. The Scriptures tell us God guides the steps of the person who chooses to serve Him. "Though he fall, he shall not be utterly cast down; for the LORD upholds him with His hand" (Psalm 37:24). Psalm 145 says, "The LORD upholds all who fall, and raises up all who are bowed down" (verse 14). With the Lord upholding us, we have great hope!

October 23 MARGARET'S CRYSTAL GOBLET

"See, I have set before you today life and good, death and evil ..." (Deuteronomy 30:15).

Early in the 16th century, Holland was ruled by Margaret of Austria. In those uneasy days of intrigue and murder, rulers took every precaution against sudden death. Margaret was no exception. She feared death by poisoning, and because it was believed that pure rock crystal would disclose the presence of poison, she would drink from nothing but a goblet made of this rare mineral.

One day a servant, handing Margaret a drink, dropped the goblet to the stone floor. The shattered crystal was carefully swept up, but one tiny fragment flew unnoticed into Margaret's slipper. The splinter of glass worked its way into her foot, which soon became painful, then grew red and swollen with infection. By the time the doctors were called, gangrene was far advanced. Immediate amputation was necessary, but the great Margaret of Austria did not survive the terrible ordeal. Ironically, she died of poisoning caused by the very crystal she believed would protect her from such a death.

Friends, did you know that many today are placing their confidence in something that not only cannot satisfy but could even cause their death? In a desire to have power and know the future, some people are seeking out the help of channelers, sorcerers, and witches. Assuming they are speaking with great people who are dead, some look for valuable information that will help them in their lives. But it is all a fraud of the devil.

King Saul, in desperation, went to the witch of Endor to supposedly speak with Samuel the prophet, who was dead. Yet God clearly commanded that spiritualists be driven out of Israel and be put to death. The Bible unmasks all spiritualism as the work of demonic and satanic forces. Saul had already rejected the counsel of Samuel, and when he inquired of God for help, the Lord did not answer. What Saul saw when he visited the witch was something that he "perceived" looked like Samuel. Since the "dead do not know anything" (Ecclesiastes 9:5), it was Satan masquerading in the form of a dead person.

The ultimate end of Saul's visit with the witch of Endor was not life and happiness, but ruin and death. He came looking for help, but had already rejected the word of God that was repeatedly sent to him. His visit with the witch, like Margaret's crystal goblet, was (he hoped) going to save him. In the end, it was a final step to the grave. Friends, don't be deceived by the devil's substitutes!

"So they picked up Jonah and threw him into the sea, and the sea ceased from its raging" (Jonah 1:15).

In 1692, the city of Port Royal on the island of Jamaica literally slid into the sea when it was struck by a massive earthquake. Many had predicted that Port Royal, a corrupt city of pirates and cutthroats, would one day suffer God's judgment and be destroyed. The disaster, therefore, surprised no one, least of all the handful of religious men who were swept to their doom along with the wicked inhabitants. One such man was Lewis Galdy. He was born in France, but left in search of religious freedom and finally settled on the island of Jamaica.

On a hot and muggy morning in June, three earthquakes rocked the island, moving two mountains nearly a mile from their original positions. But Port Royal suffered the greatest damage. It was built onto an unstable jut of land. So the city actually slid into the ocean. In just a few minutes it lay 50 feet deep in water. About 2,000 people (one-third of the city) perished. Another 1,000 died from disease after the earthquake, and eventually the city was forever abandoned.

When the first violent shock came, Galdy was buried deep beneath the earth. Amazingly, he still remained conscious and understood what had happened. Like Jonah in the belly of the sea monster, he prayed for his soul and resigned himself to death. A few moments later, the ground shook a second time and exploded, throwing Galdy high through the air and out over the churning sea. Some say he shot like a cork out of a bottle. He landed unhurt in the water and swam until a boat picked him up. Galdy lived for 47 years after his miraculous escape. He died in 1739, and his tombstone tells the story of his amazing experience. No doubt he felt like he had been resurrected.

Did you know the Bible teaches there will be two resurrections? In speaking of the coming judgment, Jesus said, "Do not marvel at this; for the hour is coming in which all who are in the graves will hear His voice and come forth—those who have done good, to the resurrection of life, and those who have done evil, to the resurrection of condemnation" (John 5:28, 29). Galdy believed judgment would come to the corrupt city of Port Royal. Jesus tells us judgment will come to the entire world.

October 25 SURPRISE BABIES

"And the Lord *visited Sarah as He had said, and the* Lord *did for Sarah as He had spoken. For Sarah conceived and bore Abraham a son in his old age, at the set time of which God had spoken to him" (Genesis 21:1, 2).*

In May 1996, Karen Watson, age 20, gave birth to a 5-pound, 12-ounce baby boy in Albany, Oregon. This would not be so remarkable except for the fact Karen had no idea she was even pregnant. Karen was en route by train to a wedding in Missoula, Montana. During the train ride, Watson became increasingly uncomfortable. Someone eventually called ahead, and they were met by paramedics at the Albany train stop to see what was causing Karen's mounting physical distress. Minutes later, Watson gave birth to a healthy baby boy.

This event took her completely by surprise, though she admitted some doctors had diagnosed she was suffering from anemia and a thyroid condition. Of course, this was not the first case of a woman unexpectedly giving birth. But it is hard to comprehend how slender, 105-pound Watson never even dreamed that the seven extra pounds she had gained could be a 5-pound, 12-ounce baby boy. What makes this even more amazing is that Karen Watson was a pre-med biology major at the University of California, Davis, with plans to go into family practice.

Did you know the Bible talks about a number of miracle baby boys that surprised their mothers? Isaac, Joseph, Samuel, John the Baptist, and Jesus were all born under miraculous circumstances. The elderly Sarah was so delighted when Isaac was born that she said, "God has made me laugh, and all who hear will laugh with me" (Genesis 21:6). Rachel, who had been tormented by her sister Leah because she had no children, said after bearing Joseph, "God has taken away my reproach" (Genesis 30:23). Hannah had her miracle boy, "and called his name Samuel, saying, 'Because I have asked for him from the Lord'" (1 Samuel 1:20). Elizabeth, the mother of John the Baptist, was also beyond the usual child-bearing years when she became with child. Her response: "Thus the Lord has dealt with me, in the days when He looked on me, to take away my reproach among people" (Luke 1:25).

The most miraculous baby, of course, was Jesus, who was born to save all those who choose to be miraculously born again in Him.

"And a vision appeared to Paul in the night. A man of Macedonia stood and pleaded with him, saying, 'Come over to Macedonia and help us'" (Acts 16:9).

On November 19, 2010, a 69-year-old woman in Paris was found who had been trapped in her own bathroom for 20 days. The door lock had snapped off, and there was no window in the bathroom or a telephone at hand. She lived alone and was unable to summon help. But, she had the never-say-die attitude and resorted to a practical gimmick to draw attention. She kept banging the pipes with whatever she could find.

Her neighbors thought she was involved in some do-it-yourself renovation work and initially ignored the banging noises! But when the disturbances continued late into the night, neighbors complained they could not sleep. They decided to start a petition to have it stopped. But some neighbors realized they had not seen the grandmother in a few weeks. That is how they eventually came to investigate the woman's apartment and rescued her. When firefighters broke into her second-floor flat they found her lying on the floor in the bathroom, badly malnourished and in a very weakened state. She had survived the ordeal with nothing but warm tap water for 20 days. The unnamed woman soon recovered in a local hospital.

In a similar way the Bible teaches we are surrounded by people who are trapped in sin and calling out for help ... but maybe we don't always recognize their signals. The apostle Paul once recognized a cry for help and responded. The Bible says, "And a vision appeared to Paul in the night. A man of Macedonia stood and pleaded with him, saying, 'Come over to Macedonia and help us.' Now after he had seen the vision, immediately we sought to go to Macedonia, concluding that the Lord had called us to preach the gospel to them" (Acts 16:9, 10).

Paul didn't hesitate to help out when the Macedonians asked for assistance. We also should respond to the calls for help when people around us are dying for the message of the gospel. Would you be willing to break down doors to help your neighbors?

RAINING BABIES

"The eternal God is your refuge, and underneath are the everlasting arms ... " (Deuteronomy 33:27).

In January 2007, Julio Gonzalez and Pedro Nevarez, two auto mechanics, caught a three-year-old boy who fell from the fifth floor of his building. The toddler, Timothy Addo, had escaped through a window while his babysitter was in the bathroom. The window had apparently been opened by the babysitter in order to have a cigarette. The men saw the child dangling from the fire escape and moved into position to make the catch. The boy only received minor injuries resulting from hitting a tree branch on his descent. "I feel like we did something good today. We were in the right place at the right time," said Nevarez.

In Detroit sometime in the spring of 1935, a young mother must have been eternally grateful to a man named Joseph Figlock. As Figlock was walking down the street, the mother's baby fell from a high window onto Figlock. The baby's fall was broken by the stunned man, but incredibly both man and baby were unharmed. This was obviously a stroke of remarkable providence, but here is where the story becomes truly astonishing. A year later, the very same baby, now a heavier toddler, fell from the very same window onto poor, unsuspecting–you guessed it–Joseph Figlock as he was again passing beneath. And again, they both survived the event!

Another story with a remarkable twist happened in the early 1900s. A lighthouse keeper in Scotland was cleaning the outside lamp window when the rusted railing gave way. The terrified man fell 130 feet. When he opened his eyes he looked up, a bit dazed, at the blue sky with white puffy clouds and wondered if he was in heaven. As he collected his wits he discovered he survived the fall because he landed on a sheep that had been peacefully grazing below the lighthouse. The sheep did not survive.

Neither did Jesus. The Bible presents Christ as the sacrificial lamb who gave His life that we might be saved. Philip once explained to a curious Ethiopian eunuch who was reading a passage about Christ, "The place in the Scripture which he read was this: 'He was led as a sheep to the slaughter; and as a lamb before its shearer is silent, so He opened not His mouth'" (Acts 8:32). When we fell into sin, Jesus offered to take the brunt of our fall with His own life.

"A certain man went down from Jerusalem to Jericho, and fell among thieves, who stripped him of his clothing, wounded him, and departed, leaving him half dead. Now by chance a certain priest came down that road. And when he saw him, he passed by on the other side" (Luke 10:30, 31).

In February 2007, police in Hampton Bays, New York, received a call to investigate a report of a home with burst pipes. Upon entering the home they were stunned to find the partially mummified body of a man who had been dead for more than a year. He was found alone in the house, sitting in a chair in front of his television, which was still on. The Suffolk County medical examiner said Vincenzo Ricardo, 70, apparently died of natural causes. A local morgue assistant said evidently the home's dry air had helped to preserve his remains.

Ricardo's wife died years earlier, and he lived alone. He had diabetes and had gone blind, but he was still very independent. The amazing thing is that he hadn't been heard from in over a year and nobody sounded the alarm. Evidently he had his bills set up to be paid automatically. Still, you would have thought someone would have observed the lights never went off and the TV was constantly blaring. In addition, his mailbox was overflowing and yet no one seemed to notice even though it could be clearly seen by others. Neighbors said they just never thought to check on him. They had assumed Ricardo was in a hospital or nursing home.

It seems that the Bible's teaching about caring for our neighbor has become a forgotten moral. A lawyer once asked Jesus, "Teacher, what shall I do to inherit eternal life?" (Luke 10:25). When Jesus asked what the law taught, the man responded by quoting the Old Testament, including the injunction to love your neighbor. But then he asked Jesus, "Who is my neighbor?" In this context, Christ told the story of the good Samaritan. In essence, the story points out, "Our neighbor is anyone around us in need."

How often has the Holy Spirit whispered to your heart to "check on your neighbor"? You might need to see if your neighbors are doing well physically, but don't neglect to be sensitive to their spiritual well-being. Share literature with people around you. Offer to pray for hurting people you come into contact with. Reach out. Don't assume everything is fine. They may be dying right next door to you.

October 29 A PARDON REFUSED

"Who is a God like You, pardoning iniquity and passing over the transgression of the remnant of His heritage? He does not retain His anger forever, because He delights in mercy" (Micah 7:18).

If you were sentenced to life in prison would you refuse a pardon? It's happened before. Way back in 1895, a young Rhode Island man named Martin Dalton was convicted of murder and sentenced to life imprisonment. After serving over 30 years, in 1930 he was offered a pardon. Incredibly, Dalton refused it. He explained that he no longer had a family, nothing to do, and nowhere to go. The prison officials were not quite sure what to do with a rejected pardon. After much legal evaluation it was determined that a pardon refused was invalidated. Martin Dalton remained in prison until his death in 1960.

Dalton and his friend, Dan Sullivan, lured a man out of town, beat him up, and robbed him of a gold watch and cash. Before the man died he identified his assailants. Sullivan was arrested a few days later, and Dalton was caught three years later. He was working in Atlanta. From the first, Dalton was a docile prisoner. His behavior in prison was cooperative, his record clean. He worked in a machine shop, then the prison laundry, and later the prison farm. When he was given a "preview visit" of life outside of prison, he was supposedly frightened. Everything had changed. Clothing was different, automobiles scared him. He had nowhere to go.

During the last 61 years of his confinement he didn't have a single visitor, and the last letter he received came to him in 1929. How sad. What's even sadder is when millions of people under a death sentence refuse to accept the pardon and eternal life Jesus has purchased for them. Paul warned the Galatians, "Stand fast therefore in the liberty by which Christ has made us free, and do not be entangled again with a yoke of bondage" (Galatians 5:1).

Jesus wants to visit you in your prison of sin. He stands at the door of your heart and knocks. Christ has purchased your freedom and will set you free. Do not refuse the pardon He offers. Eternal life outside is well worth accepting.

"For in death there is no remembrance of You; in the grave who will give You thanks?" (Psalm 6:5).

During the height of the Civil War, Sarah Pardee met and married William W. Winchester, the son of the famous rifle manufacturer. They had one child, Annie, who died about one month after birth. Then about 15 years later, William died of tuberculosis. Mrs. Winchester was deeply upset by the premature deaths of her husband and daughter and supposedly consulted a spiritualistic medium, who explained that the spirits of all those who had been killed by the rifles her family had made sought their revenge by taking the lives of her loved ones. Further, these spirits had placed a curse on her. But the medium also stated that she could escape the curse by moving West, buying a house, and constructing an ever-growing mansion to house good spirits and confound bad ones.

In 1884, Mrs. Winchester moved to San Jose, California, and purchased an eight-room farmhouse. She immediately began a never-ending building project. With much money and few responsibilities, she kept a staff of 40 to 60 servants and carpenters constantly busy. She had no master plan for a house and, according to her carpenters, built whenever, wherever, and however she pleased, always directed by the spirits. Every night, Sarah would go to her séance room to receive messages from the spirits telling her what she should build. These bizarre orders resulted in many strange creations, such as doors that open onto walls, stairs that go nowhere, a cupboard that has only one half inch of storage space, and tiny doorways and hallways just big enough for Sarah (who was 4 feet, 10 inches and of slight build) to fit through. The rambling structure has 160 rooms; 2,000 doors; 10,000 windows; and 150,000 panes of glass. It boasts 40 stairways, 47 fireplaces, and 13 bathrooms.

Sarah paid workers well to keep building continuously for nearly 40 years until her death in 1922. Sarah Winchester was a very lonely woman; there is only one blurry photograph of this eccentric recluse. In fact, when President Theodore Roosevelt came to visit San Jose, the chamber of commerce tried to get Mrs. Winchester to receive him, but she refused.

All this wasted money, labor, and years of fear were to appease the supposed spirits of the dead. But can the spirits of the dead haunt the living? The Bible says, "For in death there is no remembrance of You" (Psalm 6:5), and "the dead know nothing" (Ecclesiastes 9:5). The Scriptures clearly say "No."

October 31 FESTIVAL OF THE DEAD

"For the wages of sin is death ..." (Romans 6:23).

Halloween is observed by many on October 31st each year, on the last day of the Celtic calendar. It was originally a pagan holiday honoring the dead and dates back over 2,000 years. The name Halloween referred to "All Hallows' Eve," the evening before All Saints' Day on November 1st. This was a holiday created by Roman Catholics in an attempt to convert pagans. The Catholic Church honored dead saints on this designated day. This was to mirror the pagan traditions traced back to the Druids, a Celtic culture in Ireland, Britain, and Northern Europe.

Roots of Halloween lay in the feast of Samhain, which was held annually on October 31st to honor the dead. Samhain signifies "summer's end," or November. Samhain was a harvest festival with huge sacred bonfires, marking the end of the Celtic year and beginning of a new one. Many of the practices involved in this celebration were fed by superstition. The Celts believed the souls of the dead roamed the streets and villages at night. Since not all spirits were thought to be friendly, gifts and treats were left out to pacify the evil spirits and ensure next year's crops would be plentiful. They also dressed up in disguises to confuse the vengeful spirits. These customs gradually evolved into trick-or-treating.

Today, Halloween focuses on symbols of jack-o'-lanterns, costumes, parties, and trick-or-treating. Costume imagery is often tied to horror stories, death, evil, the occult, and mythical monsters. Candy sales average about two billion dollars annually, making it—next to Christmas—the most commercially successful holiday for stores and dentists.

So the question is, "Should a Bible Christian fear the spirits of the dead?" The Bible is very clear about what happens when a person dies. They do not come back to haunt you as a disembodied spirit or ghost. When people die, they truly are dead! "For in death there is no remembrance of You; in the grave who will give You thanks?" (Psalm 6:5). "But the living know that they will die; but the dead know nothing, and they have no more reward, for the memory of them is forgotten" (Ecclesiastes 9:5).

Christians do not need to fear the spirits of the dead, for they do not exist. People who die are in their graves, awaiting the resurrection—either to life eternal or to eternal destruction. Satan and his host of evil angels are behind all so-called appearances of dead people. But Christ promises us that His powers are greater than those of the devil. In Jesus we have no fear.

Water Creatures

"Or speak to the earth, and it will teach you;
And the fish of the sea will explain to you."
Job 12:8

November 1 HORSES OF THE SEA

"Then Moses and the children of Israel sang this song to the LORD, and spoke, saying: 'I will sing to the LORD, for He has triumphed gloriously! The horse and its rider He has thrown into the sea!'" (Exodus 15:1).

Few animals God made are more unusual than the seahorse. This bizarre creature is put together like the Mr. Potato Head of the ocean. It has the arching neck and head of a stallion, the swelling bosom of a pigeon, the grasping tail of a monkey, and the color-changing ability of a chameleon. The seahorse has a long, narrow snout like an anteater, and a little mouth to suck up tiny particles of food. It has eyes that pivot independently like a chameleon's, so that when one eye scans the surface the other can be directed downward. To top off this fantastic composition, the male is equipped with a kangaroo-style pouch from which the little ones are born.

Ranging from one inch to one foot long, the seahorse is the only fish that swims upright! It has a special "gas bladder" that enables it to keep its upright position. Seahorses are classified as fish, but they are very different from other fish because they have no scales, lack teeth, and do not have a stomach. Their food goes directly into their intestines. Their intestines process food inefficiently, so seahorses need to eat almost constantly so they don't starve.

Most seahorses are monogamous. The male and female dance together for about 10 minutes every dawn, then separate for most of the day to feed. During courtship, the female actively pursues the male until she deposits her eggs in a pouch on her mate's belly. In the pouch the eggs are fertilized and nourished for 45 days. But the most amazing paradoxical feature of all is when the male seahorse "goes into labor" and gives birth to its young. After a series of paternal spasms in which it appears every muscle convulses, the pouch is emptied and from 40 to 400 baby seahorses are born!

Did you know the Bible talks about seahorses? Well ... not exactly. "The horse and its rider He has thrown into the sea!" was part of the song that Moses and the children of Israel sang after miraculously crossing through the Red Sea and escaping their enemy, the Egyptian army. It was a song of joy and deep gratitude to God.

"And the Lord God said to the woman, 'What is this you have done?' The woman said, 'The serpent deceived me, and I ate'" (Genesis 3:13).

The leafy seadragon is a marine fish in the same family as seahorses and is found along the southern and western coasts of Australia. It gets its name from its interesting appearance. This sea creature has the ultimate camouflage outfit! It has long, leaf-like appendages growing out all over its body. These protrusions don't help it to swim but are simply for helping it hide from predators. The leafy seadragon does have pectoral fins on its neck and a dorsal fin near the end of its tail, but these fins are transparent and difficult to see. As it slowly moves about, it has the appearance of floating like seaweed. This illusion helps it blend in to its environment. It can even change its color to match its surroundings.

The name for this fish comes from its resemblance to the mythical dragon. Seadragons grow to be about 8 to 10 inches long and mostly eat plankton and small crustaceans. They have long, pipe-like snouts like the seahorse, through which they suck up small bits of food. Unlike the seahorse, seadragons do not have curled tails that can hang on to objects. They actually don't move very much and have been observed staying in one place for up to 68 hours.

The greatest threat to these beautiful creatures is man. Some people catch them to use in alternative medicine. Others simply are fascinated by them and capture them to put in aquariums, though they are difficult to maintain. Pollution has negatively hurt these little fish, and they are now officially protected by the government of Australia. In fact, the leafy seadragon is the official marine emblem of the state of South Australia.

The Bible speaks of another dragon that is a master of camouflage. Satan does not directly reveal himself but uses a variety of means to hide and deceive. From Eve in the Garden of Eden to our day, the devil is seeking to lead us astray through trickery. Jesus warns us, "For false christs and false prophets will rise and show great signs and wonders to deceive, if possible, even the elect. See, I have told you beforehand" (Matthew 24:24, 25). As the coming of Jesus moves closer, look carefully at the claims of Christians. Not everything you see is truth.

November 3 PEARL OF GREAT PRICE

"Do not ... cast your pearls before swine, lest they trample them under their feet, and turn and tear you in pieces" (Matthew 7:6).

A brooch purchased for $14.00 at a Bristol, Rhode Island, antique shop has turned out to contain a priceless purple pearl. Alan Golash, a Newport antiques dealer, claims the value of the rare pearl is supported by gem experts who examined it. His partner found the 19th-century ornamental pin while rummaging through a basket of costume jewelry at a former antique shop. Golash, who restores antique jewelry, cleaned the brooch and discovered it was made of 18-karat gold and enamel and included three small rose-cut diamonds. Based on its construction and Victorian styling, it is believed by jewelry experts to have been created sometime between 1860 and 1885.

But most notably, the brooch features two rare pearls, both of which gem experts say are all natural, purple, and produced from a type of clam known as quahogs [pronounced KOH-hog], which are extraordinarily rare. The larger of the two pearls is about the size of a marble and is a rare deep lilac-colored pearl. "We've never had a pearl like this before," said Betty Lin, vice president of jewelry at Christie's auction house. Golash plans to sell the brooch at auction in two years in Hong Kong, where pearls are highly prized. In the meantime, the pearl, named "The Pearl of Venus," was on display when it traveled with the American Museum of Natural History. The pearl is valued between $250,000 and $1 million because of its rare size.

When news first broke about the Golash brooch, Alan was swamped with reporters and actually did over 100 TV and radio interviews. Gem-quality quahog pearls are extremely rare, and when you add to this the desired lilac color, it is rarer still. Some people would say the chances of finding this are one in two million. One jeweler adviser to Christie's auction house said, "It's so rare, it's one of a kind. You cannot put a price on this pearl, because there is nothing to compare it to."

That statement almost sounds like it came from the Bible! Jesus said, "Again, the kingdom of heaven is like a merchant seeking beautiful pearls, who, when he had found one pearl of great price, went and sold all that he had and bought it" (Matthew 13:45, 46). Can you imagine selling something for $14.00 and later learning it is worth millions? Countless people do this every day.

"The statues of the LORD are right, rejoicing the heart; the commandment of the LORD is pure, enlightening the eyes" (Psalm 19:8).

The mantis shrimp is neither a mantis nor a shrimp, but derives its name from claws similar to a praying mantis and a body similar to a shrimp. These marine crustaceans, also called stomatopods, come in a variety of colors and grow to be about 12 inches long. The most colorful is the peacock mantis shrimp, with brilliant neon hues that dazzle the eye. This sea creature likes to live a solitary life, hiding in rock formations and waiting for prey to come by, though it will chase and kill for food.

The ancient Assyrians called these creatures "sea locusts." In Australia they are referred to as "prawn killers," but they are also called "thumb splitters" because of the nasty gash they can inflict if not handled carefully. Mantis shrimp sport powerful claws that they use to attack prey. These claws can spear or stun their victims. In fact, they are classified into two groups based on their claws. There are the "spearers" (with spiny appendages topped with barbed tips that stab and snag) and "smashers" (with a club-like claw that bludgeons their meals apart). The mantis shrimp's claw can strike so powerfully that its speed has been compared to that of a .22-caliber bullet. A shock wave is created as well so that if the shrimp misses its target, the aftereffect can be enough to stun or kill its prey.

What literally "stands out" in the mantis shrimp is its eyes. They are considered the most complex eyes in the animal kingdom. Each eye is mounted at the end of a stalk and can move independently. Most fascinating is that this sea animal can see both polarized and hyperspectral color. Not only that, but each eye is designed to have three regions, giving the mantis shrimp the ability to see three parts of an object from a slightly different angle. In other words, they have trinocular vision out of each eye! The optics of this little crustacean is actually being studied to improve on the current generation of Blu-ray disc technology.

Jesus once spoke about improving your eyesight. Our ability to see is directly related to our hearts. In the Sermon on the Mount, Christ said, "Blessed are the pure in heart, for they shall see God" (Matthew 5:8). When we humble ourselves before God, seeking to be cleansed from sin, our eyes will be opened to see with vision that is out of this world!

November 5 RESILIENT STARS

"Therefore those who were scattered went everywhere preaching the word" (Acts 8:4).

Starfish are the most popular creatures in tidal pools, especially among children. There are about 1,600 starfish species that are found everywhere in the oceans—from the deep, deep sea to the shallow reefs. They can range in size from half an inch full grown to 26 inches across. Starfish are unique, brainless creatures having no front, back, head, or tail, and can move in any direction without turning. Rather than using muscles to move their hundreds of tiny "tube feet," starfish use a complex hydraulic system to travel around or cling to rocks.

Because starfish are slow, they prey on slow-moving or stationary creatures, or scavenge dead ones. Starfish have a good sense of smell to sniff out any edible tidbits, and they can be voracious eaters, devouring up to three times their body weight in a day! Young starfish may eat 10 times their body weight daily! They will eat just about anything too, and this is the reason we don't usually see starfish in home aquariums.

To eat an oyster or a clam, the starfish patiently pries the two shells apart to open a tiny gap, whereupon it performs a unique feat. It turns its stomach inside out, inverting it out of its mouth into the clam, to release digestive juices and absorb the resulting soup! After the meal, it inverts its stomach back into its body. Starfish usually have five arms, but a few have less, and some species have as many as 50 arms! They are also famous for their amazing ability to regenerate, or re-grow, a lost arm. One common Pacific starfish can cast off an arm without any part of the central body attached, and that arm will slowly grow into a complete new starfish. In fact, some starfish reproduce by purposely pulling one arm off. Years ago, inexperienced pearl divers would hack up the starfish that were feasting on the oysters, not realizing they were only making more starfish.

In like manner, the caesars once tried to exterminate the Christian church by killing Christians. But the more they persecuted them, the more the church grew. The Bible says "those who were scattered went everywhere preaching the word" (Acts 8:4). Evil could not suppress the good news. Because of their deep devotion to Jesus, Christians were willing to suffer temporarily, knowing they would live again with Him in His kingdom of love.

"With long life I will satisfy him, and show him My salvation" (Psalm 91:16).

In 1835, famous English naturalist Charles Darwin collected three young tortoises about five years old from Santa Cruz Island, in the Galápagos. Darwin noted they were only about as big as dinner plates when he brought the live tortoises on the *HMS Beagle* back to England with him. He named these three subjects of scientific research "Tom, Dick, and Harry." But the young tortoises did not fare well in cold, damp England. So in 1842, one of Darwin's colleagues, John Wickham, brought Tom, Dick, and Harry to Australia aboard a whaling ship and donated the youthful 12-year-old tortoises to Brisbane Botanical Gardens.

As time went by, Tom and Dick died from unknown causes. Wanting to preserve their tortoise attractions for the next 100 years, Harry's Brisbane caretakers tried in vain to mate him with female Galápagos land tortoises. When he was in the gardens, he had to put up with people riding him. You could see the scars on his shell where people used to engrave their names on his back. Soldiers returning home from various wars even painted his shell a couple of times.

In 1952, Harry was moved to a fauna sanctuary on Australia's Gold Coast, where it was finally discovered that Harry was in fact a Harriet! Darwin evidently was not able to determine Harry's sex. Harriet made her final move in 1988 to the Australia Zoo. She loved to eat hibiscus flowers, along with zucchini, squash, beans, and parsley. At 330 pounds, Harriet spent much of her remaining days snoozing in her pond. Harriet died at 175 years of age in June of 2006. She was the third oldest tortoise in the world.

One reason Harriet survived so long is because God provides a tortoise with a natural armor in its shell. Did you know God has provided armor for Christians to preserve us for everlasting life? Paul writes, "Finally, my brethren, be strong in the Lord and in the power of His might. Put on the whole armor of God, that you may be able to stand against the wiles of the devil" (Ephesians 6:10, 11). This armor is not meant to protect against bullets and bombs, but "against principalities, against powers, against the rulers of the darkness of this age, against spiritual hosts of wickedness in heavenly places" (verse 12). With this armor in place, we can be assured of protection from death. We can live forever.

November 7 DOLPHINS

"My sheep hear My voice, and I know them, and they follow Me" (John 10:27).

Dolphins are wonderful creatures that belong to a group known as cetacean [pronounced si-TAY-shin] that includes all whales, dolphins, and porpoises. There are over 40 different species of dolphins and porpoises that can be found in most oceans and even in some freshwater rivers. Like humans, dolphins are warm-blooded mammals that breathe air and nurse their young. They are highly intelligent and usually live for about 20 to 30 years. Incredibly, dolphins can sleep in a semi-alert state by resting one side of their brain at a time. If need be, dolphins can hold their breath for five to eight minutes and can dive as deep as 650 feet.

A dolphin sheds a thin outer layer of skin every two hours. This slick, rubbery skin enables them to swim at speeds up to 35 mph. It's no wonder they can keep up with speeding boats! In fact, engineers have studied the flukes on a dolphin's tail to improve the effectiveness of submarines and boat propellers. Dolphins will always try to help sick or injured dolphins, and on several occasions have been known to assist or rescue humans stranded in the ocean, even to the point of chasing off threatening sharks.

To find their way around, dolphins use a type of sonar called echolocation to navigate through dark or murky water without bumping into anything. They produce powerful clicking sounds that travel through the water, then bounce off objects and return to the dolphin. A whopping 1,200 clicks a second can be transmitted ahead of a dolphin like a beacon. By the pitch of the returning echo, and the time it takes to get there, the dolphin can determine the shape, size, speed, texture, and density of the object. It can even view the inside of an object, almost like an X-ray.

To communicate, dolphins use a variety of noises called vocalizations that come from their blowholes. You could say that blowholes are the equivalent of a human nostril. Every dolphin has its own signature whistle to distinguish itself from its companions. Most marine biologists are convinced dolphins have a complex form of language used to communicate emotions and signals.

Jesus once illustrated His leadership in John 10 by comparing Himself to a shepherd calling sheep. If we are truly God's sheep, we will recognize the communications of the Lord. We will distinguish the messages of God and those of the devil because we are connected to Jesus. The language of heaven will be familiar to us.

"Do not look on the wine when it is red, when it sparkles in the cup, when it swirls around smoothly; at the last it bites like a serpent, and stings like a viper" (Proverbs 23:32).

Few marine animals are as mysterious and intimidating as jellyfish. These incredible creatures can be found in all of the world's oceans, and even a few varieties inhabit freshwater. They are 97 percent water and quite transparent, hence the name. Most live in shallow coastal waters, but a few can be found at depths of up to 12,000 feet! One of the largest jellyfish, the lion's mane jellyfish, can be six feet across and have tentacles over 100 feet in length!

Jellyfish have no heart, no blood, no gills, bones, or cartilage, and no brain (talk about a real no-brainer!). Scientists have determined that some jellies have primitive eyes that can detect light—amazing for an animal with no brain. Jellyfish are most closely related to corals and sea anemones, but they can move about by using special muscles to draw water into the bell and then push it out again. It's almost hypnotic to watch them swim. They're also carried along by wind, waves, and currents.

Most jellies are silent predators that kill and eat other living creatures. Usually an unsuspecting fish swims into the almost invisible tentacles, which are loaded with millions of stinging cells. These complex cells, called nematocysts, shoot out like tiny poison darts into their prey, paralyzing the victim. Then the jelly can eat its catch at its leisure through its mouth on the underside.

The painful sting of jellyfish can be deadly in some species. The sea wasp, or marine stinger, is rated as the deadliest venomous creature in the world! In the last century, this feared box jellyfish is thought to have killed more than 70 people in Australia alone. In fact, one large box jelly has enough venom to kill 60 people. Despite the stinging cells, animals such as ocean sunfish and leatherback turtles feed on jellyfish. Most jellyfish are actually harmless to man. In fact, it is hoped that some of the painful chemicals they produce may provide treatments for cancer, arthritis, and heart disease.

Did you know the Bible talks about something with a powerful sting? Drinking alcohol, it says, is a bad idea. "At the last it bites like a serpent, and stings like a viper" (Proverbs 23:32). That's one sting we can do without!

November 9 FAIRY SHRIMP

"Jesus said to her, 'I am the resurrection and the life. He who believes in Me, though he may die, he shall live'" (John 11:25).

Fairy shrimp are amazing little crustaceans that are related to sea shrimp and can be found in vernal ponds. A vernal pond is a temporary pool that usually appears in the spring. Also known as anostraca, these sea creatures are seldom more than three-quarters of an inch long and usually much smaller. They have 11 to 17 pair of legs that look more like feathery leaf-like appendages they use to a create a current for swimming, which they seem to prefer doing upside down. The current they create enables them to breathe through the front appendages, which are called gill legs. Fairy shrimp feed on algae, dead plants, and smaller animals caught in the current of water made by their appendages.

The fairy shrimp can suddenly appear in vernal ponds by the millions one year then completely disappear in the same pond for several following years. Females can produce eggs year round, which they carry in sacks behind their gill legs. But they have the uncanny ability to produce different kinds of eggs throughout the year.

For instance, just before a drought, fairy shrimp produce eggs that are encased in a hard-walled cyst or case that is so strong that the cyst-covered eggs can dry up and hatch many years later. After being exposed to water the fairy shrimp eggs hatch out in only 30 hours. Fairy shrimp eggs have been subjected to boiling water and temperatures as low as minus 310 degrees Fahrenheit and they still remained viable. Eggs have even been hatched in a laboratory after 20 years, but it is possible these resilient little eggs might last hundreds or even thousands of years and still hatch! Recognizing how durable the eggs were, in 1962 Harold von Braunhut began to market the fairy shrimp to children as "Sea Monkeys" and has since made a fortune.

We don't know how God can preserve the essence of life in a dormant egg or seed. We also don't know how He can resurrect a dead body, but when we see so many miracles of life in the natural world should we not be inclined to believe He can do the supernatural? When Christ raised Lazarus from the dead (see John 11), the response was mixed. Some believed on Jesus, others plotted to kill the Savior. Do you think this miraculous resurrection was just a fairy tale?

"Deliver me, O LORD, from my enemies; in You I take shelter" (Psalm 143:9).

Hermit crabs are curious creatures found near the coasts of Europe and the Americas. Most are aquatic, but a few species, like the coconut crab, live on land and can attain a length of up to 18 inches. Hermit crabs are sometimes called robber crabs because they are born without armor and must survive by borrowing the empty shells of dead mollusks as a protective home. These comical scavengers insert their soft abdomens into the abandoned shells they claim and drag about with them for defense. Their strong abdominal appendages are especially modified for gripping the shell firmly to their body.

As they grow, hermit crabs are often forced to seek new, bigger shells because they have outgrown their old ones. Sometimes they may change their housing whenever they chance upon a stronger shell. But these shells don't provide protection from all predators. The most feared antagonist of many hermit crabs is the octopus, which uses a parrot-like beak to pluck the hermit crabs from their shells.

But God has given a few species of hermit crabs an amazing defense against even these intelligent enemies. These clever hermit crabs will attach sea anemones to their shells. Sea anemones are armed with an array of poisonous tentacles that they use to subdue prey. The hermit crab will gently pry the sea anemone off the surface of a rock and transfer it onto its shell. The hermit crab and the sea anemone both benefit from this arrangement. The hermit crab benefits from the potent toxin of the sea anemone as a predator deterrent. Even an octopus will think twice before attacking a hermit crab smothered with poisonous anemones. On the other hand, the sea anemone can feed on food fragments produced when the hermit crabs eats. This mutual relationship, where both organisms benefit, is known as symbiosis.

Did you know the Bible teaches us about another symbiotic relationship between the Spirit and the Word? When we read the Bible with the help of the Holy Spirit, we will be led into truth that is life-changing. Jesus once explained to the Samaritan woman at Jacob's well, "God is Spirit, and those who worship Him must worship in spirit and truth" (John 4:24). Both are harmoniously at work in the heart of true believers. Together they bring us into a saving relationship with Christ that no enemy can break apart.

"Now Cain talked with Abel his brother; and it came to pass, when they were in the field, that Cain rose up against Abel his brother and killed him" (Genesis 4:8).

Sand tiger sharks, also known as ragged-tooth sharks, have a deceivingly ferocious look. They are large-bodied sharks up to 10 feet long that display a menacing mouthful of razor-sharp teeth that protrude in all directions, even when their mouth is shut. Despite their fierce appearance they are a docile, non-aggressive species, only attacking humans in self-defense.

Sand tiger sharks have another unique feature. We have all seen the ominous picture of a shark dorsal fin cutting the surface when on the prowl. Sand tiger sharks actually have a second large dorsal fin on their backs. From a distance, some who thought they spotted two sharks really saw one sand tiger shark. They also possess another highly unusual feature in sharks—a rudimentary swim bladder. This enables them to have exquisite control over their buoyancy compared with other sharks. When hunting they will swim to the surface, gulping and burping air that they store in their stomachs until they achieve neutral buoyancy. This behavior allows the sand tiger shark to hover nearly motionless in the water as they hunt for prey.

The most bizarre feature of these ragged-tooth sharks is how they are born. Although a dozen eggs might develop after mating, during the 9- to 12-month gestation period the two strongest pups will kill and feed on their remaining siblings, while still within the mother! This grisly process is called "intrauterine cannibalism." At birth, the surviving pups are already more than three feet long, and you could accurately say they are born killers!

Did you know the Bible talks about a breed of professed Christians who bite and devour their own siblings? "For all the law is fulfilled in one word, even in this: 'You shall love your neighbor as yourself.' But if you bite and devour one another, beware lest you be consumed by one another!" (Galatians 5:14, 15). Jealousy and anger led Cain to destroy his own brother. Murder truly is the end result of all selfishness and sin.

"Can you draw out Leviathan with a hook, or snare his tongue with a line which you lower?" (Job 41:1).

A few days before Christmas in 1938, a strange fish was caught in a net near the mouth of the Chalumna River in South Africa. Captain Hendrick Goosen and his crew thought the fish was bizarre enough to alert the local museum in the small town of East London. The director of the museum, Miss Marjorie Courtenay-Latimer, described the creature as "the most beautiful fish I had ever seen, five feet long, and a pale mauve blue with iridescent silver markings."

Marjorie had no idea what the fish was, but knew it must go back to the museum at once. Searching through the few reference books on hand, Marjorie found a picture that, she has said, led her to a seemingly impossible conclusion. Her specimen bore striking similarities to a long-extinct prehistoric fish! She alerted the prominent South African ichthyologist Dr. J.L.B. Smith to this amazing discovery. Professor Smith came and identified the fish immediately as a coelacanth [pronounced SEE-le-kanth]. The fish would soon be called the "most important zoological find of the century." It was nicknamed a "living fossil."

Dr. Smith, Courtenay-Latimer, and the coelacanth became overnight celebrities. When a public viewing was arranged for one day, 20,000 visitors are said to have shown up. Over the years several other coelacanths have been caught, mostly around Indonesia.

This living fossil comes from a species of fish that was firmly believed to have lived long before the time of the dinosaurs, with the fossil record dating them back over 400 million years. They were thought to have become extinct 65 million years ago, which re-dates the dinosaurs by millions of years. How could the coelacanth supposedly disappear for over 80 million years and then turn up alive and well in the twentieth century? It had also been taught that the coelacanth was a "missing link" with its "proto legs" that were evolving into limbs.

The theory of evolution continues to piece together evidence to support a flimsy framework that new scientific discoveries do not support. The best and firmest framework for understanding our world comes from the Bible, which says, "In the beginning God created the heavens and the earth" (Genesis 1:1).

November 13 GOOD SAMARITANS OF THE SEA

"But a certain Samaritan, as he journeyed, came where he was. And when he saw him, he had compassion" (Luke 10:33).

Throughout history there are many examples of dolphins helping humans in distress. The earliest record of dolphins saving people dates back over 2,000 years in ancient Greece. The musician Arion was returning home by boat after winning a handsome reward for singing. Some sailors threatened to kill him and steal his treasure. According to legend, Arion persuaded them to let him sing one last song, and as he sang, dolphins started to swim alongside the boat. Arion jumped into the water and was carried to shore by a dolphin.

There are also many modern-day stories about people being saved by dolphins from shark attacks and other desperate situations at sea. In May 1978, a boatload of people was lost in thick fog off the coast of South America. Four dolphins nudged the boat through dangerous water and saved many lives. Another story marked by the miraculous occurred in November of 1999, when 6-year-old Cuban refugee Elian Gonzalez survived a storm at sea that capsized their boat and drowned his mother. The young boy floated in an inner tube toward shore for two days and nights. When he was exhausted and began to slip, he claimed dolphins surrounded him like a contingent of angels and pushed him upward, protecting him in the shark-infested waters until he was rescued by fisherman.

Another dramatic account was reported in 2001, by a group of fishermen from South Carolina. Their boat sank 35 miles away from shore, and they found themselves surrounded by sharks. A pod of dolphins arrived and proceeded to drive the sharks away. They remained with the fishermen all night and the following day, driving off any sharks that came near. Similarly, a group of four New Zealand lifeguards were protected from a white shark by a group of dolphins who swam in tight circles around them, thus preventing the shark from attacking.

We're not exactly sure why dolphins rescue people. Amazingly, these good Samaritan dolphins have no apparent benefit to themselves. We do know it is part of their nature to help other dolphins in trouble; therefore it is possible that this instinct to help each other is simply extended to humans in danger. Or could it be that dolphins are consciously responding in a selfless way to save other intelligent creatures? Perhaps, like the good Samaritan in Jesus' parable, they have compassion.

"And Jesus said, 'For judgment I have come into this world, that those who do not see may see, and that those who see may be made blind'" (John 9:39).

Crocodiles are among the largest and longest-living reptiles on Earth. Just like a tree, they have growth rings in their scales. By counting these rings, scientists can tell the age of a crocodile and know that some males can live up to 70 and even 100 years. Female crocodiles rarely grow larger than 10 feet, but males can weigh over 2,000 pounds and measure over 20 feet in length.

Like all reptiles, crocodiles are "cold-blooded" and must lie in the sun to get warm or laze in the water to cool down. But, incredibly, they can also shut down or speed up blood flow to regulate their body temperature. A full-grown crocodile has a brain about the size of a walnut. Despite this they seem to be intelligent, learning how to quickly find prey. Powerful muscles snap the jaws closed when a crocodile grabs prey. Its jaws can open and shut, but cannot move from side to side. In other words, crocodiles cannot chew.

Saltwater crocodiles actually live in both salt water and fresh water and can swim for miles and stay underwater for up to 4 hours. A female crocodile will build a big compost nest, where she will lay up to 80 eggs. Amazingly, a baby crocodile's gender is determined by how deeply the eggs are buried in the nest and the temperature. Unlike most reptiles, a female crocodile will defend its nest to the death from any animals. When the mother crocodile hears the babies hatching, she runs over to dig them out of the nest, and then carries her babies safely to the water in her mouth.

Crocodiles have three eyelids: two leathery, protective eyelids and one clear or translucent one. They also have very good vision and can see almost 180 degrees. But in spite of this they can't see anything below their nose.

Like the crocodile, some people are blind to obvious truth right under their noses. Jesus explained this to His disciples regarding His parables. The hardhearted religious leaders did not want to hear truth. Christ said, "Therefore I speak to them in parables, because seeing they do not see, and hearing they do not hear, nor do they understand" (Matthew 13:13). When our hearts are seeking to obey the Lord we will be able to see truth, even when it's right under our nose.

November 15 GIANT BLUEFIN TUNA

"Then those who gladly received his word were baptized; and that day about three thousand souls were added to them" (Acts 2:41).

Giant bluefin tuna are the largest living species of tuna, with some reaching up to 10 feet in length and weighing 1,400 pounds. A bluefin's lifespan is believed to be longer than 20 years, but only one in a million of the hatchlings survive to maturity. They are also considered by many to be among the strongest and fastest fish. Their torpedo-shaped bodies and ability to retract their pectoral fins enable them to reach up to 25 mph in short bursts. Bluefin are found in all of the world's oceans and can migrate up to 5,000 miles of open sea in just 50 days in search of food.

Their great size and speed have also made them a popular catch for sportsmen. They have attracted the admiration of writers and scientists as well. Also called the Atlantic bluefin, it has close relatives with the Pacific bluefin, and the southern bluefin. In the UK, Australia, and New Zealand the fish was often called the "common tunny." The largest recorded catch was off Nova Scotia when Ken Fraswer pulled in a 1,500-pound bluefin. The longest battle between this fish and man happened in 1934 when 6 men fought an 800-pound bluefin for sixty-two hours!

Bluefin tuna is popular served raw as sashimi or in sushi in Japanese restaurants, where a plate of slices can command a bill of more than $75. Just one of these animals can net from $5,000 to $30,000 at the dock. In September 2000 an enormous 444-pound bluefin tuna sold at Tokyo's fish market for a record $173,600. This was the most expensive fish ever auctioned. That's right; one fish sold for $391 a pound! The tuna was reduced to 2,400 servings of sushi for wealthy diners at $100 per serving. The estimated takings from this one fish were $240,000!

Jesus told the disciples that if they followed him He would teach them to fish for men. "And Jesus, walking by the Sea of Galilee, saw two brothers, Simon called Peter, and Andrew his brother, casting a net into the sea; for they were fishermen. Then He said to them, 'Follow Me, and I will make you fishers of men.' They immediately left their nets and followed Him" (Matthew 4:18-20). In Acts 2 we see a fulfillment of Christ's training when 3,000 people were baptized in one day. Now that's a priceless catch!

"However, when He, the Spirit of truth, has come, He will guide you into all truth; for He will not speak on His own authority, but whatever He hears He will speak; and He will tell you things to come" (John 16:13).

Throughout history, sailors have told many remarkable stories of dolphins helping humans. One outstanding example is a dolphin that sailors called Pelorus Jack. For 24 years, from 1888 to 1912, this selfless animal volunteered to guide ships through the French Pass, a dangerous channel in Admiralty Bay off New Zealand. This treacherous channel, full of rocks and extremely strong currents, had been the site of hundreds of shipwrecks before the intervention of this dedicated dolphin.

Pelorus was very unique. He was a Risso's dolphin, a species not commonly seen in New Zealand waters or anywhere near land. Yet his work was so reliable that ships reaching the entrance would wait for him to appear and guide them safely through the channel. He stayed with a ship up to 20 minutes, the time it took to cross the bay, playfully swimming alongside and surfing in the bow waves. There is no telling how many human lives Pelorus saved. Even well-known figures like Mark Twain saw and wrote of him.

Then one day a drunken passenger onboard the S.S. *Penguin* drew a gun and shot at Pelorus. When the furious crew saw the dolphin swimming away with blood pouring from his body, they came close to killing the witless man. After the shooting, Pelorus disappeared and ships had to negotiate through the deadly channel without help. But fortunately a few weeks later the dolphin returned, apparently recovered from his wound, and resumed his work of guiding ships through the channel—every ship except the *Penguin*, which he stayed clear of, and which wrecked several years later.

When Pelorus Jack returned, people demanded that he be protected by law. So on September 26, 1904, a government order declared the helpful dolphin a protected animal until he vanished eight years later. It is believed this is the first sea creature in history protected by a country.

God has always guided His people. He guided the Israelites with a pillar of cloud by day and a pillar of fire by night. In this world, we face treacherous waters, but He has sent us a Guide to save us from wrecking. The Bible says that His Holy Spirit—the Spirit of truth—comes to us and will guide us "into all truth."

November 17 SALAMANDERS

"If your hand or foot causes you to sin, cut it off and cast it from you ..." (Matthew 18:8).

Salamanders are timid yet fascinating little animals that look like lizards but are actually amphibians related to frogs and toads. There are about 550 species of salamanders and newts found mainly in the Northern Hemisphere, all the way from sea level to altitudes above 13,000 feet. The name salamander comes from two Greek words meaning "fire-lizards." Ancient people linked salamanders to fire because they often saw them crawl out of logs that had been thrown onto fires, leading people to believe that these animals could walk through fire.

Most salamanders are about 4 to 6 inches long, but range from about 1.5 inches to the giant Chinese salamander growing up to 6 feet long and weighing 140 pounds! Some of these gentle creatures have long lifespans. Hellbender salamanders are capable of surviving for 25 years in their natural settings. Some fire salamanders have survived as long as 50 years in captivity.

Salamanders are earless and deaf to airborne sound, but hear by sensing vibrations from the ground. They have relatively good vision and a keen sense of smell but have little or no voice production. Most adult salamanders have saclike lungs for breathing air, but they can also use their permeable skin as a source of supplemental oxygen. They eat mainly worms and insects that are caught with a long, sticky tongue. Among the many unique characteristics of salamanders is their ability to shed their tails if a predator threatens them. Once released, the tail twitches about on the ground and confuses the attacker while the salamander slips away and later regenerates a new tail.

Jesus once spoke about symbolically losing part of your body for a good reason. When warning people about things that will cause others (or yourself) to stumble, He graphically illustrates His point by saying, "If your hand or foot causes you to sin, cut it off and cast it from you. It is better for you to enter into life lame or maimed, rather than having two hands or two feet, to be cast into the everlasting fire" (Matthew 18:8). In other words, we should go to great lengths to escape being caught in the sin of hurting others.

Interestingly, salamanders have an amazing ability to regenerate lost body parts. In just a few weeks they can grow a perfectly new limb. Whatever losses we might sustain on this earth, God will restore in the earth made new!

"The lizard you may grasp with the hands, yet it is in kings' palaces" (Proverbs 30:28 NASB).

In the jungles and rain forests of southern Mexico, Central America, and the northern parts of South America are found unusual members of the Iguana family known as basilisks. From their crested heads to their tails these reptiles can grow up to two to three inches long. They live most of their time up in the trees but are never very far from a body of water. In many ways they're just typical lizards in what they eat and where they live.

What makes them so amazing, however, is how they escape when threatened. They are famous for dropping from the trees and running out across the water. They sometimes scamper up to 15 feet across the surface of rivers or lakes in just a few seconds! To watch them perform this maneuver is an incredible sight. They actually run on top of the surface of the water. This is how the species earned the nickname the "Jesus Lizard."

So, how do they do run across water? To begin with, they have powerful hind legs that give them explosive running speed and enough momentum to get moving. Of course, the fastest runners in the world don't move fast enough to walk on water. They also have hind feet with fringes of skin that unfurl in the water, increasing surface area. But there's more. As their feet slap the water, they trap a small air pocket or bubble that briefly keeps them afloat, step by step. If they slow down or stop, they sink just like the rest of us. But that's not a problem. Their long whipping tails help the basilisk lizards to be excellent swimmers. They can remain underwater for up to 30 minutes to escape predators.

Of course, the Bible teaches that Jesus walked across water as well, but He was not the only one. "And Peter answered Him and said, 'Lord, if it is You, command me to come to You on the water.' So He said, 'Come.' And when Peter had come down out of the boat, he walked on the water to go to Jesus" (Matthew 14:28, 29).

November 19 PORT JACKSON SHARKS

"... and the Lord said to him, 'Go through the midst of the city, through the midst of Jerusalem, and put a mark on the foreheads of the men who sigh and cry over all the abominations that are done within it'" (Ezekiel 9:4).

One of the most distinctive-looking sharks in the world is the Port Jackson shark, which is found along the coastal regions of southern Australia. It has a large head with prominent ridges on its forehead, and a strange set of teeth. The teeth, unlike most sharks', are different from front to back. In the front are sharp, small pointed teeth for catching prey. The back teeth are flat and blunt and useful for grinding its diet of mostly mollusks. Its genus name, *Heterodontus,* actually means "different tooth"! Fortunately, this shark doesn't pose any threats to humans and has rarely been known to bite (though I wouldn't want to test its patience).

One of the unusual features of this shark is its ability to eat and breathe at the same time. Because of an unusual respiratory system with five special gills that transfer oxygen more effectively, the Port Jackson shark does not need to swim with the mouth open to force water over the gills. It can actually pump water through its enlarged first gill to the other four gills. In other words, it doesn't need to move to breathe. It can stay on the bottom for longer periods of time than other fish.

Perhaps the most striking feature of the Port Jackson shark is the dark brown and black markings that make it look like the shark is wearing some type of harness. This five-foot shark is easy to identify with stripes that begin around its eyes, continue up across its forehead, and then to its first dorsal fin and across the rest of its body. You can't miss this guy when he swims by, though this shark is most active at night and hides in caves and cliffs during the daytime.

God has shown that at the end of time every person on Earth will have a mark that distinguishes them as belonging to one of two groups—the Lord's people or Satan's. The Bible describes those who follow the dragon as receiving the mark of the beast (Revelation 13:16). But those who are faithful to the Lord receive the seal of God (Revelation 14:1). How will you be identified before Jesus comes?

"Again, the kingdom of heaven is like a merchant seeking beautiful pearls, who, when he had found one pearl of great price, went and sold all that he had and bought it" (Matthew 13:45, 46).

It's hard to make heads or tails of the oyster. For starters, it has no head or tail. Yet in spite of the fact that it lacks a brain, the oyster has extremely acute chemical and tactile senses and other resources that enable it to survive even though it seems one of the most defenseless creatures in the sea. The oyster has a small heart that pumps colorless blood and a pair of kidneys. But it has no brain! It draws oxygen from the water through gills, similar to fish.

The oyster "eats" by using an intricate pumping system coupled with a filtering system that sifts food from up to eight gallons of water per hour. Some oysters can even alternate their gender, male one year, female the next! And they can release over one million eggs in a season, but only a few of these eggs will likely survive to maturity. The oyster has a powerful central adductor muscle that can open or shut its shell very rapidly. It also has a "catch" inside that can keep the shell closed for a long time, apparently without getting tired.

One of the most amazing achievements of an oyster is how it makes a pearl. This brainless wonder creates a perfectly formed iridescent jewel from an irritating grain of sand. Oysters evidently used to be much bigger. A few years ago geologists found some enormous fossilized oysters that measured up to 10 feet across and weighed 650 pounds. What's even more amazing is where they were found—high in the Andes Mountains! About 500 gigantic fossilized oysters were discovered 13,000 feet above sea level in a province approximately 250 miles southeast of Lima, Peru. Can you imagine the pearl that might come from one of these monster oysters?

In describing the New Jerusalem, John saw something fascinating that boggles our minds. "The twelve gates were twelve pearls: each individual gate was of one pearl" (Revelation 21:21). Notice, each gate was not made of thousands of pearls, but of "one" pearl. How could that be? There must be gigantic oysters in heaven! But perhaps there is a deeper message for us to learn. If pearls are made through "trials" that come into the oyster's life, through little irritating bits of life that are made into something beautiful, then perhaps we too will enter the gates of heaven because we have persevered with the trials that have been our lot.

ELECTRIC EELS

"Put on the whole armor of God, that you may be able to stand against the wiles of the devil" (Ephesians 6:11).

Did you know that there is really no such thing as an electric eel? The electric eel is actually a knifefish that emits electrical discharges. This fish grows to be over six feet long and can weigh over 40 pounds. It has no scales and a square mouth. It is an air breather and comes to the surface for a gulp of air every 10 minutes or so. Even though it is called an eel, it is more closely related to the catfish. It lives in fresh water in the Amazon and Orinoco Rivers in swamps, creeks, and coastal plains. It mostly enjoys muddy bottoms in calm water and stagnant rivers.

The electric eel has special organs adapted for creating electricity. Groups of highly compact nerve endings in the abdomen make up four-fifths of its body. In small electric eels, a typical nerve-ending cell is about one-quarter inch long and has an electric voltage of 0.14 volts. The average small electric eel has about 1,000 of these nerve-ending cells per square inch of skin that are capable of developing more than 75 volts per inch. Discharges are emitted by electric fish in self-defense or to detect or stun their prey while hunting. The discharge organs of this fish include a small pilot organ that emits electricity continuously for navigation and a large, high-voltage organ that supplies most of the power for the occasional power zaps.

The most powerful discharge is emitted by the electric eel that is native to the rivers of the Amazon Basin. It is capable of emitting a discharge of 600 volts. This electric eel is even capable of stunning a horse with its shock. It can also be deadly for humans, depending on where the electricity travels through the body.

The devil also seeks to paralyze his victims before he destroys them! God warned the Israelites through Moses, "Take heed to yourselves, lest your heart be deceived, and you turn aside and serve other gods and worship them" (Deuteronomy 11:15-17). When we turn from God toward the things of this world, we become weak and vulnerable to Satan's deceptions. But when we put on the whole armor of God, we are safe against the devil's jolts.

"But one of the soldiers pierced His side with a spear, and immediately blood and water came out" (John 19:34).

The stingray, sometimes called a "pancake shark," is a unique fish that looks like a flat, flying wing, and can be found in temperate coastal waters worldwide. It's hypnotic to watch stingrays swim as they undulate their bodies like a wave or gently flap their sides like wings. They spend the majority of their time partially buried in sand, with only their eyes peering out. There are more than 65 varieties of stingrays. Their coloration commonly mimics the seafloor, camouflaging them from their hungry relatives, the sharks. Depending on their habitat, rays can live up to 25 years.

Like sharks, stingrays have electrical sensors called ampullae located around their mouths. These perceptive organs pick up the electrical impulses of potential prey that might include any small sea creature. The largest stingray is a rare freshwater version found in the Mekong River that can grow to over 20 feet long and weigh over 1,000 pounds. This is only surpassed by the stingray's deep-water cousin, the manta ray. One of these gentle giants was found to be 25 feet across and weigh about two tons.

Stingrays, normally gentle creatures, are named for their menacing barb, or stinger, located near the base of the whip-like tail. The largest spikes can grow 15 inches, but most are about half that long. With the tip as sharp as a spear, and with serrated edges, the barb can easily pass through skin and even penetrate bone. Larger stingrays have even been known, when frightened, to drive their spines through the hulls of wooden boats. The barb is covered with a sheath of toxin that is injected into a wound, which can be deadly to humans. In 2006, Steve Irwin, the "Crocodile Hunter" who spent his life protecting animals, died in a freak occurrence after his heart was pierced by a frightened stingray.

Did you know that the Bible tells about someone else who had His heart pierced? It says that after Jesus died on the cross, "one of the soldiers pierced His side with a spear" (John 19:34). Blood and water poured from the region of His heart. Before His death, His heart was pierced in another way—through our transgressions. Sin stings. Isaiah 53 says that Jesus "was wounded for our transgressions ... and by His stripes we are healed" (verse 5). That's why He came to Earth—to take away the sting and heal us.

November 23 BLOBFISH

"... from whom the whole body, joined and knit together by what every joint supplies, according to the effective working by which every part does its share, causes growth of the body for the edifying of itself in love" (Ephesians 4:16).

One of the weirdest of all fish in the world is the strange-looking blobfish. This deep-sea fish lives in the waters off the coasts of mainland Australia and Tasmania. If you think you've had a bad day, just take a look at this interesting fellow. He actually does look like a blob! The sad expression on the face of this fish might match the overfishing by trawlers that are threatening to make it extinct. Humans rarely see this deep-sea creature that grows to about 12 inches in length. It's not edible, but happens to get caught by fishermen seeking other ocean organisms at the same depth.

The female blobfish lays thousands of eggs at one time and will stay with her eggs, floating above them or sometimes actually resting on them. It's not uncommon to find a group of blobfish mothers watching over their eggs right next to each other. Scientists are unsure if they strategically hang together for protection or if they are simply too lazy to move away from each other. The blobfish is not one known for expending a lot of energy on anything.

Blobfish live between 2,000 and 3,900 feet deep. There is a lot of pressure on sea creatures at this depth. Instead of using a gas-filled bladder to maintain buoyancy, the blobfish has flesh that is like gelatin that is a little less dense than water. This keeps the blobfish floating just above the ocean floor, so it does not expend a lot of energy while slowly moving along the bottom looking for crabs and sea pens to eat. Without much muscle, this fish sort of just eats whatever happens to float in front of its face.

The blobfish describes how some Christians live. Instead of actively seeking spiritual food, they eat just about anything that floats by. And when you look at the blobfish, a fish with virtually no muscle, you can understand why some Christians are weak. In order to stay healthy as a church, the apostle Paul encourages every member to exercise their spiritual gifts (see 1 Corinthians 12). When some members do not use their God-given gifts, the body becomes weak. So use your gifts to build up the body of Christ. Don't let your church turn into a ... blob!

"Now to Him who is able to keep you from stumbling, and to present you faultless before the presence of His glory with exceeding joy" (Jude 24).

The walking catfish is a unique species of freshwater catfish found primarily in Southeast Asia and the Democratic Republic of Congo. As reflected in its name, it has an amazing ability to "walk" or scoot across land to find food or suitable environments. While it does not truly walk, it does have the ability to use its pectoral fins to keep it upright as it makes a sort of wiggling forward motion with snakelike movements. Some of these squirming migrations span well over a mile.

You might be wondering, "How does this fish manage to breathe while out of water for so long?" The walking catfish possesses a large accessory breathing organ. Tree-like respiratory structures extend above the gill chambers, enabling it to absorb atmospheric oxygen. It can survive quite a while using this form of locomotion as long as it stays moist. That's why most of these migrations happen during or after a rainfall. This fish normally lives in slow-moving (and often stagnant) ponds, swamps, streams, and rivers of the Mekong basin. When these flooded rice paddies or temporary pools dry up, its "walking" skill comes in handy for moving to other pools of water. It would be interesting to be driving down the road and see a sign that says: "Caution: Catfish Crossing!"

Knowing God can design fish to walk on land, it should not be hard for us to believe He can empower a man to walk on water. When Jesus saw His disciples in a boat on Galilee fighting a storm, He went out to them, walking on water. At first they were afraid of this strange sight, but Peter then asked, "Lord, if it is You, command me to come to You on the water" (Matthew 14:28). Jesus said, "Come."

The Lord also says to each of us, "Come." Like walking on water, the pathway to God defies the reality we live with every day. Like a walking catfish, it may seem strange, from the perspective of the world, to humble yourself and confess your sinfulness. But God will lift you up and keep you from stumbling back into the stagnant pools of this world.

November 25 THE FISH THAT HIBERNATES

"... and do not think to say to yourselves, 'We have Abraham as our father.' For I say to you that God is able to raise up children to Abraham from these stones" (Matthew 3:9).

The lungfish of South Africa is an extraordinary creature with remarkable abilities. While the lungfish has gills like any other fish, it can also breathe air through its mouth, where it is processed by a modified swim bladder that works like a lung. When water levels are high this is not so important, but during the dry season when ponds and rivers start drying up, most fish are left desperately flopping near the surface in shallow pools. Only the air-gulping lungfish is able to survive these extreme conditions.

But as the sun dries up the last muddy puddles of water, even the lungfish would bake without its other amazing ability. To avoid being cooked by the heat or eaten by predators, the lungfish digs down into the mud. It does this by squirming down into the muck like a tunnel-drilling machine. As it goes, it swallows the mud with its mouth and pushes it out through its gills. After digging deep below the surface, the lungfish curls up and begins to exude clear mucus over its body. This dries and hardens into a leathery, waterproof cocoon, leaving only a small breathing hole by its mouth. Baked into this mud tomb, the lungfish slows its metabolism to about 1/60 of its normal rate and "estivates"—a type of summer hibernation. The lungfish can survive in this condition for up to four years or until the rains return.

If you dig up one of these hibernating lungfish it will appear to be just a piece of hardened mud. This has led to some bizarre experiences for the tribal people. I'm sure more than once brick huts have been built from mud found in the river bottom. Then, when the rains return and the walls are moistened by water, the hidden lungfish come back to life. Wide-eyed children are not quite sure what to think when they see wiggling, slimy fish erupting from the bricks in their walls!

Of course, this would not be the first time someone believed rocks can be transformed into living creatures. John the Baptist warned the arrogant, unrepentant Jewish leaders not to even think of saying Abraham was their father when God could just as well make children for Abraham out of stones—and perhaps they would have had softer hearts!

"And the light shines in the darkness, and the darkness did not comprehend it" (John 1:5).

In 1895, in San Marcos, Texas, a team of well-drillers were attempting to construct an artesian well for a fish hatchery. They sank a 190-foot shaft to reach an underground stream called Purgatory Creek. With the water that came from the well also came one of the strangest creatures in the world. Living deep in the pitch-black recesses of the earth was a weird salamander, the likes of which had never been seen before. This strange salamander is called Rathbuni's salamander. It is also called the Texas blind salamander because it is found only in Hays County, Texas, and it is so rare it's on the endangered species list.

Rathbuni's salamander has no eyes. In fact, it has almost no head. Its pale, translucent body is grotesquely slender and tapers at the head to a blunt, spoon-like snout. Sticking out like scarlet antlers just behind its head are bright red external gills for breathing. It has four toes on the front feet, and five on hind feet. Its skinny legs are abnormally long, enabling it to stand tall and better sense movements made by tiny swimming organisms that make up its diet.

The amount of available food in Purgatory Creek is incredibly sparse, just a few tiny invertebrates, crustaceans, and snails. In fact, scientists are amazed that anything can exist in such a food-poor environment. Perhaps the fact that Rathbuni's salamander has a much more highly developed lateral-line organ than most other water-dwelling creatures helps it to survive. The lateral line is a series of special movement sensors that runs along the sides of water-dwelling creatures. (This is the organ that enables a school of fish to swim in such well-synchronized movements.) The more sensitive the lateral-line sensors, the easier it is for the creature to detect movement in the surrounding water.

Can you imagine living your entire life in the frigid water of a dark subterranean cave, oblivious that there was a bright world above teeming with life? Likewise, many people living in our dark world are spiritually blind, totally unaware that there is a better, brighter, more beautiful world above. When God warned the Israelites against disobeying His law, He said, "And you shall grope at noonday, as a blind man gropes in darkness; you shall not prosper in your ways ... " (Deuteronomy 28:29). When we choose to obey the Lord, we will walk in the light toward that amazing world above—heaven!

November 27 THANKSGIVING DAY

"Enter into His gates with thanksgiving, and into His courts with praise. Be thankful to Him, and bless His name" (Psalm 100:4).

Thanksgiving Day might not be celebrated in the United States today were it not for a remarkable woman named Sarah Josepha Hale (1788 -1879). It is well known that the first Thanksgiving Day was celebrated by the Pilgrim fathers in 1621 to give thanks for their bountiful harvest in the New World. In 1789, President George Washington issued a Thanksgiving Day proclamation to commemorate the first Pilgrim celebration. But Thomas Jefferson, the third president of the United States, discontinued it. After this, Thanksgiving was observed by some individual states on whatever date suited their fancy.

Then in 1828, Mrs. Hale, a patient, persistent 34-year-old widow and mother of four, began campaigning for the restoration of Thanksgiving as a national holiday. For years she wrote letters and sought appointments with national leaders, from five different presidents on down. Time after time she was politely rebuffed, sometimes being told it was "impractical" and "impossible," and sometimes being chased off and scolded and told, "This is none of your business!"

But Sarah was relentless. Finally in 1863, President Lincoln listened seriously to her plea that North and South "lay aside enmities and strife on (Thanksgiving) Day." He proclaimed the fourth Thursday of November to be the official "national Thanksgiving Day." This day was finally ratified by the U.S. Congress in 1941.

What many people do not know is that Mrs. Sarah Hale was the first woman magazine editor in the U.S., and the first person to use the word "lingerie" to describe undergarments. Sarah also helped start the first college for girls in the U.S., was the first to suggest public playgrounds, and also started the first day nursery for working mothers. But Sarah Hale is probably best remembered as author of the poem "Mary Had a Little Lamb."

The Bible encourages us to have a spirit of thanks in our hearts. Daniel thanked God for insight to understand Nebuchadnezzar's dream. "I thank You and praise You, O God of my fathers; You have given me wisdom and might, and have now made known to me what we asked of You, for You have made known to us the king's demand" (Daniel 2:23). Whether it is for God's protection, the bountiful harvest of our fields, the blessings of family, or the guidance of the Spirit, giving thanks is a habit we should express all year long.

"But he said, 'I will not let You go unless You bless me!'" (Genesis 32:26).

The giant clam is the largest living bivalve mollusk in the world. It's also one of the most endangered clam species. It is native to the shallow coral reefs of the South Pacific and Indian Oceans. Known as *Tridacna gigas*, this huge clam can weigh more than 440 pounds and can measure four feet across. (We might say it has a "giga-bite"!) It can live to be almost 100 years old.

The giant clam lives on flat coral sand or on broken coral and is found at depths up to 60 feet. Though it has the largest geographical spread of its species, it has become more and more scarce. It does have the ability to grow rapidly due to an uncanny skill of cultivating plants in its body tissue. A symbiotic relationship with algae gives the giant clam needed nutrition. During daylight hours, the clam will open its giant mouth to let sunshine inside, which helps the algae grow and flourish.

Interestingly, the giant clam cannot completely close its shell like other mollusks. Even when mostly closed, you can still see part of its inner mantle, especially in older specimens. The largest giant clam ever found measured 54 inches across and was discovered in Sumatra. The two shells weighed 510 pounds, which means it probably weighed 550 pounds alive.

The giant clam has an old reputation for being aggressive and deadly. It has actually been known as the "killer clam" or the "man-eating clam." Outdated scientific manuals once claimed this giant mollusk killed people. Even an old version of the *U.S. Navy Diving Manual* explained how to release oneself from the deadly squeeze of this huge clam. But the giant clam is not dangerous, and when it closes its shell as a defense mechanism (not to attack) it happens too slowly to be a serious threat. In fact, most of the larger giant clams cannot even close their shells all the way.

The Bible talks about a giant squeeze that actually saved someone's life! When Jacob wrestled with the Angel of the Lord (Jesus), as daybreak approached, he clung to the angel. Notice what happened: "And He [the Angel of the Lord] said, 'Let Me go, for the day breaks.' But he said, 'I will not let You go unless You bless me!'" (Genesis 32:26). The Lord blessed Jacob's faith and changed his named to Israel, which means "overcomer." If there is ever a time to squeeze tight, it is when we are clinging to the Lord.

November 29 ONE FLESH

"Therefore a man shall leave his father and mother and be joined to his wife, and they shall become one flesh" (Genesis 2:24).

One of the strangest of God's creations is the grotesque-looking deep-sea anglerfish. It makes its home throughout the oceans of the world, living more than a mile deep, where pressure over 2,000 pounds per square inch is exerted on its body. Its round body resembles a basketball, and indeed, it looks like it could easily swallow one. It has a larger mouth compared to its body size than any creature in the sea. In addition, its mammoth mouth is filled with savage, fang-like teeth. Behind powerful jaws and teeth it has a stomach that is greatly expandable, allowing it to swallow prey larger than itself. The stomach of one small black devil anglerfish contained a lantern fish nearly twice the size of the angler!

Despite its ferocious appearance, the angler's adult size is limited. Various sub-species range from about an inch to 3.3 feet. The angler name comes from the long, modified dorsal spine tipped with a light-producing organ known as a photophore. Like many other deep-water fish, the angler uses this organ like a lure to attract prey. It flashes its light on and off while wiggling it back and forth like a fishing pole. When the prey fish gets close enough, the angler snaps it up with its powerful jaws. The darkness of the deep sea makes the angler nearly invisible to prey.

Among anglers, only females have the lure; the males survive in a different way. The male is much smaller and looks like a dark jellybean with fins. It has small hook teeth that it uses to attach itself to the female. In some species, once the male is attached its blood vessels join with that of the female and it will spend the rest of its life joined to her like a parasite, getting all of its nourishment from her body. Her blood flows through his veins, in return for fertilizing her eggs. The flesh of the two fish eventually fuses and they remain permanently connected "till death do they part."

This adds a new meaning to the Scripture " ... and they shall become one flesh." Married couples don't need to go as far as the angler, but Ephesians 5:28 does say that "husbands ought to love their own wives as their own bodies." The key word in a Christian marriage is *love*.

"Behold, the LORD's hand is not shortened, that it cannot save; nor His ear heavy, that it cannot hear" (Isaiah 59:1).

The black ghost knifefish found in the Amazon Basin in Peru is a very strange-looking creature. It has no fins on the side, top, or tail. Its only fin is beneath in one long, single wave from front to back! This eight-inch fish has no tail and looks somewhat like a sideways butter knife, which narrows to a dull spear point at its back end. The one long, ribbon-like fin undulates from one end to the other. It looks something like a graceful, rippling black curtain that moves it through the water.

The knifefish has small, beady eyes and poor eyesight, but God has given this odd creature another way to see. The most unusual feature of the knifefish is its lateral line. This horizontal line of cells on its side is an electrical generating plant, producing waves of high-frequency impulses that are sent out into the water to both one side and the other. These impulses bounce off objects and quickly return, where they are sensed by other receptor cells in its skin. You might say this fish has a type of radar! The voltage of these cells is low, only about 3 to 10 volts of direct current. Yet the frequency of the impulses is high, running around 300 per second. As these impulses go outward, they create an electrical sending/receiving field of signals, which tell the fish what is all around it.

But imagine the problems that might occur when two knifefish come near each other! Both fish are sending out signals, and one might think the incoming static of confusing patterns would jam their signals, "blinding" both fish. But the Creator gave these amazing fish the ability to change wavelengths. As soon as two knifefish draw near to one another, they immediately stop transmitting impulses for a couple moments, and then both fish switch them back on, but this time tuned to different frequencies from the other.

Have you ever been praying and felt that you were on the wrong frequency? Maybe you were having a lot of background noise and static, making it difficult to concentrate. Such "noise" does not need to be sounds we hear with our ears. Static can come in the form of our thoughts as well. When we fill our minds with Bible truth, seeking to remove all the distractions of the world, we will be more tuned into the voice of God in our thoughts (Isaiah 30:21).

Technology

"The king spoke, saying, "Is not this great Babylon, that I have built for a royal dwelling by my mighty power and for the honor of my majesty?"'
Daniel 4:30

December 1 INSTANT SPEECH TRANSLATION

"Therefore, if I do not know the meaning of the language, I shall be a foreigner to him who speaks, and he who speaks will be a foreigner to me" (1 Corinthians 13:11).

Scientists in Bulgaria claim they have invented an instant translator that will allow people talking on phones in different languages to understand each other. The research team from Rousse, Bulgaria, which also worked out a computer program that translates texts, now claims to have patented the technology that converts words spoken in one language into digital code that can then be immediately interpreted into another language. The scientists claim the translator chip can be inserted into any phone. The project leader told national Bulgarian television: "A person can talk freely on the phone in their mother tongue, and at the other end of the world people can hear the translation of what they say."

The first instant speech translator was actually just fictional and popularized on a science-fiction TV series. It was called the "Universal Voice Translator." Mankind in recent decades has worked with the advancement of computer technology to make instant translation of conversations possible. Integrating three software technologies (automatic speech recognition, machine translation, and voice synthesis), newer systems actually have moved beyond "word-for-word" translation to phrases, context, pronunciation, and intonation.

Robert Palmquist was the first to develop and commercialize for public use a speech translation system. He formed SpeechGear in 2001 and has many patents to cover his work. One of the first mobile devices he created translates Japanese to English. There is a growing usage of these devices in medical facilities, schools, police departments, hotels, retail stores, and factories. These systems are usable anywhere people talk! Imagine completely removing the language barrier anytime, anywhere.

Did you know that the Bible teaches that God has had a patent on this technology for thousands of years? In fact, no matter what language we speak, even if we cannot think of the right words, the Holy Spirit can interpret the message of our minds and hearts to the throne of God. Paul writes, "Likewise the Spirit also helps in our weaknesses. For we do not know what we should pray for as we ought, but the Spirit Himself makes intercession for us with groaning which cannot be uttered" (Romans 8:26).

"So the men said to her: 'We will be blameless of this oath of yours which you have made us swear, unless, when we come into the land, you bind this line of scarlet cord in the window through which you let us down, and unless you bring your father, your mother, your brothers, and all your father's household to your own home. So it shall be that whoever goes outside the doors of your house into the street, his blood shall be on his own head, and we will be guiltless. And whoever is with you in the house, his blood shall be on our head if a hand is laid on him. And if you tell this business of ours, then we will be free from your oath which you made us swear.' Then she said, 'According to your words, so be it.' And she sent them away, and they departed. And she bound the scarlet cord in the window" (Joshua 2:17-21).

Before a bridge was built across the Niagara Gorge, several lives were lost as people attempted to ferry across the turbulent, roaring rapids. You might be surprised to learn the first step in constructing a bridge over Niagara Falls was made by a 10-year-old boy named Homan Walsh. In 1848, Homan flew a kite from one side of the gorge to the other, which won him a $10 prize.

Someone on the opposite side caught the kite and tied a little stronger string to the end of the kite string, and the new, thicker string was pulled back across the gorge. The process was repeated with an even stronger string, then a cord, then a thin rope, then a thicker rope, and eventually they had a cable across the expanse strong enough to support workers, tools, and materials. Eventually, the two nations were connected by a sturdy bridge over which trucks and trains could pass. And it all started with one tiny kite string!

The Bible also tells of a woman who saved her whole family with a little red string. Rahab, a woman of ill repute, took a step of faith in her kindness to the Jewish spies sent to gather information about her city. As she helped them escape through a window, they promised safety to her or anyone she brought into her home when they returned to ransack the city—if she tied a red cord in her window. They respected their promise, and Rahab even became an ancestor of Jesus!

THE WORLD'S MOST EXPENSIVE HOUSE

"In My Father's house are many mansions; if it were not so, I would have told you. I go to prepare a place for you" (John 14:2).

According to *Forbes* magazine, the 27-story skyscraper built in Mumbai, India, is one of the world's largest and costliest homes. Mukesh Ambani, ranked by *Forbes* with a net worth of $43 billion, is building an eye-popping home that, when finished, will be 550 feet high with 400,000 square feet of living space. The Ambanis' home, called The Antilia, will have no two floors alike in either plans or materials.

The first six stories will be dedicated to parking lots, with 168 parking spaces to pamper the many imported cars of family and guests, along with space for the 600 servants and workers. Of course, on days when the traffic is bad, they can use the helicopter pad on the roof. The Antilia's living quarters begin at a lobby with nine elevators to access the 20 palatial floors above. The Ambanis plan to occasionally use the residence for corporate entertainment, so they have one floor with a formal ballroom complete with crystal chandeliers covering 80 percent of the ceiling and silver staircase. Another floor holds the wine room and theater.

One floor features an ice room where residents and guests can escape the tropical heat to a small, cooled chamber dusted by manmade snow flurries. For more temperate days, the family will enjoy a four-story open garden with a swimming pool surrounded by flowers, trees, and lawns with hanging hydroponic plants. The four floors at the top house the luxurious living quarters for the family that will provide a panoramic view of the Arabian Sea and city skyline. The cost to build this skyscraper palace ranges between $500 million and $2 billion.

But this is nothing compared to the mansions Jesus has prepared for us. In quoting Isaiah 64, Paul writes to the believers in Corinth about heaven: "Eye has not seen, nor ear heard, nor have entered into the heart of man the things which God has prepared for those who love Him" (1 Corinthians 2:9). The costliest buildings of Earth fade in comparison to the heavenly mansions being made for us by the hand of God. More than that, we will be able to abide with Christ forever.

"For we dare not class ourselves or compare ourselves with those who commend themselves. But they, measuring themselves by themselves, and comparing themselves among themselves, are not wise" (2 Corinthians 10:12).

The race is heating up among the world's major cities for the bragging rights to the tallest building. New York City held the distinction for 40 years with the Empire State building at 1,250 feet tall. For just two years, the trophy passed to the World Trade Center, and then Chicago's Sears Tower held the title for 25 years. The twin Petronas Towers in Malaysia surpassed the Sears Tower by just 33 feet and held the record for six years. Then the Taipei 101 tower held the record for six years at 1,667 feet. In 2010, the Burj Khalifa surpassed the Taipei 101 tower by over a thousand feet, reaching a record breaking height of 2,716.5 feet. Located in downtown Dubai, the Burj Khalifa boasts more than 160 floors and contains private residences, 37 floors of office space, 57 elevators, a 160-room hotel, a fitness facility, and an outdoor observation deck. During the five and a half years of construction, 30 contracting companies and over 12,000 workers took part in the project.

But an even taller building, known as Sky City, is now on the drawing board. The company behind this building is not only seeking to surpass all the others by stabbing a little higher into the heavens—they also plan to build their 2,750-foot building in a mere 90 days!

The company Broad Sustainable Building from Hunan, China, has already proven their efficiency in construction: in 2011, they built a 30-story hotel in just 360 hours. The company uses prefabricated materials to achieve these super speeds—in the case of Sky City, 95 percent of the building will already be finished by the time they break ground in November 2012.

It is astonishing how quickly a record-setter can be surpassed—and it's a reminder of the fleeting nature of earthly glory. While taking pride in our human accomplishments is always in vain, there is something worth boasting about: "But let him who glories glory in this, that he understands and knows Me" (Jeremiah 9:24). After all, it is "not he who commends himself [that] is approved, but whom the Lord commends" (2 Corinthians 10:18). A commendation from God Himself is truly a record worth having. In addition, God's commendations come with a complimentary residence in the true Sky City!

December 5 THE PEARL BRIDGE

"I pray, let me cross over and see the good land beyond the Jordan, those pleasant mountains, and Lebanon" (Deuteronomy 3:25).

The Akashi-Kaikyo Bridge in Japan has the longest central span of any suspension bridge in the world. It was completed in 1998 and links the city of Kobe (on the mainland of Honshu) to Iwaya (on Awaji Island) by crossing the Akashi Strait. Before it was built, ferries carried people across the strait, which sometimes was lashed with bad weather. In 1955, two ferries sank, killing 168 people. The public outrage urged the government to build a suspension bridge. Construction began in 1988, and the bridge was opened for traffic in 1998.

The Pearl Bridge, as it has been nicknamed, has three spans. The center span is 6,532 feet long, with the other two measuring at 3,150 feet each, making the total length of the bridge 12,831 feet. To protect the bridge from damage, special girder systems were built to withstand winds of 178 mph and earthquakes measuring 8.5 on the Richter scale. It also has to stand against harsh sea currents. The two supporting towers rise to 928 feet high. Because of the changes in temperature, the bridge can actually "flex" by 7 feet!

Cables that hold the bridge up sink into 390,000 tons of concrete. Each cable is a whopping 44 inches in diameter and contains about 36,830 strands of wire each. There are 1,737 red, green, and blue lights mounted on the cables to illuminate the bridge; these can be changed with computer technology to many different patterns for different national or regional holidays. About 23,000 cars cross the Pearl Bridge every day.

Jesus once described the way to heaven as being narrow. Like the Pearl Bridge, it carries one over treacherous waters to the safety of God's kingdom. But not many take this path. "Enter by the narrow gate; for wide is the gate and broad is the way that leads to destruction, and there are many who go in by it. Because narrow is the gate and difficult is the way which leads to life, and there are few who find it" (Matthew 7:13, 14). Which bridge are you taking?

"Their sound has gone out to all the earth, and their words to the ends of the world" (Romans 10:18).

The first living creature launched into space was a dog named Laika. On November 3, 1957, the Soviets flew Laika inside a pressurized chamber aboard the satellite, *Sputnik* 2. Since the launching of *Sputnik* 1, the first artificial satellite in 1957, thousands of these "manmade moons" have been fired into Earth's orbit. There are currently about 200 satellites orbiting our planet, though there are thousands of unused satellites and other "space junk" circling Earth. There are a few space probes that are orbiting as satellites around the moon, Venus, Mars, Jupiter, Saturn, and the sun.

There are many different types of satellites, including military, observation, communication, navigation, weather, and research satellites. Even space stations are considered satellites since they also are objects placed into orbit by humans. Satellites do not orbit the Earth in the same way. Some are called low-Earth orbit, polar orbit, and geostationary orbit depending on their purpose. They are typically semi-independent, with computer-controlled systems that keep them on track, powered, and sending correct information to Earth.

Television uses two types of satellites for services, the fixed service satellite and the direct broadcast satellite. The first (FSS) is typically used for broadcast feeds to and from television networks with larger dishes; the second is the type (DBS) used for sending signals directly to small dishes (18-24 inches) at people's homes. These satellites are locked in a geostationary orbit. They circle the Earth around the equator at a very specific altitude that allows them to complete one orbit in the same amount of time that it takes the Earth to rotate once. As a result, these satellites stay 22,200 miles above one fixed point on the Earth's equator at all times.

Jesus said to His disciples, "Go therefore and make disciples of all the nations ... " (Matthew 28:19). Christ also explained, "And this gospel of the kingdom will be preached in all the world as a witness to all the nations, and then the end will come" (Matthew 24:14). Could it be that one of the primary means of bringing the good news of salvation to the world is through the wonder of satellites? Without a doubt.

December 7 MICROSCOPIC BIBLE

"...from childhood you have known the Holy Scriptures, which are able to make you wise for salvation through faith which is in Christ Jesus. All Scripture is given by inspiration of God, and is profitable for doctrine, for reproof, for correction, for instruction in righteousness" (2 Timothy 3:15, 16).

On December 20, 2007, Israeli scientists in Jerusalem announced that they had successfully inscribed the entire Hebrew text of the Jewish Bible on an area smaller than a pinhead. The nanotechnology experts at the Technion Institute in Haifa say the text surface measures less than 1/100th of a square inch. They chose the Jewish Bible to highlight how vast quantities of information can be stored in minimum amounts of space.

According to Guinness World Records, the tiny Bible is now the world's smallest. The previous smallest copy of the Bible originated in Australia and measured about an inch square and one quarter of an inch thick and contained 1,514 pages. With this recent Bible it only took about an hour to etch the 300,000 words of the Old Testament onto a tiny silicon surface smaller than a grain of sugar. The microscopic nano-Bible was written using a scientific device called FIB—Focused Ion Beam. With the aid of this device it was possible to blast focused beams of tiny particles called gallium ions towards a specific object. When the particles hit the object they cause the gold atoms plating the silicon surface to bounce off, thus etching it. This is similar to digging a shallow hole in the earth using a water jet from a hose. They hope to use the technology in the future as a way to store vast amounts of data on bio-molecules and DNA.

The plan of the Technion Institute was to photograph the nano-Bible using a scanning electron microscope, with the goal of enlarging the photo 10,000 times and displaying it on a giant 23-foot wall in their physics facility. It would then be possible to read the entire Bible with the naked eye.

It seems a bit strange to shrink the Bible down then blow it up! But whatever its size, the Bible is God's Word. It is living and powerful (Hebrews 4:12); it is proven (Psalm 18:30); it is "able to make you wise for salvation" (2 Timothy 3:15). Best of all, it leads us to a relationship with Jesus—the Way, the Truth, and the Life.

"You shall prepare roads for yourself, and divide into three parts the territory of your land which the LORD your God is giving you to inherit ... " (Deuteronomy 19:3).

The most advanced transportation system in pre-Columbian South America was the Inca road system. Even without horses or wheeled vehicles, a great network of 25,000 miles of roads constituted a transportation network rivaled only by that of the Romans. The roads connected all parts of the realm and made possible swift communication. Trained runners, working in relays, covered up to 250 miles per day on the roads. There was a coastal route and an inland route running north and south with many connecting roads. It covered some 1.2 million square miles of territory.

The Inca roads made quick and reliable routes for the empire's military and civilian communications. Soldiers, porters, and llama caravans were the primary users. Others required permission, and tolls were extracted at some bridges. The width of the road was between three and 13 feet, with some sections 16 feet wide. Actually, much of the road was an improvement from a previous civilization, the Wari Empire. In the steep mountains of the Andes, giant flights of stairs were built. The main 3,700-mile route ran from Quito, Ecuador, in the north past Santiago, Chile, in the south.

The ancient Roman Empire also utilized roads to help them conquer the world. At the height of its power, the Roman Empire had a road system of about 50,000 miles consisting of 29 highways radiating from the city of Rome, and a network of roads covering every important conquered province. The Roman roads were three to four feet thick and consisted of three layers of successively finer stones set in mortar, with a layer of fitted stone blocks on top. By Roman law, the right of use of the roads belonged to all of the public, but the maintenance of the roadway was the responsibility of the inhabitants of the district through which the road ran.

God asked the Israelites to designate three cities of refuge for people who accidentally killed someone. The manslayer could flee to one of these cities and find safety, only if he was not found to be guilty. Instructions were given to build roadways to these cities. Jesus Christ also came to provide a roadway to heaven. The construction of these pathways cost Him His life. Though we are all guilty of sin, He offers forgiveness and protection when we confess our sins and ask Him to forgive us.

December 9 CHEYENNE MOUNTAIN

"Come, my people, enter your chambers, and shut your doors behind you; hide yourself, as it were, for a little moment, until the indignation is past" (Isaiah 26:20).

Hidden 2,000 feet beneath Cheyenne Mountain, Colorado, is the world's most sophisticated military headquarters. NORAD, the North American Aerospace Defense Command, is a joint U.S. and Canadian command center, set up in the 1960s. Their task was to coordinate military efforts in the event of nuclear attack and monitor the skies and space for possible threats.

To accomplish this, NORAD had to be built to survive a direct hit from conventional nuclear weapons. So, 4.5 acres were excavated from solid granite to form a small city of chambers deep beneath the mountain. Twelve of these inner buildings are three stories tall. To enter the complex you must drive down a tunnel one-third of a mile long and through a pair of 25-ton steel blast doors. To resist the shock from a nuclear attack, all of the buildings in the complex are freestanding and do not touch the granite walls. The rooms are mounted on 1,319 steel springs that weigh about 1,000 pounds each. This allows the complex to shift 12 inches in any direction.

To make the compound self-sufficient, it contains a dining facility, medical facility with dental office, pharmacy, and a small clinic. It also has two physical fitness centers with exercise equipment and sauna, a small base exchange, chapel, and barber shop. Water comes from a spring within the mountain and is stored in four reservoirs that hold 1.5 million gallons each. Incoming air can be filtered to remove any harmful germs, chemicals, or radioactive particles. For backup power they have six huge 2,800-hp diesel generators. This self-sufficient design allows NORAD to provide its own power, water, air, and food for up to 800 people for 30 days.

But it is still not tough enough to survive the second coming of Christ. The Bible says about this event, "And the kings of the earth, the great men, the rich men, the commanders, the mighty men, every slave and every free man, hid themselves in the caves and in the rocks of the mountains, and said to the mountains and rocks, 'Fall on us and hide us from the face of Him who sits on the throne and from the wrath of the Lamb!' For the great day of His wrath has come, and who is able to stand?" (Revelation 6:15-17). On that day, not even a command center deep in the earth will hide people from Jesus' coming.

"He has made everything beautiful in its time. Also He has put eternity in their hearts ... " (Ecclesiastes 3:11).

The Twin Towers of the World Trade Center in New York City stood as the tallest buildings in New York City for 28 years, from their opening in 1973 to their destruction in the terrorist attack of 2001. The Twin Towers were the iconic part of a seven-building complex. None of the seven survived—following the collapse of the twin towers, a third building, known as 7 World Trade Center, collapsed, and the remaining four buildings were all torn down due to the irreparable damage. The tragedy resulted in 2,753 deaths.

Today, the site is in the process of being rebuilt. The site of the Twin Towers is marked by a memorial and a museum, and will be surrounded by six new skyscrapers. The memorial consists of two giant pools marking the footprints of the fallen towers. The largest manmade waterfalls in the country pour down their sides, and the names of the victims of the attack are inscribed at their edges.

The memorial plaza is filled with nearly 400 trees, but one tree stands out—the Survivor Tree. This tree, a Callery pear, was salvaged from the wreckage in October 2001. The eight-foot tree had just one living branch and was badly scorched and covered in ash. Nevertheless, New York City's Parks and Recreation Department took the tree to a local nursery to be replanted. Though Richard Cabo, the tree's caretaker, didn't expect it to survive, it did. Now 30 feet tall, the tree has been replanted on the memorial site. The tree not only reminds us of those who survived the attacks, but of what one survivor called "the capacity of the human spirit to persevere." In the face of tragedy and the loss of thousands of lives, our collective instinct was not to quit, but to rebuild.

Spiritually, it is the same. In spite of the tragedy of sin, something in the human spirit longs for more—as the wise King Solomon said, God has "put eternity in [our] hearts" (Ecclesiastes 3:11). We were made for more than this earthly life can offer! We were made to be replanted! Jesus Christ, the Master Gardener, knows just how to heal our burned branches and coax us back to the abundant life He designed for us in the beginning, and soon He will transplant us in the rich soil of heaven—survivor trees, rescued from the rubble of sin.

December 11 THE CORRECT WAY

"Why do Your disciples transgress the tradition of the elders?" (Matthew 15:2).

Credit for the first modern typewriter belongs to Christopher Sholes, a newspaper editor who lived in Milwaukee in the 1860s. On the Sholes and Remington, as on present-day manual typewriters, each character was set on the end of a metal bar that struck the paper when its key was pressed. The keys were arranged alphabetically.

But there was a snag. When an operator had learned to type at a fast speed, the bars attached to letters that lay close together on the keyboard became entangled with one another. One way out of the difficulty was to find out which letters were most often used and then place them on the keyboard as far from each other as possible. This had the effect of reducing the chance of clashing type bars. This was how the QWERTY keyboard was born, named after the first six letters on the top line. It first became popular on the Remington No. 2, which came out in 1878.

The first typewriter by Sholes was made with the help of his friends Carlos Glidden and Samuel W. Soule, and was patented in October 1867. Instead of four rows of keys, this typewriter only had two rows. The top line was: - 3 5 7 9 N O P Q R S T U V W X Y Z. The bottom line was: 2 4 6 8 . A B C D E F G H I J K L M. The letter arrangement changes took place over five years with several trial-and-error arrangements.

Today millions of modern computer keyboards are still using this cumbersome letter design. Studies have shown that it is helpful to have a variety of words spelled with letters used by both the left and right hand in order to give each hand a moment of rest and readiness to find the next key to press. But the QWERTY layout tends to favor the left hand, which is helpful for left-handed people but a disadvantage to right-handed operators. Though other layouts have been suggested, the QWERTY design still hangs on. Old habits are hard to break!

In a clash with the scribes and Pharisees, Jesus' disciples were accused of transgressing the "tradition of the elders" regarding the proper way to wash hands before eating bread. But Christ challenged them by asking, "Why do you also transgress the commandment of God because of your tradition?" (Matthew 15:3). When the Bible gives us clear instruction, we should set aside our own preconceived ideas. The correct way to do things is God's way!

"Now from the sixth hour until the ninth hour there was darkness over all the land ... Then, behold, the veil of the temple was torn in two from top to bottom; and the earth quaked, and the rocks were split" (Matthew 27:45, 51).

Henry Ford's mansion, named "Fair Lane," still stands in Dearborn, Michigan, filled with elaborately carved woodwork and technical wonders as an example of this unique man's innovation. For its location, Ford chose 1,300 beautiful acres overlooking the meandering River Rouge. Fifty-six rooms spread over three floors for a total of 31,000 square feet. Eight grand fireplaces stood ready to warm the inhabitants. The impression throughout is still that of magnificent design, exquisite taste, and perfect workmanship.

Constructing and furnishing this exceptional house cost about $2 million back in 1915, when a loaf of bread cost a nickel. The estate also included a summer house, manmade lake, boat house, staff cottages, gatehouse, pony barn, skating house, greenhouse, root cellar, vegetable garden, thousand-plant flower garden, ten thousand-plant rose garden, a maple sugar shack, "Santa's Workshop" for Christmas celebrations, working farm built to the scale of Ford's grandchildren, agricultural research facilities, and 500 birdhouses to satisfy Mr. Ford's interest in ornithology. Determined to be independent of public utilities, he built his own power plant connected to the home by a 300-foot tunnel. Turbines fed electricity to the entire estate, with 550 switches providing light and power at the flick of a finger. There was even extra power to sell back to the utility company.

However, in April 1947, when torrential rains lashed the Detroit area, the River Rouge went on a rampage. It smothered the fire under the powerhouse boilers and caused the electricity to fail for the only time in over 30 years. Paradoxically, that was the night Henry Ford lay dying in his bedroom. Though surrounded by engineering marvels, he left the world as he had entered it 87 years earlier—in a cold house lit by candles, and only two miles from the farm where he was born.

When Jesus died outside Jerusalem, four miles from the place of His birth, the sky went dark, the veil in the temple was ripped from top to bottom, and there was a rock-splitting earthquake. Though the Son of God was surrounded by legions of angels who could have instantly carried Him to safety, Jesus chose to die on this cold, dark planet so that we may choose to live in His kingdom of light.

December 13 LASERS

"For it is the God who commanded light to shine out of darkness, who has shone in our hearts to give light of the knowledge of the glory of God in the face of Jesus Christ" (2 Corinthians 4:6).

In 1960, an American physicist with Hughes Aircraft Corporation constructed the first working laser from a ruby crystal rod. Since that time, the laser has revolutionized every realm of modern life. The word LASER is actually an acronym for "Light Amplification by Stimulated Emission of Radiation." (I think I prefer LASER!) With an ordinary beam of light, the photons vibrate and scatter in every direction, whereas a laser beam is a tightly focused and perfectly aligned beam of light. A laser beam is produced when light bounces back and forth between two mirrors with a special medium, like ruby crystals, between them. This causes all the photons, particles of light energy, to vibrate in exactly the same synchronized phase, like soldiers in a troop.

Today lasers are used in virtually every field, from communications and industry to medicine and military. Many modern devices, including bar code readers, DVD players, and printers, use lasers. These powerful beams of light can also transmit voice or data via fiber optic cables at much improved speed and capacity. Lasers have also been used to determine very precise measurements with great accuracy. The distance between Earth and the moon was measured with lasers to within one inch. In medicine, conventional eye surgery has almost been totally replaced by the miracle of lasers. In industry, lasers are used to cut, align, and measure with great precision.

Incredibly, lasers can also produce extreme cold. Normally, when you shine light at something it heats up. But under the right conditions, laser light will actually cool atoms! In laser cooling, the laser is tuned to such a frequency that atoms traveling toward the beam get slowed down. A number of criss-crossing laser beams create a trap for the atoms, which get slower and slower, and therefore colder and colder. With this technique, researchers have used lasers to reach temperatures of nearly absolute zero.

The extremes of heat and cold produced by laser light remind us of the words of Jesus to the church of Laodicea. "I know your works, that you are neither cold nor hot. I could wish you were cold or hot" (Revelation 3:15). When the laser light of the Holy Spirit shines on our hearts, we will either be energized for Jesus, or turn away in coldness and desolation.

"The chariots rage in the streets, they jostle one another in the broad roads; they seem like torches, they run like lightning" (Nahum 2:4).

Back in 2007, a French train set the locomotive speed record by reaching 360 mph. While this record was most impressive, that bullet train was an experimental test carrying no passengers, composed of two power cars and only three rail cars. But in December 2010, a new high-speed rail in China called the "Harmony Express" broke 302 mph. That's over twice the speed of a Cessna 182 airplane. So, why is the 302 mph record so astonishing when the French reached 360 mph?

First, China's new bullet train was toting 16 cars, and a few passengers. Second, the train didn't just crest 302 and then settle back to a more sane speed. Instead, the streamlined super-train was consistently traveling at speeds of 260 mph before cranking up the turbo to pass the magic 300 number, and then finally settling back at a robust 260 mph. Passengers aboard the bullet train claim they didn't feel much difference between 150 and 300 mph.

The Beijing-Shanghai High-Speed Railway is now in service and is the world's longest high-speed line ever constructed in a single phase. It was designed to carry passengers 811 miles in about four hours, averaging 204 mph. Other parallel high-speed trains take almost 10 hours to cover the same distance. This reduced the travel time from Beijing to Shanghai by more than 50 percent. The project cost about $32 billion and carries 165,000 passengers a day. It has had its glitches, but has been providing regular service since November 2011. In 1933 it took the train 44 hours to travel the same distance.

Did you know that Bible prophecy alludes to rapid travel in the last days? Notice these words: "But you, Daniel, shut up the words, and seal the book until the time of the end; many shall run to and fro, and knowledge shall increase" (Daniel 12:4). Mankind's ability to travel quickly will also parallel a deeper understanding of prophecy. I pray the speed with which we travel these days will be matched by the depth with which we understand our Bibles!

December 15 THE BIG DIG

"Enter by the narrow gate; for wide is the gate and broad is the way that leads to destruction, and there are many who go in by it. Because narrow is the gate and difficult is the way which leads to life, and there are few who find it" (Matthew 7:13, 14).

Boston's Central Artery Tunnel Project, better known as the Big Dig, constitutes the largest construction project in U.S. history. It called for replacing an elevated six-lane highway through downtown Boston with an eight- to ten-lane underground highway directly beneath it. Engineers of this subterranean thoroughfare had to make room for 7.5 miles of underground roads that required excavating 16 million cubic yards of dirt. That's enough to fill New England's football stadium more than 15 times. This colossal project was on the same scale as the Panama Canal, or the Chunnel from Britain to France. To top things off, it had to be built through a gauntlet of existing subway lines, not to mention countless pipes and utility cables, and all this had to happen without disrupting the daily traffic flow and business life of one of America's busiest cities.

First conceived in the 1970s, the project's history spanned six presidents, seven governors, and finished five years overdue in 2005. The Big Dig also became the most expensive highway project in U.S. history. The final price is estimated at $14.8 billion. During one three-year period when construction peaked, the Big Dig was eating up $100 million dollars a month! Talk about a money pit! That's a lot of money to build a road that still has gridlock during rush hour.

Did you know the Bible tells of an even more expensive road that leads to a better city? The cost was extremely high. Jesus, God's own Son, paved the way for us with His sacrifice. But He warns us that "narrow is the gate and difficult is the way which leads to life, and there are few who find it" (Matthew 7:14). Only those who really want to find it will be successful. But, with His help, we will find that narrow gate that leads to the heavenly city and streets of gold if we search with all our hearts. With His Spirit of Truth as our Guide, we need to have our own Big Dig in the Word of God.

"Glory to God in the highest, and on earth peace, goodwill toward men!" (Luke 2:14).

Question: What was made by humans and is 8 billion miles away? Answer: Pioneer 10. This robotic space probe was launched on March 3, 1972, and is more than 9.5 light-hours from Earth. Pioneer 10 is presently about twice as far from the sun as the planet Pluto, and traveling to deep interstellar space at 28,000 miles per hour. Pioneer 10 has a number of record-making distinctions. It was the first spacecraft to travel through the asteroid belt, the first spacecraft to visit Jupiter, collect data, and transmit close-up images, the first to use a planet's gravity to change its course and to reach solar-system-escape velocity, and the first human artifact to venture beyond and explore the outer solar system. Pioneer 10 was only supposed to last long enough for a two-year mission. As it turned out, the spacecraft sent signals back to Earth for more than 30 years!

Pioneer 10's long mission has finally ended. The instruments powered by the 40-watt Radioisotope Thermoelectric Generators (RTGs) fell silent in 2003. However, the 570-pound spacecraft will continue to coast, and in only 30,000 years or so it will pass within about three light-years of a nearby star in the constellation Taurus. Pioneer 10 is no longer the most distant manmade object. In 1998, Voyager 1, speeding at 35,000 miles per hour, traveled farther from Earth than Pioneer 10. But technically, the mission of Pioneer 10 may not be completely over. You see, this space-faring ambassador carries a six-inch by nine-inch gold anodized plaque bolted to the spacecraft's main frame. It's engraved with a graphic message of goodwill from the human race, and a map showing Earth's location in the solar system. NASA says just in case "somebody out there" finds it!

Did you know the Bible teaches that there are extra terrestrials trying to communicate goodwill to Earth as well? Over 2,000 years ago in Palestine there were shepherds watching over their flocks at night, when suddenly a heavenly messenger spoke to them. This angel said, "Do not be afraid, for behold, I bring you good tidings of great joy which will be to all people" (Luke 2:10). The message was that Christ, the Savior of the world, was born in Bethlehem. Then a host of these heavenly beings broke into song on that once-dark hillside. This message was not sent from Earth into outer space. This message came from the heavens to our planet, the gospel of salvation.

December 17 THE CAN OPENER

"And the dead in Christ will rise ... " (1 Thessalonians 4:16).

Did you know it was 48 years after tin cans were first introduced before the can opener was invented? Until then, cans were beaten open with a hammer and chisel. The tin can for preserving food was patented in 1810 by a Londoner, Peter Durand. Only one year before, French confectioner Nicolas Appert had introduced the method of canning food by sealing the heated food tightly inside a glass wine bottle or jar. He could not explain why the food stayed fresh, but his bright idea won him a 12,000-francs prize from Napoleon. Appert helped Napoleon's army march on its stomach while Durand supplied the Royal Navy with canned food.

But tin canning was not widely adopted until 1846, when a machine was invented that increased can production from six cans an hour to 60. Still, there were no can openers, and the product labels would read: "Cut around on the top with a chisel and hammer." The can opener was finally invented in 1858 by American Ezra Warnet. But the can opener did not become popular for another 10 years until it was given away for free with canned beef.

The well-known double wheel-style opener was invented in 1925, and the easy pop-top lid was invented in France in 1959. Since aluminum cans made their first appearance in America in 1953, some 74 million tons of aluminum cans (about 3 trillion cans) have been produced. Placed end to end, they could stretch to the moon and back about 500 times! Still, about one quarter of all cans are recycled, some 9 million cans every hour. That is good news when you consider that it takes about 200 years for a buried aluminum can to degrade.

Did you know the Bible teaches that no matter how long Christians are buried, when their graves are opened they will come up with new bodies? We are given a sample of what it will be like when we read the story of Lazarus being raised from the dead by Jesus. When Christ stood before the tomb of His dead friend, Jesus asked for the stone blocking the entrance to be rolled away. Notice what happens: "Martha, the sister of him who was dead, said to Him, 'Lord, by this time there is a stench, for he has been dead four days'" (John 11:39). The Lord does not need a special gadget to open graves where bodies have turned to dust. At the voice of an archangel and with the trumpet of God, the dead will rise.

"I will give you a new heart and put a new spirit in you; I will remove from you your heart of stone and give you a heart of flesh" (Ezekiel 36:26).

Plastic is one of the most versatile materials in the world. Plastics can be made as hard as stone, strong as steel, transparent as glass, and elastic as rubber. Plastics are also lightweight, waterproof, resistant to chemicals and bacteria, and can be produced in a rainbow of colors. At night many of us sleep on mattresses and under blankets made of plastic materials. In the morning, we step out of bed onto polyester and nylon carpets. Plastics are used in the computers we use, the utensils we cook with, the toys we play with, the buildings we work in, and the cars we drive. For example, the average car contains over 300 pounds of plastics—approximately eight percent of the vehicle's overall weight! Telephones, textiles, paints, boats, furniture, and thousands of other products are made of plastic. In fact, by 1979 the volume of plastics produced in the United States surpassed the volume of steel produced.

Where does all this plastic come from? Most plastic is chemically fabricated from fossil fuels, such as oil and natural gas. And where did all that gas and oil come from? Our earth's great reserves of fossil fuel were formed from organic matter that lived before Noah's flood. As the tremendous forests of the antediluvian world, lush with plants and teeming with animal life—including dinosaurs—were destroyed by the flood, the wind and currents pushed their debris into immense heaps. These deposits were buried under deep layers of mud and silt, which gradually hardened into rock. After 4,000 years of heat and pressure, these enormous pockets of compost were compressed and transformed into great fields of coal, oil, and natural gas. That's right—the car you drive is not running on horsepower but dino-power! And your computer is made of ancient ferns! It's amazing to consider that so many of our modern plastic products are made from ancient plants and animals.

God is a master at converting matter. He turned water to wine and sticks to snakes. God even turned a woman into salt! But God's most amazing conversions are the ones He works on human hearts—He turned a greedy tax collector into a generous giver, and a demon-possessed maniac into a missionary. Does your heart need a conversion today? All God needs is your permission.

December 19 THREE GORGES DAM

"When you pass through the waters, I will be with you; and through the rivers, they shall not overflow you ... " (Isaiah 43:2).

It is the virtual definition of a monumental project—a dam 1.5 miles wide and more than 600 feet high that will create a reservoir hundreds of feet deep and longer than the state of Oregon. And this one dam's hydropower turbines are expected to create as much electricity as 17 nuclear power plants. In 1994, the People's Republic of China began the largest construction project in modern history, known as the Three Gorges Dam. At 3,700 miles, the Yangtze is the third longest river in the world after the Amazon and Nile. This 15-year project created the world's largest dam and hydroelectric power plant. To China's leaders, the Three Gorges Dam proves the sleeping dragon has awakened. It is propelling the nation's economy into the 21st century.

The project helps with significant flood control and safer navigation. The reservoir enables 10,000-ton ocean-going freighters to sail up the river directly into the nation's interior for six months of each year, opening a region exploding with agriculture and manufacturing. The Yangtze River has also experienced hundreds of catastrophic floods. A flood in 1998 resulted in 4,000 deaths, 14 million left homeless, and $24 billion in economic loss. The project was completed July 4, 2012, and cost the equivalent of$26 billion.

China's leaders call the dam the greatest engineering feat since the construction of the Great Wall, but to critics worldwide it is a social and environmental disaster. After the dam was completed, 13 cities, 140 towns, and over 1,300 villages were submerged by the reservoir. Ancient temples, burial grounds, and hundreds of known archeological sites were lost forever under water. To make way for the Three Gorges Dam, 1.5 million people had to abandon their homes. Then consider over 360 million people live within the watershed of the Yangtze River. If in the unlikely event the dam breaks, millions of people who live downstream could perish.

You might be surprised to know the book of Revelation predicts that a dragon will send a great flood to destroy God's church. "So the serpent spewed water out of his mouth like a flood after the woman, that he might cause her to be carried away by the flood" (Revelation 12:15). But God protected the woman, who represents the church. This enraged the dragon, who went off to make war "with the rest of her offspring, who keep the commandments of God and have the testimony of Jesus Christ" (12:17). We are still promised safety from the devil's tactics.

"Our God shall come, and shall not keep silent; a fire shall devour before Him, and it shall be very tempestuous all around Him" (Psalm 50:3).

In July 1962, the United States performed a secret test 250 miles above the earth. In this unique experiment, called the Starfish Prime, a 1.44-megaton thermonuclear warhead was detonated in space above the mid-Pacific Ocean. The results demonstrated to scientists that the magnitude and effects of a high-altitude nuclear blast were much larger than previously thought. The results of the Starfish Prime experiment became known publicly because it caused electrical damage in Hawaii 900 miles away. Hundreds of streetlights were knocked out, numerous burglar alarms were triggered, and the telephone company's microwave link was damaged.

When a nuclear device is exploded just above the earth it sends out massive gamma rays. As they pass through our atmosphere these gamma rays are converted to microwaves, causing an electromagnetic pulse, or EMP. In less than a billionth of a second this EMP will make circuits fry, power lines overload, and the electric grids collapse. Everything with a microchip stops working–including your car, cell phone, and computer. People are basically unharmed, except perhaps those depending on pacemakers. And I would not want to be flying in a jet airliner at that moment.

Major military forces of the world now have the technology to make an EMP device. Picture an instantaneous deathblow to the vital engines that power our society, delivered by a nuclear weapon designed not to kill humans, but to attack electronics. EMPs caused by solar flares have probably struck the earth many times throughout history, but that was before the world was run by microchips. If an electromagnetic pulse surged to Earth now it would paralyze every aspect of modern society's infrastructure and cause an electronic Armageddon! In a few moments the technology of mankind could be transported back to the days of horse and buggies.

It makes you wonder, will the second coming of Jesus cause an EMP? The Bible says it will be a powerful display in the elements. "Therefore, since all these things will be dissolved, what manner of persons ought you to be in holy conduct and godliness, looking for and hastening the coming of the day of God, because of which the heavens will be dissolved, being on fire, and the elements will melt with fervent heat?" (2 Peter 3:11, 12).

December 21 PEOPLE OF MANY WORDS

"But I say to you that for every idle word men may speak, they will give account of it in the day of judgment. For by your words you will be justified, and by your words you will be condemned" (Matthew 12:36, 37).

On May 24, 1844, Samuel Morse sent the first electric telegraph message from Washington, D.C., to Baltimore, Maryland. The message said, "What hath God wrought?" Mr. Morse, a devout Christian, was quoting from Numbers 23:23. For 30 years Morse code was the most cutting-edge means of communication over long distance. Then, in 1872, Joshua Coppersmith was arrested in New York City. He was charged with attempting to extort money from gullible people by convincing them to invest in an instrument that he said would transmit voice over wire. He called it a telephone. Coppersmith may not have been a con man.

What is more interesting is the reaction of the Boston newspaper that reported the case. "Well-informed people," the paper said, "know that it is impossible to transmit the human voice over wires (and) were it possible to do so, the thing would be of no practical value." Of course, within four years, Alexander Bell did send a voice over wire, and he did call it a telephone.

I wonder what that newspaper writer would have said about something that seemed even more impossible, a telephone that transmits voice without wires. An economist at Nokia's network division said there are now around 1.6 billion cell phone subscriptions. This means nearly half of all the adults in the world have cell phones. It is not uncommon to see people in India or Africa without shoes talking on cell phones. Now with a satellite phone you can make a call from virtually any spot on the globe. So with all these phones, what is everyone talking about?

God obviously considers that our words are of great importance. Jesus said that in the Day of Judgment men will have to answer for every idle word they have spoken. The Bible says, "In the multitude of words sin is not lacking, but he who restrains his lips is wise" and "Pleasant words are like a honeycomb, sweetness to the soul and health to the bones" (Proverbs 10:19; 16:24). Our words can help or hurt others; they can wound or they can heal. Our heavenly Father wants us to use our words wisely to bless others.

"Some trust in chariots, and some in horses; but we will remember the name of the LORD our God" (Psalm 20:7).

Most people would consider themselves fortunate should they get 150,000 miles out of a car engine. For Rachel Veitch, however, her car has passed the 150,000 mile mark well over three times. Her vehicle is a 1964 Mercury Comet Caliente. She bought it new off the lot for a mere $3,289. And that low price even included all the upgrades. Rachel has given her beloved car the nickname Chariot, which is fitting considering it has safely carried her thousands and thousands of miles on the original engine. Ms. Veitch confessed that she once drove her Comet up to 120 mph "just for a mile." She later had cruise control added because she kept getting speeding tickets.

On March 9, 2012, the 93-year-old Rachel Veitch parked her car for good. She said her eyesight was not sharp enough anymore to be driving. The 48-year-old car has actually outlasted her three husbands. Rachel adds, "With significantly less trouble." How many miles did she clock on her beloved Mercury? Would you believe 576,000?

What's her secret? For one thing, Rachel faithfully takes her "Chariot" in for all scheduled maintenance. We should mention she refuses to leave the Mercury's side during any servicing or inspections. She also makes sure to show the mechanics a diagram outlining all the grease fittings on the car. Ms. Veitch is also always on the lookout for lifetime warranties on any parts, and when she finds one she makes sure to use it. Rachel's car has gone through seven mufflers, three sets of shocks, and 16 batteries, all for the price of only one. Those half a million miles also included a recent trip to Rachel's 70th class reunion, a trip that added over 3,000 miles to the historic odometer reading.

If a little loving care and regular maintenance can multiply the lifespan of a car, it makes one wonder how long our bodies might last with proper care? The Lord not only wants us to be in good health (3 John 2), but would have us be prepared for the Second Coming by caring for our bodies. "Now may the God of peace Himself sanctify you completely; and may your whole spirit, soul, and body be preserved blameless at the coming of our Lord Jesus Christ" (1 Thessalonians 5:23). God doesn't want us to only care for our minds, but our whole being—bumper to bumper!

December 23 LONGEST BURNING BULB

"Then Jesus spoke to them again, saying, 'I am the light of the world. He who follows Me shall not walk in darkness, but have the light of life'" (John 8:12).

Hanging from a single electric wire in an old Livermore, California, firehouse, there is a light bulb. Not so amazing, you think? But there's more. The bulb is supplied by 120 volts and puts out a meager 4 watts of amber light. You're probably still not very impressed, until you consider this same humble light bulb was already burning when the Wright Brothers made their historic flight in 1903. This light bulb continued to persistently glow through WWI, the crash of the stock market in 1929, and on through WWII. At present this incredible light bulb has been burning for over 112 years!

The enduring bulb was originally made by the Shelby Electric Company in Ohio. The company had a legendary reputation for quality until it was bought by General Electric in 1914. This particular bulb was one of the early hand-blown models with a heavy carbon filament. Over the years there have been brief interruptions as the firehouse has been renovated and even relocated from its First Street location to the present site on 4550 East Avenue. But the same bulb went with them. With these minor exceptions it has been burning continuously as a nightlight over the fire trucks in the Livermore firehouse since 1901! This unique bulb has been declared by Guinness Book of World Records to be the oldest known working light bulb in the world.

The bulb has actually been nicknamed "The Centennial Bulb," and there is a committee that oversees its protection. When it was last moved in 1976 the bulb's cord was cut. People were concerned unscrewing the bulb might damage it. In 2001 the community celebrated the bulb's 100th birthday with barbecue and music.

Did you know the Bible speaks of a sacred light that burned for over 300 years? Moses was given instructions on the wilderness tabernacle and its services. "And the fire on the altar shall be kept burning on it; it shall not be put out. And the priest shall burn wood on it every morning, and lay the burnt offering in order on it; and he shall burn on it the fat of the peace offerings. A fire shall always be burning on the altar; it shall never go out" (Leviticus 6:12, 13). That fire and its light represent Jesus, a Light that will never burn out.

"Abide in Me, and I in you. As the branch cannot bear fruit of itself, unless it abides in the vine, neither can you, unless you abide in Me" (John 15:4).

The Northeast Blackout of 2003 was the second most widespread power outage in history. On the 14th day of a sweltering August, at approximately 4:10 p.m., parts of eight northeast states and Ontario, Canada, lost all electricity. That evening an estimated 55 million people went without power, as more than 508 generating units at 265 power plants shut down. For up to 25 hours, the blackout interrupted our modern way of life.

Thousands of people were stranded by the blackout. Airports canceled flights—traffic control centers were offline, passengers could no longer be screened, and electronic ticket information was unavailable. Amtrak service was stopped, and many gas stations were unable to pump gas. In New York City, traffic lights went out, causing a gridlock nightmare. Many commuters were stranded in the city overnight, and some slept in parks and on the steps of public buildings. Hundreds of people were trapped in elevators, as well as in stopped subway cars.

Cellular circuits were overloaded, and in some cases backup generators at cellular sites ran out of fuel. In New York City, even 9-1-1 was out of service for several 15-minute periods throughout the evening. Water supply was affected when electric pumps failed—residents in Detroit, Lansing, and Cleveland were instructed to boil their water for the next four days. In addition, sewage pumps failed, causing untreated sewage to flow into rivers and waterways near Lansing, Detroit, Cleveland, New York, Newark, and Kingston, Ontario. Unfortunately, the blackout even contributed to as many as eleven deaths. It also caused fear that blackouts might be used during a terrorist attack.

As often happens, a task force was given the job of discovering what went wrong. Eventually, industry experts reported that old and inadequate grid connections were to blame.

Life is all about our connections with family and friends, but the most important connection is with God. Just as our modern way of life grinds to a halt without sufficient electricity, our spiritual life is unsustainable when we're disconnected—our inner peace, outer witness, and ultimate salvation all depend upon a solid relationship with our Maker. Nothing could be more important than getting connected today!

December 25 LUXOR LIGHT

"Then God said, 'Let there be light'; and there was light" (Genesis 1:3).

The beam of light shooting straight up from the top of the pyramid-shaped Luxor Hotel in Las Vegas is the brightest manmade light in the world. The powerful ray of light is produced by combining 39 of the brightest Xenon lights made, each as big as a washing machine. Each light costs about $1,200, and the electricity to power them all runs around $50 an hour. Using computer-designed curved mirrors to focus the light, the intense beam generates over 42 billion candlepower of light, bright enough to read a newspaper 10 miles up in space.

On a clear night Luxor's Sky Beam is visible to airplanes up to 250 miles away. You can understand why pilots flying around Las Vegas must be very careful to avoid passing directly over the Luxor beam, or they can be temporally blinded by a blazing white flash in their cockpits. To produce this much light and cool the beacon housing requires approximately 370,000 watts of power.

No matter where you are in the Las Vegas Valley, you can see this light. Some local residents actually find comfort in seeing the bright beam shining up into space at night. Others find it to be a directional point, helping them if they get lost. Sadly, the brightest manmade light in the world is mostly wasted. When the Las Vegas desert air is dry and clean the beam does not strike any dust or clouds. It shines straight out into empty space, unseen.

The Bible teaches there is another even brighter light that is mostly unused. The Scriptures tell us, "Your word is a lamp to my feet and a light to my path" (Psalm 119:105). Brighter than the intense Luxor Sky Beam, the Bible points us to something beyond the immensity of space. It is a reliable guidance system that gives us comfort and direction in our darkest moments. We when spend time reading the Bible, no light will ever be wasted.

"This great and wide sea, in which are innumerable teeming things, living things both small and great" (Psalm 104:25).

Not all garbage ends up at the dump. In fact, Earth's largest landfill isn't on land at all. Every year millions of tons of plastic and other floating garbage is washed, blown, or dumped into the Pacific Ocean. It comes from rivers, boats, and populated beaches around the coasts of the great sea. Gradually, a constantly revolving whirlpool of ocean currents and wind gather and push these items into a virtual vortex of trash. This forms a floating rubbish convergence zone bigger than the state of Texas.

This galaxy of garbage, known as the Great Pacific Garbage Patch, stretches more than a thousand miles across the central North Pacific Ocean. It is found in ocean space between Japan and California, while hovering a few hundred miles north of Hawaii. There are places where this tangled mass of nets, bottles, and bags is so thick you can walk on it, but most of the garbage patch is a minestrone soup of rubbish. Despite its continental size, the patch is not visible through satellite photography because most of its contents are a snow of plastic confetti suspended beneath the surface of the ocean.

This swirling synthetic sea presents a deadly minefield of debris. Each year thousands of ocean-going birds, fish, and mammals are killed trying to survive near this growing gauntlet of garbage. Turtles eat the plastic bags, thinking they are jellyfish. Birds eat the plastic particles, thinking they're fish or shrimp, then starve because the indigestible polymers give them the false sensation they are full. It is estimated this nebulous, floating junk yard, also called the Pacific Trash Vortex, may contain over 100 million tons of debris, and it's growing every year. While it is the largest, the Great Pacific Garbage Patch is not unique. It is only one of five gigantic gatherings of garbage found among the seven seas of the world.

Did you know the Bible says that God will cast our sins in the depths of the sea? But the good news is that they don't float! "He will again have compassion on us, and will subdue our iniquities. You will cast all our sins into the depths of the sea" (Micah 7:19).

December 27 RIDE OF A LIFETIME

"Then we who are alive and remain shall be caught up together with them in the clouds to meet the Lord in the air. And thus we shall always be with the Lord" (1 Thessalonians 4:17).

America's first manned launch vehicle engine only produced 78,000 pounds of thrust. In comparison, the space shuttle's three main engines and two solid rocket boosters generated some 7.3 million pounds of thrust at liftoff. The energy released was equivalent to the output of 23 Hoover Dams and was more powerful than 35 jumbo jets at takeoff.

The liquid hydrogen in the space shuttle's main engine was minus 423 degrees Fahrenheit, the second-coldest liquid on Earth, and when burned with liquid oxygen, the engine's combustion temperature reached over 6,000 degrees Fahrenheit, two-thirds the temperature of the sun's surface. Two minutes of the heat energy produced by the shuttle at liftoff, converted to electric energy, would have produced enough kilowatts to power 87,000 homes for a full day. The speed of the gases exiting the nozzle was more than 6,000 mph, about five times the speed of sound.

The turbo pump on the space shuttle's main engine was so powerful it could drain an average family-sized swimming pool in 25 seconds. After liftoff it only took about eight minutes for the space shuttle to accelerate to a speed of more than 17,000 mph.

During its fiery re-entry, the underbelly of the orbiter was protected by some 24,000 heat-resistant tiles that had to be installed individually by hand. These tiles were incredibly lightweight, about the density of balsa wood, and were designed to be used for 100 missions before requiring replacement. Each tile could dissipate heat so quickly that a white-hot tile with a temperature of 2,300 degrees F could be taken from an oven and held in bare hands seconds later without injury.

The space shuttle contained all the greatest scientific and engineering skill of modern man. All of the world's greatest technology is represented in this one spaceship. Yet all this power that rocketed the craft into orbit is nothing compared to the space vehicle God is designing for the redeemed.

The Bible says that when Christ returns, those who belong to Him will all be caught up into the clouds to meet Him in the air, an event infinitely more thrilling than taking a trip on the space shuttle. Can you imagine soaring across the glorious universe with the Creator of it all? Talk about the ride of a lifetime!

"For I will not trust in my bow, nor shall my sword save me" (Psalm 44:6).

For about 500 years the Roman Empire was the undisputed military powerhouse that conquered most of the Western world. This was in part due to their heavy investment in their military and war machines. Today, there are about 195 countries in the world, and most spend something for their military budget. Of all these countries, however, the United States of America spends the most, taking up 42 percent of the world's military expenditures. In other words, almost half of the world's military investment is made by one country!

If you added up the military budgets of Europe, China, Russia, Japan, the Middle East, Australia, East Asia, and Latin America, you'd still have a sum less than what the United States spends on its armed forces. For example, just in 2010 the United States spent $680 billion on the military, whereas the country in second place, China, spent only $85 billion. Interestingly, while the U.S. military budget accounts for 40 percent of global arms spending, it is made up of 4.06 percent of its GDP, which is more than France's 2.6 percent and less than Saudi Arabia's 10 percent. It's actually low for the United States, which used 37.8 percent of the GDP in 1944. Its lowest point was 3 percent in 1999-2001. But, of course, the word "low" is a relative term when you look at the huge amount spent. No wonder the United States remains, by far, the most powerfully armed nation on Earth— and the "world's only military superpower."

The book of Revelation identifies two beasts in the last days that will try to compel a uniform international worship. It will certainly require a large military to enforce this. The Bible says, "So they worshiped the dragon who gave authority to the beast; and they worshiped the beast, saying, 'Who is like the beast? Who is able to make war with him?'" (Revelation 13:4). In describing the beast of the earth, John wrote, "He was granted power to give breath to the image of the beast, that the image of the beast should both speak and cause as many as would not worship the image of the beast to be killed" (Revelation 13:15). What nation on Earth has the power to enforce such legislation?

December 29 NUCLEAR SUBMARINES

"Beloved, I pray that you may prosper in all things and be in health, just as your soul prospers" (3 John 2).

Nuclear submarines, or "Boomer submarines," are among the most modern engineering wonders in the world. They are the equivalent to a tightly packed, self-contained city where a crew of 140 shares space equivalent to a three-bedroom house. The nuclear reactor provides heat energy, which is converted to electricity. This power is used to turn the propeller and send the submarine silently through the water. Because they carry their energy source with them, nuclear submarines are able to travel at least 400,000 miles without refueling. In addition to the torpedoes, the new Ohio class of nuclear submarines is equipped with 24 launching tubes holding warheads that may be fired from beneath the water to strike targets sometimes thousands of miles away. Each of these missiles is sufficient to completely obliterate major cities. If, God forbid, just one sub from each country fired on another nation, it would pretty much render life on this planet extinct.

Nuclear subs are deployed for months and can stay submerged for as long as 90 days. There is little contact with family during this time. This, combined with the pressure of being prepared to launch nuclear weapons, makes it one of the most stressful assignments in the military. To compensate, the Navy trains the best chefs for these subs. Notice I did not say cooks! A meal might consist of prime rib, lobster tails, sautéed mushrooms, baked potatoes, fresh bread, freshly squeezed lemonade, and real chocolate cake for dessert. And all this is done in an 8-foot by 10-foot galley that is barely larger than the kitchen in a small apartment. You can understand why submariners are the only fighting force that often gains weight during deployment.

They say an army travels on its stomach. That's why the military spends millions of dollars carefully evaluating what their soldiers eat. Then why do many Christians believe that God does not care what His soldiers eat? The Bible clearly teaches, "Therefore, whether you eat or drink, or whatever you do, do all to the glory of God" (1 Corinthians 10:31). Since our body is the temple of God (6:19), we should present our bodies as a "living" sacrifice to God (Romans 12:1, 2) and not abuse them with gluttony, especially because we are soldiers in God's army.

"At that day you will know that I am in My Father, and you in Me, and I in you" (John 14:20).

Years ago, Hollywood produced a movie about a submarine-like vessel and crew that were shrunk to microscopic proportions and injected into a human. Careening through the blood stream, the ship faced numerous obstacles before reaching the brain and wiping out a tumor. However farfetched that was, scientists are working to create tiny robots that can move through a human body to perform a variety of medical procedures.

For example, Italian researchers have designed a new, pinhead-size, radio-controlled camera pill. The camera pill is designed to be swallowed and flow through your digestive system while flashing a tiny strobe and snapping pictures. But this camera pill is immense compared to what is on the drawing board!

Have you ever heard of nanorobots? To give you an idea how small a nanorobot is, a meter is about 39 inches, but a nanometer is only a billionth of a meter. Nanotechnology is a new field that seeks to make machines millions of times smaller than what we now use. Nanotechnologists want to create nanorobots, commonly called nanobots, that could be injected into the body and programmed to seek out cancer cells and destroy them with a precision that a scalpel could never achieve. Imagine a small machine, no bigger than a germ, traveling through the bloodstream, powered by the system's natural glucose, killing cancer cells one at a time. How much better that would be than chemotherapy, which kills good cells as well! Nanobots could break up kidney stones, clean out plaque-filled arteries, and kill viruses and unwanted bacteria. The potential is endless.

Though scientists are still a long way from creating them, just remember that 20 years ago it required a building full of computers to accomplish what a handheld computer can do today!

Right now it is possible to have Jesus "in you." The Bible refers to the mystery of "Christ in you, the hope of glory" (Colossians 1:27). Jesus said, "Abide in Me, and I in you" (John 15:4). But how? His Word says, "If we love one another, God abides in us" (1 John 4:12). He also tells us, "He who eats My flesh and drinks My blood abides in Me, and I in him" (John 6:56). If we live in His love, keep His commandments, accept His sacrifice and His Word, and stay connected by spending time with Him each day, He will remain in us, giving us eternal life.

December 31 LAKE PEIGNEUR

"Therefore we will not fear, even though the earth be removed ... Though its waters roar and be troubled ... " (Psalm 46:2, 3).

Lake Peigneur was a modest, shallow lake of fresh water near New Iberia, Louisiana. Early in the morning on November 21, 1980, a drilling team was probing for oil under the lake from a large floating platform. They knew something was wrong when their drill suddenly seized up at about 1,200 feet and the large derrick began to tilt, pop, and collapse beneath them. The 12 men working the rig escaped to the shore and watched in amazement as the huge $5 million drilling platform overturned and disappeared into a lake that was less than 10 feet deep!

Slowly at first, the water around that position began to revolve, but it steadily accelerated until it became a fast-moving whirlpool a quarter of a mile across. Soon it swallowed another nearby drilling platform whole, a barge loading dock, 65 acres of soil from Jefferson Island, plus a sundry of trucks, trees, and structures. Eleven barges were pulled from that canal and swallowed by the swirling abyss. The whirlpool overtook a manned tugboat on the canal. The crew had to leap off onto the canal bank and watch helplessly as the lake consumed their boat.

Meanwhile, far beneath the lake was the Diamond Crystal salt mines, where miles of cavernous tunnels, some 80 feet high and 50 feet wide, were rapidly filling with water. Evidently the drillers had miscalculated their position and had punched a small hole into the colossal salt mines a thousand feet below. Fortunately, one of the mine workers quickly sounded the alarm and all 50 miners managed to barely escape with their lives. After three hours, the 1,300-acre lake was drained of its 3.5 billion gallons of water. Over the next two days the canal refilled the crater with ocean water, and nine of the sunken barges popped back to the surface like corks. The drilling rigs and tug boat were never found. And all this started with a little hole about a foot across.

The Bible teaches that little things can make a big difference. Achan once thought it would be OK to bend the rules just a little bit. He knew he wasn't supposed to take any of the spoils from the destruction of Jericho. Joshua later said, "Did not Achan the son of Zerah commit a trespass in the accursed thing, and wrath fell on all the congregation of Israel? And that man did not perish alone in his iniquity" (Joshua 22:20). We are deceived when we think wrong "little" sins will not affect anyone else.

Memory Verse Index OLD TESTAMENT

Memory Verse Index OLD TESTAMENT

Memory Verse Index OLD TESTAMENT

Memory Verse Index NEW TESTAMENT

Memory Verse Index NEW TESTAMENT